PRAISE FOR *BOTANY BAY: THE REAL STORY*

'Iconoclastic and refreshing … an exhilarating read'
—*The Sydney Morning Herald*

'Fascinating and compelling'—*The Weekend Australian*

'[An] amazing work … Frost has presented a powerful and compelling case.'
—*The Canberra Times*

'A nuanced, complex story'—*The Sunday Age*

'Frost's evidence is compelling, making the book essential reading for anyone
interested in Australia's European settlement.'—*The Herald Sun*

PRAISE FOR *THE FIRST FLEET: THE REAL STORY*

'Alan Frost is the myth-buster of Australian history … His work should be
studied by … anyone interested in the birth of a nation.'—*The Saturday Age*

'It is almost certain that Frost knows more than anybody else about the early
maritime history of this land … This book will surely alter the way Sydney
sees its history.'—Geoffrey Blainey, *The Weekend Australian*

'This book has rewritten the rules of First Fleet scholarship.'
—*The Sydney Morning Herald*

'Frost positively rampages through the pronouncements of earlier scholars,
smiting conventional wisdoms left and right … We need more Frosts.'
—*The Canberra Times*

'This is revisionist history at its best, immaculately researched and written.'
—*Books & Publishing*

'Highly readable, Frost's work will be enjoyed by anyone with an interest
in early Australia.'—*The Sunday Herald Sun*

'An exciting reassessment of the origins of the British colony in
Terra Australis.'—*The Courier Mail*

BOTANY BAY and the FIRST FLEET

BOTANY BAY and the FIRST FLEET

THE REAL STORY

ALAN FROST

Published by Black Inc.,
an imprint of Schwartz Publishing Pty Ltd
Level 1, 221 Drummond Street
Carlton VIC 3053, Australia
enquiries@blackincbooks.com
www.blackincbooks.com

9781760641603 (paperback)
9781743820995 (ebook)

A catalogue record for this
book is available from the
National Library of Australia

Cover design by Thomas Deverall and Akiko Chan
Text design by Thomas Deverall
Index by Michael Ramsden and Kerry Anderson
Front cover image: *Landing at Botany Bay*, John Boyne, 1786.
Depicts the Prince of Wales and members of the parliamentary
opposition landing with convicts at an imaginary Botany Bay.
Five Aboriginal people are represented in the background.
National Library of Australia. nla.obj-135300165.
Back cover and part opener image: Entrance of Rio de Janeiro (Brasil). View from the
anchorage without the Sugar Loaf bearing NW off shore 2 miles. By George Raper, 1790.
Reproduced courtesy of the Natural History Museum, London.

CONTENTS

THE FIRST FLEET

BOTANY BAY

It might perhaps be practicable to direct the strict employment of a limited number of convicted felons in each of the dock-yards, in the stanneries, saltworks, mines and public buildings of the kingdom. The more enormous offenders might be sent to Tunis, Algiers, and other Mahometan ports, for the redemption of Christian slaves. Others might be compelled to dangerous expeditions; or be sent to establish new colonies, factories, and settlements on the coasts of Africa, and on small islands for the benefit of navigation.

—WILLIAM EDEN, *Principles of Penal Law*, London, 1771

Map of Australia in relation to the East Indies and the Pacific coastlines

PREFACE

IN 1975, SHIFTING THE FOCUS OF my scholarly interest from English literature to history, I began to research the reasons for the British colonization of New South Wales in 1788.

Then, I had no real idea for how many years this quest would occupy me, and how arduous it would prove. In the 1980s and 1990s, I published a number of substantial studies which bore, to a greater or lesser extent, on the general question: *Convicts and Empire* (1980); *Arthur Phillip, 1738–1814: His Voyaging* (1987); *Sir Joseph Banks and the Transfer of Plants to and from the South Pacific, 1786–1798* (1993); *Botany Bay Mirages* (1994). Even so, I still had only a limited sense of the magnitude of the task, whose horizons kept expanding – witness *The Global Reach of Empire* (2003).

The one thing above all others that I did not know when I commenced this research was the full extent of the documentary base awaiting discovery. When I began, I naturally attended to those sources which had either been published (as in *Historical Records of New South Wales* (1892)) or cited in what were then the standard histories of the beginning of modern Australia (by Ernest Scott, Sir Keith Hancock, Sir Max Crawford, Manning Clark and A.G.L. Shaw). But as I investigated further, and in particular as I came to know better the administrative practices of British government departments in the last decades of the eighteenth century, I uncovered more and more relevant documents.

The essays in *Botany Bay Mirages* were based on some 600 documents, and in the Introduction to that work I optimistically forecast that there might be perhaps 200 more to be collected. Even so, I still had no proper idea of the actual extent of the records. I kept searching, and kept finding more documents. When in 2003 I applied for a large ARC grant to continue the process, I thought that I should probably end up with 1000. I received the grant and went back repeatedly to the Public Record Office, now the National Archives, in London. I found more and more documents – so many that at times it seemed as though there would be no end to the business. I would utter low groans each time I opened a new file to find yet another dozen or fifty that needed to be recorded.

In the end, I gathered 2500 documents (including copies). To be sure, there is often much repetition in these as, according to the practice of the times, writers summarized or repeated at length the contents of the letters they were minuting or answering. But taken together, and when combined with other sources which also reflect government deliberations (such as secondary correspondence and newspaper reports), this base constitutes a matchless record of that moment in time's long travail that led to the emergence of Australia. (These documents are now available at the State Library of New South Wales. Eventually they will be placed on a dedicated webpage. It is my hope that this will become an enduring record for the future, as new documents are added to it and as other historians make use of it for different purposes.)

The greatly enlarged documentary record means that we are now in a position to understand better than ever before why the British decided to colonize New South Wales. In this volume and its forthcoming companion, *The First Fleet: The Real Story*, I analyze this decision and how it was implemented.

As has been true generally of my past writing about British imperialism in the second half of the eighteenth century, what I am most concerned with in these studies are the political and strategic decision-making processes, and the administrative procedures by which decisions were implemented. Some of what I say here I have said before, but not in such an extensive or focused way. Also, a number of my conclusions now differ markedly from some I offered thirty years ago. I understand more now than I did then.

Much of what I say, I know, contradicts what has become received wisdom in Australian history. To some readers, it may seem the height of folly – or arrogance – to gainsay what the renowned historians of Australian colonization have said; and to do so, moreover, in polemical fashion. But this is what I am doing – in these studies I am challenging the established historiography of Australia's beginnings, which I believe to be both severely limited in its perspective and wrong in a number of its central conclusions.

In disagreeing with my colleagues and predecessors, I mean no personal disrespect. However, there is no gentle way of arguing against a whole tradition of historiography. If I intend to call it into fundamental question, then it is best that I do so directly and honestly. Only in this way is the cause of history properly served; and also that of the nation, in that we shall come to a better understanding of whence we came, and therefore who we are.

EDITORIAL PRACTICES

The documents I have located, and from which I quote here, have been transcribed and edited by Dr Natasha Weir and myself. Mostly, we have modernized spelling, capitalization and punctuation. (The principal exception is that we have left in their original form legal documents, such as Letters Patent and Acts of Parliament.) Sometimes, in the interest of readier comprehension, we have also broken up very long passages into shorter paragraphs (including in Letters Patent). While misspellings have been silently corrected, we have indicated where we have corrected obviously wrong words. We have standardized the spelling of personal and geographical names. However, I have retained older spellings when to alter them would lead to confusion (e.g., Bombay rather than Mumbai, as no eighteenth-century European source gives the modern Indian term).

Introduction

BETWEEN 1718 AND 1775, British authorities transported some 50,000 male and female criminals across the Atlantic Ocean to the North American colonies (most to Virginia and Maryland), where their labour was sold to merchants and planters for terms not longer than seven years.

This distinctive penal practice came to an abrupt halt in 1776, when many of the American colonists revolted against metropolitan rule. For the next six years, hoping that the problem would be temporary, parliament instituted an alternative sentence for felonies, that of hard labour on the harbours and waterways of the kingdom, with convicts so sentenced being held on dismasted ships ('hulks') in the River Thames. When war ended, as inclination or necessity turned numbers of the tens of thousands of soldiers and sailors returning home to crime, magistrates also returned to the older sentence of transportation; but with nowhere to send them, the number of convicts being held in metropolitan and county prisons rapidly increased, and the government was forced to expand the hulks system. By 1786, there were three hulks moored in the Thames and one each in Portsmouth and Plymouth harbours, each accommodating about 250 to 280 male prisoners.

The total number of men and women sentenced to transportation to North America or Africa or, more generally, to 'beyond the Seas' then being held in the hulks and jails of the kingdom is uncertain. It is not likely to have exceeded 4000 and may have been significantly fewer. However, there were rogues and abandoned persons enough for local authorities to complain bitterly to the central government about its failure to carry out sentences of transportation. In August 1786, the administration of William Pitt the Younger decided to establish a convict colony at Botany Bay, on the eastern coast of New South Wales, along which Captain James Cook had sailed in 1770 and of which he had taken possession in the name of the King.

The British began this colonization in 1788 with 750 convicts, 200 marines and a handful of civilian officers. In the fifty or so years to 1840, they transported about 130,000 men, women and juvenile offenders to various sites in and off eastern Australia: Sydney, Newcastle, Port Macquarie, Moreton Bay, Van Diemen's Land (Tasmania) and Norfolk Island.

The government minister usually associated with the original decision was Thomas Townshend. He had been Secretary of State for Home Affairs in the Shelburne administration (July 1782–April 1783), with convicts being one of his many responsibilities. After being raised to the peerage as Lord Sydney, from December 1783 he held this position again in the Pitt administration. To avoid confusion, I shall refer to him as Lord Sydney, and to his department as the Home Office.

For decades, historians gave only one motive for the decision: the British wished to 'dump' their criminals as far away as possible. Then, in the second half of the twentieth century, some suggested that there had also been strategic and commercial motives – a suggestion the traditionalists strongly rejected. This argument among the historians is part of my story.

*

It is possible to identify a number of phases in the historiography of this curious venture, for which there is no real parallel in modern history.

The first of these extended from the commencement of European settlement to 1880. During these years, most who reflected on the convict colonization drew not on official or private records, but rather on personal experience of life in the colonies, or on descriptions by others of this life. Inevitably, the fact of convicts dominated these would-be historians' perspective, which was often overlaid with a strong theological wash.

The author of the account that appeared under the name of George Barrington, thief in England and chief constable at Parramatta in New South Wales, for example, observed that 'in contemplating the origin, rise, and fall of nations, the mind is alternately filled with a mixture of sacred pain and pleasure'. For Barrington, the pain in the colony's beginning was that there had been so many criminals in England, and that so many of these, when transported, had 'continued incorrigible'. The pleasure was that 'some in the infancy of the Colony, will be found reforming rapidly'; and he comforted himself with the thought that 'the penitence of a Few, cannot but be acceptable to Man, since in Heaven there is *Joy over even one Sinner that truly repents*'. The primary reason for the colony's existence was to create a 'School' for 'the Correction of those unfortunate Human Beings, who, urged by various depraved motives, forfeit the protection of the Laws they have failed to observe'.[1]

Another early historian of New South Wales, John Dunmore Lang, was a Presbyterian minister there from 1823 until his death in 1878. He began his 1834 account of the colony by pointing to how the earlier transportation of British convicts to North America had been disrupted by the War of Independence. The 'main objects' of the British government in colonizing New South Wales, he asserted, had been:

To rid the mother country of the intolerable nuisance arising from the daily increasing accumulation of criminals in her jails and houses of correction;

To afford a suitable place for the safe custody and the punishment of these criminals, as well as for their ultimate and progressive reformation; and,

To form a British colony out of those materials which the reformation of these criminals might gradually supply to the government, in addition to the families of free emigrants who might from time to time be induced to settle in the newly discovered territory.[2]

This became the essential paradigm that was repeated for another fifty years. In 1862, Roderick Flanagan discussed how the successful rebellion of the American colonies had checked the British practice of transporting criminals out of the kingdom, and gave some details of the mounting of the First Fleet.[3] In 1877 Alexander and George Sutherland noted that just as Britain was presented with the problem of finding a new place to which to transport convicts, 'Captain Cook's voyages called attention to a land in every way suited for such a purpose, both by reason of its fertility and of its great distance'.[4]

But, as Babette Smith has recently shown in *Australia's Birthstain* (2008), by the middle of the nineteenth century the rhetoric of the anti-transportation movement was casting a very heavy pall over the circumstances of Australia's beginnings. In *The History of Australasia* (1878) David Blair reflected this change of outlook when he waxed indignant about the British government's reprehensible approach to 'planning a settlement in the new world which the genius and enterprise of Cook had opened up to the British people'. 'Instead of embracing the opportunity to found "a new Britannia in another world"', Blair argued, the Pitt administration's only motive had been 'that Providence had shown them a favourable opening for getting rid of their surplus criminal population'. Seeing that this 'fatal purpose' cast a 'dark shadow' over European Australia's beginning, he declared that he would pass over the story 'as lightly as the exigencies of true narration will permit. Better, a thousand times, would it be for the world, if the entire record were buried in eternal forgetfulness.'[5]

The apogee of this view perhaps came with the Sydney *Bulletin*'s denunciation of the celebration in 1888 of the one hundredth anniversary of Governor Arthur Phillip's landing at Sydney Cove. It thundered luridly that the one day among all others which has been fixed upon as the natal-day of Australia is that which commemorates her shame and degradation, and reminds the world most emphatically of the hideous uncleanness from which she sprung. The day which gave to the New World her first jail and her first gallows – the day when the festering vileness of England was first cast ashore to putrefy upon the coasts of New South Wales – the day which inaugurated a reign of slavery and loathsomeness and moral leprosy – is the occasion for which we are called upon to rejoice with an exceeding great joy.[6]

*

The second phase in the historiography of the decision to establish a convict colony at Botany Bay followed the recovery of original records in the Public Record Office in London and other archives.

George Rusden began this process with his research for his *History of Australia* (1883). It was soon afterwards greatly advanced when, in preparation for the centenary celebrations, New South Wales premier Henry Parkes, commissioned James Bonwick to undertake an extensive search for records in Britain, with a view to making them the basis of an official history. Bonwick executed his commission so diligently that the colonial government decided to publish the rapidly accumulating transcripts as a companion work to the commissioned history.[7] George Barton made early use of Bonwick's harvest with the first volume of *History of New South Wales from the Records*, published in 1889. The first volume of *Historical Records of New South Wales* appeared in 1892. When completed, this series consisted of seven densely printed volumes.

Historical Records of New South Wales provided about one hundred documents pertaining to the August 1786 decision to colonize and the mounting of the First Fleet in 1786–7. Some more were added in ensuing decades, in the various volumes of *Historical Records of Australia* and by Owen Rutter in *The First Fleet* (1937). Essentially, though, for the next sixty years and more, the documents published in *Historical Records of New South Wales* were one of the two principal pillars on which most historians' accounts of the founding of modern Australia were built.

The other consisted of complaints by English municipal and county officials to the central government about the presence in their jails of convicts sentenced to transportation. From the time peace was restored in 1783, and especially after the passage of a more comprehensive transportation act (24 Geo. III, c. 56) in August 1784, as more and more people were convicted of felonies and sentenced to transportation, these complaints grew more frequent and bitter.

The grounds of complaint were straightforward. It was the central government's responsibility to see that sentences of transportation were carried out. So long as they were not, and in the absence of any alternative means of clearing prisons, local authorities were forced to keep transport convicts in their jails. From both a security and health point of view, these jails were all too often inadequate for the purpose; moreover, there was no financial provision for the maintenance of prisoners who were not supposed to be in them. The authorities' complaints crowd the HO 42 series (George III: Domestic Papers) in the National Archives, and for decades historians considered them the only additional evidence needed to confirm that the 'convict problem' was the motive for colonization, reinforcing the explanation they found encapsulated in the documents in *Historical Records of New South Wales*.

The most distinguished of Australia's mid-twentieth-century historians who read these two classes of documents were convinced that Australia owed its beginning to a short-sighted government's irrational solution to an awkward domestic problem. Sir Keith Hancock held that 'the Government of Pitt chose New South Wales as a prison, commodious, conveniently distant, and, it was hoped, cheap; for prison labour, driven by prison discipline, would surely be able to keep itself'.[8] Eris O'Brien observed that the American War of Independence, bringing the 'traffic in convicts across the Atlantic to a standstill', was 'the real beginning of Australian history', and that the 'the reason given by Sydney for the necessity of making [the Botany Bay] settlement was the familiar one of jails so crowded as to give rise to the danger of wholesale escapes or an epidemic of fever'.[9] R.M. Crawford concluded that 'there was no escaping the fact that New South Wales was founded as a jail' and that 'necessity and not vision founded Australia'.[10] F.K. Crowley argued that 'the history of the first thirty years of British settlement in Australia certainly does not indicate the working out of any systematic plan for fostering new ventures in trade, colonization, or empire building'; that 'domestic needs rather than the implication of Imperial policies were the factors most evident in the determination of the English government to send a number of ships and convicts to the antipodes in 1787'; and that 'the hard-pressed ministers in Pitt's administration were little concerned with the importance of the undertaking. They were interested only in finding a solution for pressing political and penal problems in the home country'.[11] A.G.L. Shaw concluded that the satisfactory accommodation of the convicts 'seems to have been the government's principal concern, stimulated as it was by the loss of American plantations'.[12] And, displaying his propensity to take phrases and sentences holus-bolus from his sources, Manning Clark argued that 'one factor alone had convinced [Lord Sydney] of the need for a definite decision' about what to do with the convicts: 'the several jails and places for the confinement of felons were so crowded that the greatest danger was to be apprehended not only from their escape, but from infectious distempers'.[13]

*

In this second phase of the historiography of the decision to colonize New South Wales, then, most historians concluded that the 'dumping of convicts' motive was the only one the documentary record supported.

A number of other assumptions, sometimes unstated, accompanied this one. One was that the loss of the American colonies caused British administrations of the late eighteenth and early nineteenth centuries to lose interest in empire. Another was that the young Prime Minister, William Pitt, lacked an imperial imagination. A third was that Pitt and his ministers were incapable of either envisaging the nation's future needs, or of planning to meet them. A fourth was that these politicians responded to events, rather than acted to direct them. A fifth was that they abandoned the traditional view of convicts as a cheap source of labour from which the nation might benefit, and saw them instead in their regrettable numbers only as a domestic nuisance. Finally, there was the assumption that Pitt and his ministers decided to establish a convict colony in New South Wales in a fit of despair or of absence of mind – most likely of both! The phrase 'absence of mind' was based on a mis-reading of a comment by Sir John Seely, the eminent late-nineteenth-century historian of British imperialism: 'There is something very characteristic in the indifference which we show towards this mighty phenomenon of the diffusion of our race and the expansion of our state. We seem, as it were, to have conquered and peo-pled half the world in a fit of absence of mind.' An oversimplified inter-pretation of Seeley's statement took hold and became a widely repeated mantra, used to explain the whole sorry business.[14]

Believing the decision to have arisen from inertia and incapacity, the traditionalist historians represented it as a largely gratuitous one, prompted by Britain's loss of its North American colonies and by the social and political pressure caused by the subsequent overcrowding of prisons at home. They presented it as quite unrelated to the Pitt administration's policies in such other spheres as domestic reform, the re-establishment of colonial administration or overseas security and trade. And they saw Australia as part of the broader scheme of the British empire only after the Australian colonies had, against London's inclination, slowly attained constitutional, political and economic development similar to Britain's other colonies in North America, the West Indies and the East. As Manning Clark pointed out, when he announced the decision to the new session of parliament on 23 January 1787, the King cited only the convict motive: 'a plan has been formed by my direction, for transporting a number of convicts, in order to remove the inconvenience which arose from the crowded state of the jails in different parts of the kingdom.'[15]

*

There were occasional tinges of greenery in the otherwise dreary wasteland of official incompetence and despair described by most historians during this period.

Some of the printed records – for example, the colonization proposals submitted by James Matra, Sir George Young and Sir John Call – did lead a number of late-nineteenth-century writers to think that the British government may have had other motives for the decision to colonize New South Wales. Rusden thought that 'the mere providing of a jail was not the sole motive for the founding of New South Wales' and wondered if 'a desire to forestall the French' had not been a factor.[16] A few years later the English historian E.C.K. Gonner noted that 'it is a serious error to mistake an incident for an all-sufficing cause'. 'While the expedition to New South Wales could always be justified on the ground of present necessity,' he wrote, 'those who sent it aimed at something more important than the mere foundation of a new criminal establishment', and pointed to the commercial and political arguments advanced by James Matra.[17] Barton also observed that Matra and Young had argued vigorously for the 'commercial or political advantages' of colonizing New South Wales.[18] However, these writers made no detailed examination of these other possible motives, and their insights, tentatively advanced, failed to influence general understanding of the decision.

In 1937, Rutter revived this line of thought, writing:

Sometimes I wonder if those ministers of George III were indeed so blind as they appear to the advantages of Matra's first plan. Was all the talk of convicts and penal settlements a magnificent piece of subtlety, a splendid bluff designed to hoodwink the Dutch, who were jealously clutching their old colonial possessions in the Eastern Seas, and the French, who were avid for new ones? Did George III and his ministers, having lost a colony on one side of the world, really see the possibilities of a new one on the other side, as Matra would have had them see? To me that is a fascinating theory: and it must remain so, for I have no evidence to adduce in its support – nothing but here and there a hint as to the working of a man's mind, an implication in a sentence which the speaker or writer may or may not have phrased to conceal his thoughts.[19]

But like those unfortunate vegetables planted at Sydney Cove in the autumn of 1788, which germinated only soon to die, these tendrils of potential insight also quickly withered.

*

So, by the middle of the twentieth century, the business seemed to rest: Australia had been founded as a jail – 'commodious, conveniently distant, and, it was hoped, cheap'.[20]

Well, not quite. Like the undercurrent that can run in opposition to the habitual roll of spectacular surf, another view was also building. Although it took some time to emerge, and although those who developed it attended to different contours, this counter-current of historical thinking had as its fundamental premise the belief that governments – even incompetent ones – seldom take a particular decision entirely in isolation from others. Understanding the true historical circumstance – that it was not cheap but rather very expensive to send a large number of convicts on a voyage of eight months to a place 20,000 kilometres away, there to start a settlement from scratch – a small number of writers went against the tide and asked: 'Might it not be that the Pitt administration hoped to obtain something in return – something, that is, more than the simple removal of criminals from Britain?'

The first serious questioning of the received wisdom came in 1952, when K.M. Dallas, a Tasmanian economic historian, published a short article in an obscure journal asserting that the 'dumping of convicts' explanation was by itself 'absurd'. Because of the 'costs and risks' involved in shipping the convicts to New South Wales, and because of the availability of suitable sites closer to Britain, Dallas supposed that there was 'some deeper reason for choosing Botany Bay'. 'The dumping of convicts view is too simple', he argued. 'The emphasis should be put on *settlement* rather than on the penal aspect; on the naval and commercial realities rather than on the legal and judicial form.' Starting with the premise that during the second half of the eighteenth century 'the wealth of nations and their power depended on the gain from foreign trade; [and] foreign trade depended on possession of strategic harbours for safe refuge, for assembling convoys and for attack on enemy shipping', Dallas linked the New South Wales venture with the possibilities of trade with China, the northwest American coast and South America, and of whaling and sealing in the Pacific Ocean. He pointed, too, to the naval significance of Norfolk Island's pines and flax. He summed up his argument: 'The First Fleet was a well-planned naval expedition sent to seize and fortify a naval base; the convicts were what they had always been – the servants of mercantilist interests.'[21]

Acute as some of these points are, Dallas lacked the gift of lucid exposition, and it wasn't until Geoffrey Blainey revived them in 1966 that Dallas's views received real attention. Blainey did more than highlight Dallas's arguments, however; he went much further in support of the idea that there had been additional motives for sending convicts to Botany Bay. He too made the important point that transporting people such a distance 'was a startlingly costly solution to the crowded British prisons', and also a very slow one; and he reiterated the usefulness of a port in the southwestern Pacific Ocean to British ships. Then, deploying his wonderful facility for conveying the essence of a historical situation in modern terms, he pointed out that in the late eighteenth century 'flax and ships' timber were as vital to seapower as steel and oil are today', and that one of the concluding paragraphs in the 'Heads of a Plan', the document which went from the Home Office to the Treasury to explain the decision, mentioned this objective. The pines and flax plants on Norfolk Island, Blainey asserted, constituted the 'key to the plan to send convicts to Australia': 'Norfolk Island was the plant nursery; Australia was to be the market garden and flax farm surrounded by jail walls.'[22]

A.G.L. Shaw and Geoffrey Bolton, historians who held to the traditional explanation, responded to Blainey's arguments with disbelief. A lively debate followed, but the question remained unresolved.[23] Into the 1970s, the 'dumping of convicts' explanation reigned supreme: as one prominent historian of Australia told me then, 'Nobody believes Blainey!'

*

It was at this point that I entered the fray. On taking up my position in the English department at La Trobe University in 1970, I became aware of the controversy among historians concerning the reasons for the British colonization of Australia. Blainey's explanation made good sense to me. While working on my doctoral thesis on 'Captain James Cook's influence on the British Romantic poets', I had read widely in the narratives of Cook's voyages – in popular abridgements of them, in extracts published in such venues as the *Monthly Magazine* and the *Gentleman's Magazine*, which had wide circulation, and in geography books intended for all levels of reader, from informed adults to young children. In these varied works, the value of the islands of the south-western Pacific Ocean (New Caledonia, Norfolk Island and New Zealand) as sources of naval materials was frequently mentioned.

Let me give just two examples from the 1780s. Anna Seward – known as the 'Swan of Lichfield' – published her *Elegy on Captain Cook* in 1780. This popular work went into a fourth edition in 1784. One of the great explorer's accomplishments, Seward pointed out, was the bringing of new botanical species to Europe:

> First gentle Flora – round her smiling brow
> Leaves of new forms, and flowers uncultured glow;
> Thin folds of vegetable silk,* behind,
> Shade her white neck ...

> * *Vegetable Silk*: In New Zealand is a flag [flax] of which the natives make their nets and cordage. The fibres of this vegetable are longer and stronger than our hemp and flax; and some, manufactured in London, is as white and glossy as fine silk. This valuable vegetable will probably grow in our climate.[24]

In the *Geographical Magazine*, F.W. Martyn told readers that if this plant were to be cultivated in Britain, 'it might prove of more real benefit … than the productions of all the islands which our circumnavigators have discovered for a century past'.[25] This prospect may seem extravagant now, but at the time it accorded with the fundamental reality that Blainey highlighted. No matter how sceptically mid-twentieth-century historians viewed the possibility, it did not appear far-fetched to those who contemplated Britain's imperial needs in the 1780s.

So, when I moved into the history department, I set out to see if I could find more evidence to support this explanation. As I published the early results of my research, I received much the same reaction as Dallas and Blainey had. First Alan Atkinson and David Mackay, then Mollie Gillen, were as sceptical as the previous group of historians had been that the desire to find a new source of naval materials was a significant factor in the decision to establish the Botany Bay colony. Another lively debate followed, extending from the mid-1970s into the 1980s.[26] It is again true to say that no fundamental agreement emerged. Indeed, I must admit (somewhat ruefully) that nobody – or at least, very few – seemed to believe Frost either.

As I continued my research in the archives, mostly in Britain but also in North and South America, Europe and New Zealand, greatly expanding my knowledge of British imperialism in the last decades of the eighteenth century, I came to revise my earlier views significantly. It was not that, as you will see, I ceased to believe in the force of the 'naval materials' motive, but rather that I came to understand that this was an adjunct to a much larger plan, one developed principally by William Pitt and his closest advisers Lord Mulgrave and Henry Dundas, with the participation of Lord Hawkesbury, the president of the Board of Trade, Sir Joseph Banks and others. Their aim was to expand British commerce throughout the Indian and Pacific oceans. If this over-arching plan were to succeed, Britain would need bases and resources along or adjacent to the major sea routes, ports where ships might be resupplied and whence, in wartime, attacks against enemy colonies might be launched.

*

As I mentioned earlier, in the course of my research over the past thirty-five years, as against the hundred or so documents printed in *Historical Records of New South Wales*, I have gathered some 2500 documents relating to the decision to colonize New South Wales and the mounting of the First Fleet. It is inevitable that historical analysis based on such a vastly expanded record will differ very significantly from that based on the old, fragmentary one.

The real story of the Botany Bay decision is much more complex than the explanation that has prevailed for two hundred years. It is also much more interesting. Australians deserve to know it. It is my story here.

1.

Eighteenth-Century England: Crime

UNLESS THEY BE IMPOSED ON AN alien population by a conqueror, or by a group of religious zealots, the laws of a country do not function independently of the society from which they arise. It is therefore necessary that I say something about English society and laws in the eighteenth century before examining in detail the practice of convict transportation and the decision to colonize New South Wales. Elsewhere in this study, I use the term 'Britain' to signify the 'United Kingdom' of England and Scotland formed by the Act of Union in 1707. However, as there were significant regional differences, in what follows I mostly confine myself to English circumstances. (Some of the statistics I cite cover more than England; I have indicated this when it is so.) It is impossible to sketch the nature of a complex society in a brief compass without resorting to some platitudes, so you may find some in this chapter.

*

English society in the first half of the eighteenth century still strongly reflected the medieval structures upon which it was based. At its peak were the monarch, his or her immediate family and the nobles, both secular and ecclesiastical (the Church of England having become the established church under Henry VIII). Beneath these were the prosperous landowners and merchants; the 'middling classes' of professional people, lesser merchants, tradesmen and farmers; and the sturdy yeomen-farmers who plowed their strips and ran domestic animals on the commons, and whose wives and children augmented the family income with produce and spinning. Then there were servants and labourers, and the poor (commonly classed as either 'deserving' or 'undeserving' according to their inclination to work or to be idle).

Although political power was centred on London, in the first half of the eighteenth century English society remained predominantly rural, with the village at its core. The cultivation of grains, fruits and vegetables was widespread in the south of England, while grain fields marked its fertile northern reaches. The keeping of horses, dairy cattle, sheep and the smaller domestic animals was ubiquitous.

English rural life was regulated by a complex mixture of statute law, common law and immemorial custom. To the socially and politically very conservative Edmund Burke, contemplating the havoc wreaked across the English Channel by the French Revolution, this society was just about as near to perfection as Earth might offer. 'Society is indeed a contract', he wrote:

> It is a partnership in all science; a partnership in all art; a partnership in every virtue, and in all perfection. As the ends of such a partnership cannot be obtained in many generations, it becomes a partnership not only between those who are living, but between those who are living, those who are dead, and those who are to be born. Each contract of each particular state is but a clause in the great primaeval contract of eternal society, linking the lower with the higher natures, connecting the visible and invisible world, according to a fixed compact sanctioned by the inviolable oath which holds all physical and all moral natures, each in their appointed place. This law is not subject to the will of those, who by an obligation above them, and infinitely superior, are bound to submit their will to that law ... If that which is only submission to necessity should be made the object of choice, the law is broken, nature is disobeyed, and the rebellious are outlawed, cast forth, and exiled, from this world of reason, and order,

and peace, and virtue, and fruitful penitence, into the antagonist world of madness, discord, vice, confusion, and unavailing sorrow.

And were all this not true, he concluded, 'man could not by any possibility arrive at the perfection of which his nature is capable, nor even make a remote and faint approach to it'.[1]

Burke's view was impossibly rosy. For whatever its satisfactions, eighteenth-century English society was also deeply flawed. It exhibited vast extremes of wealth and privilege on the one hand and poverty on the other. Scant education – if any – was available to the majority of the population. The sick who could afford it might have the help of apothecaries (chemists) or doctors; but common folk were usually able to draw only on the resources of 'wise women' and their 'simples'. The parish might provide some relief to the old who had no family support and the destitute; but if the destitute were able-bodied they were put into the work house to earn their keep, and parishes were under no obligation to help strangers. The leisure of childhood was not available to the offspring of the labouring poor, who commonly went to work from the age of three or four.

While most statistics for the eighteenth century are uncertain, there were about 5 million people in England in 1750. There were a number of provincial towns and cities with populations in the tens of thousands (up to about 30,000, although it is possible that Bristol and Manchester had more) and one grand metropolis, London, which by mid-century contained perhaps 650,000 people. A number of these cities – Portsmouth, Plymouth, Bristol, Liverpool and, of course, London – were ports through which Britain traded with the world. Britain possessed an extensive merchant marine, which sailed to North America and the West Indies, around the coasts of Europe and the Mediterranean, and to West Africa and Asia. The Royal Navy was superior to the military marines of Britain's Continental neighbours. Unlike these rivals, however, Britain did not maintain a standing army, as prevailing wisdom held that this would be inimical to true English liberty, for it would give a tyrant the means to impose his dictatorship.

London was also the financial and manufacturing centre of the country, and it was here that the extremes of society were most starkly evident. A visitor moving westwards from Covent Garden saw the royal palaces, the imposing houses of parliament, the lavish townhouses of the nobility and the wealthy merchants, and great churches; not far in the other direction, in East London, there was the scarcely imaginable squalor of the poor, the unemployed and the criminal underclass. In 1751, the novelist and magistrate Henry Fielding offered this harrowing account of some of the city's notorious 'rookeries'. He drew first on the testimony of the High Constable of Holborn, who had reported:

> That in the parish of St Giles's there are great numbers of houses set apart for the reception of idle persons and vagabonds, who have their lodgings there for twopence a night: that in the above parish, and in St George, Bloomsbury, one woman alone occupies seven of these houses, all properly accommodated with miserable beds from the cellar to the garret, for such twopenny lodgers; that in these beds, several of which are in the same room, men and women, often strangers to each other, lie promiscuously, the price of a double bed being no more than threepence, as an encouragement to them to lie together; that as these places are thus adapted to whoredom, so are they no less provided for drunkenness, gin being sold in them all at a penny a quarter; so that the smallest sum of money serves for intoxication; that in the execution of search warrants, Mr Welch rarely finds less than twenty of these houses open for receipt of all comers at the latest hours; that in one of these houses, and that not a large one, he has numbered 58 persons of both sexes, the stench of whom was so intolerable, that it compelled him in a very short time to quit the place.

Fielding went on:

> I myself once saw in the parish of Shoreditch, where two little houses were emptied of near 70 men and women; amongst whom was one

of the prettiest girls I had ever seen, who had been carried off by an Irishman, to consummate her marriage on her wedding night, in a room where several others were in bed at the same time.

If one considers the destruction of all morality, decency and modesty; the swearing, whoredom, and drunkenness, which is eternally carrying on in these houses, on the one hand, and the excessive poverty and misery of most of the inhabitants on the other, it seems doubtful whether they are more the objects of detestation, or compassion; for such is the poverty of these wretches, that, upon searching all the above number, the money found upon all of them (except the bride, who, as I afterwards heard, had robbed her mistress) did not amount to one shilling; and I have been credibly informed, that a single loaf has supplied a whole family with their provisions for a week. Lastly, if any of these miserable creatures fall sick (and it is almost a miracle, that stench, vermin, and want should ever suffer them to be well) they are turned out in the streets by their merciless host or hostess, where, unless some parish officer of extraordinary charity relieves them, they are sure miserably to perish, with the addition of hunger and cold to their disease.[2]

Samuel Johnson famously said, 'when a man is tired of London, he is tired of life; for there is in London all that life can afford'.[3] And it is true that eighteenth-century London teemed with life. There was a myriad employments, some of them regular, others most precarious. There were shopkeepers and skilled workers; furniture makers and watch makers; carriers, labourers and watermen; chair-men and servants; rag-and-bone gatherers; even, God help us, dog-shit gatherers (it was used to dry leather); and of course pickpockets and prostitutes.

And all about was variegated activity. At the beginning of the 1790s, for example, William Wordsworth found the city, with its rich and imperial splendour and its street-life, a great spectacle. He viewed its grand buildings, including the dozens of churches; went to its theatres; observed its shopkeepers, labourers, beggars, criminals, prostitutes and show people; heard its notable preachers; visited parliament to hear its famed speakers; discussed politics with its liberal reporters and radical intellectuals. He was struck by the energy of the people and the place, by the city's bustle of commerce and labour, and by the variety of entertainment available in it – at the theatres, where pickpockets and prostitutes found rich returns; at more popular venues such as Sadler's Wells, with its 'singers, rope-dancers, giants and dwarfs, clowns, conjurors, posture-masters, harlequins, amid the uproar of the rabblement';[4] and in the streets, where spectators might routinely see acrobats, jugglers, exotic minstrels, dancing dogs, camels ridden by monkeys, and sometimes the new-fangled hot-air balloons.

But for many men, women and children in the great city, life was a desperate struggle for survival. Food was often meagre and of poor quality – fish, for example, was usually rotten by the time it arrived from the North Sea ports; bread was easy to adulterate with such things as peas and barley or, worse, alum, chalk, lime and white lead; good meat cost too much for the poor to be able to afford it; and, as Fielding observed, gin was the oblivion of the masses. Scurvy was endemic in winter, when many of the poor simply starved. One observer commented on circumstances at the end of 1784:

> The people in general complain of the frost since Wednesday last. It has been too cold for rain … The Thames is not frozen but on the flats and edges of the shores. Thousands are however in distress, where the poor are so many and the means of subsistence so dear. The bargemen and gardeners are in the streets crying to the windows for charity.[5]

If the ubiquitous stench of cesspits and tanneries was not enough, summer's heat added that of the open sewer that was the River Thames, causing the rich to retreat to their country estates.

Death cast a heavy pall. With little town planning and no modern understanding of the causes of disease, eighteenth-century London was repeatedly swept by epidemics of smallpox, cholera, typhoid and typhus, which wreaked terrible havoc on malnourished bodies. It is estimated that one infant in three born in London died before the age of two. In the East End, 55 per cent of children died before they were five, and the average age of death was thirty. In many years deaths in the population exceeded births, so that the total was maintained only by the annual migration of up to 10,000 persons from country areas.

*

By the mid-eighteenth century, there were changes building that would in the next hundred years transform English society. First, there were marked improvements in travel and transportation infrastructure. Roads, which while the responsibility of the parishes had often been only meandering quagmires, began to improve with the introduction of Turnpike Trusts. These were bodies set up by acts of parliament to collect tolls, which were used to keep roads in good repair. Between 1748 and 1770, the number of Trusts increased from 160 to 530, and turnpike mileage was quadrupled. Then, in the last quarter of the century, came the technique of macadamisation, which also led to better roads. The first canal was opened in 1761, and the number progressively increased. (Between 1790 and 1793, for example, some fifty-three canal navigation acts passed through parliament; by 1815 there were 2600 miles of canals.)

What is known as the Agricultural Revolution also took hold. While there is much disagreement about the nature of this change and the time of its onset, it certainly involved the recognition that large-scale farming was more efficient and productive than the immemorial culti-vation of small plots and commons grazing, and that the rotation of crops allowed farmlands to remain fertile. At the core of this change were the consolidation of established farms and the enclosure of com-mon land, and the introduction of new crops that both renewed fertility and provided fodder to support larger numbers of animals, which in turn produced more manure for fertilizing fields. As each enclosure of commons had to be legislated, the parliamentary records offer a broad indication of the growth of the Agricultural Revolution. There was one enclosure act passed between 1700 and 1710, and thirty-eight between

1740 and 1750. Between 1750 and 1800 there were 5000. The amount of land enclosed or newly brought into cultivation in this period seems to have been in the order of 2 million to 3 million acres; during the course of the century, agricultural production seems to have risen by about 40 per cent.[6]

Although it led to better farming methods, which in turn supported a larger population, the Agricultural Revolution had some disastrous social consequences, impoverishing and displacing whole classes of yeomen-farmers and agricultural labourers. As the century drew to a close, this was one of the causes of the migration of people to the cities. In his articles for the *Political Register*, William Cobbett chronicled the transformation of the English countryside and the destruction of its traditional way of life:

> from one end of England to the other, the houses which formerly contained little farms and their happy families, are now seen sinking into ruins, all the windows except one or two stopped up, leaving just light enough for some labourer, whose father was, perhaps, the small farmer, to look back upon his half-naked and half-famished children, while, from this door, he surveys all around him the land teeming with the means of luxury to his opulent and overgrown master ... We are daily advancing to that state in which there are but two classes of men, *masters*, and *abject dependants*.[7]

Such accounts may be somewhat simplistic. The population of the United Kingdom as a whole seems to have increased steadily through the century, from about 9.4 million to about 15.9 million, or by 70 per cent. By the beginning of the nineteenth century there were simply more people (particularly young people) to gravitate to the cities and towns. And gravitate they did, often to find themselves living in bitter poverty. Cobbett observed of Coventry in 1817, for example, that it had a population of 20,000, of whom more than 8000 were 'miserable paupers'.[8]

The other great change that was building throughout the second half of the eighteenth century was the Industrial Revolution, but here again we need to be careful about when we locate its emergence. It is true that Matthew Boulton started his Soho Manufactory, now recognized as a proto metal-working factory, outside Birmingham in the 1760s and that, in partnership with its inventor, James Watt, he was deploying the steam engine in the Cornish coal mines from the mid-1770s. However, the substantial effects of the Industrial Revolution, with steam power driving an increased capacity for mass manufacture, really appeared only in the last two decades of the century. James Hargreaves developed his spinning jenny in the mid-1760s, which simplified, quickened and cheapened the making of cloth; in the 1770s Samuel Crompton invented his spinning mule, which when combined with the jenny allowed the manufacture of many different kinds of yarn. In 1785, James Watt patented his fourth steam engine, the one that would be harnessed to the new spinning and weaving equipment developed by Edmund Cartwright. In 1783, Henry Cort developed his puddling process, which allowed iron to be smeltered with coal and markedly improved quality.

Even if the Industrial Revolution was only beginning to gain pace in the 1780s, however, to far-sighted people the future it proclaimed was already clear. For example, in 1787 the Prime Minister, William Pitt, the president of the Board of Trade, Lord Hawkesbury, and Sir Joseph Banks developed a plan to obtain breadfruit from the Pacific islands to feed the slaves in the West Indies, who would grow cotton for Britain's mills, which would produce cloth to be sold in East Asia. This elaborate scheme revealed an understanding that the mechanization of manufacturing offered the prospect of great returns.

The evidence of this change was soon all about. As one historian has pointed out, 'after 1782, almost every available statistical series of industrial output reveals a sharp upward turn … More than half the growth in the shipments of coal and the mining of copper, more that three-quarters of the increase of broadcloths, four-fifths of that of printed cloth, and nine-tenths of the exports of cotton goods were concentrated in the last eighteen years of the eighteenth century'. Similarly, in 1788 the annual production of pig iron was 60,000 tons; in 1796 it was 125,000 tons, the number of blast furnaces having increased from 85 to 125.[9]

By the turn of the nineteenth century, swelled by migration from the countryside, the populations of the industrializing provincial cities were growing, with those of Bristol, Birmingham, Leeds, Liverpool and Manchester now exceeding 50,000.

*

While some of the structures of authority that controlled eighteenth-century English life are quite familiar to us (the monarchy, parliament, the courts, the church), others are very strange. By and large, ours is a highly regulated society, what with the imposing role of central government, including welfare support; a plethora of laws and very extensive legal practices to govern both public and private behaviour; extensive police forces with highly sophisticated surveillance methods; and town and local councils, which provide what we have come to consider essential goods and services, and which are in turn governed by networks of laws, by-laws and regulations.

In eighteenth-century England, however, central government was only just beginning what would become in the nineteenth century and afterwards its ever-increasing regulation of public and private life. Police forces existed only in embryonic form and the law's operation was, to our eyes, perfunctory. Much more then than now, what social cohesion there was usually depended on the recognition of customary rights and the maintenance of long-standing practices that bound together servants and masters, tenants and landlords, yeomen and gentry, nobles and the monarch. Those who lay claim to authority had to negotiate it rather than assume or enforce it. Nicholas Rodger has made this point eloquently of the Royal Navy:

> In the eyes of a modern officer, the discipline of the mid-eighteenth-century Navy would appear lax to the point of anarchy. Insubordination in every form and from every rank and rating in the Service was a daily part of life. Where modern officers expect to command, mid-eighteenth-century officers hoped to persuade. The fact that this did not alarm them was partly because it was a

feature of Service life to which they were completely accustomed, and no different from the weakness of civil authority on shore.[10]

Consider this example of indiscipline. Jacob Nagle was an American who sailed on the *Sirius* to Botany Bay. In 1797, after returning to England, he enlisted in the *Blanche*, one of Nelson's Mediterranean squadron. The captain of the *Blanche* was superseded by a more senior officer, Henry Hotham. In Jacob Nagle's barely literate prose (too colourful to modernize), Hotham bore

> the name of such a tarter [i.e., one of Genghis Khan's horde] by his own ships crew, that our ship mutinised and entierly refused him. He came on board [7 January 1797], had all the officers armed on the quarter deck and all hands turned aft to hear his commission read at the capstain head. They [i.e., the seamen] all cried out, 'No, no, no'. He asked what they had to say against [him]. One of the petty officers replyed that his ships company informed us that he was a dam'd tarter and we would not have him and went forward and turned the two forecastle guns aft with canester shot.

In the face of this tumult, Hotham retired to Nelson's ship and returned with the commodore's first lieutenant. Nagle continues:

> When on b[oar]d [the lieutentant] ordered all hands aft. The ship's company came aft. He called all the petty officers out, which ware call'd by name, and pareded them in a line on the quarter deck. 'Now, my lads, if you resist taking Capt[ain] Hotham as your capt[ain], every third man shall be hung'. The crew flew in a body forward to the guns with match in hand, likewise crowbars, hand-spikes, and all kinds of weapons they could get holt of and left him, Capt[ain] Hotham, and the officers standing looking at us. They consulted for a moment and returned on b[oar]d Commodere Nelson's [ship].

The standoff was only resolved when Nelson himself came on board and assured the crew that if Hotham mistreated them, he would rectify the situation. As Nagle recorded triumphantly: 'Amediately there was three chears given and Capt[ain] Hotham shed tears'.[11]

As at sea, so on land. As R.W. Malcolmson has pointed out:

The exercise of established authority in eighteenth-century England was not only subtle and complex, it was also very uneven in its impact and effectiveness. In some parts of the country authority was unchallenged and securely enforced; in other areas the exercise of authority was tenuous, uncertain and often ineffectual ... In one type of community – perhaps a small market-town or a dominant squire's parish – we detect evidence of firm social discipline, outward deference and quiescence; in other places we uncover a social reality of dissent, frequent social conflict and plebeian independence ... For in many parts of England the formal institutions of power were neither deeply rooted nor widely respected; the populations of these places were partly withdrawn from, and sometimes resistant to, the exercise of 'lawful' authority.[12]

Let me summarize the behaviour of that class of persons that Malcolmson researched in detail. The area of Gloucester to the east of Bristol, known as the Kingswood Chase, was partly deforested and rich in coal. In the first half of the eighteenth century, the men who mined the coal and those who transported it to Bristol were notorious for their refusal to accept authority and for their more general lawlessness – notorious for, as John Wesley succinctly put it, 'neither fearing God nor regarding man'. Repeatedly, since they did not believe that they should have to pay tolls to get their coal to market, they gathered in their hundreds to destroy turnpike gates. They counterfeited coins. They broke into houses. They stole horses and sheep. They robbed travellers on the Bath and Bristol roads. They threatened violence (at one point promising to set fire to houses, and even to a whole town) to obtain the release of 'brethren' who had been arrested. Armed with clubs, staves and even muskets, they turned out in large numbers in support of other groups with popular grievances, such as the Bristol labourers and Wiltshire weavers, defying magistrates who read them the riot act. The Kingswood Chase colliers were, all in all, 'a set of ungovernable people'.[13]

*

In eighteenth-century English society, then, the bonds of civility were often fragile and easily broken, and authority was often weak or absent. It was therefore a society in which crime might easily flourish. There has probably never been an age since the beginning of the world when respectable citizens have not lamented that crime was increasing; but given the fewer checks to its progress in eighteenth-century England, it is difficult to avoid the conclusion that it impinged more on daily life then than it does now.

The greatest offence was treason – the high treason of rebellion against, or violence upon the person of the King, and the lesser treason of wife against husband, or servant against master. Below treason in the hierarchy of enormous offences were murder with malicious intent (that is, premeditated), manslaughter, rape (which, because of evidentiary difficulties, was often tried as attempted rape), infanticide, robbery with violence, burglary (heinous because it caught householders unawares at night) and horse-stealing. The common denominator linking this group of offences was violence against the person; contemporaries condemned them particularly because 'they endanger life and safety, as well as property; and ... render the condition of society wretched, by a sense of personal insecurity'.[14]

Then there were clusters of lesser crimes: breaking into a house (i.e., when no one was present); stealing without violence from the person (i.e., picking pockets); stealing from a shop or from ships in the river; receiving stolen goods; sheep- and cattle-stealing; theft of small animals and items, such as hens and ducks, turnips and fruit; sexual assault, particularly of children; coining and debasing the coinage (i.e., adding to the number in circulation, whether by forging coins or by combining fragments chipped from several coins to create new ones); forging bank drafts and wills; stealing from the post office; doing business on the Sabbath; keeping a bawdy house; poaching and the taking of wood from forests; shooting at someone, even if that person was not wounded; rioting; and vagrancy, particularly where idle and dissolute persons were suspected of 'pilfering'.

Inevitably, the great metropolis of London was where crime in all its varieties flourished. There were more people and a greater range of goods to be stolen than in smaller towns and the countryside. The buildings and narrow streets provided greater opportunity for escape and concealment, while the 'bawdy houses' and 'flash taverns' made it easier to pass on stolen goods. And crucially, the influx into the city of large numbers of feckless labourers and young people from all over the country meant that vice was more widespread and social bonds weaker than in more settled communities, where people might have known each other for decades and families lived side by side for generations.

Prostitution provides a case in point. Contemporary estimates of the number of prostitutes in London in the second half of the eighteenth century range from 50,000 to 62,000. A large proportion of these women perhaps sold themselves only occasionally; but even if we then reduce the total by half, we are left with something like 25,000 to 30,000 'working girls' servicing a male population of about 350,000, which suggests a very high incidence of paid-for sex (and this does not take into account courtesans or official mistresses). In these circumstances, it was inevitable that family and community bonds be weaker than those who lived in villages were accustomed to, and society therefore less stable.

*

In 1785 the *Edinburgh Magazine* listed the various sets and subsets of thieves, both in the metropolis and in the countryside, each of which had its particular skills and mystique.[15] At their head were the 'high-pads' or 'highwaymen', who operated on the major roads of the kingdom, frequently just outside town limits (because highwaymen too needed taverns at which to refresh, and beds in which to sleep). 'This class sit at the head of the table, pay a double share of the bill; and whenever it is necessary or expedient that one die for the credit or conveniency of the rest, the high-pads claim a preference.' Often, highwaymen went about in small gangs, such as that led by Ralph Wilson, who claimed to have operated along all the coach routes servicing London:

> One Morning we robbed the Cirencester, the Worcester, the Gloucester, the Oxford, and Bristol stage-coaches, all together; the next morning the Ipswich and Colchester, and a third morning perhaps the Portsmouth coach. The Bury coach has been our constant customer. I think we have touched that coach ten times.[16]

A romantic tinge of the Robin Hood sort often attached to these 'gentlemen of the road' or 'of the shade'. One young practitioner presented himself to a group of travellers 'dressed in a blue surtout coat, brown cut wig, a black crepe mask over his face, mounted on a bright bay gelding'. Two others, who in the space of a week 'committed many robberies on Blackheath and the Kentish roads', were 'handsome young men' who had 'all the exterior appearance of gentlemen'.[17] Crowds would gather at the haunts of highwaymen to watch them setting out on their business.

Sometimes highwaymen did conduct themselves with a peculiar sense of honour, as shown by this December 1786 story:

> A gentleman, from the west of England, went to London a few weeks ago to receive a legacy of £500, which he proposed to bring with him into the country. His servant, apprised of his master's errand, imprudently talked of it at an inn upon the road. A person in the room, in appearance a tradesman, but in reality a highwayman, overheard the conversation, and determined to possess himself of the booty. Pursuing the gentleman to London, he watched all his motions, and on his return into the country, was ready to follow him. On the other side of Hounslow, near the turnpike on Smallberry Green, the robber came up with the chaise, and passed it full gallop, but was stopped at the gate, not having a single penny to pay the toll. He appeared greatly confused, took out his handkerchief,

and begged the turnpikeman to take it as a pledge. The gentleman in the chaise having observed the transaction, on his coming up, enquired the cause; and promising to return the handkerchief to the owner, paid the penny for him. He presently overtook the highwayman, and, ordering his chaise to stop, 'Pray Sir', said he, 'is this your handkerchief? If so, I fear you are in great distress.' 'I am indeed, sir', replied the man, 'in the greatest, that is possible.' 'Allow me, then', rejoined the gentleman, 'to relieve your immediate wants'; and pulling out his purse, presented him with five guineas. 'Your generosity', said the highwayman, 'disarms me. Your five guineas have saved your five hundred'; and turning his horse, immediately rode off.[18]

But the highwaymen's strikes were not always benign. Witnessing an attack by a group of three men, a woman called out that 'she knew the rogues', who thereupon cut out her tongue.[19]

Then there were the 'collectors', the 'low robbers', or 'foot-pads', 'those who take charge of the cross ways, concurrent departments of the road, by-lanes, or wherever a purse may be taken, a pocket rifled, or a stab given with security'. These sorts of thieves, the *Edinburgh Magazine* explained, 'are bloody, cowardly villains, who lurk in the dark, loiter about hedges and old houses, and stroll out in the evenings in groups. Their orders are to take whatever they can, to strip rich and poor, and to murder or mangle whoever has nothing, gives what he has with reluctance, or makes the least resistance.' The London newspapers of the time are rife with reports of good citizens being assaulted, robbed and sometime maimed in the street, often in broad daylight, even while crossing London Bridge.

Then there was the 'rifleman' or 'budge', the person 'who is always strolling about, down lanes, up courts, lounging in unfrequented streets, and hanging in markets, or about stalls, where those who sell, and those who buy, are often over-busy, or over-careless; and he generally take aim so well, that he seldom or never misses the mark'.

The 'diver', or 'pick-pocket', 'occupies a situation of infinite danger and address. The practitioners in this branch of the system formerly went single. They were then called *bung-nippers;* because with a *horn thumb* and a *sharp knife*, they generally cut off the pocket and its contents.' These thieves were often 'well-dressed, and are constant frequenters of the theatres, the chapels-royal, both houses of parliament, and all other public places'.

The 'diver' often worked in tandem with the 'bulk'. This person's role 'was to create quarrels, in order that, by gathering a crowd, their enterprises may be carried on with effect, and without observation'.

Then there was the 'jilt' or 'ferret' or 'house-bug', a woman who, 'connected with some of the gang, takes lodgings, especially in alehouses or taverns, and with pick-locks opens all the chests and trunks to which she has access; and having selected what she likes, fastens them, discharges her lodgings, and goes off without suspicion'.

The 'prigger' or 'prancer' was he who confined his activities to stealing horses. 'This line is recruited from Newmarket, and the various mews and livery stables in the metropolis.'

The 'ken-miller' 'robs houses in the night-time, by breaking them open, getting in at the window, sprawling down the chimney, and nestling under the beds. These expeditions are generally executed by stout and resolute parties, who carry on their depredations with great system. Their implements of forcible entrance, when that is necessary, are altogether irresistible; but they generally prefer that mode which is accompanied with as little noise as possible. A watch is carefully set on every pass, and their retreat, in the event of discovery or disturbance, effectually secured.'

The 'scourers' 'are a set of people who have lately infested the houses situated on the side of the river'. Most of these were reportedly unemployed sailors, who robbed from ships and lighters.

Finally, there were the 'petty hawkers' or 'shop-lifters', 'whose chief employ is to cheapen [that is, to ask the price of or barter for] goods from place to place, till an opportunity offers of secreting such articles as are most commodious for carrying off without detection'.

*

The provincial cities, market towns, farms and sheep-walks of the country were also the scenes of other varieties of crime: riots by the labouring poor; the stealing or maiming of domestic animals; the poaching of game from gentlemen's parks; the illicit gathering of fuel; the cutting down of orchards and forest plantations. Poaching was often carried out by gangs whose members, like their city confreres, might swear oaths not to betray each other. And all along the southern coasts of England there operated smugglers intent on defrauding His Majesty's customs revenues, who frequently resorted to violence to avoid arrest.

Sometimes, as E.P. Thompson has shown,[20] this rural lawlessness arose from a sense of injustice (for instance, at sharp increases in food prices in times of dearth), or from the removal of a customary right by a rapacious landlord (such as the traditional right to gather wood in forests 'by hook or by crook'), or as a conscious act of class rebellion. At other times, however, it was simply vicious.

*

The closest contemporary Australian equivalent of eighteenth-century English society is not to be found in our well-ordered suburbs or our by and large tranquil country towns, but in the inner city of Melbourne on a Friday or Saturday night, or in the western suburbs of Sydney, with their raucous violence and warring criminal gangs.

Lord Sydney gave one indication of just how unruly life in London could be in March 1778, when he complained in parliament that crime was increasing, and that 'in the course of the winter every day furnished a fresh account of some daring robbery or burglary ... Scarcely a night passed in which there were not robberies committed in Park Lane, and firing of pistols heard'.[21] With his lavish houses, servants and carriages, however, Sydney was largely cocooned from the violence all about him. At this time, as old Bow Street officers later remembered, gangs terrorized Londoners. A constable could not 'walk in Duck Lane, Gravel Lane or Cock Lane, without a party of five or six men along with him, they would have cut him to pieces if he was alone', reported one officer. Another recalled that the members of these gangs 'used to be ready to pop at a man as soon as he let down his glass'.[22] Typical of the all-too-frequent 'atrocious' assaults was an occasion when three foot-pads slashed their victim's face with a sword ('so that his teeth and jaw-bone could be seen'), knocked him down and stole one shilling from him before running off.[23]

Mayhem was not confined to the metropolis, however. At the beginning of January 1784, 'on Monday morning early the house of Philip Martin, Esquire, near Epping, was broke open by some villains, three of whom entered the apartments, while the other stood sentry at the door. Their faces were all blacked; they were well-armed, and after behaving in a very inhuman manner to the servants, carried off plate and other valuable articles to a very considerable amount.' In January 1787, William Fitzgerald and John Millan were convicted of assaulting James Richards in the main street of Exeter and 'robbing him of a linen handkerchief and 6 shillings'.[24]

These were minor instances of the ever-present lawlessness. The two following stories show how extreme this might become. Lewis Gunner was a Hampshire gamekeeper and gang leader who terrorised his community with arrogant violence. He was, as one magistrate put it, 'of a proud, insulting and revengeful temper'. He always carried loaded pistols, and he and his men shot dogs, seized nets, lit fires and maimed farm animals. He was arrested and sentenced for shooting at an enemy, a capital offence. In response, his men rampaged, burning houses and barns. He was reprieved on condition that he transport himself out of England for fourteen years. But once he was released, he and his men intensified their violence, threatening more fires, stabbing animals and shooting at people. They coerced some of the community into signing a petition for him to receive a full pardon. As one frightened citizen complained to authorities, 'No doubt he will add names enough … for very few would have the courage to deny him. Our thatched buildings and enclosed country, my Lord, lay both our lives and fortunes at the mercy of such desperate villains.'[25]

After the Maidstone quarter sessions in January 1785, the chairman wrote to Sydney (now Home Secretary) of the particularly troubling case of Alexander Rimington, 'formerly a notorious smuggler in the neighbourhood … but later employed by the Excise officers as an assistant', who had committed a long series of outrages:

[He] was indicted at the Michaelmas sessions for an assault, and the bill found by the grand jury [that is, the indictment was found to be 'true' – valid in legal form and having substance]. He was apprehended and committed to jail; and then on finding securities for his appearance to answer the complaint, was discharged. He surrendered this session, and on his appearance in the town a man seized him, and charged him with robbing him on the highway in June last. He was accordingly tried for this fact and found guilty, and sentenced to transportation for seven years. On his return to prison, he confessed the fact.

One great reason for my troubling your Lordship with this story is that strong hints have been given that our sentence signified not a pin, for that such application would be made for him to the King, as would ensure his pardon. And as he has long been a terror to this part of the country, I thought it proper that, if such application should be made, your Lordship might not be a stranger to the story. For this man, under pretence of being an assistant to the Excise officers, but without any officer in his company – and I think it clear they cannot delegate their authority – has stopped and searched innocent persons, totally unconcerned with smuggling, with great rudeness and barbarity. He has often broke open barns at a distance from any house, and stolen corn and hay for his and his companions' horses. He has seized goods from smugglers without any authority, and converted them to his own use. And there are two miserable men, who with their families are now kept by the parish, owing to their having been totally disabled by him, having been almost hacked to pieces. These men were indeed smugglers, but unarmed, and made no resistance. In a word, the outrages he has committed in this part of the country have been so enormous, that if he is not totally removed, nobody can be safe. The sense of the people was fully shown by a burst of applause at his being convicted and sentenced, which I was never witness to before in a court of justice.[26]

This prevailing lawlessness intensified with the demobilization of tens of thousands of soldiers and sailors at the end of war. During conflict, as rogues were absorbed into the army and navy, the incidence of assaults and property crimes diminished; after it, it rose sharply. Put ashore at the Channel ports, far away from family and friends and with no other means of support, many of the demobilized men soon squandered their pay on women, alcohol and gambling; for such men, the temptation to turn their martial skills to assault and robbery could be irresistible. Stephen Janssen, who was Lord Mayor of London in 1755, observed:

> As a great many idle men and lads are taken into the sea and land service during a war, so we then find the gangs of robbers soon broken and the business at the Old Bailey gradually diminished to half its duration in time of peace nor are half the number of criminals condemned. For in some years of war they have not amounted to twenty, whereas in peace they have arisen to seventy, eighty and ninety. It is farther observable that at the conclusion of a war, through very bad policy, when we turn adrift so many thousand men, great numbers fall heedlessly to thieving as soon as their pockets are empty, and are at once brought to the gallows. The wiser ones survive a while by listing with experienced associates, by which means in a few years, those numerous and desperate gangs of murderers, housebreakers and highwaymen have been formed, which have of late stuck such a terror within the metropolis and twenty miles around.[27]

After the war of 1776–83, for example, an estimated 160,000 soldiers and sailors returned to England. Numbers of these were soon committing depredations. To give just a few examples from in and around London in 1782–3: in Dorking, a female miller was set upon by five sailors with pistols and cutlasses; two marines, similarly armed, robbed a higler (a person who sold provisions and other small items door to door); two soldiers and four sailors committed a number of robberies in Chelsea; and ten men 'armed with cutlasses and pistols, in two boats, boarded a vessel near Union Stairs, Wapping ... and stole thereabout two bales of woollens'.[28]

This lawlessness was general; as one country newspaper reported in October 1783, 'a great number of disbanded militiamen, who are too idle to return to their farming business, are robbing in all parts of the country; in Oxfordshire and Berkshire the highways are particularly infested with them'.[29] At least some of those responsible for this crime wave were soon filling the hulks and jails, and their swelling numbers was one of the factors that led the Pitt administration to resume transportation.

*

In 1751, Henry Fielding published *An Enquiry into the Causes of the Late Increase of Robbers*. Among other things, he pointed to the lower incidence of crime in the countryside than in London, where there was both more temptation and greater probability of escaping detection. Understanding that there would be less crime if people found it more difficult to profit from it, he proposed much stronger penalties for receivers of stolen goods (known as 'fences'). He urged the strengthening of community policing and recommended compensation for those bringing prosecutions, to compensate them for loss of income while they attended court.

Fielding opened his study with this striking assertion: 'I make no doubt, but that the streets of [London], and the roads leading to it, will shortly be impassable without the utmost hazard; nor are we threatened with seeing less dangerous gangs of rogues among us, than those which the Italians call the Banditti.'[30]

There are earlier instances of this word in English,[31] but Fielding's work gave it widespread currency and by the 1780s 'banditti' had become a commonplace term. In May 1781, Richard Camplin used it to describe the convict soldiers sent to Africa. One Bow Street constable spoke of the London street gangs of the time as 'the bandittis'. Another commentator complained bitterly of the 'tribes of banditti who lay the rest of the community under continual contributions'. A third bemoaned the existence of 'the dreadful banditti that infest this kingdom', 'the most formidable and dreadful number of abandoned wretches, that for a series of years have committed their depredations on the public'. Another called the foresters of Selwood, in Somerset, 'a desperate clan of banditti', and Admiral Milbanke described the Irish convicts landed at Newfoundland in 1789 as 'a Banditti'.[32] In the public imagination, 'banditti' was short-hand for those rogues who preferred a life of crime to honest labour, who as often as not operated in gangs, and who were willing to use violence, either to rob or to effect their escape. These were men who held the law in contempt, who might form 'leagues of friendship' and swear diabolical oaths, who were feared by respectable citizens and who were considered by judges to be incorrigible.

2.

Eighteenth-Century England: Punishment

IT IS NOTORIOUS THAT IN THE middle of the eighteenth century English law contained some 160 crimes punishable by death, and that this number had increased to about 200 by the beginning of the nineteenth century. These totals suggest a frightful 'bloody code'. However, simply stating the number does not represent the situation properly. As various historians have pointed out, English law was not codified, and therefore punishment needed to be specified for each variant of a general crime – for instance, the punishment for each variety of larceny needed to be stated. In the nineteenth century, as the criminal code was overhauled and more comprehensive definitions developed, the number of crimes to which the death penalty was attached fell significantly.[1]

Before discussing the punishments given for the range of crimes prevalent in eighteenth-century England, I need to explain the peculiarity in English law known as the 'benefit of clergy'. Originating in medieval times, this device permitted members of religious orders who were convicted of public offences to claim the 'benefit' of clergy, and thereby escape being severely punished by secular courts.

Applying at first only to ordained priests, it was gradually extended to include religious clerks, and then to persons who were literate. (These were required to demonstrate this ability by reading a verse from the Psalms before they were sentenced.) The extension of this practice – a legal fiction, really – allowed those convicted of felonies to escape a mandatory death sentence.

In the course of the sixteenth century, authorities removed the benefit of clergy from the most serious crimes, including treason, murder and accessory to murder, infanticide, rape, highway robbery, robbery with violence, burglary, horse-stealing, and some forms of larceny. For these offences, conviction brought the death sentence regardless of literacy.

The list of crimes punishable by death and without the benefit of clergy was expanded in the eighteenth century to include appearing armed and with face blackened in public; shooting at someone; poaching deer, hares and other animals; stealing sheep or cattle; the theft of linen or cotton cloth valued at 10 shillings or more; the theft from a ship or wharf of goods valued at 40 shillings or more; grand larceny (where the goods taken were worth more than 1 shilling); theft from a shop, warehouse or stable of goods valued at more than 5 shillings; and forgery.

For the grand and petty larcenies that remained 'clergyable', there were fundamentally two punishments. For grand larceny, this was branding on the base of the thumb, with release immediately afterwards. For petty larceny, it was whipping, either at a post or at the tail of a cart that travelled a prescribed distance in public. For some slight thefts and assault, there was the possibility of fining, which effectively involved the offender making some financial restitution to the victim. For some other forms of assault and for sexual offences there was a comparatively short imprisonment, which might also entail one period or more of 'exposure' in the pillory, a lockable wooden frame with holes for neck and arms. This last punishment might or might not be relatively benign, depending on whether the public sympathized with the criminal or not. If they did, then their throwing of rotten fruit or loose dirt might not have much effect beyond the humiliation involved. However, if the crowd was hostile, the consequences of being exposed in the pillory could be gruesome. In 1762, for example, the public turned on one old man convicted of a homosexual act, 'tore off his coat, waistcoat, shirt, hat, wig, and breeches, and then pelted and whipped him till he had scarcely any signs of life left; he was once pulled off the pillory, but hung by his arms till he was set up again and stood in that naked condition, covered with mud, till the hour was out, and then was carried back to Newgate'.[2] On another occasion, the London public threw rocks at a mannish woman who had been sentenced to the pillory for going through forms of marriage with two other women, causing her to lose her sight.

*

By the beginning of the eighteenth century, the view was widespread that the law was defective because it offered only a few punishments intermediate between death and branding or whipping. It was to remedy this defect that in 1718 parliament enacted legislation providing for felons whose crimes had not been of the most extreme nature to be transported to Britain's colonies in America for terms of seven years, fourteen years or life.

While there had earlier been some expulsions of felons from the kingdom, this act systematized the practice. The government let contracts to merchants to transport the convicts across the Atlantic Ocean on ships run and supplied at the merchant's expense. In the early 1720s, a merchant received £3 from the government for each convict taken. In 1727, this was raised to £5, though at times, when the demand for labour was strong in the colonies, the merchant might transport the convicts for no fee, knowing that he could cover his costs and make a profit by selling the labour of his charges at a higher than usual rate.[3]

On taking custody of convicts sentenced to transportation ('transports') the merchant had to sign certificates of 'jail delivery' and bonds for their safe conveyance to their destination, and for not assisting them to return to England before their sentences had expired. When he had delivered his cargo, he had to obtain certificates from the customs officer or the governor confirming that he had done so, for without these he would not receive his fees from the Treasury in London. Once in the American colonies, the merchant was able to sell the convicts' labour for the unexpired term of their sentences, up to the maximum of seven years that colonial laws permitted. Duncan Campbell, who was one of the principal merchants engaged in transportation in the 1760s and 1770s, recorded that he received on average £10 per man and £8 or £9 per woman, though for younger men, particularly those with skills such as carpentry or blacksmithing, he might receive £15 to £25.[4] And then there was the profit to be made from the return cargo, which might be timber or tobacco, or rum and sugar from the West Indies.

It was obviously in the merchants' interest to land their human cargo in as good health as possible, as the colonial merchants and planters seeking labourers did not wish to pay for those who were old or ill. And there is evidence that most of the merchants involved in the trade were usually diligent in this regard. Campbell estimated that about one-seventh of the men he transported, and one-fourteenth of the women, died between the time of jail delivery and disembarkation, mostly from smallpox and the prison scourge of typhus fever.

There were some other developments in the regimen of punishment in the course of the eighteenth century, the principal of which was imprisonment in a 'house of correction' with hard labour for periods of between three and twelve months. But for those felonies deemed not serious enough to warrant the death sentence, transportation remained the predominant form of intermediate punishment from 1718 until 1775, when the American colonies revolted.

In view of later Australian circumstances, there are other points worth making about transportation to North America. First, it was essentially a private business, for the role of central government ceased once merchants had signed contracts and taken custody of the convicts. Second, unless they did something in the colonies (such as absconding or assaulting or robbing) to give rise to a fresh record, most of the transports were simply absorbed into the general population. Presumably many of them eventually returned to Britain, but there are no figures. Third, the punishment involved in the sentence of transportation was essentially exile from Britain. From 1718, early return constituted a felony bearing the death sentence, with little prospect of reprieve.

There were ways of avoiding the forced labour that usually accompanied transportation, but these were in practice available only to those with money and influential friends. Felons might receive a reprieve if they undertook to transport themselves. For example, in 1775 Jonathan Biggott was convicted of highway robbery. He received a pardon of his death sentence on condition that he leave Britain 'within the space of two months' and not return for fourteen years.[5] Then there was the case of Nicholas Greenwell, embarked on the *Alexander*, one of the First Fleet ships. As they were on the point of sailing, he received a pardon 'on condition that he shall depart this kingdom within one month from the day on which he shall be discharged out of custody, and not to return to or be found within the same for the term of seven years'.[6] Or, persons might buy themselves out of servitude on disembarkation, by paying the contractor what he would have received for them on the labour market.

Although some authorities were expressing dissatisfaction with the practice of transportation to the American colonies in the 1760s, on the grounds that exiled felons could represent no lesson to would-be offenders at home and that it was too easy for them to return before their term was up, it was in the main a well-regarded punishment. The House of Commons committee that enquired into the resumption of transportation in 1785 reported:

> that the old system of transporting to America answered every good purpose which could be expected from it; that it tended directly to reclaim the objects on which it was inflicted, and to render them good citizens; that the climate being temperate, and the means of gaining a livelihood easy, it was safe to entrust country magistrates with the discretionary power of inflicting it; that the operation of it was thus universally diffused over the whole island, as well as this metropolis; that it tended to break, in their infancy, those gangs and combinations which have since proved so injurious to the community; that it was not attended with much expense to the public, the convicts being carried out in vessels employed in the Jamaica or tobacco trade; ... that the colonies seem to have been sensible of the beneficial consequences of this

practice; that the convicts whose labour was so purchased were usually removed into the back country, and finding none of the temptations, in that new state of things, which occasioned their offences at home, it does not appear that the police or peace of the colonies suffered in any considerable degree by them.[7]

*

What of the courts which sentenced criminals? To put the situation more simply than it was in some jurisdictions, there were essentially two levels of courts in the English counties in the eighteenth century. These were the quarter sessions, which, as the name suggests, were held four times a year. They were staffed by magistrates, who were also justices of the peace, and heard cases involving breaches of the peace, minor thefts such as of fruit and vegetables, less serious assaults, vagrancy and fraud. Often juries participated in these hearings, but sometimes cases might be heard in a 'summary' fashion by one or two magistrates sitting alone. The quarter session courts might sentence offenders to brief periods in 'houses of correction', or they might assess fines. The magistrates might also negotiate a private settlement between perpetrator and victim, which most often involved some payment in reparation, thus avoiding the need for a court hearing. As the quarter session courts did not deal with felonies carrying the death sentence, I shall not describe their workings in further detail.

The assizes constituted the second level of courts. Judges from the country's central (superior) courts conducted these hearings, twice a year in most counties (in spring and summer) but eight times a year at the Old Bailey, which had jurisdiction over London and Middlesex. In holding these hearings, the judges exercised four commissions – those of assize and of *nisi prius* (i.e., before an assize court rather than a superior one), which empowered them to deal with civil cases; and those of *oyer and terminer* ('to hear and determine') and jail delivery, which enabled them to deal with all criminal cases.

The procedure of a case coming before the assize judges was significantly different from that which we are used to, for our system employs mechanisms that were only just coming into use at the end of the eighteenth century. In effect, the victim of an assault or theft or serious fraud was also the prosecutor. He or she had to make a complaint to a magistrate, identify the nature of the crime and its perpetrator and, if possible, provide witnesses. The magistrate then turned the complainant's oral testimony into depositions. He also took depositions from the person or persons accused of the crime, without telling them of the charges against them. If the purported crime constituted a felony, the accused was imprisoned until the next assize hearing, which meant that the period of waiting for the trial might be as short as two or as long as eight months.

The assizes were conducted with a good deal of pomp, and were also the occasion of social events such as dinners and balls. Leading citizens of the municipality and county would welcome the judges on their arrival. After their commissions had been read formally in public ('published'), the judges would give the depositions to a grand jury, to determine if there was a *prima facie* case to answer. If the decision was yes, then the matter went to trial by jury, with the victim appearing to repeat their complaint and confirm their identification of the accused, and with the accused having the opportunity to challenge this identification, to question witnesses, provide an alibi, and present evidence of good character. Only late in the century did the habit develop of the accused employing a lawyer to help them challenge the evidence against them.

The English legal system in the eighteenth century was never so bloody as it now on the face of things appears. When a person was charged with and convicted of a crime (excepting the most serious offences), there was the potential for the final punishment to be mitigated. At each step the victim/prosecutor, judge and jury might collude to see that the full rigour of the law was not applied. For example, if in the indictment the stolen goods were wrongly identified as the property of William Jones rather than of his brother John Jones, the rightful owner, the case foundered. William Smith, the former chief justice of New York, attended various courts while in England after the Revolutionary War. He reported this case heard in December 1784:

Count Duroure was tried this morning at the Old Bailey on an indictment for attempting to kill Huxley Sandon by firing a pistol at him as he entered to take his wife. It was death by the Black Act … The jury acquitted him agreeable to the charge of Baron Notham, the judge. The shooting was stated to be done 4 October in a hotel kept by John Sundy and James Brewer and the proof was that it was kept by James Sundy and John Brewer. Notham said the prosecutor was not obliged to say who kept the house, but since he had undertaken it he must prove the charge as made. The Count had seduced the wife of a man who had shown him civilities.[8]

Again, if the judge and the grand jury found that while a group of poachers had been taken beside a dead deer, and while the barrel of the musket used to shoot it was still warm, if there was no witness to identify which of the poachers had pulled the trigger, none of them had a case to answer. Or a judge might advise a victim or effectively instruct a jury that the evidence was insufficient to sustain a full charge, and that a lesser one should therefore be sought. Or, out of friendship or compassion, a prosecutor might deliberately understate the value of the goods stolen, so that a guilty verdict would not bring the mandatory death sentence. Or, a jury might convict not on the whole charge, but rather on a lesser one contained within it.

These habits of 'down-charging' or bringing in a 'partial' verdict were pervasive in the eighteenth-century legal system. For example, stating the value of the goods stolen from the person at 10 pence rather than 1 shilling (12 pence) meant that a jury avoided the need to find the criminal guilty of a capital felony, as did stating the value of goods taken from a shop at under 5 shillings or from a house or a ship in the River Thames at under 40 shillings. A jury finding someone guilty of the theft of a single spoon rather than the whole dinner service they had actually taken would have the same effect.

There was often a deliberate manipulation of the legal system. For example, one woman in Sussex stole sixty-one yards of lace, which would have been worth about £100. In the indictment, however, this was valued at 8 pence and a silk girdle at 2 pence, for a total of 10 pence. Another woman who had items taken from her house 'very humanely refused to say' that they were worth more than 39 shillings. The judge at one Shropshire assize told the jury dealing with a charge of the theft of twenty-four fowls 'that the matter of fact was so fully proved that they must find the prisoner guilty, but they would do well to consider of the value'; so that the jury found him guilty of 'felony to the value of 11 pence, at which the judge laughed heartily and said he was glad to hear that cocks and hens were cheap in this country'.[9]

Even when a crime had been adjudged so serious that it mandated a capital sentence, this might still be avoided by the exercise of the 'royal mercy', whereby, having learned of mitigating circumstances, or prominent citizens having come forward with character references, a judge might recommend to the Secretary of State that the King pardon the convicted felon on condition that a secondary punishment (usually transportation) be substituted.

Sir Dudley Ryder was chief justice of the Court of King's Bench in London. He presided over four sessions at the Old Bailey between 1754 and 1756, and at various assize hearings in the Home Counties. He kept detailed notes of the cases he heard and a diary, which together give a very good insight into the sentencing system then and the exercise of the royal prerogative of mercy.[10]

At Guildford in the summer of 1754, for example, Ryder refused to mitigate the death sentences of two burglars, because 'it was a very plain and bad case', but he reprieved two men guilty of the theft of animals because the evidence was 'not clear'. He refused to accept requests for clemency from two employers of twenty-year-old Richard Gilbert, convicted of highway robbery, because Gilbert had robbed twice on the same day. Similarly, in the case of Richard Tichner, he refused requests to recommend mercy from very powerful patrons who had made a direct plea to the King, because there was 'no reason to doubt' Tichner's guilt and 'there were no circumstances of alleviation'.[11]

Ryder was certainly not uncaring, however, when he saw a clear case of necessity driving a person to serious crime. Charged with the highway robbery of a woman, Thomas Rolf came before Ryder at the Old Bailey in October 1754. As he had been apprehended at the scene, the evidence against Rolf was clear; but during the trial it emerged that he had behaved courteously towards his victim, apologizing for his action and explaining that he was destitute, with a heavily pregnant wife and two small children. Ryder told the jury that, since 'compassion could not justify finding contrary to the truth', they must convict Rolf. However, when the jurors asked Ryder to intercede on the unfortunate man's behalf, he informed the Recorder of London of the circumstances. Rolf received a free pardon.[12]

It is clear that Ryder's practice was the norm. In 1772, Theodore Janssen published details of convictions and death sentences at the Old Bailey for the period 1749–71. Of 1121 persons sentenced to death, 443 were reprieved (or died before the sentence was carried out). The breakdown of these totals shows a steady application of mercy according to the descending seriousness of the crime. For example, 72 of 81 murderers were executed; 15 of 17 attempted murderers; 251 of 362 highway robbers; 118 of 208 burglars. Conversely, only 6 of 23 shop-lifters hanged; 22 of 90 animal thieves; 27 of 63 guilty of stealing from a house; and only 27 of 80 pickpockets.[13]

The use of the royal mercy to reduce the number of death sentences continued until the end of the century. For example, in September 1772, ten persons convicted of capital felonies at the Norfolk assize had their sentences altered to transportation on the recommendation of the justices.[14] Then, the following were convicted at the Oxford assize in the spring of 1787: Thomas Court, Thomas Roberts, Thomas Gilbert, William Jenkins, Isaac Williams of horse-stealing; John Aston, Luke Mapp, John Owen, David Jones and William Watkins of sheep-stealing; William Brooks of stealing cattle; Henry Foulk and William Garrett of having returned to England before their previous sentence of transportation had expired; James Gibbard of robbery and John Ashby of being an accessory to it; Thomas Holland, Robert Crumplin, James Murphy, Annan Hudson and Thomas Spencer of highway robbery; William Smith of picking pockets; Henry Gardiner of the theft of cloth; James Cleaver of burglary; Hugh Pincot and Thomas Parker of theft from a dwelling place. These felons were all guilty of capital offences. However, since the judges recommended them 'as fit objects of the royal mercy', they were spared death on condition that they be transported to New South Wales.[15]

Indeed, sometimes a felon might receive more than one mark of His Majesty's mercy. Joseph Hall, for example, was twice reprieved from death sentences.[16] But this was unusual. More commonly, felons for whom someone was willing to speak up might expect only one mark of royal mercy. As the Under-Secretary of State commented about one criminal on whose behalf an influential friend had petitioned:

> I can see the propriety of omitting to propose any other punishment than that which Aylett is sentenced to suffer. If the Lord Chancellor thinks the man should not be exposed to the pillory, I dare say he will point out some other mode for punishing him. I think that in the course of my life I never heard of so infamous a character.[17]

Sometimes, too, such requests rankled with the officials in the Secretary of State's office, as in this October 1786 case:

> Since the receipt of your letter of the 1st inst, I have examined the report of the judge upon the case of James Hedding, in whose behalf Mr Rishton has so warmly interested himself, and I am very sorry to inform you that according to the judge's opinion it would not be proper to extend to the unfortunate convict any further mark of the King's mercy.
>
> I expect that the ships will proceed with the convicts to Botany Bay early in the next month, and I shall take care to provide for Hedding's conveyance thither in one of them, which I observe by his letter he desires may be his fate if a pardon cannot be obtained.[18]

But then, there were also instances when authorities acted to produce a result that was clearly justified. In April 1784 the *Mercury* was taking 170 convicts to North America. In a very violent rebellion, a group of the prisoners seized the ship as it was passing down the English Channel, wounding and imprisoning those transporting them. They ran it into Torbay and attempted to escape inland. William Jones, however, 'distinguished himself from the rest by a peaceable, quiet behaviour. He did not join in the insurrection and after it happened he conducted himself with humanity, sobriety and honesty'. The ship's officers recommended that he be pardoned.[19]

There were other ways for justices to determine a lesser sentence than might ordinarily have been recorded. For example, while there could be no value-mitigation where the theft of animals was concerned (that is, the crime was theft of a horse, not of one worth more or less than £10), as this crime did not usually involve violence, those convicted of it were frequently recommended for the royal mercy on condition of being transported. Persons under twenty years of age (for whom there might be some hopes of reform) and those over thirty (who were likely to have families to support) were less likely to be sentenced to transportation than unmarried, able-bodied men in their twenties. Women who were likely to have dependent children might also escape the harsher penalties.[20]

*

Let us now look at some of the felons convicted at the Old Bailey assize sessions in the 1780s who were transported to New South Wales.

Simon Hughes went to a boarding house where he was given a bed to share with two other men. After he had fallen asleep, Robert Forrester and Richard McDale robbed him of 6 guineas (£6.6.0). When he awoke at 3 a.m., Hughes found one of the robbers gone and the other preparing to leave. He also found his money gone. He told the court: 'I hallooed, and made a noise in the room, which alarmed the landlady and her daughter, they came upstairs and brought a light, and I dressed myself, and the two women went down to the houses where they thought to find the prisoners, but they could not find them then.'

When taken, the prisoners tried to do a deal with their victim by offering him 4 guineas not to appear in court. At their trial, they both denied having robbed Hughes and produced witnesses who said McDale had received 3½ guineas as part of his pension. They also found a woman to testify that Hughes had asked if he might stay with her that night. She told the court that this had not been 'convenient' since her husband was at home, so she had given him 2 pence so that he might find a bed elsewhere. But Hughes said he had never seen her before, and another witness said that she had offered him 'anything in the world' if he would help get the indictment thrown out. The accused were disbelieved and sentenced to death, but were recommended for the royal mercy on condition of being transported for seven years.[21]

Ann Green was charged with stealing nineteen china plates and a china bowl from the workshop of William Moody, valued at a total of 8 shillings. Moody's wife testified that 'I heard a noise in the back shop a few minutes after six; when I opened the door, I saw the prisoner turning from the workboard; I was in the middle room; I caught her by the cloak; she said she had made a mistake; I told her I would see what it was; I saw the nineteen plates in her hand; I immediately secured her as well as I could; I opened her apron, and found a china bowl'. Green had a very young child, and her husband had died shortly before the birth. She told the court that she did not know which had been her husband's parish – i.e., she did not know where to go for charity – and that 'I have not a friend in the world'. Clearly, all believed her story, for the prosecutor requested the court show her mercy, and the jury made the same recommendation. She was sentenced to seven years' transportation.[22] (Of course, by our standards, this was scarcely merciful; but the point is that the court pleaded successfully for her life.)

Mary Greenwood was indicted with George Partridge for the highway robbery with assault of Adam Mills, 'putting him in corporal fear and danger of his life' and stealing from him goods to a combined value of 12 shillings. However, the offence was much greater. A group of six or seven men and women first stole a £10 bank note, 7 guineas in gold, and about 15 shillings' worth of silver from Mills's pockets. When he chased them and seized one woman, Greenwood and Partridge came to her aid, striking him 'a violent blow on the side'. They then took from him a bundle of clothes also mentioned in the indictment, saying: 'Damn your eyes, you bloody bugger! If you do not give us this bundle, we will cut your bloody milt [spleen] out; I then received a hard blow on my knee, which has been very black.' Some witnesses helped him get the assailants to the watch house. The jury asked Mills if he had been sober that night, and he assured them that he had. They also asked him if Greenwood did 'aid and assist' in the robbery. He asserted that she had, and that she had 'made use of worse imprecations than the man did'. Both were found guilty and sentenced to death, but were recommended for mercy on condition of being transported for seven years.[23]

Together with James Beach and Francis Burke, Joseph Hall was charged with assaulting and robbing Sarah Stockden and her husband John in a field near a highway, putting her 'in corporal fear and danger of her life, and taking from her person, one pair of silver shoe buckles, value 7 shillings, one pocket-book, value 6 pence, and 5 shillings in money, her property'. The Stockdens were walking to Covent Garden at 6 a.m. when the thieves passed them. She deposed:

> Mr Stockden said I believe they are thieves; they are bad ones; they came back immediately, and took hold of us, and set my husband's face to Tottenham Court, and mine to Islington; I said I had a family of children; they blasted my eyes, and said, they did not care if I had twenty, they said money they wanted, and money they would have, and said my buckles were plated; they were going to sea, and blasted my bloody eyes, and said if I would not give them my money they would blow my brains out.

One took her buckles and money as another menaced her with a cutlass.[24] The Stockdens reported the assault and theft to a constable, who located the culprits at Holborn. He testified:

> I took hold of Burke by the collar, and another, and told them I had

a charge against them for a footpad robbery; there were four in company; then with that they immediately blasted my bloody eyes; they gave me a blow, and drawed their knives, and fell cutting away, I scuffled with them, and we took two; the other two made their escape; I pursued Burke and Mowatt; he is not here; I took Burke; Beach, the tall one, gave me a violent blow with the butt end of a pistol; I was hit about so, I almost lost my senses; the Bow Street people secured the other.

The three were found guilty and sentenced to death. They were pardoned on condition of fourteen years' transportation to America. Put on board the *Swift* to be carried across the Atlantic, they joined in the mutiny and Hall and another escaped into Sussex. After capture, these two were again sentenced to death (for the felony of returning before their first sentences had expired). Hall was again reprieved, on condition of fourteen years' transportation to America. Shipped out on the *Mercury* in 1784, Hall joined in the mutiny on that ship too and landed at Torbay, only to be recaptured. He was once more sentenced to death, then once more reprieved on condition of transportation for life.

Margaret Hall and Elizabeth Coleman were charged with the theft from John Jackson of a box containing '8 gold rings, value 40 shillings; 3 silver buttons, value 12 pence; 4 guineas, value £4.4.0; 6 light guineas, value £6; 1 half-guinea, value 10 shillings 6 pence; 1 light half-guinea, value 9 shillings; one moidore, value 27 shillings; 1 gold medal, value 2 guineas; 16 pieces of old silver coin, value 20 shillings ... and one promissory note of £20 from the Governor and Company of the Bank of England'. Jackson met the women at St Giles's and went to a tavern with them. He testified: 'After we had drunk, she took me to her lodgings, as I understood it to be, it was just opposite the public house; we went up stairs, and had a cup or two of some liquor, purl, or gin-hot, or something of that sort; they teased me for money ... I gave them one half-guinea, and they brought me the change ... Soon after I went to bed ... [and] I was asleep in five minutes. I slept till daybreak; when I awoke, I found nobody with me; I missed the two boxes and the silver.'

Under hard questioning from the judge, Jackson conceded that he had been 'very much in liquor', and that otherwise he would have shown 'more prudence'. Nonetheless, he maintained that he could positively identify the women charged as those who robbed him. But a witness said that Coleman had not been the second woman whom Johnson had said he wished to have sex with; and Coleman denied ever having seen him before she was charged. Coleman was acquitted, while Hall was found guilty and sentenced to death, then reprieved on condition of being transported for seven years. She too was on the *Mercury* and escaped into Exeter, only to be quickly recaptured and to have the sentence of transportation reaffirmed. Put on board the *Friendship* at Portsmouth as it waited to sail with the First Fleet, she and two others broke out of their quarters and joined the sailors. During the voyage, she was put in irons for ten days for fighting with other women.[25]

George Lisk was tried for 'feloniously assaulting John Jeffries on the King's highway ... and putting him in fear and danger of his life, and taking from his person and against his will 9 shillings in monies ..., his property'.

Jeffries, who was a poor old man, testified:

as I was coming, very nigh 11 o'clock at night, along the New Cut, that goes from John's Hill to Wapping church, the way from the New Tavern, up jumps two sailors, they came over to me directly; they were smothered with rubbish before I came, I never saw them till I came up, they threw me down at once, and I had 9 shillings and I lost it all, that man that got my money he got off, and this is the gentleman that kept me down.

He added that Lisk had held him down, and by the throat, so that he was scarcely able to cry out. Solomon Williams, who seized Lisk after hearing the watchman's alarm, said that he then found 'the old gentleman almost senseless, he kept crying out for God's sake do not hurt me, do not hurt me, he did not know what he was about, he begged he might go home to his wife and family'.

On identifying Lisk, Jeffries very magnaminously said, 'I would not have him hanged neither, because I have children of my own, and I do not know what they may come to; there is nothing too hard for God to do, he may make a good man of him yet'. Lisk was found guilty of the felony (assault), but not guilty of robbery. The judge told him:

> From the mercy of your prosecutor and the lenity of the jury, you have escaped with your life, which the offence as stated certainly affects. Considering the age and infirmity of the prosecutor and taking his all from him, your offence is very heinous. The jury have not gone to the extent of the law, but the Court thinks proper to transport you to America for seven years, and if you return and are found at large within that time, you suffer death without the benefit of clergy.[26]

*

It is one of the abiding myths of Australian history that many of those sentenced to transportation were poor people convicted for stealing a loaf of bread to feed their starving family, or a handkerchief worth a few pennies; that they were the hapless victims of a savage penal code and an uncaring, class-driven society. It seems not to matter how often or with what clarity the real situation is explained. This myth is, it seems, necessary to the maintenance of our identity as a nation forged out of dastardly oppression.

It would be silly to claim that there were never miscarriages of justice, or that harsh penalties were not given for what we should now consider minor offences. Long sentences given to children or to those made desperate by poverty still trouble the mind and hurt the heart. However, the plain fact is that the majority of eighteenth-century convicts sentenced to transportation were convicted of crimes that we continue to consider serious. When you think about it, this only makes the emergence of modern Australia the more remarkable: somehow, people not used to acting for the common good came to form a cohesive and prosperous society.

3.

Dealing with the Convict Problem: Hulks and Enlistment, 1776–83

BETWEEN 1718 AND 1775 PERHAPS AS many as 50,000 British men, women and adolescents 'left [their] country for [their] country's good',[1] the majority from London and the West Country port of Bristol. In the New World, 'planters, mechanics, and ... such as choose to retain them for domestic service' used their labour to produce raw materials cheaply for export to the mother country or in local services.[2] In the twelve years before the American Revolution, an average of about 1000 transport convicts a year made the crossing. Merchants prominent in the business at that time included Messrs Stevenson, Randolph and Cheston of Bristol and Messrs John Stewart and Duncan Campbell of London. Since they could not sell the labour of dead convicts, and were able to obtain more for that of healthy ones, it was decidedly in these contractors' interest to handle the business carefully and to attend to the welfare of those whom they transported. The most recent studies show that they did so.[3] Nonetheless, the often deplorable condition of prisoners when they were taken from the jails and the nature of the ocean passage made it inevitable that there be deaths *en route*. Campbell told the 1778 House of Commons committee enquiring into the hulks that:

on an American voyage in the transport service he has lost only 5 or 6 men out of 150; but he remembers one ship that lost 50 or 60 out of the same number; that upon an average 10 is considered a moderate loss out of 100; that upon an average of seven years, the loss of convicts in jail and on board will be one-seventh.[4]

The studies of the operations of the Bristol merchants confirm this figure.

Since he played such a large part in the creation of the system that temporarily replaced transportation to America, it is worth looking at Duncan Campbell in detail.[5] He was born in 1736 and served as a midshipman in the Royal Navy before setting up in the West India trade. In 1753 he married Rebecca Campbell, whose father owned a plantation in Jamaica, which he subsequently inherited. In 1758 he acquainted himself with circumstances in the North American colonies, at the same time as he became a junior partner of John Stewart, who possessed the government contract to transport convicts from London and the Home Counties. On Stewart's death in 1772 Campbell took over the firm and continued transporting convicts until the American Revolution. It was this association that enabled him to claim justly in 1776 that he had been 'nearly twenty years in the management of the same sort of people'.[6]

Campbell was punctilious, processing business efficiently, keeping precisely to his agreements and expecting others to do the same. But while he was meticulous, he was not grasping. In 1782, when convict numbers had fallen significantly below those he had agreed to, he offered to reduce the amount claimed at the end of his contract. And he told the Treasury in January 1785 that he had accommodated more people than he had contracted for, but that 'as the additional expense of this excess is only in clothing and provisions, which may perhaps in [the] course of my reports for the year fall as much short of that complement, I do not mean to claim on this occasion more than was paid me for the last quarter'.[7] One basis of Campbell's plain dealing was a deeply Christian outlook. After the death of a female member of his household, he described how 'without pain or fear she resigned herself to his hands who gave her life. I never saw a nobler instance of the consequence of an innocent and virtuous life. She knew herself dying and seemed much pleased at the approaching summons to her eternal happiness'.[8] Campbell brought this religious outlook to bear on his supervision of convicts.

*

From the central government's point of view, transportation to the American colonies was a neat penal practice that brought three distinct benefits. First, it 'exported' a social problem; second, it did so at comparatively small cost; and third, it benefited the nation by helping to create a supply of materials needed in Britain.

When the American colonists revolted, these smiles stopped together. Developing over more than a decade, the revolt of the American colonies had many and complex causes. By mid-1775 colonists were showing their opposition to British authority by refusing admittance to their ports of British ships and goods – and convicts. By the end of that year the British government, led by Prime Minister Frederick (Lord) North, had recognized that it must cease transporting convicts across the Atlantic, at least while circumstances in the American colonies remained unsettled.

The presence of convicts awaiting transportation in the kingdom constituted a real (if, in terms of numbers, slight) problem for the administration. While these prisoners might be pardoned or obtain remission of their sentences by the exercise of the royal prerogative, the sentence of transportation in itself could not be altered, and the administration had a legal obligation to carry it out. The sensible answer was to substitute another punishment. As the administration moved to do so, it concentrated all transport convicts in one place. In late November 1775, William Eden, the Under-Secretary of State at the Northern Department, told the Recorder of London (the most senior judge of the Old Bailey, London's central criminal court) that those in Newgate prison should be sent on board 'a proper vessel in the river [Thames] in the usual manner and as if in due course for transportation'.[9] The ship in question was Duncan Campbell's *Tayloe*. Campbell began receiving transport convicts there in January 1776 and continued to do so throughout the year. However, the administration simultaneously acted to solve the immediate problem by pardoning those men who agreed either to enter the King's service or to transport themselves beyond the seas for the remaining term of their sentence. A number of women were pardoned absolutely.[10] By December, Eden advised Campbell that there were no more transport convicts in British jails. With the last ones on the *Tayloe* having enlisted in the army or navy, left England or been pardoned, Campbell terminated his contract with the Treasury and closed the ship down.[11]

The new punishment for felonies that the North administration now adopted involved hard labour on the harbours and waterways of the kingdom. In practice at this time, however, the only place of labour was the River Thames, where the convicts were accommodated on unrigged ships moored to the east of the city.

These convict 'hulks' have had a very bad press. For 150 years, the belief that these ships quickly became extremely overcrowded and were scandalously unhealthy has underpinned the conventional explanation of the decision to colonize New South Wales. In 1916 Ernest Scott, for example, wrote:

> The prisons were wholly insufficient to hold the condemned persons … Thousands of prisoners were crowded into wretchedly insanitary hulks which were purchased to serve as receptacles. Every month saw more and more sentences of transportation inflicted, more hulks filled with offenders, and still there was no place to which they could be exiled.[12]

(In passing, consider the ludicrousness of the statement that 'Every month saw … more hulks filled with offenders'. Were this true, by the mid-1780s there would have been dozens of these convict ships. The reality is that by late 1784 there were *three* in the Thames, with one at Plymouth; later, another was added at Portsmouth.)

Historian after historian has since reiterated this view. R.M. Crawford wrote in 1952:

> So the number of convicted persons continued to rise, particularly in the more depressed areas of southern England and Ireland; and the former outlet by way of transportation to the American colonies was closed. When the jails were crowded, hulks were pressed into service, to become crowded in their turn. This was the situation which pressed Lord Sydney – not given to long views – into the action which founded Australia.[13]

In 1955 Frank Crowley claimed: 'By 1783 it was clear that the hulks had rapidly become "reservoirs and hotbeds of criminals"'.[14] Manning Clark wrote in 1962 that by early 1784, 'the escapes of felons from the hulks, as well as anxiety about the spread of jail distemper and smallpox, enabled the philanthropists and charity workers to play on the fears of those in high places, while hints and complaints of the hulks as schools of villainy and vice tweaked consciences into action'. He also stated that 'one factor alone' persuaded Lord Sydney of the need for the Botany Bay decision: 'the several jails and places for the confinement of felons were so crowded that the greatest danger was to be apprehended not only from their escape, but from infectious distempers'.[15] In 1966, A.G.L. Shaw repeated this interpretation, writing that in 1778 the hulks 'were supposed to hold only 380; but before the war nearly a thousand felons had been shipped to the plantations every year'.[16]

In 1985, writing of the recruitment of criminals into the armed forces, Stephen Conway observed, 'It was still found necessary periodically to clear both the putrid and congested jails and the equally overcrowded and insanitary hulks'.[17] In 1987, Robert Hughes claimed that when Sydney replaced North as Home Secretary in December 1783, 'he faced a rising clamour over the problem of criminal confinement – the shamefully over-crowded hulks and prisons'. The same year, John Molony wrote: 'The problem of what to do with English prisoners demanded action because of the growth in the number of persons being sentenced had resulted in crowded and unhealthy jails, particularly those in the old hulks of vessels moored on the Thames'. And in 1985 David Mackay stated that, as the number of convicts rose after 1776, one of the government's responses 'was to increase the number of hulks'. 'Another', he went on, 'was to increase the number in the hulks until they were dangerously overcrowded.'[18]

Together, these statements exemplify James Blackburn's observation (made concerning another egregious error in Australian historiography): 'Let an erroneous statement of fact, either invented or taken upon rumour, but once appear in print, and it is ever after regarded as a truth requiring no further verification, so that it is adopted by the next historian, who is copied by a third, and so on *ad infinitum*.'[19] It is also striking that *none* of these historians – commonly supposed to be pre-eminent in the field – *actually counted* the numbers of felons on the hulks during the ten years between 1776 and 1786, though Campbell's precise quarterly returns were readily available. (He was bound by law to report to the Secretary of State and the Treasury every three months; if he had not done so, he would not have been paid.) No. One writer having said that the hulks were 'shamefully overcrowded', over the next seventy years the others simply accepted the claim as fact, and repeated it.

I have counted the numbers. Here is the real story.

*

The North administration's new system for punishing felons emerged principally from discussions between Duncan Campbell and William Eden, who had a few years earlier publicized his view that the nation should receive some economic or strategic benefit from the transportation of the 'more enormous offenders'.[20] Under this new system, men who would previously have been sentenced to transportation to America would instead be sentenced to hard labour for between three and ten years. The administration enacted the legislation to make these provisions legal in April and May 1776 (16 Geo. III c. 43), to have effect for two years. With these changes, central government assumed a much greater role in the punishment of felons than it had previously taken.

Campbell had proposed that he accommodate hard-labour convicts on a ship in the Thames, where, under careful supervision, they would work from lighters (small, flat-bottomed barges) on the water and on the river bank. For £3560 a year (or some £30 per person), he offered to provide a ship of at least 240 tons to accommodate 120 convicts, together with guards, six lighters and the necessary tools, and 'to find every reasonable necessary for the people under their circumstances, medicines, vinegar etc, to wash and fumigate the vessel, for their healthful preservation'. On 12 July 1776 Campbell was formally appointed for three years as Overseer of Convicts on the Thames. For accommodation, he offered one of his own ships, the *Justitia*, of 260 tons.[21] In August he took in 85 convicts, and thereafter progressively filled up his complement of 120.

In March 1777 the administration asked him to take an additional 130 convicts. Initially he used the *Tayloe* again but in June he purchased a French frigate, the *Censor*, of 731 tons, which he fitted out 'for the accommodation and safe custody of 240 convicts and upwards'. In February 1778 he contracted for another 130, after which he accordingly filled the *Censor* to capacity, to reach a total contracted number of 380. It was arranged that these three contracts should end together on 12 July 1779.[22]

Between March and May 1778, parliament enquired into conditions on these ships and extended the 1776 act for another year (18 Geo. III c. 62). In July the Treasury asked Campbell to provide for an additional 130 convicts; he agreed, and this new contract was scheduled to conclude, like the others, on 12 July 1779. He purchased 'an old Indiaman', which he also named *Justitia*, and fitted it out to accommodate 250 people. From this point on, he was contracted to provide accommodation for 510 inmates. The actual number of prisoners aboard fluctuated around this figure for the following fifteen months.[23]

Before all four of Campbell's contracts expired together in July 1779, parliament conducted another inquiry, not only into the workings of the hulks system, but also into punishment more broadly. Sir Charles Bunbury chaired the House of Commons committee, which

heard evidence about conditions in the prisons and on the hulks, about
the prospects of resuming transportation variously to West Africa, the
East Indies and New South Wales, and about the desirability of developing a third mode of punishment, to involve solitary confinement in
'penitentiary houses' and hard labour.[24] Parliament renewed the original
1776 legislation until 1 July 1779 (19 Geo. III c. 54) as a prelude to the
introduction of a more comprehensive measure. With this new legislation, parliament extended servitude on the hulks for five years, with the
term reduced (at Campbell's suggestion) to between one and five years.
The place specified for transportation was amended to 'any Parts beyond
the Seas', and three supervisors were appointed to oversee the building
of two penitentiary houses in one of the Home Counties.

From mid-1779, then, there existed two modes of punishing those
pardoned of capital offences or convicted of non-capital felonies – servitude on the hulks, or transportation to anywhere outside Britain, even
though there was no obvious alternative to North America at this time.
How soon justices resumed sentencing felons to transportation, and in
what numbers, is unclear. In November, Campbell concluded a new contract with the Treasury whereby he agreed to provide accommodation
for 510 convicts on ships on the Thames, together with a 'receiving ship'
(*Reception*) and a hospital ship (the first *Justitia*) for twelve months.[25]

For a combination of reasons – expirations of sentences, enlistment
in the armed forces – the number of hard-labour convicts on the hulks
began to fall from the middle of 1780, to reach a low of 176 in mid-1783.
Campbell's annual contracts reflected this decline: in July 1780 he agreed
to accommodate 460; in July 1781, 440. In 1782 and 1783, he seems not to
have concluded formal contracts, but rather to have adjusted his claims
for payment according to the numbers actually borne.

In the absence of his detailed returns, it is impossible to be precise
about the base complements in these years. That for 1782 seems to have
been about 250, and that for 1783 about 200. (The average numbers were
284 in 1782 and 200 in 1783.[26]) Campbell took the *Censor* out of use in
July 1782, so that the second *Justitia* was the sole receptacle for convicts
sentenced to hard labour on the Thames.

With the return of tens of thousands of soldiers and sailors when the wars of 1776–83 ended, however, the numbers of people convicted of felonies increased rapidly and the hulks system expanded again. By 1786, Campbell was running three on the Thames, and there was one each at Portsmouth and Plymouth. Altogether, there were about 1200 transport convicts in these ships by this time, and more were being held in county jails. But this is a story for another time. For now, I wish to tell you something about the hulks system as Campbell developed it.

*

In the beginning, achieving satisfactory conditions was very much a matter of trial and error. Campbell told the 1778 House of Commons committee that in the absence of any specific directions from the Secretary of State's department, he had fitted the first *Justitia* out in the manner of ships used to carry troops, with cabins having two tiers of beds five feet, ten inches apart, providing each man with a sleeping space eighteen inches wide. This still made for crowded conditions. Other aspects of the accommodation were also undesirable. The sick were separated from the healthy only by a partition, and the sick bay was located at the upstream end of the ship, so that patients' excrement drifted past the sleeping quarters of the others.[27] The weekly food ration, which was calculated for a 'mess' of six persons, consisted of – for five days out of seven – five pounds of biscuit, half an ox cheek and three pints of peas in a soup. For the other two ('burgoo') days, each mess received three pints of oatmeal in the form of porridge, five pounds of bread and two pounds of cheese. This ration was modelled on that given in the navy, but there were certain differences. The navy diet included butter and some pork and beer (e.g., the convicts were dependent on the largesse of friends for milk and green vegetables).

This situation was one in which disease might spread rapidly, as it did in October 1776, when sixty-four convicts from Maidstone and other jails brought typhus fever with them. When the prison reformer John Howard inspected the ship at the time he found the inmates in bad circumstances, with many poorly clothed and fed, numbers of them ill and a very disagreeable smell in the sick bay. Not surprisingly, eleven of the inmates died between October 1776 and January 1777.[28]

Genuinely concerned about the welfare of his charges, Campbell moved to improve conditions. To enlarge the cramped accommodation on the first *Justitia*, he knocked down the cabins to form an open space, in which he erected a communal sleeping platform fitted with mats that allowed each person a width of two feet. Then, he replaced the mats with beds for two, six feet by four feet, with straw mattresses that were folded against the walls when not in use. He provided the convicts with more and better clothing, and more comprehensive and more regular medical attention. Simultaneously he developed a regimen of care, which he subsequently described to one of his supervisors:

> I would have you keep the convicts as dry as possible in theirs berths and let them have plenty of fresh air, but not partially as at ports; when it blows strong on the side of the ship much mischief is sometimes done by keeping the windward ports open. Have them frequently upon deck, but as they are inactive, not too long in cold and windy weather. The colds they receive by that means often create disease and serious disease too. Endeavour ever to prevent sickness, it is easier done than to cure it.[29]

These changes certainly improved matters. Visiting the *Justitia* in July 1777, Dr Solander – the Swedish naturalist who assisted Joseph Banks aboard the *Endeavour* – found the sleeping accommodation still rather cramped, but the foul smell was mostly gone, the food was good and there were few sick. When Howard inspected both ships in January 1778 the convicts told him 'that they were better used than when he saw them last', a fact he thought 'very evident by their looks'. He was impressed by their rations and the medical attention. Jeremy Bentham also reported at this time that 'no fire or candle allowed at night but the place is abundantly warm; fires kept burning all day; the ship often washed with vinegar, hardly any disagreeable smell between decks, bathing allowed at first but now prohibited as unwholesome'.[30]

Despite these measures, according to Jeremy Bentham, there was 'a very considerable sickness which Campbell says is concealed as much as possible – chiefly putrid fever and low spirits and some swelled legs, no ague'. Because of these health problems, Campbell had fitted out 'the forecastle of the *Censor* ... tolerably neat and clean for a hospital, beds very close, almost touching'. Modern knowledge shows us that such crowding is scarcely conducive to good health, and it is telling that Campbell 'declined going down' with Bentham and Howard 'into the hospital and soon called us out'. The testimony of these witnesses leaves no doubt about the improvements, but at this stage the hulks system was still not good so far as the health of the inmates was concerned. Between August 1776 and March 1778, 176 of the 632 convicts (28 per cent) received on board the ships died, but in the period of the filling of the vessels, Campbell was not responsible for the condition of those arriving from metropolitan and country jails – and as he told Bentham and the Commons committee, the mortality was 'greatest among country convicts'.[31]

In the second phase of the hulks (April 1778 to mid-1780) Campbell continued to improve conditions as he expanded overall capacity. He increased the bread ration to seven pounds per person per week in summer and six pounds in winter; he added 'small beer' to the menu, offered porridge for both breakfast and supper on 'burgoo' days, and gave each mess half an ox head per day. With these changes, he considered the whole ration to be 'better than labouring men usually had'. He began a vegetable garden on an acre of adjacent ground. He instituted a 'receiving' ship, where convicts were stripped of their vermin-laced clothes, bathed and held for four days while surgeons inspected them for signs of infection. He set up a separate hospital ship and employed three surgeons on a regular basis. He also employed a clergyman. Initially, the death rate remained high, with some 165 out of a total of 724 inmates (23 per cent) dying in the twelve months from April 1778 to April 1779. Again this rate was in large part attributable to men arriving sick – about 90, for example, died from typhus fever, 'chiefly brought by persons who came on board the hulks from the different jails'. Once the hulks' complements were reached, and the proportion of new inmates each quarter dropped, so too did the death rate. In the third phase, in the twelve months from 1 January 1782 to 9 January 1783 (as numbers declined) some 89 out of 486 died (19 per cent).[32]

In the fourth phase, the death rate was much lower. In the twelve months from 12 January 1785 to 12 January 1786, 66 of the 379 admitted to the second *Justitia* died (17 per cent), but this figure included an unusually high figure of 34 in one quarter. For the first three quarters of 1786, 20 out of 356 died (5.6 per cent). For the last three quarters of 1785, 25 out of 291 admitted to the *Censor* died (9 per cent), and for the first three quarters of 1786, 26 out of 282 (9.2 per cent).[33] These rates compare more than favourably with those from the period of transportation to North America when, as noted earlier, a 14 per cent death rate between embarkation and landing was the norm. In a more general way, and while such comparisons are notoriously difficult, it may well be that the convicts on the hulks were healthier than peer groups elsewhere in the kingdom, and certainly in London. It is also quite possible that they were better fed.

*

Contrary to long-standing belief, Campbell did not crowd convicts relentlessly into his hulks. Rather, he controlled the numbers carefully, keeping them as much as possible around the stated complements. At times, in response to 'pressing' applications from county officials, he did take on more, but this was always a strictly limited gesture. More often than not, he told importuning officials and jailers that he '[could] not at present give you directions when to bring up your people, as there are already as many convicts engaged as there is room for in the vessels'.[34]

The returns for the first and second *Justitia*, *Censor* and *Ceres* entirely confirm this point. In the twenty-four months before the decision to send convicts to Botany Bay, the second *Justitia*'s stated complement was exceeded by no more than thirty-three, and the *Censor*'s by no more than twelve. In 1786 the *Ceres*' complement was not exceeded by more than fourteen. In presenting the return for the *Justitia* for the quarter 12 October 1784 to 12 January 1785, Campbell observed that 'the pressing applications from clerks of the peace and jailers, stating their difficulties from time to time, has obliged me to exceed the number considerably, which I had limited for that vessel'.[35] He thereafter decreased this excess, although in his own defence he said he 'never failed' to relieve the county jails 'as fast as vacancies happen'.[36] Generally, however, he was punctilious about not exceeding the stated complements significantly. One reason for this was that he had contracted on the basis of a fixed number and was paid accordingly. From time to time the Treasury did lend a sympathetic ear to his requests for additional payment for the extra men, so money was not Campbell's sole reason for keeping numbers down. As we shall see, he cared for the welfare of his charges more than for profit, and successive administrations were willing to bear the cost.

When it came to transporting the convicts to their place of labour and overseeing their work, Campbell gradually developed a regimen. At first, arrangements were rather haphazard. When in October 1776 Eden asked how much sand and gravel had been raised, Campbell replied that he had so far attended rather to 'the mode than the quantity of labour'.[37] But the Under-Secretary's query stirred Campbell to place the employment of the convicts on a more regular footing. Ten days later he wrote that he would moor the vessel next to the work site at Woolwich, 'in order to make our first trial for raising sand and gravel from the banks of the Thames contiguous thereto, as being the *safest* and fittest [spot] for that purpose'. He added that the site selected was then of 'little or no utility, being nearly all overflowed every tide', so that it was 'a very convenient place for us to throw our soil upon when training the people to this labour', and that their improvements would render the area 'more valuable to the Board of Ordnance'.[38]

With experience, Campbell came to understand better what was needed. He provided lighters of 'from 35 to 45 tons burden fitted up for the employing and sheltering of twelve convicts each with the necessary bolts and securities, ballast engines to each lighter and all other implements necessary for the raising [of] sand and gravel from the River Thames', together with an appropriate number of supervisors.[39] Someone who observed the convicts at work in mid-1777 described how

> There are upwards of two hundred of them, who are employed as follows. Some are sent about a mile below Woolwich in lighters to raise ballast, and to row it back to the embankment at Woolwich Warren, close to the end of the Target walk; others are there employed in throwing it from the lighters. Some wheel it to different parts to be sifted; others wheel it from the screen, and spread it for the embankment. A party is continually busied in turning round a machine for driving piles to secure the embankment from the rapidity of the tides. Carpenters, etc, are employed in repairing the *Justitia* and the [*Censor*] hulks, that lie hard by for the nightly reception of those objects, who have fetters on each leg, with a chain between, that ties variously, some round their middle, others upright to the throat. Some are chained two and two; and others, whose crimes have been enormous, with heavy fetters. Six or seven are continually walking about with them with drawn cutlasses, to prevent their escape and likewise to prevent idleness.[40]

To guard further against escape, Campbell built a high brick wall on the landward side of the site, which also served the useful function of keeping away the curious who came to see the convicts at work. So as to allow the men to work more freely and effectively he removed the irons from all but the most recalcitrant.

The new regimen of labour meant that, in spring, the convicts worked from 7 a.m. to 12 noon, and from 1 p.m. to 6 p.m., and longer in summer. In winter they worked from 8.30 a.m. to 2 or 3 p.m. Directly or indirectly, the work they did always had a naval aspect – dredging the Thames to improve its navigation and using some of the gravel to build a new road to the Seamen's Hospital at Greenwich; building a new wharf for the Board of Ordnance at the Woolwich Arsenal; or digging moats and ditches there and performing 'other useful works', which included building new 'proof and practice butts of large extent', 'cleaning cannon' and sawing timber.[41] Always Campbell impressed on his overseers the great desirability of keeping strict control. 'Constant attention, coolness and firmness', he counselled,

> will be the sure means of keeping good order, not only amongst the convicts but amongst the ship's company. You will require to be very strict at the outset in order to obtain good habits, which if once established [are] easily maintained, while on the other hand bad habits are difficult to get the better of. In short your giving close attention to duty yourself will be an example for everybody about you to follow.[42]

Evidently Campbell had considerable success in this. The 1777 observer described with amazement how, 'so far from being permitted to speak to anyone, [the convicts] hardly dare speak to each other. But what is most surprising, is the revolution in manners: not an oath is to be heard; and each criminal performs the task assigned to him with industry, and without murmuring'.[43]

Still, the convicts did not always behave. It was sometimes necessary to flog fractious individuals, and those who threatened violence were put in irons. There were occasional riots, when desperate men sought freedom. Late in September 1778, more than 150 attempted to rush their guards and escape, but only a few succeeded in doing so. With the help of forces from the Warren, the guards put the insurrection down, killing two prisoners and severely wounding eight in the process. The next day, thirty-six convicts attempted to escape, with the result that one more man was killed and another eighteen wounded. Despite such incidents, however, most convicts seem to have behaved reasonably well in this period. Campbell's deputy, Stewart Erskine, told the 1779 House of Commons committee that they 'had behaved very well for some time'.[44] Later, the absence of any subsequent striking comment to the contrary suggests that this situation continued to prevail, though in the mid-1780s there was the inherent problem that the act under which the transport convicts were sentenced did not compel them to hard labour and they knew it.

Campbell and Erskine assessed the labour undertaken by the convicts as moderately hard, with Campbell saying that they worked as hard as labourers employed on highways, but not so hard as 'common labourers'. The real worth of the work they performed is unclear. The 1778 Commons committee accepted the estimate of £6053 as the value of their labour in the period January 1777 to March 1778. In December 1778 Campbell stated that 2680 tons of ballast had been raised in the previous seven weeks. One of the witnesses to the 1779 committee stated that:

> they had removed a mud bank, and made a very useful wharf, and a dock for barges to come in, and the river opposite was considerably deepened, so as to permit large ships to lie with convenience, where they could not lie before; that upon the whole he thought their work of great use to the Warren, and of real public service.

The committee concluded that 'the labour done appears to be of solid advantage to the public, and may be estimated at rather more than one-third of the whole annual expense'.[45] The extension, on the suggestion of Treasury Secretary George Rose, of the hulks system to the naval yards at Plymouth and Portsmouth at the end of 1785 indicates that authorities continued to see the convicts' labour as being of real economic significance.

Figures drawn up by the Home Office in 1789 for the House of Commons Select Committee on Finance confirm this. Evan Nepean, Under-Secretary of the Home Office, estimated the value of the hulk convicts' labour at 10 pence per two thirds of a man for six days a week, or £8.15.3 per year, or approximately 38 per cent of the then annual cost of £23.2.11 of keeping a convict on the hulks.[46]

*

Taking his statements at face value, a reader cannot but be impressed by Campbell's solicitude for the welfare of those whom he termed 'poor creatures'. He used the *Censor* rather than a smaller vessel because he was 'sensible from experience that more room must produce salutary effects to these unhappy people'. In summer, he repeatedly declined to enlarge the complements 'for fear of crowding the ships at this hot season'. As numbers increased, he asked for more lighters, so that men would not have to work standing in the mud and water in cold weather. In winter, he reduced the hours of labour sharply and served dinner later, so that the convicts did not have to leave the ships again afterwards. When the cold was extreme, he suspended labour entirely.[47]

More than in the simple physical welfare of the convicts, however, Campbell was interested in their psychological and social well-being. One of his earliest insights was that, more often than not, those who died succumbed to psychic rather than to physical illness. 'Our greatest loss of people arises in a great degree from a depression of spirits', he reported to Eden in January 1778, and he subsequently reiterated this to the House of Commons committee. A year later Erskine told the new committee that 'those from the country jails were apt to be more dispirited than the *London* felons'.[48] Neither Campbell nor Erskine seems to have speculated on the reason for this difference, but Campbell separately remarked that friends might supply convicts with extra food and clothing, so it may be that the *anomie* among the country convicts was to a considerable extent caused by the loss of family and social networks. Campbell sought to counter this depression by having a Methodist preacher attend the men, but he also seems to have understood that the prospect of distant salvation did little to alleviate present despair.

Loss of hope arose directly from the nature of the punishment. There was a good deal of disapproval of hard labour as a substitute for transportation, on the grounds that it was comparable to slavery and therefore anathema to English values. Sir William Meredith told parliament in 1778 that the hulks system was 'totally repugnant to the general frame of our laws', and others shared this opinion.[49] The convicts themselves seem to have been among them. Campbell observed that 'on their first coming on board, the universal depression of spirits was astonishing, as they had a great dread of this punishment'. Interestingly, they seem to have preferred the thought of transportation to North America, where they would not be shackled and where they might have the opportunity to better themselves by their labour. Erskine told the 1779 Commons committee that the convicts 'had behaved well for some time, which he attributed to an expectation they had of some alteration in their punishment, in consequence of the present enquiry, as they said they had much rather be transported'.[50]

Campbell always endeavoured to hold out some hope to the convicts, but he made clear that it was conditional on a real change in their attitudes and behaviour. He was a careful observer of his charges, as this description from mid-1777 attests: 'It seems as if each convict was most desirous of showing his readiness and his obedience to discipline, being induced thereto by one only hope, viz., that of obtaining their liberty by good behaviour, which is the only means afforded them to get their liberty before the legal expiration of their time.'[51] In January 1778, discussing with Eden how best to implement the proposed new act, he suggested a minimum term of one or two years, with a maximum of six years, on the grounds that in this time 'with proper management great alterations may be made on the habits and minds of such prisoners'.

*

There were two principal avenues by which a convict on the hulks could obtain his liberty. The first was a variation of the long-standing practice of entering the army or navy instead of being transported, of which I shall say more in a moment. The second was intriguingly modern. Hypothesizing that 'hopes of pardon … might have a good effect' on the prevailing depression among the inmates, in 1777 Campbell recommended that five well-behaved men be freed. Finding that the remaining convicts 'worked more cheerfully afterwards', he recommended another sixty men for pardon or early release. At the end of 1777 he told Eden:

I have … looked over the names of the oldest prisoners in the hulks and luckily the commander of these vessels happened just then to come to me, who much assisted my memory touching their behaviour etc; and I submit whether the ten in the last report answering to the numbers 2, 4, 5, 7, 8, 9, 10, 14, 20 and 21 may not be fit objects for the representation you was pleased to suggest. The shortness of time since I had the honour of receiving your commands prevents my being so well satisfied as to their trades, connections and the probable means of their obtaining a future livelihood; but should you think it necessary for me to give you a further information in these respects it shall be done without loss of time.

Progressively, the first arrivals on the hulks became less despondent, as they 'look[ed] forward in hopes of recommendation of pardon'. By March 1779 Campbell had secured the early release of 100 inmates and had applied for remissions or pardons for another forty-odd 'under the age of eighteen, whom he deemed proper objects'.[52]

In recommending that a convict be pardoned or have the remainder of his sentence remitted, Campbell followed a set of principles. The prisoner concerned must have shown contrition and good behaviour over an extended period, and a genuine interest in reformation after release. This usually meant that it was the longer-serving convicts who obtained Campbell's favourable report. The candidate also needed to have prospects of being able to earn a living honestly. Here it was important to have statements of support from family, friends, parish officials and prospective employers. Campbell was also sensitive to claims on compassionate grounds. On leaving, the convict received a set of clothing and a bounty (usually 2 or 2½ guineas, the equivalent of about two months' wages) to help him on his way.[53]

In July 1778 Campbell reported to the Secretary of State that James Mills

has been during his confinement very orderly and quiet, [which] promises a reformation in his future conduct. There were convicted at the same assizes, viz. Stafford March 1777, another two, John Allen and John Slater for deer stealing, who have behaved themselves remarkably well and promise very fair to reform. I have many assurances from respectable people that they can have an immediate employment and get their living in an honest way. I therefore submit whether these may not with James Mills be proper objects of his Majesty's mercy.

The balance of their sentences was accordingly remitted. At the end of 1778 he told the Under-Secretary of State that a 'poor woman' had travelled from Cornwall to beg the release of her son William Pascoe, who had been sentenced together with his father. With the father now dead, the son was the woman's only family, and she needed him to support her. Observing that 'this young man stands no. 161 in the last report' and that 'he has behaved very well since his confinement', Campbell recommended his release. Pascoe was accordingly pardoned.[54]

Campbell was by no means an easy touch, however. In August 1778, he reported of one inmate, '[he] was received … in February last. The shortness of his time on board does not admit of his being on the list with those of much longer standing who have behaved equally well, by which standard my recommendation is chiefly regulated'. In October 1779 he was particularly troubled by another request for clemency. He was, he told Eden, 'much at a loss what to say'. The convict had behaved well for the previous twelve months, and had often asked to be recommended for release. 'Had his offence been that of a common culprit', Campbell explained,

I believe ere this time he would have come in turn to my favourable mention … But his crime and the eye of the public upon that crime, his ability to do mischief should his reformation be only external, about which I think you will have little doubt, may possibly raise a question in your mind whether if he is discharged it should not be under an express condition he should transport himself out of the kingdom, and his remission made out accordingly.[55]

In June 1780 Campbell recommended against Abram Barew's release because he suspected that Barew was continuing to forge drafts on the Bank of England. Barew remained a prisoner. In August Campbell declined to recommend the pardoning of one convict whom he thought was not as sick as his friends claimed, only to relent the next day when he learned that a brewer was willing to employ the man. Still, a fresh transgression was not always an absolute disqualification in Campbell's mind. At the end of 1780 an escaped convict named Thomas Hawley applied to the Secretary of State for a pardon. Campbell reported that Hawley, who had been sentenced to three years' hard labour, had arrived in September 1777 and had behaved well until he had run away in February 1779. As Hawley's term had now expired and as he had found employment, Campbell recommended that he be pardoned.[56]

Thereafter, Campbell maintained this enlightened and compassionate outlook. In November 1781 he recommended release for William Germaine, a 'poor creature at death's door from a consumption', who was 'unfit for labour and an object of compassion' and whose life might be saved if his sentence were remitted. In December 1781 he recommended clemency for William Waples, who had served more than two years of his three-year sentence, on the grounds that he had behaved 'very orderly' and had good prospects of earning an honest living, and his family was in distressed circumstances. The balance of Waples's sentence was remitted. In February 1782 Campbell recommended in favour of Thomas Jones, who had served two-and-a-half years of a seven-year sentence, who had behaved well, and whom the chaplain said had 'shown marks of reformation'. Jones was freed on condition that he enlist in the army. Four months later Campbell recommended the pardoning of a man convicted of grand larceny whose former master was ready to re-employ him.[57]

The records do not give us a clear picture of how successful this rehabilitation programme was. At first, Campbell was well pleased with it. He told the House of Commons committee in April 1779 that of the 100 convicts who had been pardoned, 'he had never heard but of six having been accused of fresh crimes', but no later figures are available. In 1785, the Commons committee commented pointedly on the failure of the hulks system to achieve reformation in comparison to the old system of transportation, but this does not necessarily mean Campbell's efforts failed.[58] Those whom he recommended for pardon or early release were always a minority, and they gained their freedom precisely because they showed a genuine interest in rehabilitation. The great majority of convicts left the hulks only when their sentences had expired, and it may well have been true that those in this second, much larger group congregated together after their release and continued their criminal ways, as the judges claimed.

*

I mentioned earlier that another way a felon might be released from his sentence was by agreeing to serve in the army or the navy. While it is unclear how widespread this practice was before 1776, it did exist. In December 1770, for example, the King extended his mercy to Thomas Rutledge, convicted of stealing lead and sentenced to seven years' transportation, on condition of 'his entering and serving us as a sailor on board one of our ships-of-war'. And in early 1776, twenty-two transport convicts were similarly released on condition that they serve in land or sea forces 'out of the kingdom of Great Britain'.[59] Between 1776 and 1783, war – first with the American colonies, then with France from 1778 and with Spain from 1779 – created a lively demand for able-bodied men, and there were frequent draftings from the hulks and prisons. In February 1777 a small group from the hulks agreed 'to go to sea on a conditional pardon'. By 1778 Campbell had developed a standard letter to explain to local authorities the release of prisoners on these grounds; thereafter he continued to recommend this type of release for individuals as well as for groups. In November 1779, for example, he reported that George Rudrum, convicted at Norwich in 1777 of 'stealing goods and monies value £10.4.0 in a dwelling house', had 'behaved very well since his confinement, he is a stout young fellow very fit and willing to enter into the sea service'.

Thereafter the practice continued on a more regular basis. In July 1780 Campbell suggested to the Secretaries of State that the business be put on a regular footing, asking them to consider

> whether some mode ought not to be adopted so as to employ these poor creatures, who have undergone the punishment inflicted by the laws of their country, so as to keep them from returning to their former line of acquaintance and course of life. Many of them I am confident are very fit for and would make useful members of the community if employed in His Majesty's sea or land service. If the door is shut against them there what must be the consequence is easy to be conceived. It cannot be expected individuals will employ people of a description which is rejected in the different branches of His Majesty's service. What then is the alternative to those who have no friends or handicraft?

In October 1780 Campbell recommended John Russell and two others. About this time, he placed some worthy inmates on board privateers, including one he owned himself that cruised to Jamaica. In October 1781, Isaac Abraham and Francis William Hines were pardoned on condition that they serve at sea.[60]

These were rather sporadic enlistments. On at least two occasions, however, men went in significant numbers from the hulks into the armed forces. In March 1779, the army took 100 from the *Justitia* and *Censor.* 'Their general size [was] from 5 feet 7 inches and upwards, excepting a few, who have youth on their side', their recruiting officer reported. The youngest was aged seventeen; most were in their twenties, ten were in their thirties, and one was aged forty-four.[61]

In June 1781 Campbell sent another fifty-six men into the army, 'as they are willing to enlist, have most of them undergone a long confinement, and all have behaved orderly'.[62]

These men joined the two regiments of convicts then being raised for the defence of the Africa Company's fortified trading posts on the west coast of Africa, which in wartime were vulnerable to attack by the

French and Dutch. The total number enlisted in these curious regiments, the great majority of them convicts, was over 200, and what happened to them was to have strong repercussions for transportation after the end of the war. Two dozen died on the voyage out. Immediately after arrival at Cape Coast Castle in February 1782, they behaved so violently that 'their officers were afraid of their lives'. As the governor of the fort later remarked:

> from the very day these convicts were landed, their whole thoughts were turned upon rapine and plunder. The locks of the Company's warehouses, as well as those of individuals, were either picked or broke. The free Negroes' provisions and other property exposed to sale in the public market in town were stolen: nay, so abandoned were they that they even sold their muskets and ammunition, when against a Dutch fort, to the free Negroes for brandy.

He continued:

> from the immoderate use of spirits, (which being money in that country, it is impossible to keep them from) numbers of them died. Near thirty of them shortly after being landed, deserted to the principal Dutch settlement about nine miles from Cape Coast Castle, and the major part of those thirty fought against us, at the time we attacked and destroyed Fort Vredenburgh at Commenda. I saw one of them mortally wounded at the time we took possession of the fort, and who had just time to beg his life, before he breathed his last. Four- or five- and twenty of them, who were put on board a vessel bound to Commenda for the relief of our fort there, overpowered the crew, and ran away with the vessel. The far greatest part of the remainder soon died, not more than eight- and twenty or thirty of the whole (212 in number) having lived over a twelvemonth from the day they were landed in Africa.[63]

As if all this were not enough, another band turned pirates, led by the commanding officer Captain Mackenzie. They captured and plundered two neutral vessels, one Austrian, the other Portuguese. Mackenzie also forged pay receipts for men who had died, including one man whom he had tied to a cannon and blasted.

The hulks on the Thames seem havens of tranquillity in comparison.

*

Detailed investigation of British penal practice between 1776 and 1786, then, leads us to a number of conclusions. There can be no doubt that the revolt of the American colonists created a 'problem' for the British government, in that it made it impossible to continue transporting felons to the Atlantic colonies. For a number of years the North administration dealt with this problem by altering sentences in law and by instituting the hulks system. The numbers of felons held on the hulks increased steadily from 1776 to 1780, reaching a high point of about 510, then declined steadily, reaching a low point of about 180 in 1783–84. Then, with transportation re-instated as the fundamental punishment for felonies, and with the number of persons convicted increasing markedly, the number of convicts awaiting transportation rose very rapidly from mid-1784 onwards; even with a large expansion, the hulks system was unable to cope with these numbers. Contrary to popular belief, authorities did not at this time pack criminals remorselessly into the hulks. However, the jails around the kingdom did become crowded, causing local and county officials to complain bitterly to the central government.

It is most significant to understand that the decisions (taken successively by the Shelburne and Portland administrations) to resume transportation *preceded* the rapid expansion of convict numbers in the mid-1780s. In the period between July 1782 and March 1784, the number of people sentenced to transportation to Africa or America does not seem to have been significantly greater than before the Revolutionary War. Judge Frances Buller recorded that there were about forty felons sentenced to Africa in July 1782.[64] Campbell contracted to temporarily accommodate no more than 250 people who had been sentenced to transportation to America in January 1783, 200 in August 1783 and 200 in January 1784.[65] Since these figures do not include transports in other jails, or those sentenced to hard labour on the Thames, they do not offer a complete picture. Nonetheless, they appear to correlate with the average number of convictions for felonies before 1775, which was approximately 1000 per year.[66]

In viewing the hulks system itself as a distinctive penal practice, some interesting points emerge. There was considerable concern for the convicts' physical and psychological welfare, manifested in the careful regulation of numbers and in the provision of medical attention and a minister of religion. There was a strong interest in encouraging convicts to reform and to lead honest, industrious lives. There was equally an interest in obtaining some return to the nation for the cost of keeping them – as the solicitor-general asked parliament in March 1784, 'Why should they not be employed in such a manner as might defray the expense of their subsistence?'[67] Most often, as we have seen, they were employed on naval works – a point of considerable relevance to coming decisions.

4.

The Atlantic World and Beyond: Proposals for Resuming Transportation, 1782–84

BERNARD BAILYN, THE PRE-EMINENT historian of the British colonization of North America, and others have argued persuasively that a distinctive civilization centred on the Atlantic Ocean had developed by the middle of the eighteenth century.

For decades now, at Harvard University, Bailyn has conducted a seminar on Atlantic history, the central premises of which have been:

1. That before the end of the eighteenth century, the Atlantic Ocean had become 'the heart of an economy, indeed of a civilization, diverse, complex, multiple … yet essentially one';

2. That, given its multi-layered being – administrative, demographic, economic, social – it bound together Eastern as well as Western Europe, South as well as North America, the Caribbean islands and those adjacent to the western coasts of Africa, and Africa itself; and

3. That, indeed, the Atlantic Ocean was 'the inland sea of Western Civilization', 'the scene of a vast interaction rather than merely the transfer of Europeans onto American shores. Instead of a European discovery of a new world, we might better consider it as a sudden and harsh encounter between two old worlds that transformed both and integrated them into a single New World'.[1]

81

While large-scale migration and wide-ranging trading activities connected Britain to its North American colonies, it was principally the slave trade that connected Europe, West and Central Africa, the southern North American colonies, the West Indian islands, Spanish America and Brazil. Beginning in the mid-sixteenth century, this trade developed massively as Europe's demand for sugar became insatiable, and with it the need for ever more slaves to work the plantations.[2] It is estimated that in the eighteenth century European traders carried across the Atlantic some 6 million slaves from the principal areas of African supply (Senegal, the Gambia, Sierra Leone, the Gold Coast, the Bight of Benin, the Bight of Biafra, the Congo and Angola). British traders had the largest part in this forced migration, shipping some 2.5 million slaves, or 42 per cent of the total.

It is important to understand the extent to which Africans themselves dominated this trade, and so helped to shape the dynamics of the Atlantic world. In the eighteenth century Europeans, whatever their nationality, were never able to do more than establish trading posts (forts and 'factories') on the slaving coasts. These outposts were the points of interchange between European traders anxious to purchase slaves and African traders eager to sell them. It is also important to understand that, while the slave trade constituted by far the largest exchange on the West African coasts, it was not the only one. Africans willingly took muskets, spirits, metal tools and utensils, jewellery and brightly coloured cloths from the Europeans, who in turn sailed off with quantities of gold, ivory, gum, honey, bees' wax and timber.

*

The British decision to resume convict transportation when the wars of 1776–83 were over demonstrates this Atlantic worldview in interesting ways. Lord North having resigned as Prime Minister after the failure of the war in America, the Earl of Shelburne formed a new administration in July 1782, with Lord Sydney as Secretary of State for Home Affairs, Viscount Keppel as First Lord of the Admiralty, and the young William Pitt as Chancellor of the Exchequer.

The major task of this administration was to negotiate peace with the Americans and with the French, Spanish and Dutch. This was no easy matter, as the Americans had beaten the British army in North America and the Royal Navy had been unable to achieve a decisive victory over the fleets massed against it. As well, the King sternly disapproved of any political settlement with the rebellious colonists, the Dutch were unwilling to surrender any of their territories and trading monopolies, particularly that of East Indian spices, and, as on many later occasions, the Spanish wanted Gibraltar back.

Shelburne pursued negotiations into 1783. He had a vision of a trading empire rather than a vast territorial one, and was willing to sacrifice some of the gains of war in order to open previously closed markets and sea routes to British merchants. In the end, however, he was unable to explain his vision adequately to parliament and the public, and therefore to justify his concessions to the enemies, and his administration fell from power at the end of February 1783. Before it did so, however, it also made a beginning at resuming transportation, and so began a discussion that would be taken up by subsequent administrations.

*

The coming of peace meant British politicians could again pay some extended attention to the business of punishment. And it is certainly true, as the traditionalist historians have pointed out, that from the middle of 1783, as the number of people convicted of felonies rose, government ministers received a barrage of complaints from municipal and country authorities, imploring them to relieve the pressure on local prisons. Between November 1783 and November 1784, for example, complaints were received from officials in Bristol, Northampton, Lancashire, Southampton, Worcester, Morpeth and Norwich, calling on the government to resume transportation.[3]

The administration's habitual response was that there was little it could do. In December 1784, writing to Lord Robert Spencer in Lord Sydney's name, Evan Nepean explained: 'It would make me very happy to give effectual relief to the jail at Oxford, but the great difficulty which

83

has for some years past existed of carrying the sentence of transportation into execution has, I am sorry to say, been a means of crowding all the jails and places of confinement in and near this metropolis as well as the hulks in the River Thames.'[4]

Still, the complaints continued. At the end of December 1784, Mr Wallis asked that the transports in Dorchester jail be removed to the hulks. In February 1785, Henry Sedley demanded to know why Duncan Campbell had refused to take delivery of transport convicts. This same month, John Higgins told the Home Office that some prisoners in Lancaster Castle had been 'lingering here two years from the difficulty in contracting for their transportation'. On 12 April, Mr White, jailer at Winchester, advised that the number of transports being held there was 'very troublesome'. A week later, the sheriff at Shrewsbury said that his jail could not well accommodate the number of transports it was holding.[5]

In these years, there was no shortage of suggestions as to what to do with the excess of criminals. In July 1782, Robert Hurford said they should be sent to the Dey of Algiers and serve in his notorious galleys.[6] More than one person suggested they be sent into the fleet (that is, the navy), as this would satisfy the requirement that they be transported beyond the sea.[7] In 1785, Sir Watkin Lewes suggested that the convicts should be put to work in the Woolwich ropeyard.[8] More inventive, if more draconian, was the proposal from an anonymous pundit who argued that since the Lord had condemned sinners to languish in everlasting darkness, the convicts should be put to labour in the coal mines of Nova Scotia.[9]

*

In the early and mid-1780s, the ministers of the Shelburne, Portland and Pitt administrations also received a series of proposals for possible new sites of transportation within the Atlantic world. West Africa had been a minor place of transportation before the war, with some 746 convicts having been sent there between 1755 and 1776. Of these unfortunates, '334 had died; 271 had either been discharged, or had deserted, and of many there was no account'.[10] Accordingly, the region had a fearsome reputation.

English judges had resumed sentencing felons to transportation to Africa from the middle of 1782, but there was no clear destination for them. Shelburne noted in a memorandum, which was presumably intended for his Cabinet colleagues, that 'convicts require to be sent to the coast of Africa. Something must be done immediately about them, for the judges have repeatedly remonstrated'.[11] One of the complaining judges was Francis Buller, who had come to the conclusion that the practice of sentencing felons to hard labour on the Thames was a failure, 'as offenders come from [the hulks] more hardened than they went, form themselves into gangs, are ripe for all kinds of iniquity, and engage in it immediately on their discharge'. Buller also thought that imprisonment in county jails was ineffective, since many of these were 'not fit to hold any considerable number of convicts. The prisoners are idle and dissolute and their morals no means improved; and where the number is great, there will be danger of pestilential disorders and the jails will be broken open'. At present, he said, 'prisoners are set at large after receiving slight punishment only', so that the country was 'swarm[ing] with rogues'. The only solution, he told the Prime Minister, was the resumption of transportation, and therefore he was recommending certain capitally convicted felons for the royal mercy on condition of their being transported to Africa.[12] This discussion marked the beginning of the idea of sending large numbers of convicts there.

At the end of September 1782, Sydney had Nepean ask the Africa Company to take in some convicts at Cape Coast Castle. Nepean told the merchants that a number of the men the Home Office proposed to send had been sentenced to serve in the army, and that there were also some women. When the merchants asked who was to provide for them, Nepean replied that the government would give them clothes before they sailed, but that the Company was to be responsible for them after landing. After considering the proposal, the merchants said that they thought 'the transporting such people to Africa would be extremely dangerous to the Company's possessions upon that coast; that it would render the British nation odious to the natives of the country; and be thereby a means of greatly injuring the African trade'. Nonetheless, they very reluctantly agreed to take a handful.[13]

Thirteen convicts were shipped on the *Den Keyser* in November and landed at Cape Coast Castle in January 1783. The Company advised the governor of this fort that he was to follow the Home Office's instructions concerning them.[14] It was a directive that Richard Miles was soon complaining very bitterly about, and his reasons for doing so are persuasive. 'I have paid a deal of attention to what I humbly conceive to be the views of government in sending those wretches to this country', he wrote,

and the evident defect there is in the mode of transporting them. One motive is no doubt to save their lives, of which I conclude the major part have been forfeited to the laws of their own country; but the great consideration seems to be, *to get them out of Europe at all events*; without ever once adverting to the evil consequences that must attend this mode, a few of which I shall beg leave to lay before you.

The governor and council [of Cape Coast Castle] are directed to receive a certain number of convicts. No provision whatever is made for them; neither are we directed to receive them as soldiers: from which it is natural to infer that government understands it is just simply landing these people in Africa, to let them shift for themselves, and get their bread in the best manner they can. In some other parts of the world they might by their industry maintain themselves, but here it is impossible. We have no employment for them but that of soldiers (to which I shall presently state my objections). The natives have none. How then are they to be maintained? They are landed as it were naked and diseased on the sandy shore. The more hardy of them probably will plunder for a living for a few days until the climate stops their progress, and then, shocking to humanity, loaded with the additional diseases incident to the country, these poor wretches are to be seen dying upon the rocks, or upon the sandy beach, under the scorching heat of the sun, without the means of support or the least relief afforded them.

Miles went on to explain the dangers he foresaw in enlisting these men in the fort's guard, which consisted of thirty privates. 'What proportion of convicts may I with safety take in that number?' he asked:

One-third you will allow is quite sufficient, and even then I fear these would be much more likely to poison the principles of the other two-thirds, than of being themselves (by the others' example) brought to a sense of their duty. Punishments also must be much more frequent among such men, than is consistent with our feelings; and frequent punishments (more especially in this clime) are productive of enervation. Some among the ten we are to suppose so hardened in their iniquity as to be incorrigible. Their example would have a very bad effect upon the others. Again, only conceive these very men to be our guardians by night against a surprize from the enemy. Is there not every reason to apprehend that many of them would rather turn their arms against, than for us? Have we not seen an instance of it in the two independent companies sent out last year, and which chiefly consisted of these wretches? Upon the whole, I do assure you, Gentlemen, I would rather be confined to twenty good men, than have any addition to them from such a set, as we may suppose the convicts to consist of.[15]

Miles had an additional complaint. The *Den Keyser* had also landed some convicts at Gorée, further up the coast, and two of the women had made their way to Cape Coast Castle. He said that he and his colleagues would do what they could to help them, but added angrily: 'Good heavens, Gentlemen, only consider: women of our own colour landed here to be common prostitutes among the blacks. A knowledge of all the dreadful consequences of such a measure prompts me to say, that if their lives are forfeited to their country, it were humanity rather to let the forfeit be paid.' He begged the company not to send any more convicts.[16]

The company seems to have heeded this advice to some extent. In December 1784, when Lord Sydney was once again pressing the merchants to accept more transports, they agreed that men might be sent to Cape Coast Castle, but not on the Company's ship.[17]

*

North America was also still seen as a potential destination. By the end of 1782, the Shelburne administration was considering how it might resume transportation across the Atlantic. Late in December, Duncan Campbell and 'W.H.' suggested terms for transporting convicts 'to a port in North America', and for holding them on a ship until this might be done.[18] It is most unclear if this in fact then occurred; probably it didn't. However, there may have been a few small-scale ventures about this time, of the sort that Nepean arranged in April 1785, when he persuaded George Cartwright, a merchant who hunted seals and traded with the Indians in Labrador in northern Canada, to take with him four young convicts sentenced to seven years' transportation 'beyond the seas'.[19]

The first tangible efforts to resume transportation to North America came in mid-1783, when the Duke of Portland had replaced Shelburne as Prime Minister and Lord North had become Home Secretary. Rather than pursue a new initiative, North tried to revive the old system. Although the beginnings of his plan are now lost, North had clearly decided on it by the middle of the year, for on 11 July he informed the King that the merchant George Moore was willing to ship 150 convicts to Virginia and Maryland. The King replied the next day, 'the Americans cannot expect nor ever will receive any favour from me, but the permitting them to obtain men unworthy to remain in this island I shall certainly consent to'.[20]

North contracted with the London merchant George Moore to transport 143 convicts to Maryland, with the proviso that if this proved impossible he might land them in Nova Scotia.[21] These sailed in the *Swift* at the end of August, but the rogues rose while the ship was in the English Channel and about a quarter of them escaped into Sussex.

The ship finally reached Baltimore on 23 December with 104 convicts, who were presented as indentured servants to a public markedly reluctant to purchase their labour. By March 1784, many who had been hired had absconded, while many others were ill or dead. Moore and his American partner suffered heavy losses.

∗

Meanwhile, successive administrations had continued to investigate alternative sites within the Atlantic world, including other destinations in Africa. In July 1782, Justice Buller inquired about the suitability of one or another of the islands off the west African coast. He asked Duncan Campbell for information, who in turn asked William Hurford. Hurford thereupon asked traders who had resided in West Africa about the De Los Islands. These traders reported that, of the three smallest uninhabited islands, two were entirely without water, and this was only to be had on the third by sinking wells. Tamara, the largest and westernmost island in the group, had about 100 inhabitants, who barely raised enough rice to survive; the terrain was rocky and the soil sparse. Factory Island in the east had about 150 inhabitants, who raised cassava and rice. While capable of some improvement, its soil was also thin. At different seasons, rains made all the islands unhealthy. Hurford's informants thought that to found a colony on any one of them 'would be madness in the extreme'.

However, they were enthusiastic about the prospects of doing so on Banana Island, about 150 kilometres south, off Cape Sierra Leone. Indeed, they spoke of this larger island with 'rapture'. The soil was 'deep, rich and grateful'. Here, sugarcane grew spontaneously; here were 'fine meadows' and cattle in the 'greatest abundance'; here was every kind of tropical fruit, and the European fig also flourished in 'great abundance'; the coast abounded with 'excellent fish'. It was 'the very healthiest spot in Africa'. Buller passed this information on to Shelburne, who interviewed Hurford, but there is no record of the idea being pursued further.[22]

In October, the Home Office asked Portugal if Britain might send its convicts to the island of St Matthews, further out in the Atlantic, so named because, sailing for the South Seas in 1525, García de Loaysa had supposedly discovered it on the saint's day. In the 1780s it was thought to be fertile, covered with large orange groves but 'abandoned and unoccupied'. In fact, this island was a phantom, one which curiously lingered on European maps until the end of the nineteenth century. Not realising that it did not exist, the Portuguese Court curtly rejected Britain's proposal, thereby missing an opportunity to get money for nothing.[23]

The British and French had begun detailed peace negotiations in September 1782. In October, Shelburne heard from Captain Edward Thompson, who had led an attack against the Dutch sugar region of Guyana, now in French possession. The planters there were 'miserably oppressed', Thompson said, with many having taken refuge in London. He suggested that the region might provide 'a grateful asylum to the Loyalists of America', or that it might 'equally serve for the transportation of convicts, where they may be made highly useful to the plantations'.[24]

Thompson returned to this idea two years later, in August 1784, by which time William Pitt was Prime Minister. Thompson told Pitt and the Home Secretary, Lord Sydney, that if the Dutch Guyanese settlements of Demerara, Essequibo and Berbice were to be colonized with American Loyalists and convicts, Britain might export its woollens and linens, pottery and metal manufactures there, and receive in return sugar, coffee, cotton, rum, chocolate, tobacco and indigo. They might send cattle, grain, rice and timber from these areas to the West Indies, and export molasses to Nova Scotia and Newfoundland in exchange for fish and timber. In short, with settlements in Central America, the nation would not feel the loss of 'Georgia, Carolina, Maryland or Virginia'.[25]

In February 1783 Daniel Houghton, who believed Britain had scarcely begun to exploit the trade potential of West Africa, urged Sydney to consider the likely advantages of a larger presence in the Gambia. Settlers there might trade with the inhabitants of the inland districts for ivory, gold, gum, drugs and slaves. These items were also to be had on the adjacent coasts, together with rice, cotton and honey.

Tobacco, indigo, sugarcane and vegetables might be cultivated 'to the greatest perfection', and also grapes. Cattle and sheep would thrive there, and poultry and fish were available in great abundance. To these advantages was added that of 'the affability and friendly intercourse' traders had with the natives. In short, there was 'no situation on the coast more desirable'.[26]

Indeed, in the course of 1783, a number of people submitted proposals for more extensive operations in West Africa. In March, Edward Morse, formerly its chief justice, began what would come to be an extended recital of the attractions of the province of Senegambia. The Gambia, he asserted, was 'the richest spot in Africa', its produce including slaves, gold, wax, ivory, rice, palm oil, dyes, indigo, cotton and drugs. If a colony were established there, all these items (slaves excepted) might be imported into Britain. The West Indian islands might also be supplied with timber, grain and 'other necessaries', and inland exploration would open up new avenues of commerce.[27]

In July 1783, parliament enacted legislation giving the Africa Company control of all British establishments in West Africa.[28] The Company thereupon advised the Home Office of the need to rebuild its fort on James Island in the mouth of the Gambia River, which had been destroyed by the Dutch in the late war, so as to stop incursions by rivals old (French traders) and new (Americans), and to extend the slave trade.[29]

During the next twelve months, the idea of transporting convicts in significant numbers to West Africa became entwined with that of expanding Britain's presence in the region. On 23 June 1784, Morse sent Sydney his analysis of 'The Advantages and Disadvantages to be expected from the Territory in the River Gambia being in the hands of the African Company or erected into a Colony'. Among the advantages he thought likely to arise from the creation of a formal colony were that many more ships would trade to West Africa, carrying out manufactured goods and returning to Britain with the products of the region, thereby also significantly increasing the nation's fleet of ships and seamen. Morse also thought that 'a considerable number of convicts may be sent there every year and employed to great advantage', and that these would find it easy to produce enough food for themselves.[30]

Then, at the beginning of August, Edward Thompson, now commodore of the small West Africa squadron, praised the virtues of São Tomé, the island off the West African coast held by Portugal. The Portuguese had first settled it at the end of the fifteenth century and founded sugar plantations, which they had later abandoned in favour of new ones in Brazil. Its 15,000 inhabitants raised only cattle, but, Thompson asserted, sugarcane, cocoa, coffee, grain, cotton, cinnamon and tropical fruits grew in profusion. He was sure that the Portuguese Court would sell it to Britain, and that once the convicts were established they would be useful 'as mechanics and husbandmen'. 'The benefits on every scale of commerce for our manufactures, as well as the returns of produce would yield every advantage to England', he concluded.[31]

These proposals to use convicts to increase Britain's presence in West Africa, and thereby to obtain greater economic returns from that vast region's resources, validate the notion that a strong concept of an Atlantic world existed at this time. Consider that which Lieutenant Clarke sent to Pitt in March 1785. Clarke described the Gold Coast as 'rich beyond conception, and capable of rewarding most profusely any undertakings'.[32] In his view, the fundamental impediment to realizing these possibilities was the African Company's continuing control of Britain's commerce in the region. He urged that these merchants be replaced by five commissioners, that the region be opened to free traders, and that a colony of 300 convicts be established to grow provisions for visiting ships as well as rice, indigo, cotton and tobacco for export. Clarke thought that a large trade with the interior districts might be developed, with rum and Indian cloths being offered in exchange for slaves, gold, ivory, wax, spices, drugs, saltpetre and other items. Some of these goods would be shipped to Britain, but a significant proportion of them might also be shipped across the Atlantic. As well as providing slaves and tobacco, 'the Gold Coast, were it attended to, would in a short time undersell the Americans in all their southern produce, and effectually supply the [West India] islands with lumber, staves and every kind of provisions'. Also, if Britain were to lose possession of the West Indies in a future war, its Gold Coast plantations might quickly become an alternative source of sugar and rum. And, since the inland inhabitants were eager to obtain 'fine muslins, chintzes and a variety of other India goods', the East India Company 'would find an immense market for their commodities'. Such would be the increase in commercial activity that the government would easily gather an extra £100,000 in taxes.

*

In this same period, some people proposed sites beyond the Atlantic world. In September 1782, John Bindley, a Middlesex magistrate, asked the Home Office 'whether some spot of this globe at present uninhabited and uncultivated might not be found, for the reception of those whose crimes and misconduct have made it impossible [for them] to earn their bread upon these islands'.[33]

In August 1783 James Matra, who had sailed on the *Endeavour* with Captain Cook, suggested to Lord North (who was then Home Secretary) that a colony might be established at Botany Bay, on the eastern coast of New South Wales. The area's climate and soil, he said, 'are so happily adapted to produce every various and valuable production of Europe, and of both the Indias, that with good management, and a few settlers, in twenty or thirty years they might cause a revolution in the whole system of European commerce, and secure to England a monopoly of some part of it, and a very large share in the whole'. Such a colony might produce spices, sugar, tea, coffee, silk, cotton, indigo and tobacco. By opening markets in Japan and Korea, it might also lead to the development of the China trade, of the fur trade between northwest America and Asia, and of trade in wool and manufactured goods. There was also the flax on the islands of New Zealand, and trees fit for large masts.

Indeed, Matra argued:

The place which New South Wales holds on our globe might give it a very commanding influence in the policy of Europe. If a colony from Britain was established in that large tract of country, and if we were at war with Holland or Spain, we might very powerfully annoy either state from our new settlement. We might with a safe and expeditious voyage, make naval incursions on Java and the other Dutch settlements, and we might with equal facility invade the coasts of Spanish America, and intercept the Manila ships, laden with the treasures of the West.

In time, a colony at Botany Bay might 'atone for the loss of our American colonies'.[34]

At this point, Matra was envisaging a colony made up not of convicts but of displaced Loyalists from North America, those unfortunates 'whom Great Britain is bound by every tie of honour and gratitude to protect and support'.

*

By the end of 1783, then, new sites for transportation were under active consideration, a process which William Pitt's administration continued. When he took office on 19 December, William Pitt, who was then only twenty-four years old, found himself in very difficult circumstances. He had only minority support in parliament, many of whose members bitterly resented the King's decision to sack the Fox–North coalition. This administration had taken office in April 1783. Although it was headed by the Duke of Portland as Prime Minister, its real leaders were Lord North (Home Secretary) and Charles James Fox (Foreign Secretary). It was therefore a very strange alliance, for its principals held very different political views and had been opponents during the American war. George III detested Fox, whom he thought encouraged his son, the Prince of Wales, in his profligate ways. When the administration introduced legislation into parliament which would have given it inordinate power over the East India Company, the King dismissed its ministers and asked William Pitt to form a new administration.

Repeatedly, Pitt found his administration out-voted in the House of Commons. But as the nation grew weary of the political turmoil and parliamentarians came to see that the young Prime Minister was both able and determined to put the nation on a better footing after the disastrous war, the tide slowly turned in Pitt's favour and he began to obtain a majority in the Commons.

(A few weeks before he did so, Pitt was involved in a very curious incident, one that again shows the incipient violence of London life. One night, as his carriage was passing Brooks's Club, a favourite haunt of Opposition politicians, a mob, mostly made up of chairmen, but including some club members, set upon it, smashing it to pieces with poles and attempting to do the same to the Prime Minister. With considerable difficulty Pitt's servants, other chairmen and members of a rival club, White's, got him to safety. Suspicion naturally abounded that the leaders of the Opposition had connived in this assault, but when confronted about it, Fox replied blandly that he had had no hand in it; indeed, he said, he had been in bed with his mistress, 'who was ready to prove it on oath'.[35])

By this time, Pitt's ministers had turned their attention to the question of resuming transportation. A bill 'to provide places for the temporary reception of criminals under sentence of death, and respited during His Majesty's pleasure, or under sentence or order of transportation, and also sick prisoners' was introduced into the House of Commons on 2 March.[36] After the usual consideration and debate, this passed the Commons on 18 March and the House of Lords on 23 March; it received royal assent the next day.

This act (24. Geo. III, c. 12) provided for the removal of transport convicts from the county jails to hulks and, if they could not be immediately transported, for their being put to labour on the waterways. Curiously, though, this could be done only with their consent, and with the proviso that they be given half the profit arising from their labour. Also, those who had not been sentenced explicitly to transportation to Africa could not be sent there. This act was intended as a temporary measure, so as to allow time for the preparation of a comprehensive new one to provide for the resumption of transportation.

It was in the context of the passage of this act that Sydney sought out James Matra and asked him whether New South Wales might not be 'a very proper region for the reception of criminals condemned to transportation'. Matra consequently added this idea enthusiastically to his proposal. Transportation to Botany Bay, he saw, would mean that the convicts would have to remain there and to work for their subsistence; 'they cannot fly from the country', and without items to steal they must either 'work or starve'. But Matra also saw positive benefits. If upon their arrival the convicts were given 'a few acres of ground … in *absolute property*', and if they were not stigmatized for their former behaviour, it was 'highly probable that they will be useful, [and …] it is very possible they will be moral subjects of society'. As the cost of transporting them to New South Wales would be 'absolutely imperceptible, comparatively with what criminals have hitherto cost government', this would combine 'two objects of most desirable and beautiful union': 'economy to the public, and humanity to the individual'.[37]

The King disolved parliament on the 25 March 1784, ahead of a general election. Pitt was returned with a comfortable majority, and when the new session of parliament opened in April 1784 he began a legislative programme to effect much needed reforms and a diplomatic one to improve the nation's relations with the world. For example, he reformed taxation and created a 'sinking fund' to reduce the national debt. He made changes intended to improve administrative efficiency. He ordered an ambitious building programme for the Royal Navy. He set up a Board of Control to supervise the operations of the East India Company. And he set about negotiating new commercial arrangements with the United States, France, Spain and Russia.

The Pitt administration also produced a new act (24. Geo III, c. 56) to pave the way for the resumption of transportation. Passing through parliament in August, this provided for those convicted of transportable felonies, or those whose death sentence was remitted in favour of that of transportation, to be sentenced generally to 'transportation beyond the seas', with the Privy Council (King-in-Council) then fixing the place of transportation. This meant that, legislatively, the way was now clear for convicts to be sent anywhere in the world; the choice was no longer confined to places within the existing British empire.

This was a striking innovation. There evidently was some unease among parliamentarians at this last provision, on the grounds that it increased the power of the Crown. As the bill was passing, the attorney-general advised Lord Sydney that 'Lord Beauchamp intended to have objected in the House of Commons to the sending of transport convicts out of the King's dominions, but was absent when the bill came on'. In case any members of the House of Lords should raise this objection, he prepared a detailed paper to show 'that a law for this purpose existed in England from 1597 to 1714'.[38]

The passage of this act led to a fresh round of proposals for sites for a convict colony. As the bill was passing James Matra, blatantly trying to straddle the political fence, sent his New South Wales scheme to Fox.[39] Then, in September, the brothers-in-law Sir John Call and Sir George Young submitted detailed schemes for a Loyalist and convict colony in the southwest Pacific Ocean.

Drawing on the narratives of Cook's voyages, Call described New South Wales, New Zealand, New Caledonia and Norfolk Island. He wrote:

> According to the object which may be in view for making an establishment, either the coast of New South Wales, or some other part of New Holland, which on a closer examination may be hereafter discovered, cannot fail to offer a convenient situation. But if New Zealand should be deemed a more promising island either for ports or fertility, there cannot be a doubt but situations may be found attended with every convenience that nature furnishes, and perfectly adapted to receive the improvements of art. Let the choice therefore fall on either, or both, for principal establishments, it is obvious that New Caledonia or Norfolk Island will afford useful auxiliaries.

Call mentioned many of the same benefits in navigation, trade and political influence that Matra had earlier pointed to. The reason for establishing one or more secondary settlement was to obtain naval materials – masts from New Caledonia, and masts and flax from Norfolk

Island: 'the timber, shrubs, vegetables and fish already found there need no embellishment to pronounce them excellent samples, but the most invaluable of all is the flax plant, which grows more luxuriant than in New Zealand'.[40]

There were also economic and political considerations. Sir George Young advised Pitt that a settlement at Botany Bay would allow the British to open a trade in manufactured goods with South America and that, in the event of another war with Spain, '*Here is* a port of shelter and refreshment for our ships should it be necessary to send any into the South Seas'. Settlers might cultivate exotic plants and spices to commercial advantage. There was the New Zealand flax, the uses of which 'are more extensive than any vegetable hitherto known', and the products of which (cables, cordage and canvas) would be cheaper than those of Russian fibre plants. He also pointed out how Russia 'may perhaps at some future period think it her interest to prohibit our trade with her for such articles'. The British might establish an international port at Botany Bay; the Loyalists would find a home there, and it would be a suitable place to send the convicts.[41]

Matra and Young now joined forces to promote the scheme. Matra spoke to his Loyalist friends, who indicated their willingness to move to the ends of the earth.[42] Young consulted captains who had sailed East Indiamen to China. They confirmed that, once past the Cape of Good Hope, these ships might proceed through the southern Indian Ocean and, rounding Van Diemen's Land, land the convicts at Botany Bay before proceeding 'to the northward round New Ireland etc, or through St George's Channel, and so on to the Island Formosa for Canton. With a little geographical investigation, this passage will be found more short, easy and a safer navigation, than the general route to the China ships, from Madras through the Straits of Malacca'. Young and Matra then persuaded the attorney-general to take up their cause.[43]

It is clear that Pitt's Cabinet did consider these proposals, for at the beginning of November Matra asked Nepean whether the ministers had come 'to a decided resolution to reject the plan, or if there be any chance of its being entered on, in the spring season?'[44] However, New South

Wales was not the only place the ministers were considering. At the end of August, Evan Nepean asked the Portuguese ambassador if his country might take the malefactors off Britain's hands, explaining:

> that England, after the separation of America, had nowhere where it could send its convicts, and that it would much appreciate it if Portugal were willing either to send them to or to receive them in some part of its dominions, making whatever use of them which might best serve its interests.
>
> That all England wanted was to save the life of the great numbers of wrongdoers who, for their crimes, should rightfully lose it. And that this death sentence having been commuted to transportation, Her Most Faithful Majesty would be able to put them to good use as galley-slaves or in any other manner, in the settling of remote parts of her vast dominions, or in the cultivation of land, mining, or any other forced labour, no matter how difficult or arduous. And that they could also be transported to the East as soldiers, just as [Portuguese] nationals were; and that the only condition would be that they should never serve in any war on the side of the enemies of Great Britain.

A week later, the ambassador forwarded to his Court details from Duncan Campbell, who indicated how the convicts had previously been shipped across the Atlantic and how much their labour had been sold for. It was in vain, however. In October, the Queen of Portugal said she could not agree to the idea.[45]

*

Meanwhile, despite George Moore's earlier failure, the Pitt administration had sanctioned a further attempt to resume transportation to North America. On 2 April 1784, Moore's ship the *Mercury* left the Thames with 179 convicts – but this lot of rogues also rebelled, 'tak[ing] the ship from the captain and confin[ing] him and his people in chains after a very bloody resistance' and running it into Torbay on 13 April, where about 120 escaped before being quickly recaptured.[46] When at last the *Mercury* reached North America, authorities refused to accept the convicts who remained on board. In July, Moore's agent and the ship's master sailed down to Honduras with eighty-six of them, whose labour they tried to sell to the logwood cutters, only for the venture to turn out disastrously when the local magistrates refused to allow the sale. These magistrates and various others then plundered the ship.

The later deposition of Daniel Hill, Moore's agent, describing these events makes for some harrowing reading.[47] After calling at Jamaica, the ship reached Honduras in July with the convicts, twelve months' provisions and £2000 worth of goods. Hill and his colleagues asked two local magistrates where they might build a shelter for the convicts and a site at what was known as the 'Haulover' was pointed out. They set to building and landed the convicts. Then suddenly, in August, the magistrates and settlers declared that the convicts were not welcome and ordered that they be re-embarked. Anyone purchasing their labour, the magistrates announced, would be fined £100. Knowing that he could not legally return the convicts to England, Hill took twenty-two of them to the Northern River to cut timber, leaving the rest at the Haulover with his son in charge.

On his return to the Haulover, Hill was arrested as a consequence of a complaint by Henry Jones, one of the settlers at Northern River. Pleading that it was absolutely necessary that he return to Northern River, Hill obtained his release; but when he reached the timber-cutting site again, he found that Jones had persuaded the convicts to go to another, 'where he said he would show them plenty of wood, which they might cut for their own benefit; and offered immediately to conduct them to that place by which means the greater part of them were easily persuaded to follow his advice, and those that were refractory they forced along with them'. Instead of to Rio Hondo, however, Jones took the convicts to Key Chapel, a barren island where there was no timber growing, 'nor any thing else either for profit or subsistence'.

Hill then returned to Belize for the hearing of the charge against him, to find that a jury had concluded 'that Jones did very right in taking away the people and provisions, and that it was what they would have done themselves', and that the magistrates approved of this verdict.

The magistrates then persuaded Arnott, the *Mercury*'s captain, that he, rather than Hill, was in charge of the ship, convicts and cargo, prompting Arnott to bring a suit against Hill. The court found that while Arnott was in charge only of the ship and Hill of the convicts and cargo, both men were 'subject to the resolutions of the magistrates and inhabitants', and instructed Arnott and Hill to re-embark the convicts immediately.

Then, three days later, Hill said:

Arnott the master, with William Greaves his mate and part of the crew of the *Mercury*, came to my house at the Haulover, armed with blunderbusses and cutlasses, and put me by force into a boat, and carried me on board of the ship *Mercury*, where they detained me a prisoner for about six weeks; during which time all the convicts, as well as their provisions and the rest of the cargo, together even with my own wearing apparel and bedding, were made away with, the convicts being taken and employed by different inhabitants; particularly several of them by Mr McAulay [one of the magistrates], who kept them for a considerable time running wood for him; some by Mr Sullivan, some by Mr Davis, and one by Mr Potts. The goods were partly sold by the captain, and the money received by him; and about £900 worth taken by one Captain Tellet; but for none of them did I ever receive anything.

Hill tried to bring a suit to recover the stolen goods, but the magistrates told him that he must obtain a fresh power of attorney from Moore in London, a process that would take at least six months. He tried to bring other actions, but the magistrates declined to receive them, with McAulay telling him: 'Sir, you shall neither have law or justice while you stay in this country'. Hill replied that he was a British subject, entitled to the benefit of the law; whereupon McAulay responded that 'the people of Honduras had nothing to do with the King of Great Britain, that they were an independent people'.

Hill offered to show the magistrates the act of parliament authorizing the transportation of convicts to any place 'beyond the seas', whereupon the magistrates told him that 'no act of parliament was binding on the people of this country; and that they cared no more for an act of parliament than for a piece of brown paper'; and that he was 'a damned old rascal, and that if it was not for my years they would break my head'.

Hill wrote repeatedly to Moore for advice, only for the magistrates to withhold from him the merchant's replies. At last, Hill was able to get to Jamaica on a warship, and then returned to England. He said bitterly that he never received a 'sixpence' for the convicts and the cargo.

In 1785, while these events were playing out, Moore transported a further group of thirty convicts to Honduras. Leaving London towards the end of September, the *Fair American* reached its destination in December, but the settlers again refused to allow the convicts to be unloaded. After some weeks, Moore's agent landed them on the Mosquito Shore, where their fate is obscure but presumably unpleasant. Moore became bankrupt.

*

In October 1784, before the outcome of the first Honduras venture was known, Sydney observed to one correspondent: 'The more I consider the matter, the greater difficulty I see in disposing of those people, in any other place in the possession of His Majesty's subjects.'[48] This remark has underpinned the view that the British sent convicts to New South Wales because they could find no other place. This explanation has the virtue of simplicity, but also the vice of error, for it arises from a truncation of what Sydney actually wrote. Sydney's point was not that there was no other place to which the convicts might be sent, but that there was no other place in Britain's dominions, which left open the possibility of identifying a site not yet part of the empire.[49] The difference is significant. And in fact, the Pitt administration had already prepared for the solution Sydney hinted at with the Transportation Act of August 1784. Previously, parliamentary legislation had to specify the place of transportation; now, this could be decided by the King acting in conjunction with the Privy Council, and might be 'either within His Majesty's dominions, or elsewhere out of His Majesty's dominions'.[50] In searching for a place to which to transport convicts, the government could now look beyond the existing empire.

*

At the turn of the year, the Home Office received two separate but similar proposals to establish a convict settlement in West Africa. The first came from John Roberts, who had been governor of Cape Coast Castle, on the Gold Coast, between 1778 and 1782. Although fundamentally opposed to the idea, Roberts clearly knew what Lord Sydney was inclining to, and he offered his scheme in the belief that 'Africa is positively the part of the world [the convicts] are destined for'.[51]

Roberts suggested that 200 convicts be sent annually to Cape Coast Castle. There, they would be under the general authority of the governor, who would have the help of a criminal court and the power to release well-behaved prisoners from irons and, in the longer term, to emancipate them. They would be accommodated in purpose-built prisons, which would be arranged to form an interior square and which would each hold ten men. In the middle of the square would be an open shed, where they would eat. A 'pay-master' would dispense their weekly ration each Monday. There would also be a hospital capable of housing fifty men. The convicts would be guarded in their barracks and directed in their labour by 'bomboys' or 'drivers', one to each gang of ten. These would be armed and have the power to administer corporal punishment. Roberts conceded that many of the convicts would soon die; indeed, '*several hundreds might be sent* before *200* could be found to stand the climate'. However, he asserted that the hardy survivors 'would in time be useful to the state'. These white slaves would be set to cultivating cotton in the castle's extensive (but long neglected) garden:

> There is not an island in the West Indies that produces better cotton, than we every day see growing spontaneously in Africa. The Company's garden at Cape Coast in not less than five or six miles

in extent, although not three-quarters of a mile of it is cultivated by their officers and servants for the purpose of raising vegetables. I would have the convicts clear the whole spot; the labour it is true would be hard, and very trying to European constitutions, but this set of people are now got so numerous, that it seems absolutely necessary for humanity to give way in some measure to the good of our country. The ground once cleared, should be laid out in small cotton fields, or plantations, one to each gang. It might be three or four years before the good effects of such a plan would appear; but there cannot be a doubt that by that time they would be able not only to remit cotton sufficient to maintain themselves, but to pay all expenses government may be put to in establishing it.

While Roberts evidently presented this proposal to the African Committee, it is lodged among Home Office papers. How closely the Pitt administration attended to it is uncertain. It was quickly supplanted by an alternative scheme to send the convicts to Lemain, an island about 400 miles up the River Gambia (a plan which I describe below). However, the Home Office officials clearly kept Roberts's plan in reserve, for when Sydney advised the committee of the Lemain scheme, its secretary replied:

In consequence of what Lord Sydney mentioned on Saturday I ordered the African Committee to be summoned for this day, when they accordingly met, but as no letter came from his Lordship I presume he has dropped the intention of sending an additional number of convicts to the forts on the Gold Coast in case matters are not arranged for their reception at the island of Lemain at their first arrival there. I hope that plan is dropped so far as regards their being ordered to the Gold Coast eventually, as I believe [it] would be impossible to lodge them there without the most imminent danger to the forts in their present situation.[52]

The second proposal came from a group of African Company merchants headed by John Barnes, who suggested to the Home Office that convicts might be send to Lemain, which they represented as fertile and capable of accommodating 4000 persons.[53]

This was an exceedingly strange scheme. The island was to be purchased from local rulers and the convicts sent there were to be under no authority other than that they themselves might choose to create:

> [They are to] be left entirely to themselves, and before they leave the river [i.e., the Thames], be directed to elect a chief and at least four more, as a council, out of their own body, and to invest such chief with powers to appoint any subordinate officers that might be necessary for the regulation of their affairs, and to have charge of the provisions and property provided for their use, and also to try and punish any of them for crimes.

The slave traders conceded that many of the convicts would die in the beginning, but that the survivors would gradually become inured to the region's climate and diseases. These would find it impossible to escape through the country, and a guard-ship would prevent their doing so downriver. Like Roberts, Barnes predicted Britain would eventually derive significant benefits from such a colony. As it became established, it would offer more resources and become healthier, so that 'a regular succession of convicts might be sent out annually'. As for the initial cost, Barnes wrote:

> The amount [needed], admitting it to be £10,000, is really no more than the absolute and certain expense to government for the support and confinement of the same number of convicts in the River Thames for eight months. And it must at the same time be considered that the sending out a like number the second year will not, in all probability, exceed one half of that sum; the third still less, and in a short time the expense will be reduced solely to that of their conveyance thither.

As well as food, he went on, the convicts might cultivate cotton, tobacco and indigo. Once they were established as planters, they might 'take those to be sent out hereafter into their service'. And 'as they grow rich they naturally grow honest, and from the commodities which might be collected from the natives, it is more than probable that it would in a short series of years be of considerable advantage to this country. Gold is often found in the interior parts, as well as other articles of value'.

*

By December 1784, then, the Pitt administration had three distinct proposals for convict colonies outside the existing British empire, two within the Atlantic world, in the Gambia and on the Gold Coast, the third in the great world beyond, on the coast of New South Wales in the southwest Pacific Ocean.

On 24 and 25 December, in the context of a wide-ranging appraisal of Britain's strategic needs in the East (which I describe in Chapter 6), Pitt and Sydney asked Earl Howe, the First Lord of the Admiralty, for his opinion of Matra's proposals. Howe replied: 'The length of the navigation, subject to all the retardments of an India voyage, do not, I must confess, encourage me to hope for a return of the many advantages in commerce or war, which Mr Matra has in contemplation'.[54]

Nonetheless, the administration remained interested. In an agenda for a Cabinet meeting just after Christmas, Nepean outlined 'Matra's Plan':

> The erecting a settlement upon the coast of New South Wales, which is intended as an asylum for some of the American Loyalists, who are now ready to depart, and also as a place for the transportation of young offenders, whose crimes have not been of the most heinous nature;

And 'Barnes's Plan':

The transportation of convicts to the island Lemain in the River Gambia, and furnishing them with provisions, tools and implements for husbandry and for erecting habitations.[55]

The Cabinet ministers took their decision on 27 December. Two days later, Nepean wrote privately to the mayor of Plymouth, whom he knew: 'It is at last determined that [the convicts at Plymouth] shall forthwith be removed, with some others who are now in the jails in and about London, to the coast of Africa'.[56] By the end of 1784, then, the worst offenders among the convicts were destined for a most precarious future, unsupervised and unprotected, on the island of Lemain in the River Gambia.

5.

The Lemain Fiasco of 1785

IN TELLING JOHN NICHOL, the mayor of Plymouth, of the decision to send the convicts to Lemain, Evan Nepean cautioned:

> You are certainly the best judge, whether any person brought before you for a petit larceny should suffer so severe a sentence as that of transportation thither, which you know in the routine of punishment is considered as next in degree to that of death ... If you follow my advice you will sentence the convicts generally to 'transportation beyond the seas', for should the present plan, from obstacles that may hereafter appear, be laid aside, some other must shortly be adopted, and upon that general sentence you can have no further trouble.[1]

The trouble that Nepean anticipated appeared immediately, when the African trader Richard Bradley told him that he doubted that the convicts would be able to maintain themselves on Lemain and warned that 'the wretched state they would in that case be reduced to I am very certain would much hurt the humanity of Lord Sydney, and ... would excite great complaints amongst the dissatisfied people here'.[2]

Then, on 3 January 1785, Sydney had a 'long conference' with Edward Thompson 'about the state of the public jails and the disposal of the convicts', during which he told Thompson of the Lemain decision. William Pitt joined them. Thompson told the Prime Minister and the Home

108

Secretary that 'there was an inhuman appearance in the style of the business, and it would never be received by the people of England. It was in one word an African grave, and they went there devoted to death'. The ministers, Thompson recorded, 'stared, surprised at the boldness of my assertion', and replied that 'it was immediately necessary to clear the prisons'. Thompson suggested that he should locate a site in Sierra Leone, which he thought was 'a better place', where a colony might be 'cherished'. A week later, he repeated his advice about São Tomé and suggested that, despite Portugal's earlier refusal, this island might still be obtained were one of that Court's ministers given a 'proper present'.[3]

Thompson continued to discuss alternatives to the Gambia with administration figures in the next weeks. Eighteenth months earlier, he had suggested to Lord Keppel, the First Lord of the Admiralty, that he should explore the southwest coast of Africa between 20°S and 30°S latitude, 'where there was a fertile country defended north from the Portuguese and south from the Dutch by high, barren, inaccessible mountains – and between these extremes there were fine harbours'. The bay at Cape das Voltas, he had said, would 'answer in point of harbour, climate, and fertile country', and he proposed a settlement there 'for our Indiamen to call at and refit and come up with [the] SE trade [wind] in war to avoid the enemy, without returning the beaten road from the Cape, and the necessity of putting into the Rio de Janeiro'. According to Thompson, Keppel and the Prime Minister, Portland, had 'minutely attended' to the idea, but they thought 'in so infant a peace it would be dangerous to alarm our new friends by exploring, and they therefore proposed to postpone it until the succeeding year, when vessels should sail under my directions'.[4]

Nor was this the first time that the Das Voltas Bay region had been thought of as a possible place of refreshment for ships plying the India route. In January 1782, Alexander Dalrymple had urged the East India Company to survey the southern Atlantic Ocean for places of refreshment. On the outward route, these might include the islands of Trinidada, Ascensão and Tristan da Cunha; and on the homeward one, 'the *west coast* of *Africa* between the north extremity of the *Dutch districts* and the south extremity of the Portuguese territory on the *coast* of *Angola*'. Twenty months later, the Company did send the *Swallow* off on this mission, telling its commander that he was to examine 'proper places on this side of the Cape of Good Hope not in [the] possession of, or frequented by, Europeans, at which the Company's ships may be supplied with water and refreshments'; and with the particular instruction that 'the voyage must … be kept as secret as possible'. However, the voyage was aborted.[5]

Now, with the prospect of being able to utilize the convicts' labour, Thompson revived this idea. In the context of a broad discussion of the nation's strategic position in the East, he mentioned it to Charles Jenkinson on 20 February. Then, he wrote up a detailed proposal on 9 March, in which he pointed out that the Das Voltas Bay area was fertile, animals were abundant and the inhabitants friendly. He listed the site's advantages:

> 7. The superior advantage the Dutch, Portuguese and French have reaped over us in their Indian navigation and commerce, has arisen from their having more convenient ports of refreshment in their passages, for while we are compelled to Rio de Janeiro and to St Helena, where little provision is to be obtained, they enjoy with every advantage the Cape of Good Hope and the fertile kingdom of Angola, where the Portuguese and French put in, and by this means the latter have escaped our cruisers in war.
>
> 8. The bay and river of *de Voltas*, called *Angra das Voltas*, or the port, would therefore be an excellent reception for our Indiamen on their return; and the passage may be made coastways, from Guinea and St Thomas's outwards.

And he cautioned:

> 11. I could wish secrecy was observed in this matter and plan, for the moment it is divulged and committed to the public, the French will embrace the advantage and possess themselves of this country, as they have done of the Andamans in the Bay of Bengal.

Thompson presented this formal proposal to Sydney on 21 March.[6]

Despite these warnings and suggestions, the administration continued with the plan to transport convicts to Lemain. Evan Nepean arranged for the merchant Richard Bradley to go out to Africa to negotiate the lease of the island, and he asked one of the naval officers who had served on the Africa station whether he might be interested in overseeing the venture.[7]

Nepean also had John Barnes and his friends expand and refine their proposals, which became four: a description of Lemain; the terms on which they would carry the convicts out; the terms (many and convoluted) on which Barnes would keep a guardship downstream from the island, so as to prevent the convicts escaping; and the terms on which Richard Heatley was prepared to act as the government's agent in the Gambia.[8]

On 9 February, the Home Office informed the Treasury that 150 convicts were to be sent to Africa, and forwarded the merchants' proposals for appraisal. Three days later, it advised that the number would in fact be 200. The Treasury duly passed the various tenders on to the Navy Board for comment, which recommended acceptance of that for transportation, even though it was 'high', but found that for maintaining the guardship 'very extravagant', and recommended against it.[9]

At the beginning of March, the Recorder of London drew up two lists of the convicts whose place of transportation was to be changed to Africa, which Sydney sent to the Privy Council on 3 March. Orders-in-Council were issued on 11 March substituting this destination for the 'America' or 'beyond the seas' in the sentences of the convicts selected.[10]

By this time, however, having realized that it was now too late to land the convicts in Africa before the onset of the wet season, with all its unhealthiness, the administration had decided to defer implementation of the scheme for six months. On 4 March, Nepean asked Duncan Campbell to supply a ship 'for the reception and security of 250 convicts' until September. The administration quickly accepted his terms; Sydney advised the Treasury of the need on 20 March and Campbell started putting convicts on board the *Ceres* from the beginning of April.[11]

It was as well that the Home Office did defer the scheme, for news of the plan and of the issuing of the Orders-in-Council leaked out and the Opposition attacked in parliament. On 16 March, Edmund Burke sorrowfully told the House of Commons that the convicts destined for Africa had now been given sentences 'infinitively more severe' than those 'inflicted in the utmost rigour and severity of the laws'. He castigated the imposition of a worse punishment in the guise of extending the royal mercy. He also criticized the cost of transportation at a time when 'frugality and economy' were essential in national affairs. He then turned the full vigour of his renowned rhetoric on the Prime Minister. He wished to know, he said:

> what was to be done with these unhappy wretches; and to what part of the world it was intended, by the Minister, they should be sent. He hoped it was not to Gambia, which though represented as a wholesome place, was the capital seat of plague, pestilence, and famine. The gates of Hell were there open night and day to receive the victims of the law; but not those victims which either the letter or the spirit of the law, had doomed to a punishment attended with certain death. This demanded the attention of the legislature. They should in their punishments remember, that the consequences of transportation were not meant to be deprivation of life; and yet in Gambia it might truly be said that there 'all life dies, and all death lives'.

Burke then demanded to know whether the administration had signed a contract for this transportation, to which Pitt answered 'No' – which was literally true, but also a prevarication.[12]

The Opposition returned to the attack on 11 April. Lord Beauchamp pointed out that there had as yet been no report to the House of Commons on how the administration intended to dispose of the transport convicts, even though such a report had previously been ordered, and hinted darkly at a hostile motion. Pitt pleaded 'a very great hurry of public business' and asked Beauchamp the likely tenor of his motion.

Beauchamp repeated his opposition to transporting convicts outside the King's dominions, but would not otherwise be drawn.[13]

Burke then once again drew attention to the miserable fate awaiting any wretches unfortunate enough to be sent to Africa, and repeated that doing so was scarcely an example of humanity: 'the merciful gallows of England would rid them of their lives in a far less dreadful manner, than the climate or the savages of Africa would taken them'. When Pitt interjected that he was 'assuming facts without any better authority than report', Burke replied that he understood that there were seventy-five convicts aboard a ship that 'might sail before morning, and the wind would soon carry them out of the reach of the interposition of parliament'. He then sarcastically compared the full state of the 'House' of Newgate with the few members present in the House of Commons.[14]

The next day, the administration presented the Orders-in-Council of 11 March to parliament, and on 20 April the Commons set up a committee to enquire into the workings of the transportation act of the previous August. With Beauchamp as its chairman, and Burke and Fox among its many members, this was scarcely a group friendly to the administration.

The Beauchamp Committee's hearings divided into two stages.[15] In the first, from 26 April to 3 May, its members heard testimony about the state of the jails and hulks, and the suitability or otherwise of West Africa as a place of transportation.

On 26 April, Thomas Bailey, a magistrate, told of the recent difficulties in carrying out sentences of transportation. The next day, Evan Nepean testified about the administration's intentions. This was not an easy task. He explained that the African Company had refused to take any more convicts at its settlement, and that therefore 'a plan has been suggested, for the transportation of convicts to the island of *Lemain*, about 400 miles up the River Gambia'. He said that this site had been chosen partly in the absence of suggestions of others. Asked 'Whether the plan respecting the island of Lemain is finally determined on', he replied that it was 'under the contemplation of government, and preferred [to] every other plan, though not finally resolved on'. He added that it would have been put into effect were the season for sailing not so far advanced and described the scheme in detail.

Nepean was followed by John Boon, a surgeon who had lived in Senegal for three years, who told of how 'putrid fevers' and 'fluxes' were very prevalent among Europeans in the area. Someone who labours in the field, he said, 'could not live a month, unless he had an able surgeon with him'. Moreover, 'no reliance could be placed on the faith of the natives', who 'would rob any settlers that might be sent there of their tools, and of everything they could lay their hands upon, particularly iron'.

The committee then heard from John Barnes, who announced that the Lemain idea was originally his, and that he and Home Office officials had worked out its details in conversation. Barnes testified to the healthiness and fertility of the area, to the friendliness of the natives and to the usefulness of the scheme proposed, concluding that Britain was likely to receive distinct benefits from it.

John Call and the Recorder of London testified on 28 April. Call said that he had visited both Senegal and Gambia in 1750, and that Europeans there 'almost generally laboured under fluxes or fevers'. He thought that convicts sent from England were likely to arrive debilitated and unfit for work, that conflicts with the natives would certainly follow; and that the inevitable mortality among the crew of the guardship would diminish its effectiveness. The Recorder described the workings of the new transportation act, with its provisions for fixing the place of transportation by Order-in-Council.

Sir George Young, Mr Sturt, Edward Thompson, Henry Smeathman and John Barnes appeared on 2 May. Young cited his four tours of duty on the Africa station, and said that it would be impossible to restrain 'a colony of convicts without order or government'; if the convicts were armed, he warned, they would 'probably kill and rob the natives, or if unarmed, the natives would rob and kill them'. The Gambians were 'very peaceable, if well treated, but very revengeful, if insulted', while 'death would be the consequence of [European labourers] continuing an hour exposed to the sun'.

Sturt, who had accompanied the convict regiments to Cape Coast Castle in 1782, told of the soldiers' bad behaviour and desertion. Thompson reported that the area was generally unhealthy and that the natives were likely to kill the convicts. If they didn't, fevers and the climate would. Moreover, he said, a convict settlement needed more control than a guardship stationed downstream could provide. Smeathman, who had lived in Sierra Leone for four years, described the natives there as 'exceedingly vindictive'. Barnes offered what opposing views he could, but by this point the overall tenor of the testimony had become clear. Jonathan Nevan and Thomas Nesbitt added to it the next day, when Richard Akerman also gave details of the crowded state of Newgate prison.

Beauchamp then prepared a report of this stage of the committee's hearings, which he presented to the Commons on 9 May.[16] The administration can scarcely have been happy with it. The committee had heard from a stream of witnesses, administration supporters among them, who had tellingly exposed the weaknesses and callousness of the Lemain scheme, publicly confirming the severe criticism Edward Thompson had made of it at the beginning of the year. With the tabling of this preliminary report, it became impossible for the administration to proceed with the scheme.

*

The Beauchamp Committee began the second stage of its hearings on 6 May, when James Matra testified about the suitability of Botany Bay.[17] While the minutes of this day's hearings have not survived, Matra evidently presented members with his fully-fledged scheme for a Loyalist colonization of New South Wales. It is also possible that they were given details of Sir George Young's scheme, which he had had printed on 21 April, obviously in preparation for the committee's hearings; however, there is now no indication that Young appeared to testify about it. (It may be that his brother-in-law John Call, who was a member of the committee, instead distributed copies of the printed version.)[18]

Matra appeared again on 9 May. Committee members opened their questioning with an enquiry about numbers:

> Supposing colonization to be out of the question and that the only object was the inquiry of this Committee, viz., to send criminals out of the kingdom, that a guardship and some marines being sent to control them 300 or 400 might not be sent in proper transports and established in a situation where by hard labour, [and] if furnished with proper tools and seeds, they might be able to provide convenient residence and future subsistence for themselves and those appointed to govern and direct them?

Matra replied that 500 convicts might be safely sent, provided the guardship remained.

Although the scope of its enquiry was limited, it is interesting that the committee did not rule out a free colonization of New South Wales. Could both sorts of settlement co-exist, at sufficient distance from each other that there need be no intercourse between them, a member asked. Matra was certain that they could. He thought that the initial colonizing expedition should leave England not later than the beginning of August and that, given necessary stops for provisions at the Cape of Good Hope and other places, the voyage would take a minimum of six months. He described how on Cook's first voyage they had been on the coast of New South Wales between April and July and had found the climate 'perfectly agreeable to [the] European constitution'. He said that the inhabitants of New Caledonia and Tahiti were 'of a quiet nature' and as happy 'as human nature generally are'. As Tahitian women preferred European men, he added, they might be brought to the new settlement 'in any number'. A committee member then raised a point that was later to be of considerable significance: 'Do you think government would run any risk in attempting this plan without further examination than you or anybody you know could give them of that country?' 'I think they would not', Matra replied. He added that rather than see the idea dropped he would, if the administration wished, 'undertake it not on the footing of a contractor, but as an officer under the government, to be the conductor and governor'. On being asked whether he meant 'as a sober regular colony or as a colony of convicts', he replied, 'Either or both'.

If the decision were for a colony of 500 convicts, Matra continued, he would need a force of 200 marines and a guardship (a 40-gun ship 'of the old build' would be most suitable). The colony would need to be under military law, and ministers of religion should be sent. He concluded by saying that he had not calculated the likely costs of transporting convicts to New South Wales, but that the seeds and livestock needed might be purchased at the Cape of Good Hope, Madagascar and the Moluccas.

Sir Joseph Banks appeared before the committee the next day (10 May). The members told the now-famous naturalist that they would be glad to know 'whether in your voyage with Captain Cook it occurred to you that there were any places in the new discovered islands to which persons of such description [i.e. convicts] might be sent in a situation where they might be able by labour to support themselves?' Banks replied that he had 'no doubt that the soil of many parts of the eastern coast of New South Wales between the latitudes of 30°S and 40°S is sufficiently fertile to support a considerable number of Europeans who would cultivate it in the ordinary modes used in England', and that Botany Bay was 'in every respect adapted to the purpose'.

Banks confessed himself ignorant of the Aborigines' language and form of government, so that he could not advise about negotiating the cession of an area, but he said that fish were plentiful on the coast, and that there were no wild beasts. The timber appeared 'fit for all the purposes of house-building and ship-building'. He thought European cattle would thrive there, as would grains and legumes. Women for the 500 convicts might be brought from the Pacific islands. He concluded by saying that 'from the fertility of the soil, the timid disposition of the inhabitants and the climate being so analogous to that of Europe, I give this place the preference to all [others] that I have seen'.

Charles Coggan, the East India Company's chief shipping official, and Duncan Campbell appeared before the committee on 12 May. Coggan gave members some idea of the likely costs of transporting to

New South Wales, by providing those of sending troops out to India. His figures showed this to be on average £25 per man, but he pointed out that this sum did not include the cost of a surgeon's services on the voyage, of food and accommodation, and of some other minor expenditures.

Campbell followed Coggan. He briefly described how he had transported convicts to North America, and his trading activities there. He explained that, on average, he had received £13 for the sale of each convict's labour; and that he had had the advantage of a homeward trade in tobacco. He thought that he would have required a minimum of £12 per person, if he had been unable to obtain a return cargo and been 'obliged to come back in ballast'.

A committee member friendly to the administration (who may have been John Call) then asked Campbell a series of questions prepared by the Home Office:[19]

If you were to carry convicts a voyage of probably six months to a place where no kind of trade is carried on, how much per man would you contract for?

I think the ship ought not to be of less tonnage than 700 or 800 for this purpose. It ought to carry out 300 convicts exclusive of crew. Then if she goes alone I apprehend 70 or 80 men would be enough to man her. I must reckon on a 15 months' voyage; provisions for the ship's company for that time; for convicts for the outward voyage, for 7 months. I think it could not be contracted for less than £30 a man.

If the ship carried only 200 what could it be done for then?

About £40 a man.

In the calculation do you include the expense of a surgeon and medicine?

Yes, all expenses and a profit to the undertaker of the plan.

The committee received a follow-up letter from Campbell 'relative to the expense of transporting convicts into the southern ocean beyond the Cape of Good Hope' when it next met on 23 May.[20] Its members had some more questions for Matra:

Do you conceive that cattle, sheep, poultry, hogs and other live stock may be obtained more easily and expeditiously both for consumption as well as propagation from countries much nearer to New South Wales than the Cape of Good Hope?

I do, from Savu and the other Molucca islands. I believe any quantity may be obtained, at a very easy expense and at a very short space of time, and from the Friendly and Society islands hogs and poultry may be obtained.

Don't you think that grain of some kinds, vegetables and fruit may be also obtained from these and other islands in the neighbourhood?

At the Moluccas there is the greatest abundance of all kinds of grain that grow in the east. There is a Dutch agent resident in each of the islands, who gives permission to trade and of whom the permission may be purchased.

Though Mr Campbell seems to think that a ship that should take on board 300 convicts would not be able to take stores, provision and water, can you suggest any other mode by which that difficulty may be obviated?

If the ship be burden of about 800 tons she will certainly carry stores and provisions sufficient for the voyage, and sufficient to bring her crew back, especially if she is under convoy of a frigate, and in case it is meant to retain them there under any kind of government, then undoubtedly a storeship would be necessary.

When you [were] examined upon a former occasion touching the propriety of sending convicts to New South Wales did you give any information of that country being taken possession of by Captain Cook in the name of His Britannic Majesty?

I don't recollect that any such question was put to me, but Captain Cook regularly took possession not only of the different parts of the coast, but also of the strait which separates it from

New Guinea, and there are no accounts known to the public of any European powers having visited them previous to our discovery, nor is there the least trace to be found among the natives of any European manufactures or utensils.

Have you any doubt that the Dutch will supply us with those necessaries from the Moluccas for the purpose of such settlement?

I don't imagine there would be any difficulty at first, as there is but a single agent. I think we might even [have traded] without assistance when we were there in the *Endeavour*. We found no difficulty, and I imagine that if he acted properly we might get as much at the first supply as would be necessary.

Anyone witness to the committee's enquiry to this point would have been in no doubt that its members would recommend Botany Bay as the new site of transportation. All the testimony they had heard in this second phase had related to this region, and that testimony had provided the basis for a well-founded scheme. Yet this did not happen; instead, the committee opted for another site in Africa. Some aspects of this abrupt change of mind remain obscure, but enough details are extant to provide a fascinating glimpse of behind-the-scenes manoeuvring.

At the end of June, when the committee's final report had been written but not yet presented, Lord Beauchamp observed darkly in parliament that 'he, as chairman of the committee, should have stated some place [as the site for transportation]; but a particular circumstance occurred during the sitting of the committee, that rendered it improper for him to mention it at the time'.[21]

What had happened was that the Pitt administration had abandoned the Lemain proposal in favour of Das Voltas Bay, that site on the southwest African coast recommended by Edward Thompson. In a tantalizingly incomplete memorandum, which, while also undated, must have been written about the time of the committee's presenting its first report to parliament (9 May), Evan Nepean suggested this alternative:

> As so much noise has been made and so many objections started to the sending the convicts to the island of Lemain, on account of its very unhealthy situation, it may be advisable to change the place of their destination. The southern coast of Africa at or near Angra das Voltas between the latitudes … is not subject to the same objections, the climate being nearly the same as that of Lisbon, and although the interior part is very little known or indeed even the coast, it has been ascertained by ships that have touched at places upon that coast that the natives are not inclined to act with hostility, and that they are amply …[22]

While Nepean does not state the other attractions of the Das Voltas Bay region, as he is so obviously paraphrasing Thompson's proposal, we may know that these were strategic and commercial.

Events in the next weeks show that the administration adopted Nepean's suggestion, and Africa remained its preferred destination for the convicts. As Lord Sydney remarked to Lord George Cavendish, a member of the committee, on 20 May, 'transportation to Africa is the sentence of many of these convicts, and the wish of many others, who are sensible that no climate is worse than that of a jail'. He added: 'But there are those who are disposed to make transportation to that part of the world impracticable'.[23] It was in keeping with this outlook that, on 13 May, the administration issued new Orders-in-Council nominating Africa as the place of transportation for an additional number of convicts.[24]

Signs of the administration's change of plans soon appeared. When the Beauchamp Committee met on 25 May, John Call brought 'a paper containing information with regard to the western part of the southern coast of Africa, accompanied with some observations of his own'. The copying of sentences and paragraphs from these documents into the committee's final report shows that they were Thompson's Das Voltas Bay proposal of 9 March 1785, and Call's New South Wales proposal of September 1784.[25]

The committee members asked Beauchamp to seek further information about the southwest coast of Africa from the Home Office and from published narratives of exploration, and to form 'such a report as he conceives they may be warranted to make relative to the coast of New South Wales or the west coast of Africa between the latitude of 20°S and 30°S'.

Beauchamp had this report ready by 21 June, and he presented it to parliament on 28 July.[26] After an initial complaint about lack of co-operation from Lord Sydney, the report began by deploring the problems afflicting jails and hulks, asserting that:

> the extraordinary fullness of the jails makes a separation of offenders impracticable, and that by constant intercourse they corrupt and confirm each other in every practice of villainy; that the hulks, however necessary they may have been as a temporary expedient, have singularly contributed to these mischievous effects; that they form distinct societies for the more complete instruction of all newcomers; who, after the expiration of their sentences, return into the mass of the community, not reformed in their principles, but confirmed in every vicious habit; that when they regain their liberty, no parish will receive them, and no person set them to work; that being shunned by their former acquaintances, and baffled in every attempt to gain their bread, the danger of starving almost irresistibly leads them to a renewal of their former crimes.

In the committee member's view, these evils arose from the discontinuation of transportation to North America, which they saw as having 'answered every good purpose which could be expected from it':

> it tended directly to reclaim the objects on which it was inflicted, and to render them good citizens; that the climate being temperate, and the means of gaining a livelihood easy, it was safe to entrust country magistrates with the discretionary power of inflicting it; that the operation of it was thus universally diffused over the whole island, as well as this metropolis; that it tended to break, in their infancy, those gangs and combinations which have since proved so injurious to the community ...

Transportation to North America had also, the committee noted, been comparatively cheap.

The report pointed out that the committee members had not considered the idea of sending convicts to labour under foreign governments, as the negotiations that would be required were the legal responsibility of the administration of the day. It then set forth the criteria the members considered necessary for a new site of transportation:

That the climate and situation ought to be healthy; as, although many of them have forfeited their lives by their original sentences, it is implied, by His Majesty's conditional pardon, that their transportation shall not expose them to any imminent danger of their lives; that unless they are removed to a considerable distance, from whence the means of returning may be rendered difficult, the end of their transportation will be defeated; that, subject to this caution, a coast situation is preferable to an inland one, for the convenience of supplying the settlers until they are able to provide for their own subsistence, as likewise to furnish them an asylum, if any natives should be disposed to annoy them.

The report then stated the committee members' strong opposition to the common premise of Banks's 1779 proposal, Call's proposal, and Barnes's scheme:

it was their decided opinion, that the idea of composing an entire colony of male and female convicts, without any other government or control but what they may from necessity be led to establish for themselves, can answer no good or rational purpose; that such an experiment has never been made in the history of mankind; that the outcasts of an old society will not serve as the sole foundation of a new one, which cannot exist without justice, without order, and without subordination, to which the objects in question must of necessity be strangers; that confusion and bloodshed would probably soon take place among them; and that no spot, however distant, can be pointed out by the Committee, in which the mischiefs of realizing so dangerous a project might not be felt on the trade and navigation of these kingdoms.

The report then enunciated the principles that committee members had had in mind in pursuing their enquiry, the most important of which were that the new site should not offer temptations to further crime, but rather hold out the means of social redemption; that the convicts' labour should there be 'employed to the most useful purposes', by which they meant the obtaining of strategic and commercial advantages; and that these advantages should repay the nation the cost of establishing a colony there.

Accordingly, the committee had considered:

First, those parts of Africa which already belong to the Crown of Great Britain, or which may probably be acquired for the purpose in question; secondly, the provinces as well as islands which are subject to His Majesty in America; and lastly, such other parts of the globe as have been already, or which may be, taken possession of for the object under consideration (if policy warrants the measure) without violating the territorial rights of any European potentate or state.

The report gave details only of the committee's findings on Africa. They thought that grave disadvantages would attend transportation to either the Gambia or Guinea, but that the area about the Das Voltas River was promising. No other Europeans had settled or claimed it; the local inhabitants were evidently peaceful; and it was highly probable that these would cheerfully lease as much land as was required. The site was coastal; it was fertile and had abundant water; there were great herds of horses, cattle and sheep; and the climate was healthy. There was copper in the nearby mountains (of strategic significance now that warships were being sheathed with this metal), and a 'fine bay and harbour for the shelter of shipping'. A settlement here might become a very useful port of supply for ships returning from the East, since (copying Thompson):

the superior advantage which the Portuguese, Dutch and French have reaped over us in their Indian navigation and commerce has arisen from their having more convenient ports of refreshment in their passages; for while we are confined to Rio de Janeiro and Saint Helena, where little provision is to be obtained, they enjoy with every advantage the Cape of Good Hope and the fertile kingdom of Angola, by which means the French Indiamen have often escaped the British cruisers in war; that the bay and river of Das Voltas would be an excellent place for the homeward-bound Indiamen; and that the passage may be made coastways from Guinea and Saint Thomas's outwards.

As well, it was only about ten days' sail from Das Voltas Bay to the coast of Brazil, where whales abounded. A settlement at Das Voltas Bay might also 'promote the purposes of future commerce or of future hostility in the South Seas' – that is, along the western coasts of the Spanish colonies in the Americas.

The committee members thought that the site would be suitable for the Loyalists as well as the convicts, but added that if the administration established a convict colony, the settlers should be properly equipped for their tasks with food, tools, seeds, etc. They recommended that the colony be policed by marines and a prudent officer put in charge, with the 'most absolute control over the settlers', and recommended Edward Thompson 'as the fittest person for the service'. They qualified all this by noting that they proposed this venture 'so far only as the commercial and political benefits of a settlement on the southwest coast of *Africa* may be deemed of sufficient consequence to warrant the expense inseparable from such an undertaking'.

Yet at the same time as they issued this caution, the committee members appealed to the nation's imperial inclinations, pointing out (copying Call):

That all the discoveries as well as great commercial establishments now existing in distant parts of the globe, have been owing to the enterprise and persevering exertions of individuals, who at great personal risks, frequent losses, and in some cases total ruin, have opened the way to the greatest national advantages; that the first settlements in North America were undertaken under every circumstance of an inhospitable climate and an ungrateful soil, as well as the fiercest attacks from the natives; yet, in the space of two hundred years, a new world has sprung up, under many untoward circumstances to which the undertaking in question does not appear to be exposed.

In recommending Das Voltas Bay, the Beauchamp Committee gave the Pitt administration what it wanted, and the government quickly moved to implement the scheme. On 22 August, Sydney formally asked the Admiralty to direct Edward Thompson to investigate the area, 'in order to fix upon a proper spot for making a settlement upon that coast, if such a measure should hereafter be judged expedient'.[27] Thompson had been expecting these instructions for some time. Late in the previous year, he had begun to gather officers skilled in survey work and had asked Admiral Howe for a suitable ship, so that he might accurately chart parts of Africa's western coast.[28] Howe now approved the idea; he added the smaller *Nautilus* to Thompson's command, and the Navy Board proceeded to fit the little squadron out. In secret instructions, the Admiralty told Thompson that, after inspecting the various forts in West Africa, he was to send off the *Nautilus*:

directing her commander to use every means in his power to obtain the best survey or intelligence that he possibly can respecting the navigation at the entrance of and in the said river or bay, as well as upon the coast contiguous thereto and to examine, as minutely as circumstances will admit, the face and produce of the country, the character and disposition of the inhabitants; and, in general, to use his utmost diligence in gaining every sort of information that may be requisite to be acquired previous to [a colonization].[29]

Sir Joseph Banks arranged for Anton Hove, a Pole with training in languages, botany and medicine, to sail on the expedition, and drew up detailed instructions for him. Banks advised him that his general mission was to find out if the country was 'fertile or barren'. If it were inhabited, he was to 'take especial notice of the lands cultivated by the natives, what is the nature of the soil, in what manner and with what kinds of implements they practice their tillage; whether they use any kind of manure to increase its fertility, and, if they do, of what kind; and whether their crops are rank and strong, or poor and weak; [and] to collect specimens of every plant, root or fruit which is cultivated'.

He was, moreover, to 'attend to the general appearances of the country – whether mountainous, hilly or plain; rocky, stony, gravelly, sandy or morassy; whether heathy, like the moors of England, [or] shrubby, grassy or covered with wood'. He was to investigate with an eye to locating land that might be able to be cultivated; and he was to collect specimens of all other plants for the King's garden at Kew.[30]

The expedition sailed at the end of September. As it did so, the administration received two proposals for a settlement on the southeast coast of Africa, about 500 miles to the east of Cape Town. On its voyage back from India, bad weather had forced to *Pigot* to take refuge at Krome River, about 150 miles to the east of Plettenberg Bay. A Dutch farmer had fed the ship's company from his abundant harvests and herds for several weeks. While they waited to resume their voyage, two of the military officers on the ship had looked about them with a careful eye and then written lengthy reports for the East India Company.

Henry Pemberton said that the bay into which they came offered shelter for many ships, and abounded with fish. The surrounding country was:

free from brush or underwood, a most luxuriant soil, with regular hills and dales containing the most beautiful sheep walks which extend many miles up the country, and only wants the hand of the ploughman and gardener to produce everything that grows in Europe, or indeed in the world. It is free from all kinds of wild beasts, excepting wolves, which are not numerous or troublesome, abounds with all kinds of cattle and game, the largest and fattest sheep and oxen we ever saw, and in the greatest number besides. Deer, goats and hogs, excellent horses of a small kind and tractable, all kinds of grain, excellent wheat and barley, European and tropical fruits, and vegetables, potatoes, cabbages, etc etc, with milk, butter, fowls etc, all equal in their several kinds to the best in Europe. The climate [is] as mild as the south of France, neither experiencing extreme heat nor cold, and productive of the choicest vines.

He pointed out that, from the English Channel to the coasts of India, the British did not possess 'a single port capable of affording shelter and protection or refreshment to their ships', and that therefore one on the southeast coast of Africa would be 'an object of national importance'. He also stated that the area was a suitable one to which to send the convicts because, surrounded by the Kaffir tribes, they would not be able to escape, while its temperate climate and ready means of obtaining food meant that they would not die in droves.[31]

Colonel William Dalrymple wrote to his wife ahead of his arrival home, telling her to draw up a proposal in his name and send it to William Devaynes, the deputy chairman of the East India Company, who should give it to Pitt. Dalrymple reiterated Pemberton's glowing praise of the area:

It is the finest soil I ever saw, with a divine climate ... It requires no clearing, as in America; only ploughing and sowing wheat, corns, cabbages, potatoes, etc, etc, and abounding with cattle, game of all sorts, and plenty of fish; producing also oranges and a tolerable wine from the grape.

'We should in a few years derive every advantage from a settlement here that the Dutch have from the Cape', he asserted, 'and in time of war, and returning home, would refresh here: with this additional advantage, that the French would not be so likely to capture our ships, as they could not know whether they would touch at St Helena or at the settlement.' 'We are at a loss where to send our convicts', Dalrymple continued, 'to send them to this country would indeed be a paradise to them, and settlers would crowd here'.[32]

Devaynes duly passed this proposal on to Henry Dundas and Pitt, saying that it deserved to be considered seriously, and that he believed that if it were to be pursued, this should be done *secret and out of hand*'; he had therefore not told the East India Company's Court of Directors of it.

Pitt and his colleagues did consider these proposals. Pitt asked his cousin W.W. Grenville's opinion at the beginning of October, pointing out that such a settlement would 'answer in some respects the purposes of the Cape, and ... serve also as a receptacle for convicts'.[33] But – presumably because Das Voltas Bay was their first choice, and because Thompson had already sailed – the administration does not seem to have pursued this idea further at this time.

6.

Thinking about the Whole Globe

IN THE PERIOD 1782–85, up until the Pitt administration's decision that Das Voltas Bay would be the new site for convict transportation, the thinking of ministers about penal practice had been conventional and had proceeded within accustomed parameters. They had attempted to resume transportation to Nova Scotia, Virginia and Maryland, Honduras and the west coast of Africa, and had considered various islands. These prospects all represented variations on the old practice of exporting a domestic problem to somewhere else in the Atlantic world, and of obtaining an economic benefit by doing so.

The Das Voltas Bay decision represented a striking departure from this thinking. First, because for the first time the proposed solution to the convict problem bore on Britain's imperial endeavours in the larger world beyond the Atlantic one – in the Indian and Pacific oceans, and along the coasts that bordered these vast realms. And second, because the government itself would be the employer of the convicts.

*

What premises underpinned this change in thinking?

As always with broad assertions about a new outlook, it is difficult to fix a precise beginning. However, so as to avoid taking readers back to Drake, and before him to Magellan and Columbus, let me begin this part of my story in the early eighteenth century.

From the time of the War of Spanish Succession (1702–13), British administrations had progressively enlarged the role of the Royal Navy. After capturing Gibraltar (1704) and Minorca (1708), and after augmenting existing dockyard facilities or creating new ones at these bases, the British turned to deploying a squadron permanently in the Mediterranean. In the 1720s and 1730s they built extensive facilities at Port Royal, Jamaica, and English Harbour, Antigua, which then became bases for the West India squadron. In 1739, at the commencement of the war with Spain, they sent Edward Vernon with a squadron to ravage the enemy's Caribbean settlements. In the middle of the 1740s, they established a permanent squadron in North America. Between 1745 and 1749 they kept a squadron in the East Indies based on Trincomalee, in Dutch Ceylon.

Daniel Baugh has succinctly delineated the general nature of this expansion:

The growth of the British navy in the eighteenth century was to a large extent the direct result of its radically enlarged strategic commitments in foreign waters. Between 1689 and 1714 England assumed a role in Continental conflicts which, whether she liked it or not, she could not renounce, and as a natural consequence of this role the Mediterranean turned into a major theatre of operations for the British navy. Simultaneously colonies and foreign trade prospered, and Whig governments were neither able nor inclined to deny colonists and merchants the protection they demanded from piracy, privateering, and raids of plunder. Moreover, naval strength had to be found, not only to defend the empire, but also to support a policy of expanding its boundaries by conquest. All of these things had been necessary at one time or another before. But where a cruiser had sufficed in the seventeenth century, it was now often necessary to employ a squadron; what had been a squadron's task now seemed impossible without a fleet; and what had been accomplished by an expedition now required a permanently stationed force.[1]

During the Seven Years' War (1756–63), the British developed a distinctive strategy, first of paying allies to engage enemies on the continent of Europe, rather than committing their own troops there; and second, of using their naval strength to attack those enemies in their shipping and overseas colonies. In the end, this strategy saw the British emerge triumphant from the conflict with their naval dominance confirmed, and with the French having lost colonies in North America, the West Indies and India, while the Spanish had suffered the ignominy of the capture of their two great hubs of empire, Havana and Manila. The success the British had in Europe, in North American waters, in the West Indies, off West Africa and around India, together with the accompanying land actions in French and Spanish colonies, meant that the Seven Years' War was a great watershed in European imperial rivalry. And in developing this strategy, British planners had been required, really for the first time, to think on a very broad scale – as the Duke of Newcastle remarked in 1758, 'Ministers in this country, where every part of the world affects us, some way or another, should consider *the Whole Globe*'.[2]

As the British expanded the scope of their maritime operations in the Seven Years' War, the problems of building and maintaining a sufficient number of ships and of their operating ever more widely became more apparent. Throughout the war there were delays in obtaining new ships. There was a shortage of masts in 1757, and the next year one of frame timbers. In the warm waters of the West and East Indies, barnacles and seaweed enveloped hulls, and the marine borer *Teredo navalis* ate them away. The disadvantages of inadequate bases in the East Indies became clear, as the squadron there was repeatedly rendered ineffectual by the lack of dockyard facilities, of naval stores (masts, spars, canvas, cordage, pitch) and of harbours to give protection from the northeast monsoon. Bitter indeed were the complaints about these deficiencies from desperate commanders charged with repulsing the French in the seas about India. And, always, there were the problems of finding men to crew the ships, and of keeping them healthy in a climate where 'living a fortnight or three Weeks on [salt meat] will throw half a ship's company down in the scurvy'. At the turn of 1762, Admiral Cornish took his squadron out from Bombay round to Madras. He lost 600 men to scurvy during the passage, and on arrival sent another 1400 to hospital.[3]

Still, the Seven Years' War was a naval triumph for Britain. Spain lost ten line-of-battle ships and twelve frigates – a fifth of its navy – at Havana, and France's navy was similarly crippled. Immediately on the return of peace, both these nations looked to rebuild their fleets in preparation for yet another war in which they might redress their losses and humble their inveterate enemy; but the process went slowly, and it was only in the mid-1770s that they were once more in a position to contemplate renewed naval conflict.[4]

*

When these enemies did take the side of the rebellious Americans (France in 1778 and Spain in 1779), they found circumstances much more favourable than during the Seven Years' War. As there was no conflict on the Continent, they were free to pursue naval war undistracted. They had modernized their navies since the last war, so that for a time, combined, they in fact out-matched the British. And when Britain declared war on Holland in 1780 in an attempt to stop Dutch ships supplying its enemies with naval stores, France and Spain obtained the use of Dutch colonial bases in addition to their own. Meanwhile, Britain was distracted by a fratricidal conflict in North America, which required that it maintain an army there, with the attendant problems of supply, including of food.

In September 1779, the Earl of Sandwich, then First Lord of the Admiralty, summed up the situation:

> It will be asked why, when we have as great if not a greater force than ever we had, the enemy are superior to us. To this it is to be answered that England till this time was never engaged in a sea war with the House of Bourbon thoroughly united, their naval force unbroken, and having no other war or object to draw off their attention and

resources. We unfortunately have an additional war upon our hands, which essentially drains our finances and employs a very considerable part of our army and navy; we have no one friend or ally to assist us, on the contrary, all those who ought to be our allies, except Portugal, act against us in supplying our enemies with the means of equipping their fleets.[5]

Gradually, the British did manage to bring more ships into commission, so that by the end of the war they were matching their enemies' squadrons; but it was lack of money in France's and Spain's treasuries, rather than decisive defeats, that forced these nations to negotiate for peace in 1782.

*

In particular, the wars of 1776–83 showed the British just how vulnerable they were in the East when opposed by well-resourced naval enemies.

To service the very long route between Europe and India the Dutch had the incomparable Cape of Good Hope, which formed a fulcrum of the southern oceans' wind and current systems. The colony's two bays provided anchorage for most of the year, and while the dockyard facilities at Simon's Bay were not extensive enough to permit either careening or rebuilding, they were adequate for other repairs. Cape Town's fortifications were sound, its climate healthy and its agriculture abundant. On the southeast coast of India, the Dutch had Negapatam, which gave reasonable anchorage for half of the year and some food; and on the northeast coast of Ceylon, Trincomalee, the only port in European possession that faced the Bay of Bengal and offered safe anchorage year round. Trincomalee had a fine natural harbour, but its hinterland was unproductive jungle, and the Dutch had not developed its naval potential much, nor fortified it extensively. In the East Indies, they had a network of minor bases and major ones at Malacca and Batavia (Jakarta). Batavia was notoriously unhealthy, but it stood at the junction of busy sea routes and offered sheltered anchorage, efficient dockyards and abundant food and naval supplies.

France possessed a major base at Mauritius (also called Ile de France) and a lesser one at Bourbon (now Réunion). Although authorities made concerted efforts to improve the situation in the 1770s, Mauritius was not self-sufficient in food, with quantities having to be imported from the Cape of Good Hope and Java (and to a lesser extent from Madagascar). As well, the climate was unhealthy, the weather unpredictable, and reefs and prevailing winds made the approach to the island hazardous. However, it had a good harbour, with adequate dockyards that the French kept well supplied. Bourbon was of limited use, for it too had the disadvantages of sparse agriculture, hazardous approaches and unhealthy climate, and lacked a good harbour. However, both islands lay adjacent to outward as well as homeward shipping routes, and while their distance from India detracted a little from their usefulness, they together constituted a satisfactory springboard for war or trade. On the coasts of India, the French had only minor anchorages at Mahé, Pondicherry and Karikal.

While the old papal division of the non-European world between Spain and Portugal meant that Spanish ships did not operate in the Indian Ocean, in the western Pacific Ocean the Spanish had Manila, the centre of an extensive and productive realm of islands.

Between Europe and India, by contrast, Britain possessed only St Helena to assist its shipping. This small island had no harbour, only an open roadstead. It was not self-sufficient in food and authorities had to import supplies from the Cape. As the winds prevailed from the southeast, it was not easily approached from Europe, and ships sojourning there were very vulnerable to attack by cruisers sailing out of Mauritius or the Cape. In India, the British were better served at Bombay (Mumbai), which had a good harbour, dockyards, an established shipbuilding industry and an extensive hinterland to supply food. They were less well placed on the eastern coasts, however, for though Madras (Chennai) and Calcutta (Kolkota) were also fed by extensive hinterlands, these places offered poor dockyard facilities and inadequate shelter to large ships during the northeast monsoon.

All the maritime powers encountered severe problems in keeping the naval arsenals at these bases adequately equipped. The Cape of Good Hope was deficient in timber, so the Dutch sent building and naval varieties of wood from Europe, as well as other stores. They made more use of local materials at Batavia, but also brought out European ones. The French supplied their dockyards at Mauritius almost entirely from Europe, sending out timber, masts and spars, cables and cordage, and canvas. The British sent the same items to Bombay, despite the fact that the Indian artificers they employed otherwise used teak and other regional materials. The Dutch, French and British all obtained saltpetre (used in gunpowder) in India.

As a consequence of this habit of being supplied from Europe, these bases were often severely limited in their ability to meet the calls on them. A yard's having supplies depended first on the goods' availability in Europe, then on navy officials having obtained adequate quantities, then on their having shipped them out with foresight. It depended, too, on store ships surviving tempests and shoals and reaching their destination. The safe arrival of a cargo, however, did not in itself guarantee that stores would be available. Sails mildewed in the tropical heat; masts and spars rotted in the warm ponds; a cyclone might see a carefully compiled supply reduced at once, with no prospect of its being rapidly replaced. In peacetime, the Europeans partly countered these problems by drawing on each other's resources; in war, the difficulties of supply often had a marked effect.

This was so in the naval war in the East between 1778 and 1783. After the declaration of war on Holland, the British sent an expedition to capture Cape Town, but this failed. In May 1781, Admiral Hughes, the commodore of the East India squadron, resumed patrols in the Bay of Bengal. He and land forces captured Negapatam in November, and then Trincomalee in January 1782. Upon his return to Madras, Hughes learned that his French counterpart, the Bailli de Suffren, had arrived. The squadrons met in full battle four times this year (17 February, 12 April, 6 July and 3 September), fierce encounters with no decisive result, and both commodores were left desperately searching for materials to repair their damaged ships.

In 1783, both having been reinforced, the squadrons met again on 20 June. Hughes had eighteen line-of-battle ships, Suffren fifteen. The British ships were faster, but as thousands of the British sailors were afflicted by scurvy the French were better manned. The outcome was again inconclusive, the damage to ships again heavy. Hughes described returning to Bombay in December 1783 with 'the nine sail of His Majesy's line-of-battle ships ... not a serviceable lower mast on board any of them, nor a fish for a mast or a spar for a topmast to be found but at Bombay'. He reported again in September 1784 that the 'line-of-battle ships in these seas are in the greatest want of cables, no supply of that article or any naval stores having been sent to India for these eighteen months past'.[6]

*

Distant though the Indian theatre of war was from Europe, Britain's strategic needs were soon of concern to William Pitt and his principal advisers.

The first months of the young Prime Minister's tenure of office were difficult, and not only because he faced a hostile House of Commons. Taken all in all, his Cabinet ministers were a mediocre group. Later in life, Pitt's cousin W.W. Grenville made a scathing assessment of them, to which historians have added. Earl Howe, the First Lord of the Admiralty, was perhaps the finest fighting officer of the day, but his character was otherwise 'cold and repulsive', his thinking about civil matters was 'clouded and confused', and he took little part either in the 'councils of the government' or 'the general business of the country'. Earl Gower, the Lord President of the Privy Council, was a sociable man who 'lent his prestige rather than his efforts' to the administration. Lord Camden, who became Lord President in 1784 when Gower moved to Lord Privy Seal, was 'experienced and shrewd, but indecisive and rather tired'. The Duke of Richmond, the Master-General of the Ordnance, had considerable intellectual ability but was 'capricious in his disposition', 'uncertain' in his opinions and 'visionary' in his thinking. Lord Thurlow, the Lord Chancellor, was a notable lawyer but an 'irresolute and timid' statesman who 'shunn[ed] with studied ingenuity the labour and the hazard of decision'. Thurlow disliked Pitt and was in turn disliked and distrusted by the Prime Minister. Lord Sydney and Lord Carmarthen, the Home and Foreign Secretaries, 'were unequal to the most ordinary business of their own offices'.[7]

Grenville was certainly right on this last point: Sydney was manifestly not up to his work. For example, the India Act made him the formal chairman of the Board of Control, but within four weeks he told Pitt that he was 'ready to abandon it to the ambition of those who like the department'. 'Lord Sydney never attends [an India Board meeting], nor reads or signs a paper', Dundas told the governor-general of India in July 1787. Even more telling is the observation by William Smith, who personally experienced Sydney's inertia in 1786 and felt for his loyal and diligent Under-Secretary: 'Poor Nepean! He knows not what to say, and is willing to conceal Mr Pitt's contempt of the Secretary of State'. He added: '[Pitt] is really the Minister at least over that Office [i.e., the Home Office], which dare not it seems show any resentment'.[8] I have spent decades reading through the papers of the ministers of the first Pitt administration, and noted only one consideration that roused Sydney from his prevailing torpor: the prospect of obtaining preferment from the King for members of his family.

And poor Nepean, indeed! To him fell the major burden of directing the work of the Home Office and of composing its extensive memoranda. There are exceedingly few of these papers in Sydney's hand, in sharp contrast to the many written by Pitt, Dundas and Mulgrave, for example, in the records of other departments. If he had ever spoken candidly about it, I think Nepean too would probably have said that he held his political master in contempt.

Pitt eventually dropped these unhelpful ministers when political circumstances allowed, but the first did not go until mid-1788. In the early years of his administration, he was forced to adopt another strategy for overcoming their deficiencies. This was to let them direct the ceremonial and mundane business of their offices, but to instruct or bypass them in matters involving the national interest.

As First Lord of the Treasury and Chancellor of the Exchequer, Pitt watched over the nation's financial affairs. From the beginning of his tenure, he also supervised foreign affairs, especially those which involved Holland and France, frequently drafting despatches for the Foreign Secretary to sign and sometimes even having the Under-Secretary send them off without the minister's having seen them. He also oversaw much colonial business.

But if Pitt became 'essentially the government in all its departments',[9] he did not determine the reforms intended to strengthen Britain's position both at home and abroad alone. Rather, he sought the help of a small group of men outside the Cabinet who were masters of their business, and in whom he had confidence – Henry Dundas, W.W. Grenville, Constantine Phipps (Lord Mulgrave) and Charles Jenkinson (Lord Hawkesbury). He discussed matters privately with these men and he put them on the administrative bodies he set up to develop detailed policies. On particulars he sought the advice of the trusted and efficient department heads, whom he also used to implement policies – George Rose and Thomas Steele at the Treasury, Evan Nepean at the Home Office, William Fraser at the Foreign Office, Philip Stephens at the Admiralty, Sir Charles Middleton at the Navy Board.

Pitt's procedures meant that he and his close colleagues conducted much of their initial planning in conversation, of which there is often no detailed record. Let me give one example of how they dealt with business. At the beginning of 1786, East India Company authorities in Bengal sent Colonel Charles Cathcart off to Mauritius to negotiate with the French governor-general a settlement of some disputes arising from differing interpretations of the 1783 peace treaty. Having done so, Cathcart reached England in mid-August and gave the Secret Court of Directors details of the agreement he and the governor-general had reached. The directors sent Cathcart's information to the India Board and Pitt, Dundas and Mulgrave read the various papers formally on 26 August. They then gathered privately at Dundas's Wimbledon house to consider the convention clause by clause. 'Mr Pitt and Lord Mulgrave are here', Dundas told Hawkesbury on 16 September, and he advised William Eden twelve days later, 'I only drew the first sketch, but Mr Pitt and Lord Mulgrave lived with me on the subject for a week at Wimbledon'. On 16 September, Pitt gave Carmarthen the 'heads of a despatch' to send to Eden if he 'concurred', adding: 'I have sent to Fraser a letter to Eden to accompany this despatch if you send it.' Carmarthen duly forwarded these papers.[10]

The fact that so much was done in conversation can make it difficult for the historian. After Pitt's death, a would-be biographer asked Henry Dundas for relevant papers. Dundas replied:

I don't recollect amidst the many years in which we lived almost unremittingly together that I ever had a walk or a ride with [Mr Pitt] that a very considerable part of the time was not occupied in discussions of a public concern, and for the same reason it is that most of the useful knowledge I possess of his sentiments either as to men or measures does not exist in any written documents, but rests upon my memory and recollection, and must die with myself.[11]

*

Still, despite the inevitable gaps it is possible to reconstruct a good deal of these politicians' thinking.

As events and a later extended elaboration by Dundas make clear, from the mid-1780s Pitt and Dundas envisaged the development of a global trading network, the centrepiece of which would be a triangular exchange across the Pacific Ocean. One of the perennial problems facing the East India Company was that the Chinese would take little but silver for their goods. This meant that the Company's ships usually sailed from Europe with empty hulls. Silver bullion, moreover, was often very expensive to buy and at times impossible to obtain, as during the wars of 1776–83.

If British ships could carry manufactured goods to Spain's American colonies, these might be sold for silver, which might then be used to purchase Chinese teas, silks and porcelains for sale in Europe and Spanish America. At this time, there seemed also to be a demand in northern Asia for sea-otter pelts from the northwest Pacific coast; if merchants could sell these and other wares (woollen clothing, pots and pans) to Korea and Japan, they might again obtain bullion for trade with China and expand their economy at the same time. The British were also eager to extend their trade in cotton goods with China. To achieve these things, they needed to revise the terms of the East India Company's charter, which gave it a monopoly of all British trade between the Cape of Good Hope and Cape Horn, and to extinguish the South Sea Company's charter, which gave it the right to trade with Spain's American colonies. Then, they needed to negotiate trade agreements with China, France and Spain. As we shall shortly see, the Prime Minister began to set steadily all these things in train.

If they were to succeed in realizing this grand scheme, Pitt and his colleagues also needed to strengthen Britain's resources in the Indian and Pacific oceans and on the very long sea routes to and from them. They now turned their minds to this matter, and did so with five particular points in view.

The first was the crucial importance of the Cape of Good Hope to ships going to and coming from India – as the chairmen of the East India Company had pointed out in 1781:

> that the power possessing the Cape of Good Hope has the key to and from the East Indies, appears to us self-evident and unquestionable. Indeed we must consider the Cape of Good Hope as the Gibraltar of India … No fleet can possibly sail to or return from India without touching at some proper place for refreshment, and, in time of war, it must be equally necessary for protection … Not only the Company's possessions in India, but also the immense trade between Britain and that part of the world will be hazarded and in extreme danger, if the Dutch and French are permitted to hold possession of the Cape of Good Hope.[12]

Second, possession of Bombay was similarly important to operations in the seas about India – as Admiral Hughes pointed out at the conclusion of the war:

the safety of Bombay is of the utmost importance to the safety of the whole [British establishment in India], for at no other port or place in our possession could the ships of the squadron be even properly refitted, much less repaired. At Bombay, as the only place of refit, are deposited all the masts and other stores for the ships, and it not only furnishes a great number of expert native artificers, but its docks are of the utmost consequence. In short, without Bombay or some other as convenient harbour in our possession, no squadron of force could be kept up in this country.[13]

Third, there were intelligence reports that the French were pursuing a treaty of defensive alliance with the Dutch, and, following a scheme of Admiral Suffren, were forming a settlement at Acheen (Ache), on the northern tip of Sumatra. Suffren considered that possession of Acheen and Trincomalee together would give France 'the quiet dominion of Hindustan'. So did the members of the Pitt administration, with the Foreign Secretary observing that French possession of 'Trincomalee on the western and Acheen on the eastern side of the Bay of Bengal would indeed render the safety of the British interests in that part of the world to the most alarming degree precarious'.[14]

Fourth, if British ships were to ply between Asia and South and North America, they would need resources in the Pacific Ocean.

And fifth, the administration believed that India would be the principal theatre in any future war. As Henry Dundas put it in November 1784, 'our force now, and hereafter, must be regulated by the intelligence we have of the force kept up by our European rivals, at the Mauritius, Pondicherry, Ceylon or other places in India. Taking it for granted that India is the quarter to be first attacked, we must never lose sight of keeping such a force there, as will be sufficient to baffle all surprise'.[15]

*

At Christmas 1784, with the Cabinet about to decide on what to do with the convicts, Pitt asked the First Lord of the Admiralty's opinion of a series of proposals (probably nine) for strengthening Britain's position in and about the Indian Ocean. These included a scheme to build a new harbour near Calcutta, the taking possession of the Nicobar Islands, and Matra's (and perhaps Young's) proposals for the colonization of New South Wales. Howe replied that the idea of building the harbour was 'a wild scheme'; that the Nicobar Islands in the eastern Bay of Bengal were 'much the most eligible station for ships of war, were commercial purposes less in contemplation for fixing at Acheen', but that 'it would require a long time before magazines could be formed for keeping a squadron on that side of India, all the year'; and that the length of the voyage to New South Wales, 'subject to all the retardments of an India voyage', did not encourage him 'to hope for a return of the many advantages in commerce or war, which Mr M. Matra has in contemplation'.[16]

Howe's unenthusiastic responses by no means put an end to the Pitt administration's consideration of these options, however. Mulgrave, who had held a very unusual appointment during the war, serving as one of the Lords Commissioners of the Admiralty at the same time as commanding a ship of the Channel squadron, was very knowledgeable about maritime affairs. (He is said to have had the finest naval library in England.) His particular role on the India Board was to pursue naval strategy concerning India, and a series of moves from 1785 onwards were the direct results of his efforts.

On 9 April 1785, meeting in secret session, the India Board instructed the East India Company's Bengal presidency to survey the Nicobar Islands with a view to occupying them, noting that in the hands of an enemy 'their situation would give the greatest alarm to our possessions, and the most effectual check to our operations in a future war'.[17] The manuscript copy of the Beauchamp Committee's second report, with its recommendation for a settlement at Das Voltas Bay to 'promote the purposes of future commerce, or of future hostility in the South Seas', is dated in Pitt's hand 'June 1785', and in another hand '21 June 1785'.[18] On 27 June, the India Board told the Bombay presidency to survey and occupy Diego Garcia, in the western Indian Ocean, and to advise 'the best manner of settling it, [so as] to make it a place of refreshment for ships'.[19]

By the end of June 1785, then, the Pitt administration was moving decisively to secure the shipping routes from the Atlantic into the Indian and Pacific oceans.

*

In 1782, as war was drawing to a close, British governance structures had been revised. The Secretaryship of State for American Colonies was abolished, and the old Northern and Southern departments reorganized into the Foreign and Home offices, the latter becoming responsible for (among many other things, of course) convicts and colonies.

Partly because he was Home Secretary at the time, and partly because he signed the letter to the Treasury formally announcing the decision to use convicts in the colonization of Botany Bay, historians have been wont to see Lord Sydney as the prime mover in that decision. Manning Clark declared that 'one factor alone had convinced [Lord Sydney] of the need for a definite decision: the several jails and places for the confinement of felons were so crowded ...', and he was followed by a legion of historians repeating the same view.[20] However, it is a misguided legion, for this was another matter that a reforming Prime Minister took out of an incompetent Secretary of State's hands. Let me tell you how it really was.

It is evident that Sydney had some role in developing the Lemain scheme; just how significant this role was, however, is another matter. John Barnes told the Beauchamp Committee that 'I did propose to government some time ago a plan for transporting [the convicts] to Lemain in the Gambia, not a regularly formed plan, but from different conversations with Lord Sydney and at the Secretary of State's Office such a plan may have been formed'.[21] Sydney personally informed Edward Thompson of the plan. But there is also evidence to suggest that it was in fact Evan Nepean who put the proposal together from the advice offered by the slave traders. Be this as it may, Sydney was closely associated with it; and when opposition to it swelled, Pitt was left to defend what was indefensible on humanitarian grounds, to his own embarrassment in parliament. When the Beauchamp Committee roundly condemned the scheme, his embarrassment was increased.

Although we can now see only some points in the process, there is sufficient evidence for us to understand that, from this point, Pitt took over the business of finding a place to which to send the convicts. First, by December 1786, the mounting of the First Fleet had progressed as far as convicts being embarked. Thinking that he might be questioned about it when parliament resumed, Pitt became anxious to have a clear idea of the cost of the venture. He therefore had Evan Nepean find this out. Nepean wrote to Middleton at the Navy Board on 12 December, explaining that he was 'desired by Mr Pitt to request that he will order a statement to be made of the expenses which it is supposed will be incurred under the direction of the Navy Board for the providing of provisions, clothing, implements, etc for the convicts, and sending them out to Botany Bay, including the expenses incurred for the detachment of marines'. He added that he had also requested details from Philip Stephens at the Admiralty and Augustus Rogers at the Ordnance Board. All three sets of estimates reached Pitt by the end of December.[22] That is, instead of Lord Sydney, the minister responsible for convicts and colonies, acting to ascertain the costs of the coming Botany Bay venture, the Prime Minister, William Pitt, was the one who did so.

The second indication of Pitt's central role is rather tangential, but nonetheless offers additional insight. During the same period, Pitt was pursuing the plan to bring breadfruit plants from the Pacific Ocean to the West Indies. This was a complex business. The breadfruit would provide food to maintain a larger number of slaves, who would produce greater amounts of cotton for Britain's burgeoning manufacturing industry. With the cultivation and manufacture of these species of cotton favoured by the Chinese, more cloth might be sold to them, provided Britain could obtain freer access to the Chinese market.

The *Bounty* voyage, the first of the breadfruit missions, is beyond famous, and the second – which succeeded in transferring the breadfruit after the *Bounty* was lost – is quite widely known. What is much less well known is that in 1787, on behalf of the Board of Trade, Sir Joseph Banks sent Anton Hove to India to collect cotton seed, and that, also in 1787, acting as the India Board, Pitt, Dundas and Mulgrave sent

Colonel Cathcart to China to negotiate a new trade agreement – an initiative that came to nought when Cathcart died *en route*. Initially, the breadfruit scheme involved Botany Bay: after unloading, one of the First Fleet transports was to sail on to one or other of the Pacific islands. In line with this idea, Governor Phillip reminded the Home Office in March 1787 that his instructions should include the provisos that 'I send one of the ships to Charlotte Sound, in the island of New Zealand for the flax plant, and to the Friendly Islands for the breadfruit; and as women will be there procured, that I put an officer on board such transport'.[23] Banks later recorded that he was 'employed by Mr William Pitt to arrange for him a plan for bringing the breadfruit from the South Sea islands to our western dependencies', and that he gave the 'original plan' of the voyage to Pitt, together with 'the instructions intended for Governor Phillip which were to guide him in framing instructions for the master of the vessel originally intended to have been despatched from Botany Bay'.[24] But then, partly at Phillip's suggestion, Banks decided that the ship would be much better fitted out for the task in England. So, under the command of William Bligh, the *Bounty* sailed for the breadfruit separately, after the First Fleet had left. But in initially tying the breadfruit voyage to the Botany Bay venture, Banks was following Pitt's wishes.

Though tantalizingly brief, the third indication of Pitt's role is the most significant. As they waited for the results of the *Nautilus* survey, the Home Office prepared for the resumption of transportation. In May and June, Nepean obtained estimates of costs from merchants. When he asked the Treasury to scrutinize these, he stated: 'It seemed to me to be Mr Pitt's intention at all events that if Cape Voltas was not found to correspond with our expectations for the settlement of the convicts, that some other spot should be fixed upon to the southward of the Line, and as that is his determination ...'[25]

This statement by Nepean has never received due attention from historians of Australian colonization, yet it is illuminating for two reasons. The first is that it shows clearly that Pitt had taken the business away from Sydney. The second point is that in any event the site for the new convict settlement was to be *to the southward of the equator.* That is, it was to be the point of departure and resort for British merchant ships and warships plying between the Atlantic world and the greater one beyond. Far from being merely a dumping ground for convicts, the new colony was to play a crucial role in the expansion of British trade.

*

It is true that there is no written statement from the mid-1780s by Pitt or his colleagues overtly linking the various elements of their far-reaching plan. But the fact that they did not write the plan down does not mean they did not have it. Consider the analogy of a wagon wheel. The rim equates to those places in the far reaches of the world to which these planners turned their attention – the West Indies; the southwestern and southeastern coasts of Africa; the islands of the western Indian Ocean and the Bay of Bengal; China, Korea, Japan, Kamchatka; the northwest American coast; the western coasts of Spanish America; the islands of Polynesia; New South Wales and New Zealand. The spokes that were to link these distant places to the imperial hub were, variously, sea-going merchants interested in carrying goods between one place and another; control of sea routes; possession of islands, harbours and bases where ships might refresh; the transfer of breadfruit and other exotic foods from one hemisphere to another; cotton and flax; convicts; slaves; the industrialization of cloth manufacture; and negotiated access to new markets.

All these things we know because we have written evidence for them, since administrative procedures had to be followed in order to effect them. For example, the India Board couldn't send Colonel Cathcart to China to negotiate agreements without giving him formal instructions and arranging his travel. Pitt, Dundas, Mulgrave and Hawkesbury's plan to expand British commerce into northern Asia involved obtaining from the Chinese the use of a base further north than Canton. In instructing Cathcart for his mission, the India Board told him that he was to assure Chinese officials that Britain wanted only 'a place of security as a depot for our goods' – 'a small tract of ground, or detached island, in some more convenient situation than Canton'. If the merchants who would reside there enjoyed the 'protection of the Chinese government', the site would not need to be fortified. This modest request was possible because Britain's 'views are purely commercial, having not even a wish for territory'. If the Chinese should mention 'our present dominion in India', Cathcart was to point out that it had 'arisen almost without our seeking it'. If permission were granted for a new base, Cathcart was to 'endeavour to obtain free permission of ingress and regress for ships of all nations'.[26]

At this time, the phrase *ships of all nations* was shorthand for 'free' trade, having gained wide currency following the publication of Adam Smith's *The Wealth of Nations* in 1776. In analyzing Europe's trade with the East, for example, Smith commented:

During the greater part of the sixteenth century, the Portuguese endeavoured to manage the trade to the East Indies ... by claiming the sole right of sailing in the Indian seas, on account of the merit of having first found out the road to them ... But since the fall of the power of Portugal, no European nation has claimed the exclusive right of sailing in the Indian seas, of which the principal ports are now open to the ships of all European nations.[27]

It was Smith's strong view that if the mercantilist trading system, which gave exclusive rights to national trading companies, were replaced by one of 'free ports', then ships of all nations might enter them, to the infinite benefit of economic activity.[28] These ideas were very influential. In 1786, for example, the Board of Trade discussed the establishment of 'free ports' to which 'ships of all nations' might resort, and this duly happened in Jamaica, Dominica, New Providence and Grenada in 1787.[29]

*

It is not, then, that we lack documentation for the various spokes. What we lack, rather, is a description from its builders of the central hub from which the individual spokes extended, a hub constructed by, variously, strategic, commercial, diplomatic and philosophical considerations. We may, however, gain insights into the nature of this hub from actions taken and from the remarks of people who were closely involved in shaping it.

In the mid-1780s, the Pitt administration began the process of opening the areas of the charter companies' monopolies to independent traders. After reports that the Russians, who were already involved in the north Pacific fur trade, were commencing extensive whaling operations, the Board of Trade held hearings which resulted in Britain's Southern whalers receiving permission to go east of the Cape of Good Hope into the Indian Ocean south of 26°S latitude as far as 15°E longitude, and round Cape Horn into the Pacific Ocean no further than 500 leagues (c. 1500 miles or 2400 kilometres) west of the South American coast.[30]

In October 1786, reflecting on the Botany Bay scheme, in which he had had the greatest organizational hand, Nepean wrote:

> some of the timber is reported to be fit for naval purposes, particularly masts, which the fleet employed occasionally in the East Indies frequently stands in need of, and which it cannot be supplied with but from Europe. But above all, the cultivation of the flax plant seems to be the most considerable object.[31]

And in 1787, at Mulgrave's urging, the members of the India Board planned a comprehensive survey of shoals, islands and coastlines of the Indian Ocean. They did so because they considered that

> it is of the greatest importance to ascertain the most proper stations for the shelter, refitting, refreshment or protection of squadrons and ships-of-war, as well as convoys and East India ships during the different seasons under various circumstances in the East Indies, in case of a future war; as well as the places most worthy of attention either for offensive or defensive operations in the extensive possessions of this country in that part of the world.[32]

The political turmoil caused by the King's illness delayed the beginning of this survey for eighteen months, but when it was at last undertaken it produced much valuable information.

When he outlined his plans for a massive transfer of plants between the Eastern and Western hemispheres (including, but not limited to, the breadfruit), Sir Joseph Banks also left an insight into the central plan. Writing as he was overseeing preparations for the *Bounty* voyage, Banks stressed the potential for economic expansion in the East:

If we consider but for a moment that the greatest part of the merchandizes imported from India have hitherto been manufactured goods of a nature which interferes with our manufacturies at home; that our cotton manufacturies are increasing with a rapidity which renders it politic to give effectual encouragement and that a profit of 100 per cent is to be got with certainty upon the importation of the raw materials of cottons and probably on many things besides. How is it possible for us to encourage even sufficiently everything which tends to the cultivation of raw materials? In India labourers are abundant, their labour incredibly cheap. Raw materials of many sorts: dyeing drugs, medicines, spices, etc sure of a ready market and of producing a most beneficial influence upon the commerce of the mother country. Why then should not raw materials of every kind furnished by the inter-tropical climates except perhaps sugar be sent to us from the East Indies cheaper than they can be from the West where the immense price of labour performed by slaves purchased at extravagant rates more than compensates for the difference of distance and consequent enhancement of freight and charges in bringing the produce home.

If we look towards the Chinese market we shall see a still more flattering prospect. The immense population of that enormous empire ensures a consumption for very large quantities of all those things which necessity, fashion or prejudice have brought into vogue among them and the vegetable productions which their junks fetch from countries situated very near the confines of the

[East India] Company's territories we know by experience to be numerous.

That drugs the natural produce of this island [i.e., Britain] as chamomile, valerian, peppermint, penny royal, etc, though plentifully to be found in the fields and woods, are carried to market by those who cultivate them for that purpose cheaper and better than by those who collect them wild is well known; and the same will certainly be the case in India where labour and land are so much cheaper than in England. Why should not we then, if proper means are taken to discover and obtain the plants which produce the articles they want and if by means of the garden the cultivation of them is set on foot, why should we not, I say, be able to undersell the Chinese in these articles at their own markets and diminish at least if not annihilate the immense debit of silver which we are annually obliged to furnish from Europe?[33]

*

Events during the Nootka Sound alarm and in its aftermath show the interrelation of these things.

In 1789, the Spanish naval officer Estéban José Martínez seized a number of British trading vessels at Nootka Sound on Vancouver Island. When news of this action reached Britain early the next year, the India Board and the Home Office organized for one frigate to sail out from England to New South Wales, to be joined there by the *Sirius*, and for both to link up with a third warship sent from India. Mulgrave's input into this scheme was again central. However, when Lieutenant John Meares arrived home claiming that the Nootka had requested British protection and that he had taken formal possession of territory for Britain, the Pitt administration decided instead to bring Spain to heel by a massive show of force in European waters. As Pitt had continued the building programme begun towards the end of the wars of 1776–83, the Royal Navy was in very good condition; and when dozens of British warships exercised off its coasts, Spain capitulated.[34]

The convention that the two nations then negotiated opened the way for British traders to sail much more widely in the Pacific Ocean; and the Board of Trade set about giving them permission to do so. Calling them to hearings in January 1791, it examined the whalers at length about the possibility of extending their operations. One of the Board's questions was:

> Do you conceive that it would be for the interests of the merchants concerned in the Southern Whale fishery to send a ship across the Line into the Pacific Ocean, upon the joint venture of fishing etc, and to trade with the natives on the western coast of North America?

Another was:

> In case permission was granted you to carry on your trade and fishery in all the seas and on all the coasts of the west and east of South and North America ... would it operate as any detriment to the said trade or fishery, if the owners, masters, or others concerned therein, were bound by bond not to carry on any illicit trade, contrary to law or treaty?[35]

The whalers answered that they did indeed want permission to operate north of the equator in the Pacific Ocean, and that they also wished to go east of the Cape of Good Hope, south of 15°N latitude and as far as 'the eastern side of New South Wales, so as to include our settlements on that island'. They added that they 'would not request this extension of limits, if they did not know that whales were in great plenty within the limits they have requested, and that the French and American whalers will have that fishery to themselves, without [i.e., unless] the English whalers have the same privilege'.[36]

In fact, wishing to see more extensive trade, the politicians had a much greater range in view – as Grenville wrote to a colleague, 'Our general idea ... is to enable any persons to carry on that trade under certain licences, to which are to be annexed as conditions such regulations as are, *bona fide*, necessary to secure the East India Company's monopoly of the tea trade to these kingdoms, the only one of the objects under the charters I have mentioned that is of real importance'.[37] Further, what they wanted was for independent traders to be able to enter the Pacific either via the Cape of Good Hope or Cape Horn, and to touch at

> any part of the western coast of the continent of America, not occupied by Spain . . . or [at] any part of the Pacific Ocean, for the purpose of trade and fishery; and to sail from thence to any of the ports of China, or to any part of the coast of Asia north of China, or to any islands to the east of the longitude of Canton, for the purpose of selling there any articles the produce of such trade or fishery.[38]

The members of the Board of Trade persuaded the chairmen of the East India Company to agree to these changes, only to have the Company twice renege.

Instead, the Company proposed that the whalers should not trade in Asia north of Canton; that they should be able to off-load goods they obtained on or off the western coasts of the Americas only at Canton; that those proceeding east of the Cape of Good Hope would need to be licensed; and that they might operate in the Pacific Ocean south of the Tropic of Capricorn (23½°S latitude) and only to the east of 140°E longitude; and that only the Company should trade from Asia to the Americas.[39]

The politicians were furious. Hawkesbury asked, rhetorically, whether it was right that British subjects should be able to enjoy freedom of navigation and trade only with the permission of a private company. And he pointed out that the Company's proposal to restrict the private traders who wished to operate south of Canton to the waters bounded by 23½°S latitude and 140°E longitude would 'exclude these ships from the Philippine Islands and from the principal part even of New Holland ... [And it] will also exclude them from another part of New Holland, from New Guinea, as well as from the Moluccas, with respect to which the chairmen thought it was not our business to lay these ships under any restrictions.'[40]

In the end, the conflicting parties reached a compromise, whereby the whalers might operate in the south and north Pacific Ocean to the east of 135°E longitude and would not need licences if they sailed via Cape Horn. However, they were required to give any trade goods other than whale products they acquired to the East India Company at Canton, for transhipment to Europe.

*

Together, these comments and actions provide insights into the grand scheme Pitt, Dundas and their colleagues pursued from the mid-1780s, a scheme which involved securing a more reliable supply of naval materials for British ships in Indian waters; a base on the southwestern edge of the Pacific to facilitate war or trade; a trading base in northern China; the transfer of useful plants from one hemisphere to another; the manufacture in England of cotton goods for export to China; and increased freedom for independent traders, so that they might operate successfully in the East.

What does all this mean for Botany Bay and our understanding of its origins? In Pitt, Dundas and Mulgrave (and Middleton, Hawkesbury and Banks) we have a group of exceptionally far-sighted men. This is best illustrated by another spoke in the wheel of their scheme, one I've not yet mentioned. By the 1780s, it had become clear that the forests of Europe would not go on supplying naval timbers forever. As more ships were built, and as these grew ever larger, oaks – which supplied frame timber and planks for hulls – were cut in greater numbers. As it takes a good one hundred years and more for an oak tree to reach maturity, this rate of ship building was not sustainable. Pitt, Dundas, Mulgrave and Middleton began discussing the possibility of building warships from Indian teak in the mid-1780s,[41] and at the beginning of 1788 they drew up what we would call a 'White Paper' on the subject. 'Few of our naval stores except those of metal are produced in Great Britain', they pointed out:

We have our hemp, our masts, deals, plank and part of our iron from abroad at a very considerable expense, independent of freight. We have at present an interest in India. We want to make it useful to us in such a way that will not impoverish the country; and we are willing to spare as much as possible of our own oak timber for fifty or sixty years to come. Whatever helps therefore India can afford, whatever supplies we can prudently draw from it, we should readily accept, and freely use. Nor should any article be sent out from England for the equipment of India guardships, that can be procured on the spot, or in the adjoining settlements.[42]

The India Board pursued this scheme for over twenty years.[43]

How probable is it that such men, otherwise so capable in their thinking and so alert to Britain's commercial interests, were indifferent to the potential value of convict labour? It is inconceivable that economic considerations should not have influenced their approach to dealing with the convict problem. And having developed the Das Voltas Bay scheme in 1785, with its clear strategic and commercial rationales, is it likely that, upon learning that the site was not suitable, these planners lapsed into hopeless incompetence? Can they really have suffered 'a fit of absence of mind' and decided simply to dump the convicts as far away as possible?

In defending the administration's hard line with Spain over Nootka Sound, Dundas told the House of Commons that 'we were not contending for a few miles, but a large world', by which he meant networks of transoceanic trade linking Europe, the Americas and Asia.[44] The 'dumping of convicts' view fails as an explanation of the Botany Bay decision, for it does not comprehend the Pitt administration's intention that New South Wales should also play a role in this 'large world'.

Had he been present the day Dundas spoke in parliament, Arthur Phillip would have understood his remark that the Pitt administration had been 'contending ... for a large world'. In mid-1788, as the First Fleet transports were leaving New South Wales, he wrote a series of letters home. As he had then received no new despatches from England, what he said can only reflect understandings he had been given before sailing in May 1787. Phillip told Sydney how in January he had had the 'satisfaction' of finding Port Jackson to be 'the finest harbour in the world, in which a thousand sail-of-the-line may ride in the most perfect security'. After describing the initial problems the settlers had encountered, he told Shelburne (now the Marquess of Lansdowne), 'I think that perseverance will answer every purpose proposed by government, and that this country will hereafter be a most valuable acquisition to Great Britain, from its situation.' And he sent a chart of Sydney Harbour to Middleton, which he said 'will show that hereafter, when this colony is the seat of empire, there is room for ships of all nations'.[45] The *finest harbour in the world ... from its situation ... the seat of empire ... ships of all nations*: these were signifiers of a scheme comprehending very much more than the dumping of convicts.

7.

Voices Prophesizing War

AS THE *NAUTILUS* SAILED TO INVESTIGATE the suitability of Das Voltas Bay, on the southwest coast of Africa, as a site for a convict colony, the political situation in Europe turned sharply against Britain, as France prepared for another war. At stake were Britain's dominance of the seas, generally but particularly around India, and its commercial supremacy in the sub-continent. France had lost a great deal of valuable overseas territory to Britain in the Seven Years' War, and had not had victories decisive enough in that of 1778–83 to regain it. This rankled, and even as the French ministers negotiated an end to hostilities in 1782–83, at least some of them were already preparing for another contest that would restore the nation's pride, humble its enemy and increase its wealth.

In September 1783, when the ink on the peace treaty was scarcely dry, the Secret Committee of the East India Company forwarded to the Bengal Council copies of Marquis de Bussy's scheme for joining with Indian rulers to overthrow the British there, and of the French Crown's instructions for his 1781–83 expedition. In doing so, the Secret Committee warned that while the peace treaty might mean these plans were now in abeyance, they could easily be taken up again in the future.[1]

There is a superabundance of evidence that in the mid-1780s French ambitions and British anxieties centred on India. At the very beginning of 1784, Lord Carmarthen, the Foreign Secretary, told Anthony Storer, one of the officials at the embassy in Paris, that it was a matter of urgency to have details of 'the sailing of ships of force, under the usual disguise of being *armés en flûte* [i.e., with guns de-mounted and carried in the hold], for the East Indies, the French West India islands, the coast of Africa, but more particularly for the first of these destinations'. Storer was therefore 'to obtain any information, which by any means you can acquire of a nature to be depended upon, as to the ships of force which may have sailed from Brest, or any other ports of France, in the course of the last three months'. The Foreign Secretary added that 'this enquiry is of so much importance that any reasonable expense to obtain accurate and authentic accounts will be allowed'.[2]

In April, the British heard that the French King had given three warships *armés en flûte* to merchants trading to the East. This information prompted Pitt to emphasize to the Foreign Secretary the importance of knowing what naval forces the French and the Dutch intended to maintain in Indian waters.[3] Twelve months later, when the French had reconstituted their East India Company, such reports became more ominous. In June 1785 Daniel Hailes, another of the Paris embassy officials, passed on a spy's report that a 64-gun ship *armé en flûte* had sailed for Bourbon, carrying naval stores and 300 troops. The next month he advised that the French were planning to send out two more such ships. In August, he reported that 'the property of the ship-of-war the *Dauphin* is transferred by the King to the East India Company, under whose direction she is to make a voyage to China'. He warned: 'Should any of the 64-gun ships intended to be laid up, as it is said, be hereafter converted to the service of the Company, I shall be apt to think that that establishment is meant to mask designs much more hostile than commercial'. Four months later, he reported that the French navy was supplying all the Company's ships.[4]

The sailing of these old warships to the East was not the only ominous sign of French intentions. In mid-1784, British authorities received intelligence reports that the French intended to order Admiral de Suffren back to India. Carmarthen asked Hailes to investigate, remarking that 'sending an officer of his abilities and high rank in a time of peace would certainly give rise to suspicions of something more being meant'.[5]

Then, in July, the Duke of Dorset, the British ambassador at Paris, reported that France had successfully negotiated with Sweden to establish a naval depot at Gothenburg, which was to be stocked from the Baltic regions.[6]

Such reports would gain in significance if there were unusual activity in French dockyards. In September 1784, Hailes sent details of naval works at Cherbourg, which seemed designed to increase France's ability to command the English Channel. In October, Dorset wrote that three new two-deck ships had been launched at Toulon, and that others were under construction. Carmarthen then instructed Dorset to obtain 'the fullest and most accurate intelligence of the present state of the French marine, of the particular force now fit for, or preparations for service, both at Brest and Toulon, as well as what ships of war may have sailed from either of those ports since June last, and as far as possible the respective destinations of such ships'. Again, the Foreign Secretary said that 'no expense can be reckoned ill-bestowed which may be laid out in the procuring such useful information as this must be if really authentic'.[7]

By this time, however, the inner council of government had acted to obtain 'authentic' information in another way. On 14 October, Captain Arthur Phillip, who spoke French fluently, asked the Admiralty for a year's leave, so that he might go to Grenoble to settle some 'private affairs'. This reason was a blind to cover one of national significance. One month later, Evan Nepean recorded paying Phillip £150 'to enable him to undertake a journey to Toulon and other ports of France for the purpose of ascertaining the naval force, and stores in the arsenals'. Phillip reported to Nepean at intervals thereafter. In January 1785 he advised that the French were paying the 'greatest attention' to their navy. They were fitting fourteen line-of-battle ships at Toulon, and eleven frigates and storeships. They were recruiting additional shipwrights and importing naval timber from Albania.[8]

There was other evidence of France's intentions. In April 1784, Hailes reported that the French were investigating setting up 'a communication with India by the way of Alexandria, Suez and the Red Sea'.

Dorset also reported this in July. Twelve month later, he wrote that 'there is much reason to believe that the French Cabinet have serious designs of making an establishment in Egypt whenever a favourable conjunction shall offer itself'. In December 1785, Sir Robert Keith, the ambassador at Vienna, relayed Joseph II's information that 'France is firmly determined to strike a bold stroke by making herself mistress of all Egypt'. The Emperor asserted that he knew this 'with certainty from more quarters than one', adding: 'Monsieur Toff himself told me at Paris that he had travelled through all Egypt by order of his Court to explore that country in a military light, and to lay down a plan for the conquest of it'.[9]

The British knew only too well that possession of Egypt might be the means to a much greater end. As one commentator put it to the India Board:

> France in possession of Egypt would possess the master key to all the trading nations of the earth. Enlightened as the times are in the general arts of navigation and commerce, she might make it the emporium of the world. She might make it the awe of the Eastern world by the facility she would command of transporting her forces thither by surprise in any number and at any time – and England would hold her possessions in India at the mercy of France.[10]

Accordingly, the Board moved to set up its own courier service via Suez and the Red Sea.[11]

*

Such reports could not but give the British grave cause for alarm, for they confirmed the ministry's central assumption, namely that in the next war, France's principal aim would be to expel the British from India. As Dundas had told Sydney in November 1784:

> Our force now, and hereafter, must be regulated by the intelligence we have of the force kept up by our European rivals, at the Mauritius,

Pondicherry, Ceylon, or other places in India. Taking it for granted that India is the quarter to be first attacked, we must never lose sight of keeping such a force there as will be sufficient to baffle all surprise. In that shape, I believe, the attack will first be made.[12]

The next month, the British received the report that the French were pursuing Suffren's scheme for a settlement at Acheen, on the northern tip of Sumatra. As mentioned, the French admiral considered that possession of Acheen and Trincomalee together would allow France to control Eastern trade.[13] Carmarthen wrote urgently and confidentially to both Dorset and Hailes on 23 December, asking for details (which they were to forward by a specially hired 'packet', i.e., express boat) and observing that Acheen's situation made it 'of the utmost importance to British interests should it ever fall into the hands of France or Holland'.[14] Dorset replied five days later that all seemed tranquil. Hailes responded on 15 January 1785 that he had been unable to confirm this report.[15] Before the administration had this advice, however, Pitt had commenced that far-reaching review of Britain's strategic needs in the East described earlier.

*

Other circumstances, too, conspired to confirm these beliefs. The 1783 peace treaties had left for future negotiation the question of what naval establishments Britain, France and Holland would maintain in the Indian Ocean. In February 1784, Carmarthen asked Dorset to obtain from the Comte de Vergennes, the French Foreign Minister, 'the most explicit declaration ... of the number of ships they mean to keep in those parts'. With each side chiding the other for being dilatory, and with each suspecting the other of duplicity, discussions were protracted. The British repeated their request in July. At the beginning of October, Carmarthen again asked for information, saying that 'as the time is drawing near when the Navy estimate will be prepared, it will be necessary to know what force the French propose keeping up in India in order that we may be enabled to ascertain the number of ships to be employed by us in that quarter of the world'. One month later he suggested that it would be in both nations' interest not to maintain a line-of-battle ship in the East, to which – surprisingly, on the face of things – Vergennes readily agreed.[16]

There was a reason why the French Foreign Minister might be accommodating on this point. The issue was not simply what naval force the French intended to maintain in the Indian Ocean. As the Dutch had lately been the allies of the French, there was also the question of what Holland's force there would be. At first the British enquired about this via the embassy in Paris, but, having no satisfaction, at the beginning of 1785, the Foreign Secretary told Sir James Harris, the ambassador to The Hague, that details were needed 'in order that we may know what number of ships it may be necessary for the King's service either to leave, or to send out, in proportion to the marine establishment of France and Holland in that quarter of the globe'. Again, however, the Dutch were slow in providing details – a tardiness Harris attributed to the French influence over them, an influence that caused him to warn: 'Our wealth and power in India is their great and constant object of jealousy; and they never will miss an opportunity of attempting to wrest it out of our hands'.[17]

*

In Europe, the central diplomatic strategy pursued by the French was to persuade the Dutch to abandon the neutral stance they had maintained until the British had declared war on them in 1780, and to become professed allies. It took the French more than two years to conclude the treaty that achieved this.

This was mostly because, in the aftermath of the war, Dutch politics were even more confused than British politics. Resentful of the humiliating peace terms the British had insisted on, the merchant-based Patriot party, which controlled the States General (parliament), sought to gain ascendancy over the hereditary ruler (the Stadholder) and his aristocratic followers.

Backing intrigue with money, the French supported the Patriots and proposed that the nations reach a formal agreement. Hailes reported in June 1784 that the treaty was to be one of defensive alliance but not of commerce and that, 'though believed to be in great forwardness, none of the particular stipulations are known'. In July, Carmarthen advised Dorset that, 'so far as any progress has been made in the projected alliance between France and Holland, the most serious consequences to this country (in regard to our oriental possessions) are to be guarded against, the mutual guarantee of foreign possessions being plainly concerted with a view to future hostilities with us in that quarter of the world'. Soon afterwards, Carmarthen obtained a draft of the proposed treaty, and on 26 August Dorset reported that 'the French Cabinet now presses very much the conclusion of the Treaty of Alliance with the Dutch, according to the plan proposed'. The difficulty of Holland's being in conflict with Austria, France's partner in another treaty, over navigation rights in the Scheldt, then delayed the French concluding the negotiations.[18]

Deeply disturbed by the rising French influence in Holland, the British counter-moved. Having been given a large allocation of secret-service money, in August 1785 Harris sought 'to discover if it was possible, not only to separate the interests of the Dutch East India Company [the Vereenigde Oost-Indische Compagnie, or VOC] from those of France, but to unite them with those of Great Britain'. He assured representatives of the VOC, which was then in severe financial difficulties, that Britain had no plans for commercial expansion in the East Indies that would harm their activities. He underlined this point by tentatively suggesting that Britain might choose not to exercise its right, given in the peace treaty, to navigate freely through the eastern archipelago.[19]

In September Harris made a friendly contact with the Zealand directors of the VOC and soon after developed a close understanding with Mr Boers, its solicitor. The directors suggested that one way for Britain to increase its influence over their company would be to arrange for the English East India Company to make them a large loan, for which they would offer three ships loaded with tea as security. If the VOC's financial position did not soon improve, they said, they would be forced to accept the terms which the Patriots were making a condition of financial help. Harris and Carmarthen were in favour of the English company's providing the funds, but Pitt ruled against it, unless the Dutch could offer something more advantageous in return.[20]

Despite Harris's efforts, this diplomatic struggle in Holland went badly for Britain in the autumn of 1785. With advice from the French, the Austrians and the Dutch settled their dispute. This cleared the way for the French to advance the treaty negotiations, which they did vigorously. In early September Harris told Carmarthen he was attempting to fling 'delays and difficulties in the way of the French alliance'; but only a week later he had to report 'a manifest intention to make us feel the close intimacy which subsists between the Republic [Holland] and the Court of Versailles'. On 8 November he wrote that 'all appearances' indicated that the nations would 'inevitably and expeditiously' conclude a treaty and that he saw little hope of 'saving' Holland. The next day French and Dutch representatives signed preliminary articles, which the States General then accepted. The nations exchanged acts of ratification at Versailles on 21 December 1785.[21]

*

In September and October 1785, as negotiations for this treaty neared conclusion, one of the French emissaries, the Comte de Grimoard, urged upon both Vergennes and Castries, the French Minister of Marine, his idea that the nations should make a secret treaty to strengthen their position in Asia. This idea found immediate favour with Castries, who very much wished to see the British humbled. He considered that, by themselves, the French would always find it difficult to defeat their enemy, but that they might do so with the help of the Dutch, particularly if they were able to use the Dutch bases in Africa and the East.[22]

Castries saw that three steps would be necessary to achieve this aim. First, the VOC must hand over control of its colonies' naval and military affairs to an independent officer. Second, this general commanding officer must be French. And third, the Company must increase its forces in the East. He considered that if the two nations agreed either that each should maintain six warships and 6000 troops, or that Holland should contribute the twelve ships and France the 12,000 men at the eastern bases, they would have a force sufficient to overwhelm the British at Bombay, Madras and Calcutta.

It is here that we see France's cunning. By the treaty of peace, Britain and France had agreed to maintain only a token naval force in the Indian Ocean. However, as Holland had made no such commitment, it might station a strong squadron there. If it were to do so, Britain would be in a difficult situation. If Britain kept the agreement with France, and the French then took charge of the Dutch forces, it would be heavily outnumbered. But if it broke the agreement with France, the French would be justified in increasing their forces and the imbalance would remain. In February 1786, Carmarthen advised Dorset to tell the French that the French and Dutch squadrons in the East should together not exceed the strength that the British and French had agreed to. A week later, he instructed Harris to tell the Dutch the same thing. It was a futile hope. In April, Vergennes advised that it was impossible that the French and Dutch squadrons should be counted as one. The British had been outmanoeuvred.[23]

Even then, the British did not know how close the French were to pulling off this plan. The French did indeed ask the Dutch to make a French officer effectively the governor-general of their colonies in the East and the commander of their armed forces. The person they had in mind was the Marquis de Bouillé, but to their irritation a Dutch aristocrat thought that he was the man for the job.

The Rhinegrave de Salm was very keen to see the British brought low and driven out of India. His plan had many facets.[24] He proposed that Holland should conclude treaties for the mutual defence of eastern possessions with France and Spain, and perhaps also with Portugal. (As Portugal was Britain's longest – and sometimes only – ally in Europe, this last move would have isolated Britain even more and denied its ships the use of Rio de Janeiro in wartime.) Holland and France should increase their forces in the East, and he should assume command of the

VOC's. France should send a representative to India to confirm old treaties or negotiate new ones with rulers hostile to Britain. These should then make war on the British settlements, so as to destroy the East India Company's military power and ruin its trade. If France and Holland were to achieve all this, Salm thought, Britain would have the unenviable choice of giving up its claim to control Indian politics and commerce, or of losing its position anyway in an all-out war.

In the middle of the diplomatic struggle between Britain and France for control of Holland, a copy of a French memorandum fell off the back of a cart into British hands. In it, the central issues were stated with stark clarity. 'Our politics and our views', the author wrote, 'are and must be principally directed against our maritime rival [i.e., Britain]. [We] must prepare the way, at the first occasion for a rupture, for decisive blows on the coasts of India in concert with the United Provinces.'[25]

*

In the mid-1780s, then, in the aftermath of the war of 1776–83, those who governed both Britain and France believed that a new war was inevitable, and that this time it would centre on India.

In 1786, the British received ominous signs that hostilities were imminent. At the beginning of February, Sir James Harris warned from The Hague:

> The intentions of France in forming a connection with this country are too evident to admit of a doubt. The Patriots are in the plenitude of power and concur heartily with the Court of Versailles in all its operations and designs. If the direction of the East India Company falls into their hands (and I very much fear it will) you may be assured that all its force, wealth and resources (without any regard being paid to its commercial interests) will be employed against us in India the moment France chooses to give the signal.[26]

Then, in letters that reached the India Board in the spring, John Macpherson, temporarily governor of Bengal, warned of the arrival of a warship with 450 soldiers at Pondicherry, and of French interest in the Andaman Islands. Three months later, Hailes advised that he had now learned that 'a certain government' – either the French or the Dutch – had asked the Austrians to cede their outposts in the Bay of Bengal. Now that they had obtained effective control of Trincomalee, gaining control of additional settlements, particularly any in the Nicobar Islands, would enable the French to close the eastern Indian Ocean to British shipping. As Hailes observed, 'the situation of the Nicobar Islands, commanding the entrance into the Straits of Malacca, and if joined with Trincomalee, [is] likely to render truly formidable the French and Dutch power in the Bay of Bengal'.[27] The Foreign Office sent this information to Pitt and the Admiralty and India boards.

Then, in mid-June, the Board received Macpherson's reports of incidents in Bengal that boded very ill. On the face of things, the problems had arisen from differing interpretations of the relevant article of the peace treaty, by which Britain had agreed to give France back the trading posts and territories it had possessed prior to 1749, and that France should enjoy 'certain, free and independent commerce' on the eastern and western coasts of India and in Bengal.[28] But this was a vague and faulty stipulation. Before 1783, the British had had a monopoly of the saltpetre and opium trades in Bengal. Europeans pursuing other commerce had had to submit to British control, to pay customs duties and to permit their cargoes to be inspected. Now, the French claimed that the treaty clause meant that they were no longer subject to these restrictions, and also that their ships might sail up the Ganges River unhindered.

Asserting these supposed rights, in November 1785 the French agent in India sent a cargo vessel into the Ganges for the upriver outpost at Chandernagore. When the captain attempted to pass the British fort at Budge Budge without stopping, the fort's commander, who had reports that the ship was carrying a cargo of saltpetre, fired cannon balls across its bow. The master stopped and allowed the British to search the ship, and they did not in fact find the suspected cargo. Two weeks later, the captain of the French frigate *Espérance*, which was leaky and in urgent need of repair, also attempted to pass the fort without stopping. Again,

British cannonfire brought it to a halt. The delay proved too much for the decrepit ship, which sank.

The Bengal Council of the East India Company reported these events in a series of letters that reached the India Board in mid-June 1786.[29] In doing so, the Council members stressed how weak Britain's naval position in the East was. 'The French have ships at Mauritius', they pointed out; 'they have cruisers in the Gulf of Persia, and they sometimes have frigates on the Coromandel coast. The Dutch too have a fleet in India, while the English are without any, or at least will be so on the expected departure of the ships now commanded by Captain Hughes.' In the absence of a British squadron, they asserted, two enemy warships would be sufficient to stop them supplying Madras and Bombay; and since these centres were dependent on Calcutta 'for the means of carrying on war, we shall be involved in the most serious dilemma if at the commencement of hostilities there shall not be a British marine force in India equal to that of our enemies'. They then reiterated the point that had greatly concerned the British ministers for the previous two years:

> By the Indian Seas we should certainly understand the seas east of the Cape of Good Hope, and every precaution should be taken that no large French ships *armés en flûte* should visit these seas, for they may soon be fitted out at Mauritius as ships-of-the-line, and unless the engagements between France and Holland are fully known to our ministers, and provided against, the squadron of the States General may on any sudden rupture between us and the Dutch or between us and the French, act against us.[30]

To the authorities at home, as well as to those in India, the provocative gestures in the Ganges seemed intended to create a pretext for war. And no sooner had they learned of them, the British had even more unwelcome news. On 1 August 1786, Sir James Harris wrote that he understood that the French ambassador to Holland had received 'some very important instructions, relative to the future plans of the French in the Dutch East Indies', and that there would soon be a major development.

Harris said he gathered that the French intended to send troops to the Dutch bases in the East. Three days later, he reported again:

> The Court of Versailles is to represent, ministerially, to the Republic the defenceless state of the Dutch settlement in India; and to insinuate that if Their High Mightinesses expect France to fulfil the article of the late treaty by which she guarantees to them their possessions in that part of the globe, it is absolutely necessary to put their military establishment there upon a more respectable footing – that is to say (according to a plan given in some time ago), to raise it to 14,000 European troops.
>
> The States [General], on receiving the representation, are to send it to the East India directors. These are to repeat what they have already said, 'that the exhausted state of their finances puts it out of their power to increase their expenses, and that they cannot supply a fund for more than 9,000 men'.
>
> To this the States [General] (supposing the power of the pensionaries equal to the work) are to reply, 'that they will furnish the money'; and France is to lend the 5,000 men deficient in the complement, which are to be carried out by the Rhinegrave de Salm, who is to take upon himself the supreme command of all the Dutch forces in Asia.

Both these reports reached the Foreign Office on 7 August and were passed on to Pitt. In a letter of 8 August, which arrived four days later, Harris said that 'the crisis which ... is to determine the political existence of this Republic is drawing nearer and nearer every hour'.[31]

Then, Colonel Cathcart reached London from Mauritius on 15 August. He brought the convention he had negotiated with the French governor-general and other relevant papers, which he gave to the Secret Committee of the Court of Directors, which passed them to the Secret India Board, whence they went to the Foreign Secretary and then to the King. Cathcart also brought information about France's naval capacity in the East, which he gave to Sydney. Sydney sent an account of their interview to the King at 3.25 p.m. on 16 August, and George III replied three hours later that 'France certainly under the name of *flûtes* can soon collect a considerable naval force in the East Indies'.[32]

*

British authorities were thus confronted with a complex jigsaw of international politics in the aftermath of the wars of 1776–83, and there were two more important pieces to be dealt with. The first was that in mid-1785, the French mounted an ambitious expedition to complete whatever exploration Cook had left unfinished in the Pacific Ocean. This expedition was, as Cook's were, a monument to Enlightenment science; but, inevitably, it also had political and strategic implications, with the French Court instructing the commander, the Comte de Lapérouse, to report on the commercial potential of the lands in and about the great ocean, and on the purpose of any settlement the British might have formed in its southern half.[33]

The French government spared no expense to equip Lapérouse's expedition for its scientific work, but Britain's diplomats and spies in France reported that the voyage had a secret purpose. Dorset wrote in early May 1785 that he had heard on some authority that Lapérouse had

> orders to visit New Zealand with a view to examine into the quality of the timber of that country, which is supposed by the account given of it in Captain Cook's *Voyage* may be an object worthy of attention. This plan is recommended by Monsieur de Suffren, who says that ships may with little difficulty go from the Mauritius to that country. It is believed that the French have a design of establishing some kind of settlement there if it shall be found practicable.

A month later, he reported further that 'sixty criminals from the prison of Bicêtre were last Monday conveyed under a strong guard and with great secrecy to Brest, where they are to be embarked on board Monsieur de Lapérouse's ships, and it is imagined they are to be left to take possession of that lately discovered country'. Lord Dalrymple also sent this intelligence, advising that the convicts were to be landed in New Zealand, a move that left 'little room to doubt of their being a design to make a settlement in that country'.[34] Comprising two ships, the expedition sailed in August 1785.

Consider, then, the situation that British planners thought they faced in August 1786. Including that at the Cape of Good Hope, the French would have at least five bases adjacent to the shipping routes to the western and eastern Indian Ocean, bases which would be stocked with naval materials from New Zealand; and they had a significant number of warships and former warships which might rapidly be converted back to their original purpose at Mauritius. This network of bases and these ships would allow them to dominate at sea and therefore also on land, as foreign troops and munitions reached the coasts of India only by sea. It was a grim prospect indeed; and once established in New Zealand, the French might also dominate the eastern route into the Pacific Ocean.

*

The other remaining piece of the jigsaw concerned Britain's troubled relationship with Russia.

In mid-1785, in an effort to contain the French, who were then consolidating their alliance with the Dutch, the Pitt administration pursued a surprising, and risky, course. Believing that 'France ever must be considered as our natural and inveterate rival at best, if not our declared and open enemy', the Foreign Secretary instructed Alleyne Fitz-Herbert, the minister at the Russian Court, very discretely to sound out the Empress Catherine about forming a triple alliance with Austria, as a means of preventing France from increasing its influence further in Europe.[35]

Nothing seems to have come of this approach and by the end of the year the Pitt administration had in turn become anxious about certain Russian activities. On 20 December, Carmarthen asked the ambassadors to European countries (except France) to ascertain:

1. Whether the Court of Russia has taken, or is taking, any measures for the encouragement of a Southern whale fishery, and particularly whether the Empress has granted any, and what bounties for that purpose.

2. Whether any ships have sailed, or are intended to sail, from any of the ports of Russia, for the purpose before-mentioned, and what success such ships as have already sailed, on this fishery, may have had.

3. Whether the Court of Russia is giving any encouragement to the consumption of whale, or other animal oil, with the Russian dominions.

4. Whether that Court is negotiating with the United States of America for the admission of whale or other animal oil, produced by the fisheries carried on by the people belonging to the said States into the dominions of Russia.

The unstated background to these queries was that Britain and Russia needed to negotiate a new commercial treaty, as that concluded in 1766 was due to expire in June 1786. Russian expansion into the southern oceans and a trading alliance with the United States would increase the existing pressure on Britain arising from a large trade imbalance in favour of Russia, one caused particularly by Britain's heavy dependence on Russian hemp.

In 1968, downplaying the significance of the naval stores motive in the Botany Bay decision, Geoffrey Bolton asserted that 'diplomatically ... 1786 was by no stretch of the imagination a crisis year in Anglo–Russian relations', and that 'it is very doubtful whether the trade in flax and hemp was affected by the commercial treaty'.[36] In fact, the very opposite was true. Towards the end of 1785, Fitz-Herbert presented the Russian Vice-Chancellor with a draft treaty very largely based on the previous one. The Russian Court was slow in responding. Fitz-Herbert wrote of a 'species of lethagy', but subsequent events strongly suggest that the delay was deliberate. In January 1786, Fitz-Herbert conveyed in 'civil, but pointed language' Britain's unease at the delay.[37]

When it came, Russia's response concerned the British greatly. Many of the articles taken over from the earlier treaty were now worded in a 'new and exceptionable … manner'; and some of the newer ones were very objectionable. One of these was that the bulk of the trade should be conducted only in Russian ships. Another was that the tariff differential should be widened – i.e., that Russian merchants should pay lower duties than previously, and British merchants higher ones. A third was that Britain should not insist on searching Russian ships in time of war (and the criteria for determining what was a Russian ship and a Russian sailor were also widened). As Carmarthen observed, some of the new articles were 'contrary to the rules of maritime law, stipulated in former treaties, and others directly contrary to the laws of this country'. In particular, the British thought that that concerning Russian ships and sailors was likely to be 'productive of the most dangerous and fatal consequences in time of war'.[38]

Negotiations became protracted. In the hiatus, the Russian Court agreed to extend the provisions of the previous treaty for six more months; but the business gave the Pitt administration much trouble. Various officials produced very detailed analyses of the Russian proposals, with the Board of Trade repeatedly asking Fitz-Herbert for further information.

As the business dragged on, the Russians gave the British a demonstration of just how vulnerable Britain's dependence on Russian hemp made it. As spring burgeoned in Europe, and evidently with the encouragement of the Empress, Russian hemp merchants formed a cartel to withhold supplies from British buyers, so as to drive up the price – very much in the same way as the Middle Eastern oil-producing countries did in the mid-1970s. They also had merchants buy up supplies on the London markets. As it happened, the Navy Board was holding sufficient quantities of hemp to meet its immediate needs, but private shipping merchants and hemp manufacturers were very badly affected, with the price per ton rising from £23 to £32. The owners of thirty-four ships who had contracted to bring hemp from St Petersburg at the old price were facing heavy losses, and hemp manufacturers had no materials to continue their business.[39]

By August, the situation had become acute. Perhaps on the very day that the Cabinet ministers decided to colonize New South Wales, one of the London newspapers published a long account of the situation by an observer recently returned from Europe:

Upon coming to town on Friday last, and paying a visit to a rope-maker in Sun Tavern Fields, I found him very busy discharging his workmen, who all appearing in the utmost distress, I naturally enquired the cause, and received the following very melancholy answer.

That a monopoly in the article of hemp took place in April last; and that the engrossers had advanced the price six or seven shillings per hundredweight. Their agents abroad had purchased considerable quantities, and had influenced the sellers to demand very high prices for the rest. These agents had again disposed of great part to foreigners, purposely to reduce the quantity that might otherwise have been sent to this market, so that the regular trader, not supposing it were possible men in credit would form engagements so contrary to the general rule of trade, ... had not taken measures to counteract any such proceedings, the transactions abroad, if not amenable to the laws of this country, are to those of Russia. The buying Russian products, and selling them again in the country, is confiscation of the whole property. Thus by art and injustice, both here and abroad, our poor labouring subjects are deprived of the means of supporting themselves and families; for it is an incontrovertible fact that the manufacturer cannot purchase under a monopoly more hemp than he has fixed the price for when manufactured. The consumption is hereby greatly reduced; and many hundred labouring men, during the course of the ensuing winter, will be left without employment.[40]

The Pitt administration made the consideration of Russia's proposed terms of the new treaty the first item when the reconstituted Board of Trade commenced hearings on 24 August. The Board interviewed

Edward Forster and Godfrey Thornton, two members of the Company of Merchants trading to Russia, who said that 'of hemp, little comes from any other country. Of flax, a small quantity comes from the Prussian dominions, the rest from Russia'; and that the other maritime powers were mostly supplied from Russia too. When asked what would be the effect if Britain had to purchase supplies of Russian hemp in another country, the pair replied that it 'probably would not receive so good a price, or be so well paid'; and they also pointed out that, whereas British merchants gave extended credit for the goods they exported to Russia, Russian merchants were paid in cash for the goods they sent to Britain.[41]

One of the changes the Empress was proposing was a reduction in customs duty levied on goods sent to Britain in Russian ships, and the merchants confirmed the Board's suspicion that this would sharply lessen the number of British ships involved in the trade, and therefore the trade itself. Accordingly, the Board of Trade asked the Customs and Admiralty boards for details of 'all iron, hemp, flax, flax in yarn, pitch, tar, turpentine, tallow, timber, masts, yards and bowsprits, sail cloth and cordage imported into this kingdom from the year 1763'. The Navy Board responded with details of prices the next March.[42]

It was in the context of this wide-ranging consideration that Pitt asked Sir Charles Middleton for advice about the naval stores situation. Middleton replied on 29 August that

> the consumption of hemp in the year 1779 on the part of the Navy was about 9000 tons, but when at the highest in 1781 – 12,000 [tons], including about 2,000 tons of Riga. But I am of opinion 10,000 tons will be a sufficient quantity under a proper management of the fleet in any future war.
>
> The annual consumption at present is about 3,000 tons, and the quantity in store about 2,800, exclusive of 4,600 contracted for and to be delivered in this and early in the next year. Great Britain consumes very near 2/3 of what grows at St Petersburg.
>
> It does not occur to me that any inconvenience can attend a neutrality but in the article of naval stores. In that article neither

France nor Spain can be supplied in time of war but by the consent or inactivity of Great Britain. And if permitted by neutral vessels, it will exceedingly strengthen the operation of their fleets against this country. It is incredible how much they suffered in the two former wars from our command of the Baltic trade.

Middleton wrote further a week later that 'it is for hemp only that we are dependent on Russia. Masts can be procured from Nova Scotia and iron in plenty from the ores of this country. But as it is impracticable to carry on a naval war without hemp, it is materially necessary to promote the growth of it in this country and Ireland'.[43]

On 21 September, James Mitchell, another merchant, told Hawkesbury the Russians had achieved their monopoly by controlling supplies at home and buying up those available in London. He suggested that a short-term solution to the problem of idle ropeyards would be for the Navy Board to release some of its reserve, but added:

As to future means, I leave to your Lordship's wisdom and commercial knowledge. To me the prospect is dark, and the evil without remedy, whilst St Petersburg shall remain the almost only market of that necessary commodity for the completion of a maritime equipment. We must depend on Russia, unless we cultivate our own plains, or promote the growth of hemp in some other quarter of the globe, to rival that emporium of commerce in naval stores.[44]

The crisis subsequently faded, when an overabundant harvest forced Russian merchants to open the market again and the two nations at last concluded a new agreement. But the whole business had provided a powerful insight into the importance of Russian hemp to Britain's maritime endeavour, and how vulnerable it was because of this dependence.

*

In mid-August 1786, then, to Pitt, his Cabinet ministers and his principal advisers, war with France over India seemed both inevitable and imminent. What's more, they now understood that Britain's bitter rivalry with France extended into the Pacific Ocean. Russia, too, had turned antagonistic. It was at this time that the Pitt administration decided to establish a colony at Botany Bay. It is simply fantastical to suppose that there was no connection between these politicans' perceptions of the international situation and this decision.

And, indeed, there is quite explicit documentary evidence that they were connected. First, the proposals for the colonization of New South Wales were considered in the strategic review of Britain's situation in the East that Pitt undertook at Christmas 1784.[45] Second, when the administration sought the East India Company's agreement to the venture (which it was required to do by the Company's charter), it pointed out, ominously, that this move would 'be a means of preventing the emigration of our European neighbours to that quarter, which might be attended with infinite prejudice to the Company's affairs'.[46] And third, when the First Fleet was preparing to depart, Arthur Phillip was instructed to occupy Norfolk Island so as to 'secure the same to us, and prevent its being occupied by the subjects of any other European power'.[47]

The historians who have proffered the traditional explanation for the Botany Bay decision have ignored this clear evidence, and have thereby mistakenly represented it as quite unconnected to events in the world at large. Just as did Pitt and Dundas's scheme for trans-Pacific trade, the political and commercial situation in Europe and the strategic situation in the eastern seas bore directly on the decision.

A convict colony in New South Wales would certainly solve an irritating domestic problem. Much more importantly, however, it would increase Britain's ability to combat France, Holland and Spain in the Indian and Pacific oceans; and it would assist British traders in the coming competition with the Americans and Russians for the resources of these distant regions of the world.

8.

An Overseas Convict Colony:
Investment and Return

As Gary Sturgess has acutely pointed out, the binary concepts of investment and return on investment are central to any real understanding of the reasons for the establishment of an overseas convict colony.[1]

If undertaken as a state venture, building such a colony from scratch would cause the government much time, trouble and expense. Not only would there be the cost of transporting the convicts themselves, there would also be those of carrying out and paying the officials and guards; of building materials and agricultural equipment; of medicines; of food (even if some native supplies might be found); and of domestic animals. The further away from Britain the colony was, the higher these costs would be. Moreover, they would remain high until the colony achieved self-sufficiency or at least approached it. And in the first years, before agriculture, trade or other activities had developed, there would be no return cargoes.

In the eighteenth century, as now, governments usually did not spend large amounts of money on ventures that would need years of support unless they thought the nation would receive benefits in return. It is significant that all the proposals made for government-sponsored overseas convict colonies in the 1770s and 1780s involved the notion of return on investment. This was present, for example, in William Eden's

1771 suggestion that 'the more enormous offenders ... might be compelled to dangerous expeditions; or be sent to establish new colonies, factories, and settlements on the coasts of Africa, and on small islands for the benefit of navigation'.[2] And it was present in the proposals – no matter how fantastical they now seem – for convict colonies in the Gambia or elsewhere in West Africa, which were represented as likely to lead to much more extensive trade, which in turn would generate greater revenue for the state.[3] It was present, too, in the proposals for a convict colony on the southeast coast of Africa. As Pitt himself observed in asking Grenville's opinion, such a settlement would 'answer in some respects the purposes of the Cape, and ... serve also as a receptacle for convicts'.[4]

This notion was also prominent in the decision for Das Voltas Bay. Edward Thompson told Pitt and Sydney that 'the superior advantage the Dutch, Portugueze and French have reaped over us in their Indian navigation and commerce, has arisen from their having more convenient ports of refreshment in their passages'; and that 'the bay and river of Das Voltas, ... or the port, would ... be an excellent reception for our *Indiamen* on their return'.[5] In recommending Das Voltas Bay as a site for a convict colony, the members of the Beauchamp Committee cautioned that they did

> so far only as the commercial and political benefits of a settlement on the southwest coast of Africa may be deemed of sufficient consequence to warrant the expense inseparable from such an undertaking, at the same time that it restores energy to the execution of the law, and contributes to the interior police of this kingdom.[6]

*

So, on the one hand, the establishment of an overseas convict colony needed to deal with the crime problem in Britain, and, on the other, to produce commercial and 'political' – i.e., strategic – benefits. What, then, were the returns that the Pitt administration might reasonably have expected from a convict colony at Botany Bay?

First, there was the solution it offered to the convict problem. As Evan Nepean put it, from 'the fertility and the salubrity of the climate, connected with the remoteness of its situation (from whence it is hardly possible for persons to return without permission)', it seemed a country 'peculiarly adapted to answer the views of government, with respect to the providing a remedy for the evils likely to result by the late alarming and numerous increase of felons in this country, and more particularly in the metropolis'.[7] And if properly planned, such a colony would be able to absorb new drafts of convicts year after year, with the costs of sending them out diminishing as it became established.

These benefits are the only ones traditionalist historians have offered to explain the Botany Bay decision. However, they pertain only to the domestic side of the investment/return equation. What of possible external – that is, commercial and strategic – returns on the investment? As the evidence I present in the following chapters makes clear, the Pitt administration envisaged benefits in the areas of naval materials, access to the Pacific Ocean, and desirable products.

The most immediately realizable of these external benefits would be a maritime one: a convict colony in New South Wales would help to improve Britain's naval stores situation. In order to establish this point, it is necessary that I examine this situation in detail. In the second half of the eighteenth century, the Royal Navy experienced repeated shortages of masts and spars, cables, cordage and canvas. Just as I have counted the numbers of convicts on the hulks, so too have I counted the numbers of masts and spars and amounts of timber and hemp in the Royal Navy's dockyards in the 1780s. They tell an interesting story.

The merchant and military ships of the European maritime powers grew progressively larger in the course of the eighteenth century. The increase was not only in number, but also in size. Ships built after 1755 were typically 40 per cent larger than those built in the first half of the century. Britain's merchant marine, for example, increased in capacity from some 473,000 tons in 1755 to 588,000 tons in 1774 to 752,000 tons in 1786. Although the records are very imperfect, roughly the same degree of increase seems to have occurred in the merchant marines of

France and Spain. Between 1775 and 1790 the volume of shipping above 500 tons displacement in the Royal Navy rose from 327,300 tons to 458,900 tons. In the French navy this volume rose from 190,000 tons to 314,300 tons. Altogether, in this period European warship tonnage increased by approximately 46 per cent.

The consequence of this expansion was an ever-increasing demand for timber and fibre. After all, in an age before iron hulls and steam power, a large, ocean-going ship could not be built without frame, hull and deck timbers, nor sailed without masts and spars, cables, cordage and canvas. Blainey was perfectly right: in the eighteenth century, these materials were as important to military and commercial powers as steel and oil are today.[8] And the demand for them inevitably increased sharply in wartime, thus exacerbating the underlying problems of supply.

This was the general situation. Let me now give details only for the 1770s and 1780s.

Responding at the end of 1781 to criticism of his performance as First Lord of the Admiralty, Lord Sandwich commented that when he had taken office in 1771, he 'came to the management of a fleet that had been exceedingly neglected for some years past, [and] was greatly out of repair; that there was scarcely any timber in any of the dockyards, and a total despondency at the Navy Office as to means of procuring it, it being generally understood that the timber of England was exhausted'.[9]

There was no doubt some embellishment here for political purposes, but there was also a good deal of truth. Many of the ships of the great fleet assembled during the Seven Years' War were in disrepair by its end, and they had not thereafter been properly maintained. As Sandwich's ally Admiral Palliser pointed out, 'the bad condition of those ships ... is best shown by the small number of them that remained at the beginning of 1778'.[10]

It was not that Sandwich had done nothing to rectify the situation; in fact, he had done a considerable amount. He had broken a cartel of timber merchants, thus freeing up supplies, which he had had the Navy Board purchase. In 1771, the Admiralty and Navy boards and parliament had adopted a policy of maintaining approximately three years' supply of naval timbers in the dockyards – that is, 66,000 loads, where a 'load' was approximately one ton, the usual product of a substantial oak tree.

For a time, authorities were able to meet this goal. At the end of 1778, there were some 72,000 loads in the dockyards. But thereafter, due to wartime demands and the building programme that continued through the 1780s, there was a sharp decline in the amount of timber held. In 1784, there were 29,157 loads of English timber and 274 loads of foreign timber in store; in 1785, 21,186 loads of English and 216 of foreign; in 1786, 15,880 loads of English and none of foreign.[11]

In the early 1770s, British authorities also sought to build up reserves of masts, spars and bowsprits. But the pine and fir forests of the Baltic countries had been harvested for centuries for the benefit of the maritime powers of Western Europe, and increasingly they were unable to offer 'sticks' (as masts and spars were then commonly called) of large dimensions. Between 1764 and 1770, the British obtained 'great masts' (of 38 down to 30 inches diameter) for the largest warships from New England, but the American war disrupted this supply. By November 1777, the Deptford yard had no sticks larger than 30 inches. In the course of the war, the number of smaller masts and bowsprits held in the dockyards also declined very sharply. Moreover, those that did arrive were often defective, with knots, other faults and excessive sap.

In this emergency, the Navy Board turned to 'making masts' – that is, shaping smaller sticks and binding them with iron or rope about a central spindle. Depending on its size, a 'made' mast might require six to eight small sticks. In the wars of 1776–83, the Navy Board was forced to make masts not only for line-of-battle ships, but also for vessels as small as 20-gun frigates and sloops. In the period 1780–83, the Deptford yard made eighty masts and bowsprits.[12] This method was labour-intensive and time-consuming and, being less flexible and less reliable, made masts were much less satisfactory than single-stick ones. Sir John Jervis voiced the heartfelt plea of the service in 1783 when, as one justification for peace, he cited 'the want of sticks of a proper size for masts, which occasions most tedious process in making them'.[13]

The situation was similar when it came to hemp products, which European producers – particularly Russia – supplied to Britain's enemies as well. Early in 1782, James Durno, the consul at Memel, sent home a plan for 'engrossing for His Majesty's navy, masts and hemp, the produce of those parts, which are at present supplied to France and Spain'. 'Nothing less than purchasing all the naval stores that are brought into the Baltic' could prevent the evil, he thought. The Foreign Office passed this suggestion on to the Admiralty, which consulted the Navy Board, whose members considered that it would be both very expensive and also impractical, given the problems of storage. As Sir Charles Middleton later remembered, about this time 'the idea prevailed in the Cabinet of purchasing all the hemp that could be procured at St Petersburg and Riga, but finding it impracticable, it was given up'.[14]

In the wars of 1776–83, the consequences of the shortages of naval materials were even more apparent on tropical colonial stations, which were also beset by the problems of distance from the major sources of supply; the destructive forces of cyclones and shoals; seaweeds and barnacles, which weighted down hulls, and marine borers, which ate into them; and warm air and water, which hastened the deterioration of masts, cables, rigging and sails.

The situation in India is indicative. After sailing from England to take command of the India squadron in March 1779, Sir Edward Hughes wrote home in April 1780, 'should the storeship not be arrived we must be very much distressed by the want of canvas, running rigging, cables, sticks for topmasts and spars of all sorts, as there is not one to be got in Bengal, or on either of the coasts [i.e., Coromandel and Malabar]'.[15] The *York* did arrive with its precious cargo three months later. The next year, after he had taken his ships round to Bombay for repairs, Hughes wrote that without the storeship 'it would have been impossible to have refitted the squadron for sea, as there was not anywhere in India, so much as a spar fit to make a jib boom for a 64-gun ship, nor any timber to be had of a size to make an anchor stock for a line-of-battle ship'. He pointed out that he now needed another cargo of stores, and complained that sails 'never arrive in condition for service, always rotten, and not answering the proper dimensions'.[16]

Throughout 1782, Hughes contended with his French counterpart Suffren for naval supremacy in Indian seas. In January, having reached the Bay of Bengal first, he was able to capture Trincomalee, thus giving his ships a secure anchorage, though the area otherwise offered very few resources.

As described in Chapter 6, the French and British engaged four times this year in the Bay of Bengal.[17] These were fierce contests, and Hughes reported after the clash on 6 July that, with their masts, spars, rigging and sails shattered, the majority of his ships were 'greatly disabled and in general ungovernable'.[18] He retired to Negapatam roadstead, but finding few resources there sailed on to Madras, with spars 'only secured sufficient to prevent them falling in the short passage'. At Madras he also found replacement naval stores just about non-existent. He wrote, 'our distress for anchors, cables, cordage and spars of all sizes is still very great, no naval stores having been imported at this place since the arrival of the *York* storeship in July 1780'; and warned that the squadron was in 'great straits'.[19] Because of this shortage of spares and stores, Hughes could not effect repairs quickly enough to put to sea again before Suffren, who occupied Trincomalee. After the battle on the 3 September the British ships were once more in desperate need of repair. Again finding it impossible to obtain materials at Madras, Hughes was forced to abandon his eastern position and retire to Bombay. [20]

*

In the war of 1776–83, then, the British experienced severe shortages of naval materials, particularly of large sticks for great masts and bowsprits, and of cables, cordage and canvas. This continued to be the case in the next years.

Partly because of the innate problems of supply, and partly because of Pitt's continuing the extensive building programme that had commenced in the later years of war (which included two ships of 98 guns, fifteen of 74, one of 64, two of 44, three of 36, three of 32 and nine of 28), in the mid-1780s the Navy Board was far from achieving its aim of maintaining three years' supply of ship's timber in its yards. As mentioned, in 1786 the reserve was a mere 16,000 loads rather than the 66,000 it should have been. It was only in 1790 that holdings again approached the desired reserve figure.

At this time, the Navy Board also found it impossible to obtain New England sticks of a size for great masts. In 1788, when the Board set new targets for peacetime reserves, its holdings in its yards were: of masts between 30 and 38 inches diameter, only two of the twenty-seven required; of bowsprits between 30 and 38 inches, twenty-nine of a total of forty-nine (but only two of these were larger than 33 inches). In general, the stocks of smaller sticks approached and in some cases exceeded the reserves stipulated; however, as the officials noted, since these had been 'a long time in store, it is supposed that the greatest part are in a defective state'.[21]

The situation was similar with larger Riga sticks, with those greater than 20 inches in diameter continuing in short supply. In April 1786, for example, the Chatham officers asked the Navy Board for sticks of 21 to 24 inches to make masts for the *Bellerophon*, for the Board to reply that 'sticks of large sizes are become very scarce, and there being a great stock of masts of smaller sizes, we shall send [you] by the coach in a day or two models for making masts for a 74-gun ship, … [and direct you] to maturely consider each method and give us [your] opinion which [you] think advisable to adopt'.[22]

As described in Chapter 7, there was also a crisis in the supply of hemp and flax at this time. Indeed, in the middle of 1786 it seemed that Sir George Young's prophesy – that Russia may at 'some future period think it her interest to prohibit our trade with her for [hemp and flax]' – was coming true.[23]

The situation remained similar on the colonial stations. Hughes reported from India in September 1784, for example:

> the line-of-battle ships in these seas are in the greatest want of cables,
> no supply of that article or any naval stores having been sent to India

for these eighteen months past, and what cables are brought out for sale on the Company's ships are few and too small for 64-gun ships, and unless a supply of cables arrives at Bombay before March next, the line-of-battle ships must be reduced to the use of coir cables.[24]

Clearly, then, new sources of trees suitable for great masts and large spars, and of hemp and flax for canvas, cables and cordage, would be very beneficial to Britain's maritime endeavours generally, but particularly where India was concerned.

It was here that the islands of the southwestern Pacific Ocean, with their towering pines and New Zealand flax, might play an important role. As Sir George Young and Sir John Call pointed out in asking for permission to colonize Norfolk Island, '[this enterprise] will prove of great utility, by furnishing a supply of those valuable articles of *cordage* and *masts* for your shipping in India, which are now obtained at a most enormous expense; and from their scarcity have often reduced the maritime force employed in the East Indies to great inconvenience, and even distress.'[25]

True, it might well be expensive to harvest these materials at places so distant as New Caledonia, Norfolk Island and New Zealand; however, a convict labour force would lessen the cost. And in any case, cost was not necessarily the final consideration – as the East India Company instructed its officials in Bengal in 1791:

We are desirous of obtaining the best information you may be able to afford touching the present state of the growth of hemp and flax in any of the districts within your government. In respect to the former, if considered only commercially we are aware that no successful [competition] can be set up against the Russians; but as a plentiful supply of these articles from every possible quarter is of the highest importance to the well-being of the British nation we recommend this object to your very serious notice.[26]

*

The second benefit to be expected from a convict colony in New South Wales was also a maritime one: it would serve as a base for ships proceeding into the Pacific Ocean.

In 1786, the worsening political situation in Europe and India, the scheme to establish a trans-Pacific trading empire, and the existing threat of competition from the French and the emerging one from the Russians and Americans for this ocean's resources meant that it was necessary for Britain to create new maritime resources on the route to it.

'New resources' comprehended not only a harbour and naval materials, but also food, wood, water and personnel. Being adjacent to the route taken by Cook in his second and third voyages, and evidently fertile enough, Botany Bay appeared a suitable site. A population of convicts become yoemen farmers might raise domestic animals and cultivate grains, fruits and vegetables, and also supply replacement seamen.

Such a colony might therefore become most useful for commercial and military purposes, as James Matra had pointed out in 1783:

The place which New South Wales holds on our globe might give it a very commanding influence in the policy of Europe. If a colony from Britain was established in that large tract of country, and if we were at war with Holland or Spain, we might very powerfully annoy either state from our new settlement.

We might with a safe and expeditious voyage make naval incursions on Java and the other Dutch settlements, and we might with equal facility invade the coasts of Spanish America, and intercept the Manila ships laden with the treasures of the west. This check which New South Wales would be in time of war, on both those powers make it a very important object when we view it in the chart of the world with a political eye.[27]

Sir George Young reiterated this point to Pitt in 1784:

Botany Bay, the part that is proposed to be first settled, is not more than twelve hundred leagues from the coast of New Spain, with a fair, open navigation; and there is no doubt but that a lucrative trade would soon be opened with the Spaniards for English manufactures. Or suppose we were again involved in a war with Spain: here is a port of shelter and refreshment for our ships should it be necessary to send any into the South Seas.

From the coast of China, it lies not more than about seven hundred leagues, and nearly the same distance from the East Indies; from the Spice Islands about five hundred leagues, and about a month's run from the Cape of Good Hope.[28]

A convict colony in New South Wales, then, would meet the criteria enunciated by the Beauchamp Committee in July 1785, that it should 'promote the purposes of future commerce or future hostility in the South Seas'; and that, thereby, it should bring benefits as 'may be deemed of sufficient consequence to warrant the expense inseparable from such an undertaking'.[29]

*

The third benefit to be expected concerned cotton, which by the mid-1780s the British were intent on manufacturing in much greater quantities.

At this time, India was the heartland of cotton production. People had grown cotton on the flood plains of the Indus Valley since time immemorial and, using simple but highly effective technology, they had developed a very successful manufacturing industry. By the first century of the Common Era, Arab traders were selling cotton goods in Italy and Spain, and these had become available in Northern Europe by the Middle Ages.

When the English East India Company established a presence in India in the seventeenth century, its officials began sending fine fabrics back to England. Naturally they became aware of the extensive local export trade in 'piece goods' (i.e., bales of cloth) to China. One of the perennial bugbears of Britain's Eastern trade was that the Chinese showed no interest in European manufactured goods, which meant that the British were compelled to offer silver in exchange for tea, silk and porcelain, and that their ships therefore had little outward cargo. As discussed earlier, these problems might partly be solved if the British could manufacture cotton goods at home and export them to China. In the mid-1780s, the industrialization of spinning and weaving offered these prospects, and with them arose another grand scheme, this time overseen by Sir Joseph Banks.

This *Bounty* scheme developed over a dozen years and more, with West Indian planters first requesting a supply of breadfruit in the early 1770s.[30] As I have outlined, the intention was to provide more food to support more slaves, who would increase supplies of cotton to be manufactured in England. The first concrete plan for obtaining breadfruit plants involved Governor Phillip's sending a convict transport on from Botany Bay to one or other of the central Pacific islands. Banks accordingly drafted instructions for Phillip and the gardener who was to oversee the business at the beginning of March 1787; but then he decided that the ship would be better fitted out in England.

At the same time, Banks arranged for Anton Hove, whom he had sent out to southwest Africa on the *Nautilus*, to go to India. Ostensibly, Hove was to present himself to the Indians through whose territories he travelled as a poor student interested in medicinal plants. However, in 'private' instructions issued in March 1787, Banks told him that collecting plants for Kew Garden was a 'secondary' consideration, as 'the real object of your mission is to procure for the West Indies seed of the finer sorts of cotton'. A couple of weeks later, Banks added that Hove was particularly to seek out that variety of cotton having the colour of 'nankeen cloth which is imported from China'.[31]

Hove had a very chequered time in India. Going directly against Banks's advice, at the urging of local people he surrounded himself with a retinue of servants and guards, so that he far exceeded his budget. Still, he returned with seeds of some 170 species, including twenty-three varieties of cotton, and samples of dyes. He also returned with fourteen kinds of grain for 'food and fodder', which Banks considered 'might prove a greater blessing to the [West India] islands than the breadfruit'.

And he brought back 'the nutmeg of Banda, the balm of Gilead, and the mangosteen of Malacca', which Banks also considered might prove of 'inestimable value' if introduced into the West Indies.[32]

It was James Matra who had first suggested the possibility of growing cotton in New South Wales. Given the latitude, he pointed out, New South Wales should be capable of producing, as well as spices, 'tea, coffee, silk, cotton, indigo, tobacco, and the other articles of commerce that have been so advantageous to the maritime powers of Europe'.[33] A convict population might produce these items cheaply, and thereby obviate the need for Britain to purchase them from others.

*

The fourth benefit to be expected – albeit a less urgent and less immediate one – from a settlement in New South Wales was a supply of spices.

Strictly controlling the production of aromatics (cinnamon, cloves, nutmeg, etc.) on various islands in the East Indies, the Dutch had long enjoyed a virtual monopoly of the spice trade, which they guarded jealously. One of the Patriots' reasons for detesting the recent peace treaty was a clause that gave the British the right to a 'free' navigation through the eastern archipelago, which directly threatened this monopoly.

One means open to European nations wishing to lessen their dependence on the Dutch for spices was to harvest them themselves at settlements in the East Indies. In January 1785, the merchant George Smith stressed to Henry Dundas the advantage of forming an outpost at Acheen, partly because it already produced goods for which there was demand throughout India – pepper, beetle, gold, Benjamin (benzoin gum or oil), camphor and sugar; partly because with careful cultivation it might also produce coffee, indigo, cinnamon, cassia, cloves and nutmeg; and partly because it would form a base for warships on the eastern side of the Bay of Bengal, and for merchantmen going to and coming from China.[34]

Such a move, however, would inevitably create resentment that might lead to war. A less risky, though a more difficult and expensive, means of solving the problem was for European nations to cultivate spices in other suitable locations. In the 1760s and 1770s, the French botanist Peter Poivre began doing so in his botanical garden at Mauritius. Fifteen or so years later, production was promising to meet all of Europe's demand for cloves and nutmeg by the end of the century.[35]

Joseph Banks was very aware that, when it came to transferring plants from one hemisphere to another and managing their acclimatization, the French were decades ahead of the British, and he was determined to rectify the situation. As well as expanding the botanical gardens at Kew and on St Vincent in the West Indies, he oversaw the establishment of others on St Helena and at Calcutta, and he brought plants to them from all over the world. The *Bounty* voyage, for example, was intended to comprehend much more than the transfer of breadfruit. Banks directed Bligh to take on a range of Pacific island fruits, along with, from the East Indies, 'mangosteens, duriens, jacks, nancas, lansas, and other fine fruit trees of that quarter, as well as the rice plant which grows upon dry land'. If the French would permit it, Bligh was to leave examples of the breadfruit at Mauritius and take on spice trees in exchange.[36]

If Britain were to produce spices in New South Wales, it would not need to insist on the right to a free navigation among the East Indian islands, which would mollify the Dutch; and it might in time become independent of them for these desirable condiments.

It was James Matra again who pointed out this possibility:

as part of New South Wales lies in the same latitude with the Moluccas, and is even very close to them, there is every reason to suppose that what Nature has so bountifully bestowed on the small islands, may also be found on the larger: but if contrary to analogy it should not be so, the defect is easily supplied, for as the seeds are procured without difficulty, any quantity may speedily be cultivated.[37]

In the matter of spices, too, a colony of convicts, with their free labour, might make a contribution to Britain's economy.

*

These, then – naval materials, a new base and desirable products – were the specific external returns that the Pitt administration might reasonably expect from the necessarily substantial investment in a convict colony in New South Wales. In attending only to the domestic one of getting rid of the convicts, traditionalist historians have failed to understand a much more complex situation.

9.

Towards a Decision: August 1786

THE FIRST DAYS OF AUGUST 1786 were difficult ones for Britain.

On Wednesday 2 August, believing that the kingdom had been stolen from her and that if it were not returned, 'England would be drowned in blood for a thousand generations', Margaret Nicholson attempted to assassinate King George III. The King escaped unharmed.[1]

This disturbing event preoccupied the administration for several days. Lord Sydney organized for Nicholson to be interrogated at length by Evan Nepean and William Fraser, who ran the secret service in Europe, to determine her motives for the attack. The Under-Secretaries of State decided that she was not the agent of a foreign power and the doctors who examined her concluded that she was mad. (It seems that she became disordered after a lover rejected her.) The Great Cabinet of the Privy Council confirmed these findings after a lengthy interrogation on 8 August and announced them to the nation. As news of the attack spread, Lord Sydney received dozens of petitions from individuals and corporations expressing horror at this dreadful attempt and relief at His Majesty's providential deliverance. As duty required, he laid these before the King and returned the monarch's gracious thanks to the petitioners.

'Deeply impressed with the protection of the Almighty', the King took a country tour to Oxford, to restore his and his family's agitated nerves – and also to avoid being in London on his profligate heir's birthday! Lord Sydney too retired to his country seat for the weekend to

193

recover from this 'disagreeable and alarming event', which, as he told a correspondent, 'you will easily imagine must have taken up my whole time and attention'.[2]

Meanwhile, the *Nautilus* had returned from its voyage to Das Voltas Bay, sailing into Portsmouth on 23 July, and T.B. Thompson had immediately travelled to London to report the results. The need for the ministers to deal with the assassination attempt, however, meant that it was some weeks before he was able to tell Sydney officially that he had found 'no bay, river, or inlet' in the vicinity of Das Voltas Bay, and that he had followed a frequently fog-bound coast north to 16°S latitude 'without finding a drop of fresh water, or seeing a tree'. On 15 August, Thompson advised the Admiralty, 'I have received my dismissal from my Lord Sydney'.[3]

*

In August 1786, then, the Pitt administration needed to consider again where to send convicts sentenced to transportation. Within two weeks, the ministers had decided that this should be Botany Bay.

There are fundamentally two perspectives from which we can view this decision. The first is negatively, as one taken in a slough of despair – as Mackay put it, as 'a reckless act on the part of a desperate ministry'.[4] The second is positively – that is, as one taken in the belief that there were benefits (in addition to that of getting rid of the convicts) to be gained from colonizing New South Wales.

The first perspective rests on the claim that, in the whole globe, there was simply nowhere else to dump the convicts – as Shaw misquoted Sydney's earlier comment, 'the more I consider the matter, the greater difficulty I see in disposing of those people'.[5] This view would lose any substance it might have if it were to emerge that Botany Bay was not the only place the Pitt administration considered once it had received the disappointing information about Das Voltas Bay.

There is such evidence. In June 1786, as the administration awaited the results of the *Nautilus* survey, the *Edinburgh Magazine* reported that one of the ministers had drawn up a plan for 'regulating the quota [of convicts] that it is imagined might be sent without hazard to Quebec and Montreal, Halifax, Jamaica, and all the Leeward Islands; and also to the British settlements in Africa, in which last they are not designed to be soldiers, as heretofore, but in another way, in the commercial and inland trade'.[6]

On 8 August, the Portuguese envoy in London reported to his Court the results of the Das Voltas Bay survey. He added that the Cabinet ministers were now uncertain 'whether they might send the convicts to the Cunene River, without violating the rights of the Portuguese Crown, or whether they should transport them instead to Cape Breton'.[7] Whether the North American destination being considered was limited to Cape Breton (or Cape Breton Island) or was in fact the broader region identified in the *Edinburgh Magazine*'s report does not give any cause to doubt the general authenticity of Souza's information, which in all likelihood he had directly from Evan Nepean, who had repeatedly discussed the convict problem with him.

Simultaneously, John Blankett, a naval captain with political connections, wrote to Lord Howe: 'as I understand that the sloop from Africa is returned, without the success there was reason to expect, I may venture to suppose that the finding a proper place to send our convicts may again become a naval question'. He proposed Madagascar, because 'it would serve as an *entrepôt* between Europe and Asia for the refreshment of all ships going to and from India', and therefore become 'a great resource and recruit for the navy in India in any future wars', and a centre of trade with the countries facing the western Indian Ocean. Four days later, Blankett told Nepean of his suggestion, adding, 'I have reason to think that if it becomes a naval question that the idea will be adopted. I just hint it to you, in case you have any other plan which it might cross.' On 16 August, explaining that he believed that 'the Minister [i.e., the Prime Minister] might imagine it a naval question', Blankett wrote to Howe again about sending felons to Madagascar.[8]

'In disposing of the convicts,' Blankett observed, 'two objects seem to present themselves. The first is to send them from this country at the least expense possible; and the second [is] to make their future labour and subsistence serviceable to the state.'[9] As this view of investment and return was the same as that being simultaneously enunciated by Evan Nepean in Heads of a Plan, it may be that Blankett and Nepean had discussed the matter. In any case, however, Blankett was well placed to know the administration's thinking. He was in close contact with Captain John Leveson Gower, Howe's protégé on the Admiralty Board; and in 1787 Nepean sent him as Phillip's replacement to spy in France. Most significantly perhaps, on 19 August, probably the day on which Cabinet decided for Botany Bay, Howe asked him if 'he would be willing to undertake the direction of the plan … in case the conduct of any similar voyage of discovery and settlement of the convicts should be tendered for his acceptance?'[10]

Then there was the proposal put forward in the autumn of 1785 by William Dalrymple and Henry Pemberton, and considered by Pitt, Dundas and Grenville, for a settlement on the southeast coast of Africa, in the vicinity of the Krome River. True, there is no explicit evidence that this proposal was under notice again in August 1786, but we might claim that it had dropped entirely out of sight only if there was no subsequent attention to it. In 1789, however, the administration planned another survey of islands and coasts of the southern Atlantic Ocean, including of the east African coast 'from the eastern limit of the Dutch possessions, to the Portuguese settlement at Mozambique'.[11]

So, far from lacking alternative sites for convict transportation, in mid-August 1786 the Pitt administration had suggestions for at least seven:

1. Nova Scotia (or perhaps Lower Canada more generally)
2. The West Indies
3. West Africa
4. The area at the mouth of the Cunene River in southwest Africa (17°S latitude, 12°E longitude)
5. The southeast coast of Africa (east of Plettenburg Bay, in the Krome River area, c. 34°S latitude, 26°E longitude)
6. Madagascar
7. Botany Bay

While no purposeful analysis of the situation survives (if one was ever written down), we may plausibly suppose that the ministers would have viewed these alternatives with varying degrees of enthusiasm. For instance:

1. Nova Scotia was a comparatively short voyage from Britain, and ships sailed outwards regularly in the spring and summer, so it would be cheap to transport convicts there. However, there were no clear commercial advantages to be gained from doing so, and in any case the Canadians had already objected to the idea. A convict settlement in North America, moreover, would not meet Pitt's desire for a new base 'to the southwards of the Line'.

2. The West Indian islands were also a comparatively short voyage from Britain, and the route was a busy one, so again transportation to one or more of them would be comparatively cheap. However, these islands already possessed a slave labour force. If the response of the settlers at Honduras to convicts in 1784–6 was any indication, the West Indian ones might also object. Again, none of these islands was of any help to ships sailing to or returning from India.

3. The annual voyages of the slave traders to West Africa provided a ready-made method of transporting convicts to the Africa Company's forts, but these could not be sent there in sufficient numbers to solve the domestic problem, and there was abundant evidence of the perils of sending them in any numbers at all. And then, parliament's 1785 condemnation of the Lemain scheme really precluded any further attempts. Nor were these forts situated south of the equator.

4. A settlement on the southwest coast of Africa would certainly help British ships sailing to and from the Indian and Pacific oceans, but the Portuguese were likely to object to any settlement in or adjacent to Angola. Another survey would be needed, and transportation to the area would be significantly more expensive.

5. The same considerations applied to a settlement on the southeast coast of Africa. The Dutch might well object to it, and it would also

be within the territorial limits of the East India Company. A survey would be necessary, and, again, transportation there would be expensive.

6. There were similar arguments for and against a settlement on Madagascar. It would give increased access to the Indian Ocean but, as Blankett himself observed, the East India Company would probably object.[12] A survey would be needed, and transportation would be expensive.

7. New South Wales was very distant from Europe, so transporting convicts there would be even more expensive. However, Britain had a preliminary right to possess this territory, and Cook's, Banks's and Matra's descriptions rendered a further survey unnecessary.

Whatever the comparative advantages and disadvantages of each of these sites, the fact is that in August 1786 the Cabinet ministers had a number to consider – that is, they had a choice.

*

Beyond that of an individual site, however, these ministers had a much more profound choice to make.

Considering it as a whole, the scheme reported by the *Edinburgh Magazine* was essentially one in the old mode, since it would have involved using private contractors to ship convicts to places already under British control – places where some structures of authority already existed, where merchants and planters might make use of the convicts' labour, and where the contractors might obtain a return cargo. The government's involvement, and therefore the cost to it, would be minimal.

However, none of the individual destinations mentioned in the *Edinburgh Magazine*'s report, nor probably all of them together, would have been able to take convicts in the numbers required to solve the problem, particularly if each succeeding year brought hundreds more. On the other hand, a properly planned new convict colony might do so; but if begun from scratch and if located at a great distance from

Europe, it would cost the government a great deal of money. The site chosen therefore needed to be one that would offer returns on this investment.

*

It is now time to offer a detailed analysis of what made Botany Bay a suitable site for a convict colony. (In doing so, I draw only on knowledge available in 1786.)

First, it was thought to offer a sheltered anchorage, and one able to be fortified.[13] Cook had described it as 'capacious, safe and commodious', with an entrance through narrow-set heads and 'steep rocky cliffs next [to] the sea', and therefore 'tolerably well-sheltered from all winds'. It had a channel giving 2 to 2½ fathoms of water at low tide, and anchorages of from 5 to 7 fathoms.

Second, according to Cook's, Banks's and Matra's descriptions, the environs had the potential to meet the needs of the colonists and of ships that might visit. There were the native resources – on land, a kind of spinach, a kind of cherry, 'large quantities' of quails and parrots; and in the bay, a plethora of shellfish and fish. There were a number of streams, and while there were some areas of swampy ground, much of the land might be easily improved. The timbered areas were 'free from underwood of every kind and the trees are at such a distance from one another that the whole country, or at least great part of it, might be cultivated without being obliged to cut down a single tree'. Away from the marshes, the soil was 'a light, white sand' that produced 'a quantity of good grass'; and there were areas of a 'much richer … deep black soil', which bore 'besides timber as fine meadow as ever was seen', and which might produce 'any kind of grain'. Colonists might cultivate these areas in 'the ordinary modes used in England', Banks said. 'In this extensive country', Cook wrote, 'it can never be doubted but [that] most sorts of grain, fruits, roots etc of every kind would flourish here were they once brought hither, planted and cultivated by the hand of industry, and here are provender for more cattle at all seasons of the year than ever can be brought into this country'. The large trees seemed to offer an abundant supply of fuel and building materials, and the stone was also 'very proper' for building.

It is worth digressing here, so as to lay to rest another of the enduring misconceptions of Australian history, which is that Cook falsely described the Botany Bay region, and that with the passage of time Banks overlaid the barren landscape with a romantic tinge. 'The fine meadows talked of in Captain Cook's *Voyage* I could never see, though I took some pains to find them out', John White complained bitterly in 1788. Two hundred years later, L.A. Gilbert suggested that the passing years 'had given New South Wales a new lustre in Banks's mind'.[14]

But consider. Unless weather patterns are disrupted by the *el niño* phenomenon, the Sydney region usually receives a good deal of rain in autumn. Cook, Banks and Matra were at Botany Bay in the first week in May 1770. Reflecting recent rains, there was abundant groundwater and fresh growth. Fish had come inshore to feed on the nutrients the flowing creeks were carrying into the bay, hence the presence of the large stingrays, come to feed on the fish, which the Europeans caught. (Their first name for the harbour was 'Stingray Bay'.)

The First Fleet, however, reached Botany Bay in late January 1788. There had obviously been little recent rain, for the ground was dry and creek-flows meagre, and, being at the end of their annual cycle, the native grasses had withered. Whether the local Aborigines were in the habit of burning off to encourage fresh growth when the rains arrived is unknown; but, if they were, this would have been another factor influencing the appearance of the country at different times of the year. Clearly, the landscape about Botany Bay in January 1788 was very different from that in May 1770. But rather than calling the accuracy of Cook's and Banks's descriptions into question, historians should have looked out their windows – or, if you like, attended to the state of the track at Randwick's autumn carnival!

Returning to our list and the third point in Botany Bay's favour, the region's climate appeared healthy. Cook observed that the Aborigines of New South Wales lived 'in a warm and fine climate and enjoy[ed] a very wholesome air'. Matra told the Beauchamp Committee that the

Endeavour people found the climate 'perfectly agreeable to [the] European constitution'. Clearly, Botany Bay should prove no 'white man's grave', in the manner of the Gambia or Batavia.

Fourth, the British might claim New South Wales without violating the decorums of European politics. Cook's discovery and charting of the continent's eastern coast were the first recorded by the representative of a European state. (We may discount here any prior discovery by Portuguese or Spanish navigators, for which there is no good evidence.) Cook's taking formal possession of the territory gave Britain a preliminary right among its neighbours to claim it. By settling it, Britain would make actual this preliminary right, thus precluding a claim by either the Dutch or the French.

The fifth attraction of Botany Bay was one that time and changed consciousness have rendered problematic. The British believed that there was only a sparse Aboriginal population in New South Wales. Banks reported that he and Cook had encountered only a few Aborigines at Botany Bay, never more that '30 or 40 together'. Although given to hostile gesturing, these had seemed not 'at all to be feared'. They had only the most insubstantial of dwellings and appeared nomadic. He believed that they wandered 'like the Arabs from place to place, set [their shelters] up whenever they met with [an area] where sufficient supplies of food are to be met with, and as soon as these are exhausted remove to another, leaving the houses behind, which are framed with less art or rather less industry than any habitations of human beings probably that the world can show'.[15] They did not keep domestic animals, and they did not plant. According to European ideas of the time, as they had not mixed their labour with the land, they had not established a right to possess it. New South Wales was for the claiming.[16]

Sixth, Botany Bay was adjacent to the route into the Pacific Ocean pioneered by Cook on his second and third voyages – that is, down the Atlantic Ocean to the Cape of Good Hope, east through the southern Indian Ocean, then east and north into the Pacific Ocean. Though longer than the Europeans' usual western one through the Straits of Magellan or round Cape Horn, this eastern route was significantly less arduous because of the direction of prevailing winds and currents. Ships might refresh their wood and water at New South Wales, Van Diemen's Land or New Zealand – and, with a bountiful colony, also replenish their food supplies.

And then, Botany Bay was not inconveniently far from the East Indies and India. Matra described it as 'about a month's run to the Cape of Good Hope; five weeks from Madras, and the same from Canton; very near the Moluccas, and less than a month's run to Batavia'.[17] Sir George Young told Pitt the same things. From Botany Bay, the British might attack the Dutch in the East Indies by a 'safe and expeditious voyage', and the Spanish in Manila with equal facility. Moreover, as Cook was returning from his second voyage, it took him just five weeks to sail from Princess Charlotte Sound in the south island of New Zealand to Tierra del Fuego – so that, as Young again told Pitt, a settlement at Botany Bay would facilitate trade with Spanish America and, in the event of another war, provide 'a port of shelter and refreshment for our ships, should it be necessary to send any into the South Seas'.[18] This was advice the Prime Minister kept in mind. Twenty years later, with war again imminent, he indicated places around the world that might be attacked, and by what means. Against Valparaiso in Chile he recorded: 'New levies or otherwise from New South Wales'.[19]

And, seventh, the islands in the southwestern Pacific offered the prospect of a supply of naval materials for ships in the eastern seas. These islands ranged from New Caledonia to New Zealand, but attention centred on Norfolk Island, about 1600 kilometres to the northeast of Botany Bay. This small island is of volcanic origin; it has two peaks of about 300 metres and is some 36 square kilometres in area. Its coastline is abrupt and jagged, and it offers a reasonable landing at only one spot – and then not when the sea is heavy. Shoals and reefs cluster about it. The French navigator Lapérouse, who was unable either to anchor or land there in 1788, described it as 'only a place fit for angels and eagles to reside in'.[20] But in the late eighteenth century, Norfolk Island had two most valuable attributes: towering pine trees rose above it, and the New Zealand flax plant spread over it. These were manna to

a maritime nation which would send its ships into the oceanic reaches
of the world.

*

Traditionalist historians have been dismissive of the naval stores motive
for the colonization of New South Wales. Documents from the time,
however, show decisively that those involved in the Botany Bay decision
were well aware of this likely benefit.

When the *Endeavour* reached New Zealand in 1769, Cook and
Banks were struck by the towering trees of the River Thames region –
'the finest timber my eyes ever beheld', Banks wrote.[21] They were struck,
too, by the flax plant that flourished in many places:

> But of all the plants we have seen among these people that which is
> the most excellent in its kind, and which really excels most if not all
> that are put to the same uses in other countries, is the plant which
> serves them instead of hemp and flax … Of the leaves of these plants
> with very little preparation all their common wearing apparel are
> made and all strings, lines and cordage for every purpose, and that
> of a strength so much superior to hemp as scarce to bear a compari-
> son with it. From the same leaves also by another preparation a kind
> of snow white fibres are drawn, shining almost as silk and likewise
> surprisingly strong, of which all their finer cloths are made; and of
> the leaves without any other preparation than splitting them into
> proper breadths and tying those strips together are made their fish-
> ing nets. So useful a plant would doubtless be a great acquisition to
> England …[22]

On his second voyage, Cook also drew attention to the pine trees of
New Caledonia and the Isle of Pines. But what particularly took his
attention was Norfolk Island. He and his companion William Wales
wrote that the flax was so abundant on the island's jagged shores that it
was 'scarce possible to get through it', and that the 'spruce pines' grew in
'vast abundance and to a vast size, from two to three feet diameter and

upwards', and were superior to those of New Zealand and New Caledonia for 'masts, yards, etc'. Here was an island, they said, 'where masts for the largest ships' might be obtained, and Cook fashioned one tree into a yard for the *Resolution*.[23]

Banks brought samples of New Zealand flax back to England. Furneaux, who returned from the second voyage before Cook, brought seeds, which Lord Sandwich sent to the King, saying that this 'remarkable flax plant … is very likely to grow here', and that Banks advised that 'the sooner it is put into the ground the better'.[24] On the *Resolution*'s return in 1775, J.R. Forster, one of its naturalists, gave some specimens of the plant to a 'foreign lady' to work, and the result was 'a degree of fineness and whiteness which could be little expected'. When Forster showed the results to the Admiralty, they asked Cook to obtain some samples of seeds and plants on his forthcoming voyage, 'that farther experiments may be made of it'.[25]

In their published accounts of the voyages, Cook himself and a number of his companions (among them Sydney Parkinson, Georg Forster and James Matra) suggested that the islands of the southwestern Pacific Ocean might in future supply naval materials.

This perception was soon a commonplace in the secondary accounts of the voyage. Here are some examples to add to those I gave in the Introduction.

Immediately on the return of the *Endeavour* to England, the *Gentlemen's Magazine* reported that 'among the curiosities brought home by Mr Banks and Dr Solander, there is some hemp seed of a new species, which is reckoned to have twice the strength of any other yet discovered, and as it grows in a dry, light soil, it promises to be of the greatest utility to our agriculture and navigation'.[26] When John Hawkesworth's compilation of the recent Pacific voyages had appeared, this magazine borrowed from it to report that when the British landed in New Zealand 'the Indians laughed at their nets, and showed them one of theirs five fathom deep, and not less than three or four hundred fathom long, made of a kind of grass which is very strong'. Cook and Banks, the report continued, found in the woods trees of an incredible size, one of which meas-ured 19 feet 8 inches in the girt, 6 feet above ground, and from the root to the first branch 89 feet, and as straight as an arrow, and tapered but very little in proportion to its height. Between the woods in which these trees grow, there runs a river not unlike the Thames, where ships of any burden might ride in safety, and load with all imaginable ease.[27]

In 1776, this magazine reported further that at Norfolk Island Cook and his officers had found 'trees large enough for the masts of 3rd-rate men-of-war'.[28]

Two years later, also summarizing Hawkesworth, C.T. Middleton told readers:

Among all the trees and shrubs, of which there are many, bearing beautiful flowers, and highly aromatic, there is not one that pro-duces fruit; but there is a plant worth them all, serving the natives instead of hemp and flax. Of this plant there are two species; one bearing a deep red flower, the other a yellow. The leaves of both resemble flags, but the blossoms are not so large, and their clusters are more in number. They make all their clothes of the leaves of this plant, and also all their strings and cordage, which are at once glossy, elastic, and so strong, that nothing made of hemp can equal them. From the same, by another process, they draw out long, slender, strong fibres, white as snow, and shining as silk; of these they make their better cloth; and, by slitting the leaves in proper breadths, and tying them together, they make their fishing nets. This plant seems to grow best in boggy grounds; there is every reason to believe that it would thrive well in England, and could we transport it here, it would be a great acquisition.[29]

In 1782, G.H. Millar advised that in New Zealand 'are forests of great extent, crowded with trees, the straightest, cleanest, and largest ever seen. They are rather too hard and heavy for masts; but if they could be lightened by tapping, as it is probable they might, they would make the finest masts for shipping in the world'.[30]

What is especially significant here is the opinion of experts who had a hand in the Botany Bay business. For example, Brook Watson was commissary to the British army in America during the Revolutionary War and had very large trading interests in the Canadian colonies, including in naval stores. As Sheriff of London, he had frequent contact with Home Office officials, and as an MP he had close ties with Pitt. His firm, Rashleigh and Company, supplied some of the items sent on the First Fleet. In 1785, Watson told a Canadian acquaintance that if the flax from the southwest Pacific might 'be introduced and accord with your soil, it would be better than the mines of South America to Spain'. And in 1789, when he was assisting the Board of Trade to obtain details of a new French method of manufacture, he told Hawkesbury:

> The more I consider the nature of hemp, the capability of our country to produce it and the consequences of its being so produced, and the peculiar advantages which would accrue to our manufacturers from bringing it to them in its best form, by the mode recently discovered for doing it – the more anxious I am for its being carried to the highest pitch of improvement. To this desire your Lordship must attribute the repeated applications with which I trouble you. The specimens of New Zealand hemp which I have seen are so far superior to any other I have beheld that I most earnestly entreat your Lordship to take the best and most speedy means for procuring some of its seed from that country.[31]

*

One of A.G.L. Shaw's reasons for rejecting Blainey's point about the significance of naval stores in the Botany Bay decision was that

> We might expect some contemporary commentators to have discussed the hopes, ill-founded though they may have turned out to be, of obtaining naval supplies from the Pacific. ... But no. Neither

the *Annual Register* nor the *Gentleman's Magazine*, for example, refers to hopes of naval stores from 'New Holland'.[32]

This claim is wrong. When London publications reported on the mounting of the First Fleet in October 1786, they did draw attention to the prospect of obtaining naval stores from the islands of the south-western Pacific Ocean. On 13 October, the *Morning Chronicle* advised that Botany Bay was 'within a fortnight's sail of New Zealand, which place is covered with timber, even to the water-edge, of such an enormous size and height, that a single tree would be much too large for the mast of a 1st rate man-of-war'. The next day, the *London Chronicle* told its readers:

> To the other important benefits which the settlement of New South Wales affords, is to be added, that very valuable article of New Zealand hemp or flax plant, an object equally of utility and curiosity. Any quantity of it might raised in the settlement, in as much as it grows spontaneously in New Zealand. This plant is so admirably disposed by nature, that it will serve the various purposes of hemp, flax and silk, and is easier manufactured than any one of them. In naval affairs, it could not fail of being of the utmost consequence; a cable of ten inches being supposed to be of equal strength and durability with one of European hemp of eighteen inches. Some of this flax is now in England, and the manufacturers are of opinion, that canvas made of it would be infinitely superior in strength and beauty to any at present in use. ... The advantages that might accrue from this article would be important beyond belief.

That newspapers considered it significant to report these things is another indication of the importance of naval materials to Britain's imperial and commercial endeavour.[33]

*

To understand how a convict labour force was relevant to the creation of a new source of naval materials, we need to know how hemp and flax were manufactured in the eighteenth century.

As I have discussed, the progressive expansion of the military and merchant marines of Western Europe created a constant, and indeed insatiable, demand for canvas, cables and cordage. While there was some cultivation of *Cannabis sativa* in England, Scotland, Holland, France, Spain and the lands behind the Adriatic coast, by far the most important region was that around the Baltic Sea, extending from what are now Germany and Poland into Russia. There, each year, farmers planted and harvested vast fields of hemp, selling it to merchants who in turn sold it to dealers and manufacturers in Holland, France, Spain and Britain.

Cut and bundled, the leaves or 'flags' of hemp were soaked in water ('retted'), until the hard outer layer (the 'harl') disintegrated, exposing the fibres. These were then beaten ('scutched') to remove the residual harl, then untangled and separated by being passed through a comb ('hackle'). Depending on their size and quality, these fibres were then either woven into canvas or kneaded and twisted into cordage and cables, which were 'tarred' (mostly with oil from Baltic pines) to make them impervious to water. An additional use of hemp came with the shredding of old ropes and cables to produce 'oakum', which was used to caulk ships' planks.

Dismissing the importance of the naval stores motive, David Mackay asserted that 'the beating and dressing of flax and hemp, and the manufacture of ropes and sailcloth were technically difficult and labour-intensive processes in the eighteenth century', with the implication that these would not have been considered suitable tasks for convicts.[34] Well, he was half-right. The manufacturing of hemp and flax and the 'picking' of oakum were certainly 'labour-intensive' work; but while they were dirty, they did not require particular skills.

How Mackay could make this extraordinary claim is mystifying, for by the 1780s there was a long tradition in Britain of setting the poor and criminals to this work. It was one of the duties of the overseers of the poor to provide 'a convenient stock of flax, hemp, wool, thread, iron and other ware and stuff' for those ordered to the parish workhouses to process.[35] In the course of his inspections in the 1770s, John Howard found prisoners beating and weaving flax and hemp and picking oakum in the London, Tothill Fields, Dartford, Cambridge, Warwick, Southwell, Peterborough and Thame bridewells.[36]

In 1779, the Bunbury Committee heard testimony that the setting of criminals to beating hemp and picking oakum was a frequent practice in local jails – for example, at Clerkenwell, Maidstone, Southwark and St George's Fields. It also received Benjamin Crook's proposal for employing convicts to make cordage for the navy. In turn, it recommended that those confined to the proposed new penitentiary houses should be employed at tasks

in which a competent knowledge may be acquired with little applica-tion, and to which no apprenticeship is necessary; in which many may be kept to labour by the supervision of few; and in which it is difficult to embezzle the materials: such, for example, as the sawing of stone, the making of cordage, or picking of oakum.[37]

In line with this recommendation, in mid-1785 Sir Watkin Lewes, member of parliament and sheriff and alderman of the City of London, told the administration that he was willing to employ between 300 and 600 transport convicts in making annually 1500 tons of cordage for the Royal Navy.[38]

That convicts might be set to manufacturing the flax growing on distant Pacific islands was a natural extension of this thinking.

*

Now, all this would be irrelevant if in the mid-1780s British authorities did not consider the possibility of obtaining naval materials from the islands of the southwestern Pacific Ocean. There is clear evidence that they did so.

1. There are the reports of the prospects by Cook and his companions on his three voyages, concerning the timber and flax growing on Norfolk Island and the New Zealand islands.
2. Then, there are the favourable opinions formed by experts in England, particularly of the virtues of the flax.
3. There is the attention drawn to the prospect in the proposals of Matra, Young and Call.
4. There is the specific adoption of these proposals. Nepean listed 'Matra's scheme' in the agenda for Cabinet's discussion of the available options; and it is seldom noticed that the mode of settlement pursued – a main colony on the coast of New South Wales and a secondary one on Norfolk Island – was that proposed by John Call.

*

As I show in the next chapter, there is abundant evidence that in August 1786 members of the Pitt administration hoped that the investment in a convict colony in New South Wales would result in those returns discussed in the previous chapter. Before proceeding to consider this evidence, though, I need to point out a peculiarity in the manner of this decision.

Normally, questions relating to colonization would have been referred to the Privy Council's Committee of Trade and Plantations, but there is no evidence that this was done in the case of New South Wales. In mid-August 1786, when the decision was taken, administrative arrangements were in a transitional state. In 1782, when it had become clear that the war in America was lost, the Committee of Trade and the Secretaryship of State for American Colonies had been abolished, with the new Home Office becoming responsible for colonies.

Then, in March 1784, finding that he had no adequate forum in which to discuss colonial questions, develop commercial policies and formulate trade agreements, Pitt had revived the Committee of Trade, this time as a standing committee of the Privy Council. By mid-1786, it had become apparent that the role of this body needed to be expanded, and that a more permanent structure was needed. The reconstituted

Committee of Trade and Plantations commenced on 23 August 1786, with Charles Jenkinson, raised to the peerage as Lord Hawkesbury, at its head.[39] (For convenience, I have used the modern title Board of Trade when referring to this committee.)

It seems that the administration was anxious to conclude some pieces of colonial business before this new committee took legal effect. On Wednesday 16 August, Sydney asked William Fawkener, the clerk of the Privy Council, to arrange for Hawkesbury to reach town 'on Friday morning early enough to hold a Committee of Trade before the Levée, to consider of Lord Dorchester's instructions'. Pitt, Sydney, Hawkesbury, Carmarthen, Grenville and Effingham accordingly met on the Friday and approved the Home Office's draft of those instructions.[40]

We must conclude that a decision about Botany Bay was part of this 'tidying-up' of colonial business, for the decision not to refer it to the new Board of Trade must have been deliberate. No known document casts any direct light on this puzzle. It may be that, on 18 August, when the Home Office was still formally responsible for colonies, the Cabinet ministers considered that this gave them sufficient authority to take a decision, and that they were in a position to do so because the proposal had been closely examined in 1785 by the House of Commons committee, and because Evan Nepean had subsequently developed detailed costings.

All this may have been so. Still, it is difficult to avoid the conclusion that something deeper was involved, something which caused the administration not to want the new Board of Trade to consider Botany Bay. Such consideration would have delayed the decision by months, perhaps by many months if other sites were proposed, during which time both the number of transport convicts and public resentment at the central government's failure to ship them out of the country would have increased. As parliament had risen and would not sit again until late January 1787, by taking the decision in mid-August the administration had six months to get the convicts away before there might be any sustained scrutiny of its decision for Botany Bay.

This analysis may seem cynical – but then, political machinations often justify a degree of cynicism. However, there are other things to keep in mind when trying to understand the Botany Bay decision. First, although again there is no explicit evidence for it, I think Pitt told his ministers what he wanted – i.e., to use the convicts to build a base south of the equator – and that they agreed. As I have shown, by mid-August 1786 the international political situation had become very threatening to Britain's situation in Europe and India. It had become important to secure possession of New South Wales and the adjacent islands with their naval materials before the French occupied them. Moreover, Pitt's extensive scheme for expanding British commerce in and about the Pacific Ocean would require bases if it were to succeed. Because of the certain domestic and international opposition that would arise once the parameters of this scheme became known (from the East India Company on the one hand, and France, Spain and Holland on the other), it is not surprising that the administration would have avoided publicizing its thinking. This does not mean, however, that these concerns were not important, or that they did not give an extra urgency to the Botany Bay decision.

It is, I know, all too easy to invoke secrecy to indulge fantasy. However, in the 1780s there *was* a deal of secrecy about plans to increase Britain's strategic resources along the India route. The commander of the *Swallow* was instructed to keep the purposes of his voyage 'as secret as possible'. In presenting his Das Voltas Bay proposal, Edward Thompson stressed: 'I could wish secrecy was observed in this matter and plan, for the moment it is divulged and committed to the public, the French will embrace the advantage and possess themselves of this country'. The Admiralty subsequently issued him with secret orders, and the *Nautilus*'s stores were augmented to eight months' supply at sea, so as to conceal the true length of its voyage. In presenting his plan for the Kaffir Coast, William Dalrymple said, 'What I write must be kept secret, as the Dutch would make every exertion to seize the country if they had the least idea of our intentions of setting in the neighbourhood.' And in passing this proposal on to Dundas, Devaynes said: 'I am of opinion if anything is done it should be *done secret and out of hand*', adding, 'I have sent a copy of it to Mr Pitt, and have not communicated [it] to our Court [of Directors] or any other person.'[41]

Similarly, there was a deal of secrecy about Botany Bay. Indeed, there is one curious newspaper report that the Pitt administration leaked rumours of the plan's having been modified or even abandoned, so as to conceal its real intentions.[42] Then there was the choice of Arthur Phillip as the colony's governor. Given his extensive covert career, Phillip was just the sort of 'able and discreet officer' whose appointment the Home Office had called for when it wrote to the Admiralty about the post.[43] Phillip spoke five European languages fluently. He had spied not only in Europe but also in South America, and had sailed on at least one secret expedition intended to subvert Spain's authority in its colonies.[44] The decision to appoint such a man as governor is significant.

There is also the uncommunicative manner in which Phillip conducted himself on the voyage out to New South Wales. David Collins, who sailed with the First Fleet as the colony's new deputy judge-advocate, reported to his father from Rio de Janeiro that:

Our governor has not as yet announced himself as such, nor did he communicate any of his powers or instructions to Major Ross, until a week after our arrival here. Major Ross, I apprehend, will write to you, and if he does, no doubt he will inform you fully of these circumstances, indeed more amply than is in my power, for I am wholly in the dark respecting them. Neither know we anything of his future plans or intentions. We understand they are to be developed when we leave the Cape of Good Hope, between that port and New South Wales. I do imagine this secrecy is calculated to prevent any discovery of them by letter from the officers of the new settlement to their friends at home, until they begin to be put in execution. How far this is wise or necessary I will not take upon me to decide, but if any plan or design is kept secret now, I can only say it is the first circumstance of the kind to be met with in our history.[45]

Robert Ross complained bitterly that Phillip did not confide in him: 'I could not, I confess, but feel myself much hurt at his Excellency's not having given me the most distant hint of his intention [to go on ahead], prior to our quitting the Cape.' And Ross's friend Captain Campbell repeated this complaint: 'This man will be everything himself. [He] never, that I have heard of, communicates any part of his plan for establishing the colony or carrying on his work to anyone.'[46]

In what were evidently acrimonious exchanges with the marine officers, Phillip insisted opaquely that, as a consequence of its 'situation', the colony would 'in time become the Empire of the East', a view his opponents held in contempt; but then, they were not privy, as he was, to the administration's thinking.[47]

There are two more major points about the Botany Bay decision with need simple reiteration here. The first is the central role played by the Prime Minister, William Pitt. By late 1785, Pitt had clearly taken charge of the business of establishing a new convict colony, and Evan Nepean, the Under-Secretary at the Home Office, was working according to his direction. As was the case with the business of India, where convicts were concerned Lord Sydney had become invisible.

The second is that by this decision members of the Pitt administration shifted their thinking about where to send the convicts, from the Atlantic world to the much greater one beyond. In doing so, they abandoned the old mode of dealing with the problem, that is, exporting it, with the central government playing only a minimal role, and adopted a new one, in which the government's role would be dominant. This was a radical departure, which we may now see as an early manifestation of one of the most striking features of the modern state, which in the past two hundred years has progressively extended its control over the lives of its citizens.

10.

The Decision for Botany Bay

And so to Botany Bay.

By mid-August Evan Nepean was busy working up Duncan Campbell's earlier estimates of the cost of transporting 750 convicts, three marine regiments and a handful of officials to the harbour 33° south of the equator, on the coast of New South Wales, seen by Captain Cook, Sir Joseph Banks and James Matra in May 1770.[1] He considered the figures again and again, until he had worked out that, for the voyage out and in the first three years of the colony, the cost for a male convict would be about £32 per annum, or only about £4 more than that of keeping him on a hulk.[2]

Having arrived at this satisfactory figure, Nepean then drew up the document entitled 'Heads of a Plan for effectually disposing of Convicts, and rendering their Transportation reciprocally beneficial both to themselves and to the State, by the establishment of a Colony in New South Wales'. This region, he wrote, seemed 'peculiarly adapted to answer the views of government'. Its climate was good, and its soil fertile enough for agriculture. The colonists might obtain livestock from the Cape of Good Hope and the Molucca Islands. If they were industrious, they should become self-sufficient in food in three years. In any case, when set against the 'great object to be obtained by it', the difference in cost between placing the convicts at Botany Bay and that of keeping them on the hulks was 'too trivial to be a consideration with government'. And

215

Botany Bay's remoteness meant that the convicts would scarcely be able to return to Britain without permission.[3]

The expedition to establish the colony should consist of a warship and a tender of about 200 tons and transport ships; officials, comprising a governor, lieutenant-governor, deputy judge-advocate, surgeons and others; marine guards and their officers; and convicts. After they had excorted the transports out, the governor might use the warships to obtain livestock, and perhaps Polynesian women to redress the sexual imbalance. The marines, who would maintain order among the colonists and protect them from the natives, should include skilled workmen – carpenters, sawyers, blacksmiths, potters and farmers.

William Pitt's Cabinet usually met on Tuesdays and Fridays. However, Gary Sturgess has established that the ministers met more frequently in the week beginning Monday 14 August 1786 – on Wednesday 16 August, in the morning of Friday 18 August and again that evening, and then in the morning of Saturday 19 August. On these occasions they considered the crisis in relations with France in Europe and the East, the problems with supplies of naval stores from Russia, and a suitable destination for the convicts. It is likely that they decided to establish a convict colony at Botany Bay on either 18 or 19 August.[4]

On Monday 21 August, when he was back in the office, Evan Nepean drafted the letter announcing the decision, which went with Lord Sydney's signature and a copy of the Heads of a Plan to the Treasury. Nepean instinctively dated this letter the 21st, but then back-dated it to the 18th. This change was necessary because the Treasury Board had risen for its summer recess on 18 August – and then as now, government departments needed Treasury approval to spend money. Nepean's counterparts at the Treasury, George Rose and Thomas Steele, duly recorded Sydney's letter as having come before the Board on the Friday, and approval having been given the same day.[5]

*

So we come to the central question: why did the Pitt administration decide to establish a convict colony at Botany Bay? Traditionalist historians have long woven their explanations out of four strands: 1) the inability to continue transporting convicts to North America; 2) the domestic pressure caused by their accumulation in large numbers in local jails and on the hulks; 3) the sheer inability to find any other place in the whole world to which to send them; and 4) Botany Bay's distance from Britain, which would make it extremely difficult for these failed citizens to return.

It is here, however, that the point made decades ago by Dallas and Blainey becomes very relevant. While these factors may well explain why the British authorities decided to use convicts in the Botany Bay venture, only the last begins to account for the choice of site.[6]

To understand this choice, we have to look to the other factors, at the other historical contexts that I have analysed. These involved Britain's naval needs in the southern Atlantic, Indian and Pacific oceans, and included the roles a settlement at Botany Bay might play in trade or war, as outlined by James Matra and Sir George Young in 1783–4. It is true that, at the end of 1784, Earl Howe, the First Lord of the Admiralty, was sceptical about the envisaged benefits, although, significantly, he didn't entirely rule out such a move, for he began his advice to Sydney with: 'Should it be thought advisable to increase the number of our settlements on the plan Mr M. Matra has suggested …'.[7] However, between December 1784 and August 1786 there were a number of planning and political developments which combined to make a colony in New South Wales seem advantageous. Indeed, it may not be an overstatement to say that these developments made it necessary that the British establish a colony in the region so as to obtain formal possession of it.

As discussed, these developments included pressing military and material concerns, and the grand scheme formulated by Pitt, Dundas, Grenville, Mulgrave, Hawkesbury and Banks to promote a massive expansion of British trade in the Indian and Pacific oceans, including with the countries of eastern Asia, the Spanish colonies in the Americas and the inhabitants of the northwest Pacific coast and the Kamchatka peninsula. To bring this scheme to fruition the politicians needed to carry out a number of interrelated projects – surveys of coastlines and islands, the creation of new bases along shipping routes, liberal new trading agreements with European nations and China (and, they hoped, Japan), and the reduction or removal of the monopolies of the East India Company and the South Sea Company. As I have described in detail in *The Global Reach of Empire*, it would take thirty years and two global conflicts for this scheme to be achieved. Nonetheless, Pitt and his colleagues began the task in the mid-1780s and pursued it into the early 1800s. The colonization of New South Wales is part of this larger story.

*

The traditional historians have repeatedly claimed either that there is no good evidence or no evidence at all to relate the Botany Bay venture to these very broad considerations. In this, they have been simply wrong. There is an abundance of relevant evidence.

Let me start by considering the Heads of a Plan and the letter that accompanied it when it was sent to Treasury. These documents have been the central exhibit in the long-running debate over the administration's motives. Signed by Sydney but written by Nepean, the letter begins:

> The several jails and places for the confinement of felons in this kingdom being in so crowded a state that the greatest danger is to be apprehended, not only from their escape, but from infectious distempers which may hourly be expected to break out amongst them, His Majesty, desirous of preventing by every possible means the ill consequences which might happen from either of these causes, has been pleased to signify to me his royal commands that measures should immediately be pursued for sending out of this kingdom such of the convicts as are under sentence or order of transportation.[8]

The Heads of a Plan begins:

> Heads of a Plan for effectually disposing of Convicts, and rendering their Transportation reciprocally beneficial both to themselves and to the State, by the Establishment of a Colony in New South Wales …[9]

Rendering their transportation reciprocally beneficial both to themselves and to the State – yet the traditionalists would have us believe that the sole benefit to Britain from this venture, which might be effected only with great effort and at very considerable expense, given that Botany Bay was half a world away, would be the riddance of its criminals. In fact, however, the last three paragraphs of the Heads spell out three other advantages to be derived from it:

It may not be amiss to remark in favour of this plan that considerable advantage will arise from the cultivation of the New Zealand hemp or flax plant in the new intended settlement, the supply of which would be of great consequence to us as a naval power, as our manufacturers are of opinion that canvas made of it would be superior in strength and beauty to any canvas made from the European material, and that a cable of the circumference of ten inches made from the former would be superior in strength to one of eighteen inches made of the latter. The threads or filaments of this New Zealand plant are formed by nature with the most exquisite delicacy, and may be so minutely divided as to be manufactured into the finest linens.

Most of the Asiatic productions may also without doubt be cultivated in the new settlement, and in a few years may render our recourse to our European neighbours for those productions unnecessary.

It may also be proper to attend to the possibility of procuring from New Zealand any quantity of masts and ship timber, for the use of our fleets in India, as the distance between the two countries is not greater than between Great Britain and America. It grows close to the water's edge, is of size and quality superior to any hitherto known, and may be obtained without difficulty.[10]

Let me deal with the middle of these paragraphs first. 'Asiatic productions' here means principally spices and cotton. As discussed, the Pitt administration was certainly interested in reducing Britain's dependence on the Dutch for these sought-after spices, and in supplying its cloth manufacturers with greater amounts of cotton.

The first and last of these three paragraphs have become famous in the historiography of the Botany Bay decision, as writers have argued over their status and the validity of the explanation they offer. The traditionalist historians have concluded that, coming as they do at the end of the document, and with their conditional verbs ('it may not be amiss …', 'it may also be proper to attend …'), they were merely 'tacked-on', a sort of 'window-dressing', and that the motive they announce is therefore inconsequential. These historians have also argued that the 'dumping of convicts' explanation, coming as it does at the start of the letter to the Treasury, is the only real and true one for the decision.[11] Those who have challenged the traditional view, however, – principally Geoffrey Blainey and I – see these paragraphs as most significant, for they clearly state a motive other than the convict one, and one, moreover, which accords with the needs of the time.

The traditionalists' stance here has been decidedly odd. They have implicitly downplayed the importance of Heads of a Plan because of its title, and have dismissed the significance of the final paragraphs because of their position within the document. But there are no logical grounds for doing so, unless one wishes only to confirm a deeply held view, and not to consider information that might contradict it. As a number of other such documents from the period demonstrate, the title 'Heads of a Plan' means precisely what it seems to – that is, a concise enunciation of the major points of a plan.[12] There are no grounds for giving more weight to one paragraph than to another according to their position within the document. And if we dismiss the significance of the third last and last paragraphs of the Heads, we obliterate from the record what Evan Nepean considered the principal benefits Britain was expecting to derive from the Botany Bay colony (apart from that of sending criminals out of the kingdom).

Nepean's view should not be dismissed as inconsequential. Far from being some underling requested to find an excuse for a fundamentally unjustifiable decision, he was the government official most involved in the decision and in the mounting of the First Fleet. If anyone other than Pitt and his closest advisers knew what the motives for these things were, it was Nepean.

In fact, the 'naval stores' paragraphs of Heads are perhaps the two most significant ones of all for understanding the business. As Bolton pointed out, they are very largely direct quotes from James Matra's 1783 proposal, which we know was considered by Cabinet at the end of 1784. Apart from these two instances, they appear nowhere else, and so are unique in the records of the Botany Bay decision.

On the other hand, the opening paragraph of the letter to the Treasury, with its alarmist notes concerning the convicts, appears again and again. I have found some nineteen examples of this generic paragraph in documents from the 1770s and 1780s. The first of these is in a January 1776 letter from William Eden to the Secretary of State:

> The number [of transport convicts] [was] so great in London that it became necessary in order to avoid pestilential disorders to remove near 140 aboard a vessel in the River; and I hear this morning that, exclusive of the inconvenience of keeping them in this severe weather, several have died aboard, in consequence of the complaints contracted in prison, and that it is much to be wished for the sake of all that the crowd could be lessened.[13]

Nepean used it again at the beginning of 1783, and while his letter is now seemingly lost, his Treasury colleague's reply indicates its tenor, and also conveys the historical fact it reflects:

> my Lords [Commissioners of His Majesty's Treasury] understanding that the jail of Newgate is crowded with prisoners to a very inconvenient degree and that an infectious distemper has broken out among them, are of opinion that it is highly important the convicts there should be removed immediately without waiting to settle the terms for transporting them to America ...[14]

In the mid-1780s, whenever the Home Office wrote to the Treasury or Admiralty boards or Duncan Campbell concerning the need to expand the hulks system or that to resume transportation, the writer – that is, Evan Nepean – invoked this generic paragraph to justify the request. It appears, for example, in North's letter to Campbell of 24 August 1783; in Sydney to Campbell, 23 January 1784; in Sydney to the Admiralty, 29 May, 9 and 11 June 1784, and 10 November 1785; in Sydney to the Treasury, 9 and 12 February, 20 March and 10 November 1785.

Neither is it always placed at the head of these letters. It appears in the body of Rose's letter to Nepean of 3 January 1783. Indeed – dare I mention it? – on one occasion it is placed *last*, in Sydney's letter to the Treasury of 10 November 1785: 'I will only beg leave further to mention to your Lordships, that the jails are in so crowded a state that it is absolutely necessary for the Public safety that this measure should be carried into execution.'[15]

Of course the danger of typhus fever on the hulks was real. There were repeated outbreaks between 1776 and 1786, most often when infected convicts arrived from county and local prisons, where they had been kept in very squalid conditions and their clothing had become infested with vermin. However, when we see the phrase 'may hourly be expected to break out' repeated over two years and more, we may understand the rote nature of the opening paragraph of the letter to the Treasury.

That is, this paragraph is mostly a rhetorical flourish, whereas the last paragraphs of Heads of a Plan give vital insight into the thinking of the Pitt administration. But having taken the opposite view, the traditionalists absolved themselves of any need to investigate the other historical contexts of the Botany Bay decision. They thereby failed to understand that the need for more, and more secure, naval supplies was indeed a major factor in it.

*

Some of Nepean's arrangements for the First Fleet and the colony once the decision had been taken confirm the centrality of this motive.

In October and November 1786, he asked William Sharrow, a Birmingham manufacturer, how the New Zealand flax should be worked.[16] He and other officials saw that the necessary equipment was sent on the ships, including 'the necessary articles for dressing flax' – viz., '9 hackles for flax; 9 hackle pins; 3 flax-dressing brushes; 127 dozen combs; 1 machine for dressing flax, with ironwork and brushes;' and a 'loom for weaving canvas complete'.[17] At the beginning of November, Brook Watson passed on to Nepean a recommendation that Lieutenant William Dawes go out to New South Wales, as someone competent to attend to 'the flax from New Zealand, or any other important article of commerce which that country may produce'. In addition to Dawes, a master weaver, Roger Murley or Morley, joined the expedition as a free man.[18]

Then, at the end of October, writing to the Irish government, Nepean outlined what the venture was to involve. According to those who had been with Cook when he visited the area in 1770, it offered a good climate, fertile soil, wood, water and seafood, and was therefore a suitable site for a settlement. The founding expedition would consist of two warships and transports for 750 convicts, 200 marines, the civilian officials and the stores. Upon arrival, the convicts would be employed in building and agriculture.

Nepean explained that the scheme was to be 'reciprocally beneficial'. 'Besides the removal of a dreadful banditti from this country,' he said, 'many advantages are likely to be derived from this intended settlement':

Some of the timber is reported to be fit for naval purposes, particularly masts, which the fleet employed occasionally in the East Indies frequently stands in need of, and which it cannot be supplied with but from Europe. But above all, the cultivation of the flax plant seems to be the most considerable object. This plant has been found in that neighbourhood in the most luxuriant state, and small quantities have been brought to Europe and manufactured, and, from its superior quality, it will it is hoped soon become an article of commerce [i.e., export] from that country.[19]

This paragraph has an additional significance. Nepean states explicitly that the naval materials obtained in the Pacific would be sent to India – a detail not mentioned in the Heads of a Plan. India was the destination suggested by Young and Call in their June 1785 request for permission to colonize Norfolk Island. In giving this destination, Nepean revealed an evolution in the administration's thinking, whereby New South Wales had become part of the long-term policy being developed by the India Board to obtain materials for the India guardships 'on the spot, or in adjoining settlements'.[20] Nepean's comments also gainsay Manning Clark's assertion that 'everyone associated with the execution of the [Botany Bay] decision named the overcrowding in the jails as the only motive' – clearly, this simply isn't so.[21] There is no doubt that when they took their decision in August 1786, British authorities were interested in obtaining naval materials from the islands of the southwestern Pacific Ocean. In their eagerness to dismiss or downplay this interest, the traditionalist historians have either denigrated or simply ignored a considerable body of evidence.

*

There is also evidence that the Pitt administration's plans extended beyond Botany Bay. The Orders-in-Council that specified New South Wales as the place of transportation provided for one or more secondary colonies, stating as they did that the destination was to be 'Botany Bay, on the eastern coast of New South Wales, or some one or other of the islands adjacent'. And Phillip told Nepean in March 1787 that his instructions should include the provisos 'that I send one of the ships to Charlotte Sound, in the island of New Zealand, for the flax plant, and to the Friendly Islands for the breadfruit'.[22]

Then there are Phillip's instructions, which included these directions:

Norfolk Island ... being represented as a spot which may hereafter become useful, you are, as soon as circumstances will admit of it, to send a small establishment thither to secure the same to us, and prevent its being occupied by the subjects of any other European power, and you will cause any remarks or observations which you may obtain in consequence of this instruction to be transmitted to our principal Secretary of State for plantation affairs for our information.

And:

as it has been humbly represented unto us that advantages may be derived from the flax plant which is found in the islands not far distant from the intended settlement, not only as a means of acquiring clothing for the convicts and other persons who may become settlers, but from its superior excellence for a variety of maritime purposes, and as it may ultimately become an article of export, it is therefore our will and pleasure that you do particularly attend to its cultivation, and that you do send home by every opportunity which may offer samples of that article, in order that a judgment may be formed whether it may not be necessary to instruct you further upon this subject.[23]

Phillip told Lieutenant Philip King on 1 February 1788 – that is, within a week of his hoisting the flag at Port Jackson and of Lapérouse's arrival, and before he had landed the bulk of the convicts and unloaded the ships – that he was sending him and a specialist party (which included the master weaver and convicts experienced in the business) to occupy Norfolk Island and commence harvesting the flax. King sailed fourteen days later, with orders that, 'after having taken the necessary measures for securing yourself and people, and for the preservation of the stores and provisions, you are immediately to proceed to the cultivation of the flax plant'.[24]

Finally, there are the comments of the officers when the hopes for Norfolk Island failed to materialize – as one reflected, 'the scheme of being able to assist the East Indies with naval stores, in case of a war, must fall to the ground'.[25] Clearly these hopes were real. There is more to the flax scheme, for, as with the breadfruit venture, British authorities did not give up their hopes when it did not initially succeed; but I have told you enough for you to know that it was an important motive in the decision to colonize New South Wales.

*

Cotton also figured in arrangements for the expedition. There are a number of indications in Phillip's letters that he began to consult Banks about the colony immediately on being offered the governorship of it in September 1786. On 30 October 1786, he reminded Nepean of the need to obtain cotton seeds. Nepean accordingly wrote to William Singleton, a Wigan manufacturer, who replied that he was sure 'cotton will thrive in [the] South Seas', and offered to supply different kinds of seed for trial plantings. Phillip subsequently took on more seeds and plants at Rio de Janeiro. Following Phillip's explicit instruction, King planted cotton immediately on landing at Norfolk Island, but this evidently did not succeed, for Phillip later reported that 'of the cotton seed brought from England very little vegetated'.[26]

Phillip also took on some cochineal insects and the nopal (prickly pear) plants they live on at Rio de Janeiro on the voyage out. The story of these insects and the reddish-purple dye derived from their bodies is a curious one. On conquering Mexico, the Spanish found the Aztecs using the dye, and, keeping its origins secret, they gained a monopoly of it. By the mid-eighteenth century, there was strong demand for it in Europe, where it sold for more than 14 shillings per pound. From 1759 onwards, the British Society of Arts, Commerce and Manufactures offered a prize to whoever might produce twenty-five pounds in a single year in Jamaica.

Then, at the beginning of the 1770s, the Portuguese found colonies of the insect on Santa Catarina Island off the southern coast of Brazil. The viceroy established a large plantation there, from which he dispensed plants and insects freely to ships and to other parts of Brazil. Phillip conducted breeding experiments in his cabin while in the Portuguese navy, but his insects died during the winter when he patrolled off Colonia in the River Plate. Nonetheless, his experiment convinced him that the insects might be 'carried into our West India islands and there bred to the great advantage of the nation, as well as to the very great profit of the planter'.[27]

On the way to New South Wales, Phillip repeated his experiment. These insects survived the first winter in New South Wales, but there is no mention of them thereafter. But the purport of Phillip's having carried cotton seed and cochineal insects on the voyage out is clear. If cotton would grow in New South Wales, and if the insects could be established there, Britain would have another source of fibre for its manufacturing, and a sought-after dye, both of which might be produced cheaply by a convict labour force – in other words, New South Wales had a role to play in the *Bounty* scheme.

There is no overt evidence in the way in which the First Fleet was equipped that the Pitt administration intended to make New South Wales an immediate source of spices. When we consider the range of plants that Banks sent out to New South Wales on the First Fleet and later, though, and those that Phillip and others sent back to him, we may readily see that he intended the colony to participate in the global exchanges he was pursuing.[28] The introduction of spices and Asian fruits into the antipodean colony would have been a logical, and short, next step.

*

It is clear, then, that Pitt and his colleagues did indeed anticipate significant returns from the government's investment in a convict colony in New South Wales. Rather than a simple 'dumping of convicts' scheme, the plan bore on Britain's commercial and strategic endeavours in the vast oceanic world between the great capes.

It was a scheme that carried considerable risks and, given the distance from England and from other sources of supplies, and also the nature of the colonists, it might easily have failed. But it did not; rather, despite the early difficulties, it succeeded beyond expectation. When we consider modern Australia, we may see that the Botany Bay scheme has been the most striking penal experiment in history.

Conclusion

There are a number of central points to be made about the Pitt administration's decision to establish a convict colony at Botany Bay.

First, the decision to resume transportation was a deliberate one. It was by no means inevitable that it should have been taken. In 1779, consequent upon the Bunbury Committee's recommendations, the North administration had begun preparations to build two large 'penitentiary houses', where men and women convicts would be forced to contemplate their misdeeds and set to useful tasks. True, by 1786 progress in building these had been so slow as to be almost non-existent. Still, the Pitt administration might have continued with the project, and thus advanced the emergence of the modern prison as represented by Millbank (1816) and Pentonville (1840–2) by some decades. This would have constituted a very significant change to British penal practice, which Pitt and his colleagues chose not to undertake. Rather, they decided to legislate the encompassing penal act of August 1784 (24 Geo III, c. 56), with its provision that convicts might be transported anywhere beyond the seas.

In part, this act represented a deliberate return to a long-established practice, that of 'exporting' an intractable social problem. It also represented an affirmation of William Eden's view that convicts 'might be compelled to dangerous expeditions; or be sent to establish new colonies, factories, and settlements on the coasts of Africa, and on small islands for the benefit of navigation'.[1] This rationale was endorsed in

1785, when the Beauchamp Committee recommended that a convict colony be established at Das Voltas Bay, but with the important qualification that this should be done 'so far only as the commercial and political benefits of a settlement on the southwest coast of Africa may be deemed of sufficient consequence to warrant the expense inseparable from such an undertaking'.[2]

With the 'in principle' decision to resume transportation, the real question became: to where? Honduras proved a fizzer; public opinion forced the administration to abandon the Lemain scheme; and Das Voltas Bay turned out to be unsuitable. As Pitt told parliament in February 1786, 'the great difficulty lay in fixing upon a fit place for the transportation of convicts'.[3] There is some evidence that, at this point, Pitt and his colleagues did contemplate making a permanent change to Britain's punishment for lesser felonies, with Pitt remarking that 'if it should happen that the mode prescribed by the act should not be thought literally practicable, His Majesty's servants would very soon substitute another mode of punishment in its stead'.[4]

But they did not do so. In choosing Botany Bay, Pitt and his colleagues signified that they thought it a suitable site for transportation. It is sometimes asked why they didn't send a survey ship out, as they did to Das Voltas Bay? The answer is straightforward. Cook was the finest navigator and chart-maker of his time, and Banks a pre-eminent naturalist. What reason did Pitt and his colleagues have to think their reports were unsound?

Neither was the decision for Botany Bay hastily taken. It developed over seven years, the idea having first been raised in by Banks in 1779, and thereafter considered at intervals until August 1786. It may even have had a longer gestation, given that it turned in part on knowledge produced by Cook's voyages, particularly the first (1768–71) and second (1772–5). It is noteworthy that both Cook and Banks pointed out that the Thames River area of the north island of New Zealand was suitable for colonization.[5]

As K.M. Dallas and Geoffrey Blainey said long ago, while the fact of the convicts may explain why they were used in the colonization, it does not explain the choice of the site – in Dallas's words, 'The First Fleet was a well-planned naval expedition sent to seize and fortify a naval base; the convicts were what they had always been – the servants of mercantilist interests'; and in Blainey's, 'Two questions should be involved in explaining why Botany Bay was settled in 1788. The first is why Britain in the 1780s sought an overseas place to which convicts could be sent … The second question is why Britain selected Australia rather than another land of exile'.[6]

*

The traditional account of the reasons for colonizing New South Wales developed in the nineteenth century. Advanced by the most notable historians of Australia's development, it had gathered great force by the middle decades of the twentieth century. The views of Dallas and Blainey did little to diminish this force and this old explanation has continued strong, despite mounting evidence of its severe limitations. More recently, it has been repeated by David Mackay, Alan Atkinson and Thomas Keneally.

And yet – to use an expression beloved of Manning Clark – it is fatally flawed. The major reason for this is that it does not connect the Botany Bay decision to anything other than the loss of the American colonies and the accumulation of British criminals at home. In one of the poems of his old age, when he thought his facility was fading, W.B. Yeats had the circus ringmaster plead, 'What can I but enumerate old themes?'[7] This is just what the traditionalist historians have done. With the old, supposedly tried and true, explanation in mind, they went to the documents in *Historical Records of New South Wales* and found it confirmed. The many complaints by county authorities to the Home Office and by local jailers to Duncan Campbell offered a second confirmation – if one were needed. And there the historians let their investigations rest. They did not seek among the voluminous records of the 1780s for other factors, specifically those of commercial ambition, international politics, strategic imperatives and naval needs. By neglecting these factors they were able to dismiss the significance of the last paragraphs of the Heads of a Plan, and to deny that these other motives had anything to do with the decision to colonize New South Wales.

Within this severely limited perspective, there were many specific instances of omission and blindness. Let me indicate some of these.

I'll start with the business of cost. In the mid-1780s, it was costing the government about £28 per year to keep a male convict on a hulk in the Thames (not taking into account the value of his labour). In August 1786, Evan Nepean produced figures to show that the cost over three and a half years (i.e., a six-month voyage and three years in the settlement) of sending the initial draft of 750 convicts to New South Wales would be about £34 per person per annum. By December, however, responding to a request from Pitt for more details, he and Sir Charles Middleton had revised this figure upwards to £45; and it increased further as more and more items were added to the First Fleet. By 1790, the cost of this first expedition had risen to £63 per convict per annum. (This last figure excludes the cost of the *Guardian*'s voyage.)[8]

Contrary to the traditionalists' claims, the Botany Bay venture was an expensive one. Pitt knew this at the time the First Fleet was mounting; and he implicitly conceded as much in parliament in February 1791, when the Third Fleet was gathering and voices were raised against continuing transportation to New South Wales. Having invested heavily in establishing the new colony, he argued, it made sense to continue to use it:

> no cheaper mode of disposing of the convicts, he was satisfied, could be found. The chief expense of the establishment of the colony was already passed and paid. Why, then, were they, unless strong reasons indeed operated to enforce the measure, to begin *de novo*, and make a new colony? And where it could be made to more advantage he really was stranger.[9]

In one of those curious omissions the traditionalists are given to, Shaw seized on only part of this statement, arguing: "'no cheaper mode of disposing of the convicts could be found", declared Pitt in the House of Commons, and that has to be explained by those who urge that other reasons were more important'.[10] But Pitt was speaking in 1791, not 1786, and he was discussing the cost of the Third, not the First, Fleet. His point was that the major expenses of establishing the colony having already been met, there was *now* no cheaper way of disposing of the convicts. The difference is significant.

When I was interviewed before receiving my first grant to research the Botany Bay decision in British archives, one member of the panel remarked that he hoped I would not spend (he meant, 'waste') my time going through files others had already investigated thoroughly. We know that the traditionalists had read through the files in the HO 42 series (Domestic Papers of George III), for these contain the many complaints from county officials about the government's failure to clear their jails of transport convicts. It's a good thing I did not heed this advice, for these files also contain Duncan Campbell's and Evan Nepean's calculations of the likely cost of the Botany Bay venture, calculations which show that the decision was not taken overnight, and that it was carefully prepared for.

The traditionalists missed more things in these and other files. There is Evan Nepean's suggestion that, in view of the opposition to Lemain, the administration look rather to Das Voltas Bay (HO 42/1). There is John Call's long proposal for the colonization of New South Wales or New Zealand, and Norfolk Island or New Caledonia, so as to obtain naval materials. This was published anonymously and incompletely in *Historical Records of New South Wales*, but the manuscript version was annotated by Nepean: 'Copy of a paper left with Lord Sydney by Colonel Call' (HO 42/7). There are the letters between Nepean and William Sharrow concerning how the New Zealand flax should be worked (HO 42/8, 9, HO 43/2). There is the version of the letter to the Treasury Board, drafted by Nepean on 21 August then backdated to 18 August (HO 35/7). Most notably, there is Nepean's letter of June 1786 to the Treasury Secretaries, in which he indicates that Pitt has determined that the convicts should be used to establish a settlement south of the equator (T 1/632). Why did the traditionalists not see these things?

In general, the traditionalists limited their enquiries to familiar things. Why did none of them analyse in detail how Duncan Campbell kept the convicts on the hulks? (Actually, it is only proper to point out that one person did. As a young man, Wilfrid Oldham went from Adelaide to London in the 1920s, and wrote a doctoral dissertation on transportation and the hulks system. However, this study was not published until 1990, long after his death. Oldham's conclusions were very similar to mine. I believe that if his study had been published earlier, it would have been impossible for Clark and his colleagues to write of the origin of the New South Wales colony as they did.)

Why did none of them investigate the actual situation concerning naval materials, in England and in India, to see if the paragraphs in Heads of a Plan reflected a clear historical need?[11]

Then there are the distortions. I have already given two instances by Shaw. Here are two more. Early in the first volume of *The Europeans in Australia*, Alan Atkinson ringingly dismisses the naval stores motive, declaring that 'Nothing could be further from the truth'. He then vaguely tells readers that the British occupied Norfolk Island 'during 1788'. Not until 141 pages later does he mention that Phillip had been instructed to do so; and he does not mention at all that this instruction was intended to prevent any other European power from possessing it. Neither does he point out that this threat was made real by the arrival of Lapérouse's ships at Botany Bay on 25 January 1788. Nor does he explain why European maritime nations should have been interested in Norfolk Island, a remote speck in the Pacific Ocean. If he had, he would have had to admit that it had only timber and flax to offer, and that these were therefore the only possible reasons for Britain's and France's being interested in it. Had Atkinson admitted these things, he would have been unable to write so dismissively: '[New South Wales] was so far from Europe that transported men and women would find it hard to get back. Also, it was useless. Because it was useless the people who were sent there would work for nothing but their own survival.'[12]

In his recent first volume of *Australians*, Thomas Keneally also briefly mentions the controversy over the naval materials paragraphs of

Heads of a Plan, only to conclude: 'The document declares itself at its opening sentence: "Heads of a plan for effectually disposing of convicts."'[13] His failure to give readers the second half of the title: 'and rendering their transportation reciprocally beneficial to themselves and to the state, by the establishment of a colony in New South Wales' must have been deliberate.

There are also plain errors in the traditionalist account. It was simply wrong for Shaw to claim, in rejecting Blainey's views, that flax 'played no particular part' in the consideration of a new commercial treaty with Russia. As I have shown, it was a central consideration in August and September 1786, at the time of the Botany Bay decision. It was also wrong of him to say that no one knowledgeable in the business of working flax went on the First Fleet.[14]

Then there are the outrageous statements reflecting nothing but prejudice and a desire to shock. Robert Hughes had no evidence for his calumny that Duncan Campbell was 'crooked'; and John Molony's statement that 'the British decision to send Governor Arthur Phillip to found a penal settlement at Botany Bay ... was made with breath-taking nonchalance and almost criminal negligence' was equally ill-considered.[15]

Publishers, too, have wilfully promoted these old and blinkered views. For example, Melbourne University Press keeps reissuing Manning Clark's *A History of Australia* in various forms, the first volume of which appeared in 1962. Some of the analysis in it was outdated at the time, and this situation hasn't improved in the succeeding decades. Clark's views are also regularly recycled in school texts and newspaper articles, as though no new insights have emerged since the mid-twentieth century.

*

What, you might well ask, enabled me to see past these old assumptions when the leading historians couldn't? The answer is curious.

As he responded to Blainey's arguments, Geoffrey Bolton grew more willing to entertain the possibility that there may have been motives other than the 'dumping of convicts' one, conceding at one point that he and his colleagues might 'have all missed a number of considerations obvious to a fresh mind coming to the question unencumbered by the presuppositions which specialists in the period may form'.[16]

I think that my having been trained in English literature put me in the way of doing so. Not having been educated in the prevailing view of modern Australia's origins, I was able to see its limitations, and to approach the records with a mind not directed by deep-seated assumptions. And, as I mentioned in the Introduction, these records proved very much more extensive than historians had previously known. Also, my reading of eighteenth-century geography books gave me the means to understand how informed people then viewed the world beyond Europe.

So far as I can tell, the traditional explanation of Botany Bay became so powerful because, with a strong sense of how the nation had developed socially, politically and economically, the historians looked back from the mid-twentieth century to its 1780s beginning and saw a mass of convicts. I have tried instead to put myself in the place of the economic and strategic planners and politicians who guided Britain's affairs in the last decades of the eighteenth century, and looked outwards from London – to Europe, with its intense national rivalries; about the watery Atlantic world, with its islands and coastlines and shipping routes and raw materials; far across the Levant to South and East Asia; and to the Pacific Ocean beyond, which then offered large opportunities for economic expansion.

Different perspectives can produce sharply different analyses, and our unexamined assumptions can limit historical understanding. As Philip Lawson has pointed out, if we go by the length of the relevant parliamentary debates and reports of public discussion in Hanoverian Britain, 'India took up far more time in public and private deliberation than America, at least up to 1774.' A preoccupation with America, Lawson thought, had quite distorted the study of Britain's mid-eighteenth-century history: 'The obsession with America has been evident in works on the eighteenth century since the last [i.e., nineteenth] century, and the justification for this bias is never questioned or ... even acknowledged.' Then, with the work of new generation of historians in mind, he asked:

> Is the American obsession to continue? If so, then scholars will continue to be victims of an old mythology. To break out of this tiresome framework, the scope of the debate needs expanding. The 1760s and 1770s are special not simply because of the American problem but also for the imperial questions raised elsewhere, India and Quebec in particular, which proved equally intractable and difficult to answer. In the narrow focus on America, historians have ... been misleading their audience for far too long.[17]

The same general point can be made about the mid-1780s and the Botany Bay decision: historians have overlooked India, strategic needs and commercial ambitions in their preoccupation with the convict problem. It was not accidental that Pitt should have made his first major task the legislating of a satisfactory system for the government of India. Nor was it mere idiosyncrasy that led Henry Dundas, effectively if not formally the Secretary of State for India,[18] to tell Sydney, the nominal head of the new India Board, that they must take it 'for granted that India is the quarter to be first attacked', that they 'must never lose sight of keeping such a force there, as will be sufficient to baffle all surprise'; nor to tell parliament after Nootka Sound that the administration had been 'contending not for a few miles, but a large world'.[19]

With the notable exceptions of Dallas and Blainey, what the historians of the Botany Bay decision have missed is its imperial dimension. It was always wrong of the traditionalists to proceed on the assumption that Botany Bay was entirely unconnected to concerns and activities elsewhere. They would probably respond that they were simply not persuaded by the evidence of other motives. To continue this disbelief into the twenty-first century, however, is to fly in the face of now-abundant information.

Still, such distortion has a long history in Australia. After two and a half years of effort at Sydney, in the face of an initially recalcitrant labour force, surly marine officers, the wreck of supply ships and a long *el niño*-induced drought, Phillip had achieved some social cohesion and made substantial progress in establishing a food supply for the colony. In July 1790, he told Banks that he had had 'many as fine figs as ever I tasted in Spain or Portugal'. In April 1792, he wrote that 'all our fruit trees thrive well, and I have this year gathered about three hundredweight of very fine grapes … I have oranges but they are not yet ripe … We have now vegetables in abundance. At Parramatta they are now served daily to the convicts.' 'Still', he cautioned, 'you may be told that the country will not produce a cabbage.'[20]

In 1792, on his way to Sydney, Major Grose met some disgruntled officers at the Cape of Good Hope, who told him he was going to a place of dearth and despondency. On arrival, he found the reality quite different. Indeed, he was astonished by the verdant and productive state of the colony – as he reported to Nepean, 'instead of the rock I expected to see, I find myself surrounded with gardens that flourish and produce fruit of every description. Vegetables are here in great abundance, and I live in as good a house as I wish for. I am given the farm of my predecessor, which produces a sufficiency to supply my family with everything I have occasion for.'[21]

*

There is a lesson here. Only when we have replaced clichés repeated without examination from one generation to the next with accurate analysis of the full documentary record, and broadened our perspectives to include the imperial dimension, shall we at last have an authentic understanding of the beginnings of modern Australia.

In its intricacies and its extensions, the real story of the Botany Bay decision is very different from the meagre one the traditionalist historians have told, and much more interesting. I hope you have enjoyed it.

THE FIRST FLEET

Thus, under the blessing of God, was happily completed, in eight months and one week, a voyage which, before it was undertaken, the mind hardly dared venture to contemplate, and on which it was impossible to reflect without some apprehensions as to its termination. This fortunate completion of it, however, afforded even to ourselves as much matter of surprise as of general satisfaction; for in the above space of time we had sailed five thousand and twenty-one leagues; had touched at the American and African continents; and had at last rested within a few days' sail of the antipodes of our native country, without meeting any accident in a fleet of eleven sail, nine of which were merchantmen that had never before sailed in that distant and imperfectly explored ocean: and when it is considered, that there was on board a large body of convicts, many of whom were embarked in a very sickly state, we might be deemed peculiarly fortunate, that of the whole number of all descriptions of persons coming to form the new settlement, only thirty-two had died since their leaving England, among whom were to be included one or two deaths by accident; although previous to our departure it was generally conjectured, that before we should have been a month at sea one of the transports would have been converted into a hospital ship.

—DAVID COLLINS,

An Account of the English Colony in New South Wales, 1798

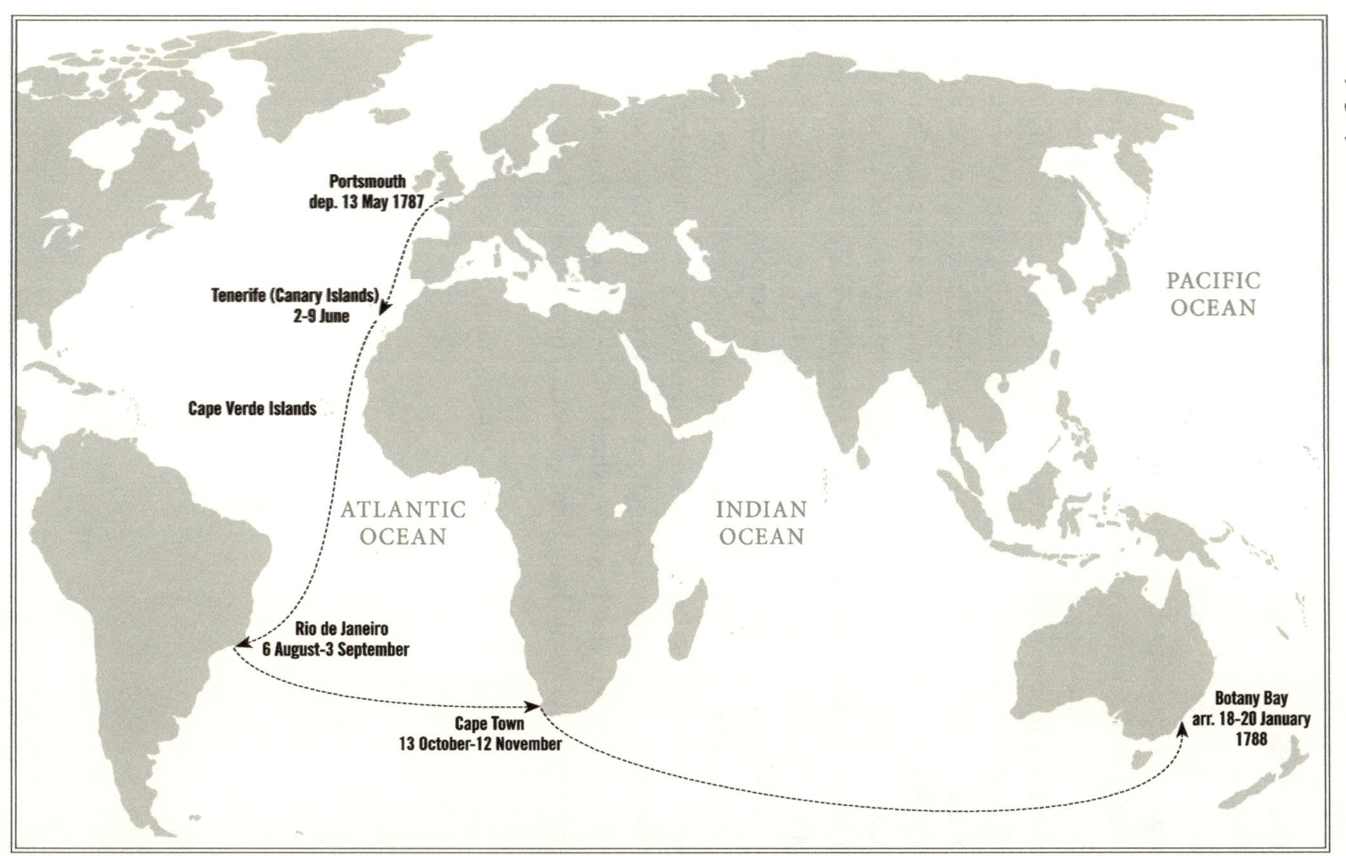

PACIFIC OCEAN
ATLANTIC OCEAN
INDIAN OCEAN
Portsmouth dep. 13 May 1787
Tenerife (Canary Islands) 2-9 June
Cape Verde Islands
Rio de Janeiro 6 August-3 September
Cape Town 13 October-12 November
Botany Bay arr. 18-20 January 1788

Preface

Surprising as it is, this is the first extended study of the mounting of the First Fleet that carried the officials, marines and convicts who began the British colonization of New South Wales in 1788.

It is based on some 2500 documents that I have collected over the past thirty-five years, and that Dr Natasha Weir and I have transcribed and edited. I have told the story of this gathering in *Botany Bay: The Real Story*. While this long process may reflect no particular merit except persistence, it is also true that such a study as this could not properly have been undertaken without a detailed knowledge of the extended documentary record.

Despite its being so extensive, it is clear that even this record is not complete. Much of the planning was undertaken in conversations among officials at the Home Office, Treasury, Admiralty and Navy Board, and First Fleet officers such as Arthur Phillip (governor) and John White (chief surgeon). Also, numbers of the documents that were created are now lost to history. But while some aspects of the venture remain obscure (e.g. Phillip's appointment), most can now be elucidated in considerable detail.

Editorial practices

In editing the documents we have mostly modernized spelling, capitalization and punctuation. (The principal exception is that we have left in their original form legal documents, such as Letters-Patent and Acts of Parliament.) Sometimes, in the interest of readier comprehension, we have also broken up very long passages into shorter paragraphs. While misspellings have been silently corrected, we have indicated where we have corrected obviously wrong words. We have standardized the spelling of personal and geographical names.

To avoid repetition, I have throughout referred to the Treasury and Admiralty Boards simply as Treasury and Admiralty, but retain the full titles for the Navy Board and Board of Trade.

INTRODUCTION

THE FIRST FLEET CARRYING the Botany Bay colony's officials, marines, convicts, animals, plants and supplies set out from Portsmouth harbour in the early morning of Sunday, 13 May 1787.

Comprising eleven ships – two Royal Navy ships, six convict transports and three storeships – it wasn't really a 'fleet'. A more accurate characterization would be 'squadron' or, better, 'convoy'. Still, 'fleet' is how it is known in Australian history, so that is the term I shall continue to use.

The First Fleet has had possibly a worse press than the decision to establish a convict colony at Botany Bay. Manning Clark wrote that 'an indescribable hopelessness and confusion dominated the scene' as the ships gathered at Portsmouth.[1] A.G.L. Shaw thought that the government 'did not seriously consider the needs of a new settlement, penal or otherwise'.[2] Jonathan King wrote that 'bureaucratic sloth, poor communications, faulty equipment and bad conditions' delayed the departure of the Fleet.[3] David Mackay held that 'the despatch of the First Fleet to Botany Bay was a reckless act on the part of a desperate ministry … The expedition itself was poorly organized and badly equipped'.[4] Robert Hughes found that the planning of the expedition was marked by 'muddle and lack of foresight'.[5] John Molony spoke extravagantly of 'criminal negligence'.[6] Mollie Gillen first pointed to 'muddled' preparations and 'real deficiencies in preparing for the settlement', then reached a crescendo with the view that the very colonization was a 'monstrous crime'.[7] Charles Wilson strained to equal her in hyperbole:

> The execution of everything essential … to the satisfactory despatch of the Fleet and its successful transportation of its passengers and their settlement on arrival in New South Wales rested more [than with Phillip] with an ill-chosen, ill-organized, contentious and unwilling body of what passed for public servants in a dozen ministries and institutions, and a venal and corrupt body of private contractors.[8]

*

Underlying such comments are the same instinctive assumptions and lack of attention to detail that characterized the historians' treatment of the decision to colonize New South Wales.

There is also a myriad mistakes. Clark wrote luridly that, at Portsmouth, 'the women convicts lolled on the decks in indescribable filth and their all too scanty clothing'.[9] This false assertion is based on something Governor Arthur Phillip wrote: 'the situation in which the magistrates sent the women on board the *Lady Penrhyn* stamps them with infamy – though almost naked, and so very filthy, that nothing but clothing them could have prevented them from perishing'.[10] But Phillip was commenting on the condition of the women as they arrived from regional jails to the holding one in London before being put on board the *Lady Penrhyn* in the Thames. It is not a description of how they were neglected at Portsmouth. Once under the supervision of the First Fleet officers and surgeons at Plymouth and Portsmouth, the women were bathed, clothed, fed properly and had their ailments treated. Clark grossly misrepresented the real situation.

Mind you, he has some distinguished company. Hughes thundered that 'the Fleet was under-victualled by its crooked contractor, Duncan Campbell'.[11] He was wrong on three counts here. As I show in *Botany Bay: The Real Story*, Campbell was not 'crooked'.[12] Neither was he the contractor for the First Fleet: William Richards Jr was; and he did not stint the rations. William Bowes Smyth, the surgeon on the *Lady Penrhyn*, wrote that 'few marines or soldiers going out on a foreign service under government were ever better, if so well provided for as these convicts are'. The marine officer Watkin Tench recorded that 'the provisions served on board were good, and of a much superior quality to those usually supplied by contract'. When the colonists were at last on land at Sydney, David Collins, the deputy judge-advocate, wrote: 'the high health which was apparent in every countenance was to be attributed not only to the refreshments we met with at Rio de Janeiro and the Cape of Good Hope, but to the excellent quality of the provisions with which we were supplied by Mr Richards Jr, the contractor'.[13] Whom should we rather believe – the art critic whose historical research was inadequate; or people on the spot who knew what they were taking about?

Shaw, too, comprehensively panned the organization of the venture: 'No farmers were sent out, no skilled craftsmen or mechanics, no person "knowledgeable in flax-dressing" ... no anti-scorbutics ... insufficient surgical supplies, even for the marines ... overcrowding on the ships'.[14] The trouble is, none of these charges is true, as I shall show.

There's an obvious way of showing up the falseness of these views and assertions. Altogether, the people on the First Fleet numbered at least 1420 on embarkation; and with deaths and births *en route*, about 1373 reached Sydney.[15] David Collins wrote:

Thus, under the blessing of God, was happily completed, in eight months and one week, a voyage which, before it was undertaken, the mind hardly dared venture to contemplate, and on which it was impossible to reflect without some apprehensions as to its termina-tion. This fortunate completion of it, however, afforded even to ourselves as much matter of surprise as of general satisfaction; for in the above space of time we had sailed five thousand and twenty-one leagues;[16] had touched at the American and African continents; and had at last rested within a few days sail of the antipodes of our native country, without meeting any accident in a fleet of eleven sail, nine of which were merchantmen that had never before sailed in that distant and imperfectly explored ocean: and when it is considered, that there was on board a large body of convicts, many of whom were embarked in a very sickly state, we might be deemed peculiarly fortunate, that of the whole number of all descriptions of persons coming to form the new settlement, only thirty-two had died since their leaving England, among whom were to be included one or two deaths by accident; although previous to our departure it was generally conjectured, that before we should have been a month at sea one of the transports would have been converted into a hospital ship.[17]

Now, Duncan Campbell said that a good result for a convict voyage across the Atlantic Ocean was a 10 per cent death rate, but that the average over an extended period was about 14 per cent.[18] Yet, during a much longer and more difficult voyage, the First Fleet death rate was about 2 per cent. It would have been impossible for Phillip and his officers to have achieved this success if the ships were as poorly equipped and provisioned as the historians have claimed.

Behind such individual errors lies an abiding fault in the writing of history in and of Australia. All too often, later writers have simply accepted what earlier ones have said without ascertaining its accuracy, so that mistakes have been passed from one generation to the next.

The identification of the *Sirius* as an East Indiaman offers one good example of this habit. This characterization was evidently first made by M. Barnard Eldershaw (the *nom-de-plume* of Marjorie Barnard and Flora Eldershaw) in *Phillip of Australia* in 1938.[19] It was thereafter frequently repeated, including by me, when I simply followed what those before me had said.[20] Graeme Henderson and Myra Stanbury corrected it in 1988, when they pointed out that Philip King's description of it as an 'East country man' meant that it was built for the Baltic rather than the East India trade, a point confirmed by details of its construction. Yet still the mistaken characterization goes on, most recently by David Hill in *1788*.[21]

Let me give a more serious example of this persistent failure to assess evidence rigorously. In 1935, W.S. Campbell published a very short article, in which he announced confidently that he had 'solved' the puzzle of why Arthur Phillip was appointed governor of the Botany Bay colony: he felt 'sure that Phillip's appointments were due to the influence of Sir George Rose', for the pair had been neighbours near Lyndhurst in the New Forest.[22]

Showing all the enthusiasm of the amateur, and none of the discrimination of the professional, and also showing no awareness of the ironies of his story, Campbell related how he had recently travelled to Lyndhurst; and that he had 'failed altogether to obtain any information respecting Phillip, or whereabouts his farm was situated. 'The whole place has been altered,' he reported, 'and the fine mansion once occupied by Sir George Rose at Chuffnells [actually, Cuffnells] has been converted into a hotel'.

Nonetheless, Campbell pressed his case. Rose, he said, had been 'Head' of the Navy. (Wrong. Lord Howe was the First Lord of the Admiralty, and Philip Stephens Secretary of the Admiralty Board. Rose was Secretary of the Treasury.) After citing Howe's unfavourable response to Sydney's advice that Phillip was to be appointed, Campbell quoted a supposed reply from Sydney (which I don't believe is in fact by Sydney; but as Campbell gave no source, it is impossible to verify this); and he then identified Rose as the 'Minister'. (Wrong again. William Pitt was the Prime Minister.)

Campbell then told how he went to the Admiralty and the Public Record Office in search of information about Phillip's appointment, only to draw a complete blank. Mystifyingly, he therefore concluded, 'This all tends to show … that Sir George Rose appointed Phillip, but that he made no record of the appointment'.

Well! So we have an explanation of an historical 'puzzle', but one entirely lacking in evidence, except *perhaps* the circumstantialities that Phillip and Rose were neighbours in the New Forest, and that Phillip named the area to the west of Sydney that we know as Parramatta 'Rose Hill'.

It was routine for eighteenth-century explorers to name geographical features of a new country after prominent public figures, who may or may not have been patrons. Phillip named Sydney Cove (after Lord Sydney);

the Carmarthen Hills (after the Marquess of Carmarthen, the Foreign Secretary of State); the Lansdowne Hills (after the Marquess of Lansdowne, the former Prime Minister); the Nepean River (after Evan Nepean); and Pitt Water, an expanse in the mouth of the Hawkesbury River (respectively, after William Pitt, the Prime Minister, and Lord Hawkesbury, the President of the Board of Trade). His naming Rose Hill might be evidence of a connection to George Rose, were it supported by some documentation, such as letters between them. However, while Phillip wrote many letters from New South Wales to Sydney, Nepean and Banks, and at least one to Lansdowne, none is known to Pitt, Carmarthen, Hawkesbury or Rose. Campbell's idea was a will-o'-the-wisp, which should never have been pursued nor publicized.

But it was, and it developed a corporeality it simply didn't deserve. In 1938, Barnard Eldershaw repeated it. True, they were circumspect, saying that 'nothing definite is known', and that it was only 'possible' that Rose was Phillip's patron;[23] but their very mentioning the idea gave it legs. Then, in 1962, Manning Clark gave it a gee-up when he said that Phillip 'was again farming at Lyndhurst when Lord Sydney offered him the position of governor of New South Wales', an assertion for which, once more, there is not the thinnest shred of evidence. J.J. Auchmuty heeled it along in his edition of *The Voyage of Governor Phillip to Botany Bay* in 1970; and John Moore set it going again in 1987.[24]

The currency of this idea now extends through more than seventy years, with David Hill repeating it in 2008: 'There is some indication that Sir George Rose, the Under-Secretary of the Treasury, was the minister responsible for making the decision. Rose's estates were at Cuffnels [sic] near Lyndhurst, so he was a near neighbour of Phillip, who was then a gentleman farmer in the same district'; and by Tom Keneally in 2009: 'A neighbour of Phillip's in the New Forest, Sir George Rose, Secretary of the Treasury, was involved in the costing of the enterprize, and he supported Phillip's appointment'.[25]

But consider. So far as we know, Phillip, with his wife, was on the Vernals farm at Lyndhurst only from 1766–68. The parish register shows that he became an overseer of the poor in April 1766; that he paid another to undertake this duty in April 1768; and that he ceased to hold the office at the end of July 1768.[26] In 1769 he and his wife concluded a formal separation.

Rose did not purchase the Cuffnells estate until 1784; and how frequently and for how long he was in residence thereafter is unknown, although clearly his duties at the Treasury kept him in London for much of the year. In the first half of 1784, Phillip was sailing back from India, reaching England again in late April. From October 1784 into 1785, Nepean had Phillip spying in France. In October 1785, he again obtained leave to travel in France – i.e., to spy – for another twelve months. Precisely when he returned to England again is unknown, but presumably he was there by the beginning of October 1786. Whether he returned of his own accord, or was summoned back by Nepean to prepare for Botany Bay, is also unknown.[27]

On the face of things, then, it is extremely unlikely – look, given the sixteen-year gap, let me say impossible! – that Phillip and Rose were ever 'neighbours' near Lyndhurst; and therefore, in the sheer absence of any other evidence, it is also most unlikely that Rose had any hand in Phillip's appointment.

There is in fact one piece of evidence that confirms conclusively that George Rose had nothing to do with Arthur Phillip's appointment as governor, and therefore that my criticism of the historians is valid.

In late November 1786, after first approaching Rose about the business, Newton Fowell's mother wrote to Evan Nepean, asking that the young man, who had just obtained his lieutenant's passing certificate, be appointed to one of the Royal Navy ships going out to New South Wales. Nepean replied:

Captain Phillip, who is to command on the expedition to Botany Bay, offered to take with him any young gentleman I might think fit to recommend, as a midshipman, and conceiving himself under some obligation to me, for what I know not, he promised, that if the young man behaved well, he would make him an officer, if a vacancy offered during his command.

Mr Rose, knowing my intimacy with Captain Phillip, desired me to ask him to take out a young man who had been recommended by Mr Justice Buller, which Captain Phillip refused to do, declaring that his complement of persons of that class had been completed long before. I met Mr Buller soon after, and finding that he was particularly interested in the success of his application, I offered to give him the vacancy which had been reserved for my nomination and [I] can assure you that I was particularly glad to find it was in favour of your son, Newton.[28]

Nepean's letter tells us two things. First, if Rose had engineered Phillip's appointment, he would not have had to ask the favour via Nepean; and second, Phillip would not have refused it. Nepean's having employed Phillip as a spy, and the resulting close connection between them, is an infinitely better explanation of Phillip's appointment. But like a worn-out old nag, the idea that George Rose was involved keeps limping around the Australian historical farm.

*

The desire to avoid such errors was one of my principal motivations in my long quest to recover original documents. The historiography of the First Fleet has been based on a very incomplete documentary record. True, as well as those documents published in *Historical Records of New South Wales*, historians have made use of many more – e.g., those published in *Historical Records of Australia* and in Owen Rutter's *The First Fleet*. They have used, too, many of the journals and letters of those who went on the voyage, and numbers of the unpublished sources in the British National Archives, the British Library and elsewhere.

However, even when taken together, these records still constitute an inadequate basis for making judgments about the mounting of the First Fleet and the equipping of the colonists. In 1980, I remarked: 'No one has yet described adequately the mounting of the First Fleet … A comprehensive description of this mounting would lay to rest the myths that the Pitt administration was generally indolent in assembling the Fleet, that it equipped the colonizing party poorly, and that these features reflect its callous disregard of the convicts' welfare'.[29] Now, another thirty years on, this present work fills this wide gap.

As before remarked, this is the first full-scale analysis of the *mounting* of the First Fleet. Most of the earlier works which might from their titles seem to deal with the subject, such as those by Victor Crittenden and Jonathan King, are narrative collations of original records rather than analytical studies, and are in any case concerned more with the voyage than the equipping of the expedition. They are also far from comprehensive or accurate. The relevant chapter in David Hill's *1788* is replete with error, and wildly wrong in its general conclusions. A.K. Cavanagh's account of the return of the ships is precise, but deals only with that aspect.

Only two previous studies have been soundly based. The first is that by Charles Bateson (1959, 2nd ed. 1969), but his concern was solely with the ships that constituted the fleet, which he dealt with in a few pages. The other is that by Roger Knight, which is based on an extensive knowledge of relevant records and Navy Board procedures, but which was never intended to be more than a conference paper.

In essence, the documents I have gathered have allowed me largely to reconstitute original series which have become scattered over more than two hundred years. Sometimes, original papers sent from one government department to another were returned, without copies having been taken. Attachments became separated from their covering letters. It was by no means uncommon for senior administrators in the eighteenth century to consider state papers as their own, and to take them when they left office. Later, when these private collections were dispersed, the migration of individual pieces was often widespread.[30]

Nonetheless, by the later eighteenth century, the British bureaucracy had developed firm record-keeping procedures. While it is always possible to find earlier foreshadowings of such practices, let me locate their substantial beginnings in the second half of the seventeenth century, when the two revenue-collecting departments of Customs (tax on imported and exported goods) and Excise (generally, tax on domestic produce and goods, either at the point of production or of sale) were gradually placed on a secure footing. By the turn of the eighteenth century, these branches of government were showing many of the features that we associate with a modern, professional civil service: senior officials' tenure was independent of whichever party held political power; these officials were paid a salary rather than given fees based on the revenue collected; lesser posts were no longer in the gift of politicians; those holding them were examined to ensure they had the requisite skills, particularly in mathematics; continuity of employment meant the accumulation of a broad body of experience; the collection of revenue proceeded in accordance with the law; and meticulous records were kept of goods produced or imported, and of the taxes paid on them.[31]

During the course of the eighteenth century, other government departments adopted these practices. Senior administrators held their positions for extended periods. (In the 1780s, for example, George Rose and Thomas Steele at the Treasury, Evan Nepean at the Home Office, William Fraser at the Foreign Office, Philip Stephens at the Admiralty, and Sir Charles Middleton at the Navy Board served under a series of administrations.) Again, as the sphere of operations of the Royal Navy progressively enlarged, the Admiralty and Navy Board needed to have to hand details of ships, men, supplies and finance, not only in Britain but also in North America, the West Indies, the Mediterranean and India. So the Admiralty needed to collect and file all the logs kept by the admirals, captains, commanders and lieutenants who served on its hundreds of ships, and all the correspondence to and from these officers.

The Navy Board needed to know where the ships were, what was their state of repair, who comprised their crews and when these crews were paid. As a result, there are tens of thousands each of reports, musterbooks and paybooks. The Board needed to know how many masts were in the dockyard ponds; and what were the quantities of cables, cordage, canvas and hemp in the warehouses. It needed to maintain annual contracts for the delivery of English oak, American and Baltic masts and spars and Russian hemp; and to let a myriad specific contracts for the provision of equipment, food and clothing. It needed to have details of the 'warrant' officers – masters, carpenters, gunners, cooks, surgeons – whom it appointed to the hundreds of ships; and to maintain an army of workmen, not only at the major home yards of the Thames, Portsmouth and Plymouth, but also those at New York and Charleston, Jamaica and Antigua, and Gibraltar.

The meeting of all these needs gave rise to another vast body of records. For example, the Deptford yard in the Thames was the main place for the inspection, repair and fitting out of Royal Navy ships in Britain. There are thousands of folio-sized letterbooks, each with hundreds of pages, recording the Deptford officers' correspondence with the Navy Board in the eighteenth century.

The situation was similar in other government departments. Let me give only one particular example now. After the reorganization of the old Southern and Northern Departments of State into the Home and Foreign Offices in 1782, one of Evan Nepean's tasks was to run the secret service in France, Spain and elsewhere in southern Europe. This espionage had a number of aspects. There were informers in the government departments and armed forces of the European countries, who passed information to local spies, who sent it on, directly or indirectly, to Nepean. Embassy officials and patriotic private citizens also reported back – as in mid-1785, when the ambassador to France (the Earl of Dorset) and Lord Dalrymple, who was in Paris on private affairs, sent details of a secret purpose to Lapérouse's coming voyage.[32] Nepean also often received information about the movement of enemy shipping from naval officers serving at sea, masters of merchant vessels, and smugglers. And, at moments of need, he sent agents fluent in European languages into these countries to obtain particular information – as in 1784–85, when he had Arthur Phillip report on activity in the French dockyards.[33]

In 1790, after news reached Europe that Spanish officers had seized British trading ships at distant Nootka Sound, on Vancouver Island, relations between Britain and Spain reached flash point. At the height of this crisis, Nepean was receiving, from a variety of sources, weekly reports of the number of ships in the Spanish fleet and the disposition of these ships, information which he carefully collated and entered into the registers that he controlled, information which was then available to the politicians who were contemplating ending the crisis by destroying the enemy's fleet.[34]

The growth of this administrative competence means that the records of British government departments in the 1780s are voluminous. Indeed, even a comparatively minor matter might generate a lengthy sequence of correspondence. (For example, from mid-October to mid-December 1786, the Admiralty, Navy Board, Deptford officers and its commander gave extended consideration of what size cannon the *Supply* should carry, which has left a sequence of twenty-two documents.) Even when a particular document has been lost or was not copied, given the mode of minuting then (which involved summarizing the contents of the document being responded to before recording the decision), it is often possible to know what was in the missing one.

*

It is a curious thought that the records I have gathered now allow us to know more about the mounting of the First Fleet than all but three people knew at the time. Two of these were Sir Charles Middleton, the Comptroller (Head) of the Navy Board, and Evan Nepean, the Under-Secretary of State at the Home Office. For reasons which will become clear, Nepean's view of the business was significantly broader than was Middleton's. Nonetheless, both these men knew a great deal about it; and they often took steps ahead of the necessary formalities. For example, in December 1786, somewhat irritated that Nepean had questioned his proposed disposition of people and stores on the ships, Middleton told him, 'I trust and hope that when any business of this kind is agitated again, that I may have some notice of it before it is sent officially'; and in March 1787, when Phillip was insistent, both that the convicts on board the ships at Portsmouth should be fed fresh food while they waited to depart, and that the expedition should receive more medical supplies, Middleton advised Nepean that he had 'given directions agreeable to [your] letter concerning provisions, essence of malt, wine etc., trusting to official authority in due time'. And each sympathized with the other concerning 'this disagreeable and troublesome business'.[35]

Arthur Phillip was the third person possessed of a comprehensive knowledge of the mounting of the First Fleet. Sometimes to the annoyance of other officials, he had a hand in just about every aspect of it; and, as I shall show, it was largely due to his efforts that it was as well-equipped as it was.

In general, the various lesser officials involved in the business had no significant overview of it. For example, Joshua Thomas and George Teer, the Navy Board officials most concerned with the fitting and provisioning of the ships, were not involved in the making of the legal arrangements for the colony. This was the work of the Law Officers and the Privy Council. Conversely, the personnel of these departments had no idea of the trouble the Navy Board was at in gathering the ships and fitting them out. Similarly, the marine officers who sailed on the ships had no notion of Phillip's instructions, nor of private understandings he had been given about the colony's purposes.

The documentary record I have assembled allows a much more comprehensive understanding of the venture than any previous one. It forms the basis of the story I tell here of the First Fleet – the real story.

PART ONE:
PLANNING A CONVICT COLONY

1.

Announcing the Decision

As I explain in *Botany Bay: The Real Story*, William Pitt's Cabinet met on 18 and 19 August, and decided to establish a convict colony at Botany Bay, on the eastern coast of New South Wales. No minutes of this decision, so momentous in its consequences, are known. However, the administrative steps that followed immediately afterwards confirm the fact of it.

As Home Secretary, Lord Sydney was responsible for calling Cabinet meetings. In practice, this meant that it was Evan Nepean, the Under-Secretary (or, in our terms, permanent head) of the Home Office, who summoned other Cabinet ministers and drew up agendas. While he certainly was at some, whether Nepean was present at all Cabinet meetings is unknown. However, it was not necessary for him to attend these meetings to know what the ministers were thinking. Inevitably, he was in close contact with Sydney, and, as we shall see, also with William Pitt, the Prime Minister.

Then as now, government departments could not undertake new initiatives without knowing that there was money to pay for them. On Monday, 21 August, Nepean went into the office and drafted a letter to the Treasury formally announcing the Botany Bay decision, and giving details of the scheme for colonization.[1]

When Lord Sydney had signed this letter, it went to the Treasury together with a copy of the Heads of a Plan, the three enclosures to that plan, and another two enclosures, as outlined in Sydney's letter:

- Estimate of provisions to be provided for the intended settlement on the coast of New South Wales
- Staff establishment for the settlement at New South Wales
- Messrs Turnbull, Macaulay and T. Gregory's letter of 21 August 1786 (offering to contract for the venture)[2]
- List of the tools, utensils etc. for the convicts and marines intended to proceed to New South Wales
- Estimate of clothing to serve a male convict for one year[3]

George Rose and Thomas Steele, the Treasury Secretaries,[4] received these items the same day, and entered them in the minute book as though the Board had considered them on 18 August. The reason for this subterfuge was that, by Monday, the Treasury Board had actually adjourned for the summer recess. The Secretaries also recorded that Pitt and two other Board members had on 19 August 'read and approved the minutes of yesterday'; and that the Board would next meet on 10 October. Until this date, they proceeded 'by the direction of Mr Pitt', who held the two financial portfolios of First Lord Commissioner of the Treasury and Chancellor of the Exchequer.[5]

The nature of the administrative procedure and range of the business are best conveyed by the minute itself. After summarizing the contents of Sydney's letter, the Treasury Secretaries listed the following points:

My Lords, impressed with the necessity of sending a number of convicts out of the kingdom immediately, are pleased to direct a letter to be written to the Commissioners of the Navy to take measures for providing a proper number of vessels for the conveyance of 680 male and 70 female convicts to Botany Bay in New South Wales, together with the provisions, necessaries and implements for husbandry which are judged requisite for the use of them and the marines who are to go to the same place on duty, giving notice that one of the ships must be fitted up for the accommodation of the above-mentioned number of women so as to keep them separate from the men.

Acquaint the Commissioners that the marine corps will be supplied during their passage out by the Victualling Department, but that provisions must be sent for their use after their landing, and that the daily rations for them, for the convicts, and for some women who it is expected may be prevailed upon to come to the new settlement from the neighbourhood will amount to one thousand, and that a quantity equal to two years consumption must be provided for them over and above the provisions for the convicts during the voyage.

Acquaint the Commissioners of the Navy that my Lords are of opinion it will be most advisable to give notice that they are ready to receive proposals for the passage, and the victualling the convicts during the same, and for a stock of provisions to be landed equal to two years consumption at the rate of one thousand rations a day.

Transmit to the Commissioners a list of the tools and utensils of husbandry to be provided for the marines and the convicts, and a list of the clothing and bedding, and acquaint them that my Lords will approve of their directing the person who shall take the contract on terms the most advantageous to the public, to purchase the same on the commission usually allowed. When my Lords have the particulars of the surgeon's instruments, medicines and necessaries for the sick, they will direct the same to be provided under the inspection of the Commissioners for the Sick and Hurt.

Acquaint Mr Nepean for the information of Lord Sydney that if the commanding officer who shall be entrusted with the care of the service shall draw bills from the Cape Verde Islands or from the Cape of Good Hope for the purchase of cattle, seed grain or other necessaries, my Lords will order the same to be paid, representing to his Lordship however the necessity of the commanding officer's transmitting vouchers of such expenditure.

Acquaint Mr Nepean also that when my Lords are informed of the particulars of the quantities and kinds of merchandize which it will be necessary to put on board the ship of war or tender previous to their sailing, my Lords will order the same to be provided, and that my Lords have already given directions for taking up the ships, and for providing the provisions, tools and other necessaries for the marines going out and for the convicts, and that they wait only to be acquainted with the particulars of the surgeon's instruments, medicines and necessaries for the sick, to order them also.

On 31 August, Nepean drafted a similar letter for Sydney to sign to the Admiralty, informing it of the decision and enclosing a copy of Heads of a Plan.[6] This letter advised that the Treasury had been asked to arrange for a number of vessels to convey the convicts to Botany Bay, 'together with provisions and other supplies for their subsistence, as well as tools to enable them to erect habitations, and also implements for agriculture'. It requested that the Admiralty provide 'a ship of war of a proper class' and a tender of about 200 tons burden*, both to escort the convoy and 'for other purposes after their arrival'. It further advised that three companies of marines should be sent to preserve order and to guard the settlement. (Attached to this request was the advice that these would 'be properly victualled by a commissary immediately after their landing', a proviso which was to cause considerable trouble before the Fleet sailed.) The marines' term of service was to be three years, and volunteers were to be given first preference. They were to be provided with the necessary tools and equipment. As their service while on land would be 'entirely unconnected with maritime affairs', they were then to be responsible to the Home Office.

The East India Company also needed to be told of the decision, as its royal charter gave it the exclusive monopoly of all British trade in the vast region between the Cape of Good Hope and the coasts of the Americas. Nepean drafted and Sydney signed a letter to the Company giving details of the proposed colony and asking for its agreement on 15 September, with which went the Heads of a Plan (without the attachments). The letter pointed out that the Court of Directors' 'concurrence' would not

---

* 'Tons burden' is not the weight of the ship; rather, it is a mathematical estimate of its carrying capacity.

only please His Majesty, 'but will be a means of preventing the emigration of our European neighbours to that quarter, which might be attended with infinite prejudice to the Company's affairs'. The Chairmen referred the request to the Court of Directors, which agreed on 21 September.[7]

Despite this quick agreement, there may well have been considerable opposition to the venture among the shareholders of the Company. In early October, William Richards, who was supplying the transports, told Pitt that 'the whole interest of a certain set of gentlemen that are materially affected by its adoption, have been employed to thwart every means of its being obtained'; and a few days later, the *Daily Universal Register* advised that the Company's directors were unhappy that, while the government was paying Richards £7 per ton for his ships on the outward voyage, they were paying £10 per ton for the homeward one.[8]

*

By this time, the public had also been made aware of the Botany Bay decision.[9] On 19 September, for example, the *Public Advertiser* announced that it was 'the design of government to form a settlement at Botany, on the east side of New Holland, in the Indian seas, for the reception of male and female felons sentenced by the laws of this country to transportation'; and it offered a very detailed description of the Botany Bay area taken from Hawkesworth's compilation of Cook's and Banks's journals.[10] Other London and country newspapers did likewise, often simply repeating one another's words.[11]

In the next weeks, more details of the planned expedition came out. Towards the end of the month, the *Daily Universal Register* informed readers that Captain Arthur Phillip was to be the colony's governor, with a salary of £500 per annum; and that 700 male and 150 female convicts were to be transported.[12]

The public's attention was also drawn to other motives for the decision. On 25 September, the *Birmingham Daily Gazette* reported that there were some who thought that 'besides providing a place for our convicts, from which all escape will be impracticable, the settlement may be otherwise highly beneficial to our Asiatic commerce'.[13] In the middle of October, the *Morning Chronicle* announced that the government was pursuing James Matra's scheme, then quoted two paragraphs from it, those dealing with the centrality of New South Wales to future naval operation against the Dutch and Spanish empires in the Indian and Pacific oceans. It also pointed to the prospect of obtaining masts from New Zealand. Also quoting from Matra, the *London Chronicle* told readers about 'that very valuable article of New Zealand hemp or flax plant'.[14] In December, the *London Chronicle* announced that 'the Botany Bay expedition may in the end keep in this island much of the money now sent to Holland for spices', which resonated both with Matra's scheme and the second last paragraph of Heads of a Plan.[15]

In December, there were a number of reports that the principal site of settlement was to be Norfolk Island rather than Botany Bay. The *St James's Chronicle* was the first to say so, followed by the *Daily Universal Register*. The latter paper also subsequently reported that one ship would sail ahead to the island 'to find the properest station for the first landing of the convicts'. Administration records make clear that this was never the case; but the fact that it was reported indicates that there was some knowledge abroad of official interest in the island's potential as a source of supply of naval materials. And, indeed, the *Daily Universal Register* advised the correct situation early in January 1787, when it said that the governor had 'discretionary power to land the convicts at Botany Bay, or Norfolk Island, or elsewhere, as he shall think proper. He is not particularly bound to Botany Bay; on the contrary, his command on that head is not limited'.[16]

Some of the papers were supportive of the decision. After pointing out the inconvenience of continuing to keep the convicts at home, and the impossibility of sending them to America or Africa, the *Morning Chronicle* praised Botany Bay as a site, saying that, since the convicts 'may become useful to the empire', it was reasonable to spend some public money establishing them there.[17] The *Public Advertiser* held that 'the banishment of the convicts to Botany Bay is an instance of modern humanity, for it will be little else than freedom in a new country, and a plentiful store of implements to till the land, and labour for a sustenance'.[18]

In January 1787, a number of papers advised readers that

the expedition to Botany Bay comprehends in it more than the mere banishment of our felons. It is an undertaking of humanity, for in all the islands of the South Seas, there is not a four-footed animal to be found but the hog, the dog and the rat, nor any of the grain of the other quarters of the world ... By the number of cattle now sending over of various sorts, and all the different seeds for vegetation, a capital improvement will be made in the southern part of the New World; and our ships, which may hereafter sail in that quarter of the globe, must receive refreshment in greater plenty that from the exhausted soil of Europe, considering that all New South Wales is formed of a virgin mould, undisturbed since the creation.[19]

However, public approval of the venture was certainly not general. Some reporting of it was doubtful, if respectful. In November, for example, the *Daily Universal Register* said that there was some question of the expedition's being abandoned, on the grounds of cost; then, a few days later, it gave readers figures that it must have received from Nepean, demonstrating that the difference in cost between keeping a male convict on a hulk and sending him to New South Wales was only £4 (£28 as against £32).[20] In December, however, this paper came out against the decision, on the grounds, first, that the colony would shortly become a nest of pirates, who would ravage Britain's eastern trade; and second, that the colonists would soon demand independence in the manner of the ungrateful Americans.[21]

Other notices heaped scorn upon the decision. The *Gentleman's Magazine* said that 'this plan is so wild and extravagant, that we can hardly believe it could be countenanced by any professional man after a moment's reflection'; and it pointed out that 'it is notorious that the Dutch East India ships lose more than half the recruits they take on board for their settlement in India in crossing the Line'.[22] The *Bath Chronicle* was particularly scathing:

Botany Bay still continues to be a subject of town talk, without anybody seeming to know anything about the matter. First, it is Botany Bay where the convicts are to be transported to; then it is not Botany Bay in that huge island New Holland, but the small rock called New Norfolk in the South Sea! Then it is both Botany Bay and Norfolk! Then it is neither of them, but the commodore may conveniently dispose of them at Botany Bay, or New Norfolk, or the Lord knows where! Wherever he can shoot his rubbish!

If we could really believe such folly reigns among statesmen, as to adopt any of the schemes above alluded to, we should say, it is very little difference to the bulk of the destined wretches which of those remote places they are bound for. We believe the first land that two-thirds of them will reach will be the bottom of the sea, there to make their final deposit in the bosom of the great deep; and probably there will be but a dark account of the remaining third part.[23]

*

News of the decision was soon abroad in Europe. On 19 September the Portuguese ambassador in London informed his Court of the expedition, and that Captain Arthur Phillip, who had served in the Portuguese Navy, had been given command of it.[24] In mid-October, the Spanish ambassador sent a selection of newspaper reports of the business to his Court.[25] There were persistent rumours that the Dutch government was opposed to the venture. For example, in early October one correspondent told the *Public Advertiser* that from his conversations during a recent trip to France and Holland, he thought it likely that both nations would oppose the venture, perhaps even by arming the Aborigines. Ten days later, the *Hampshire Chronicle* reported that 'the East India companies in Holland pretend to have a property in [New South Wales], though they were ill-used by the inhabitants when they attempted to settle themselves there'. There was one report that the Dutch government intended to object formally, on the grounds that Dutch navigators had been the first Europeans to discover New Holland. A number of other papers repeated this claim. At the beginning of 1787, the *Hampshire Chronicle* followed up with:

> Private letters from Holland mention that the Dutch have at this instant, either in Botany Bay, or within a few leagues of that place, several transports and two men of war, with troops, to preserve their prior claim to that part of the world. Government must certainly have heard of this, as the matter of sending out the troops last spring was notorious, although their destination was not generally known. Spain means to support Holland in this scheme; and therefore the probable consequence of our Minister's inexperience, and juvenile obstinacy, may involve this country in a war.[26]

I have never found any official correspondence to confirm this claim of Dutch opposition; however, it is by no means impossible, even though some of the details in these reports were fantastical. No diplomatic record of any such protest has ever been found, however.

*

After the ministers had drafted it and Pitt had read it at the Cockpit the evening before, the King delivered his address to open the new session of parliament on 23 January 1787. His Majesty assured members of both Houses that 'the tranquillity of *Europe* has remained uninterrupted, and that all foreign powers continue to express their friendly disposition to this country'. He announced that Britain had concluded a commercial treaty with France; that such negotiations were continuing with other nations; and that agreement had been reached with Spain concerning a disputed article in the peace treaty. He introduced budget estimates, and asked that they be voted; and that revenue and administrative reform continue. He also announced: 'My Lords and Gentlemen: A plan has been formed, by my direction, for transporting a number of convicts, in order to remove the inconvenience which arose from the crowded state of the jails in different parts of the kingdom; and you will, I doubt not, take such farther measures as may be necessary for this purpose.' In their addresses-in-reply, both Houses assured His Majesty that they would adopt this plan.[27]

Historians holding to the traditional view of the reasons for founding the Botany Bay colony have made much of the fact that at this time the King mentioned only the convict motive.[28] But this is a naïve view of what to expect in such a public address. Were the King and Cabinet really going to announce: 'We are establishing a naval base at Botany Bay, the better to conduct offensive operations against the Dutch and Spanish colonies'? To do so would have mightily alarmed Britain's recent Continental adversaries. Were they really going to say: 'We are establishing a base at Botany Bay in order to expand British trade throughout the Pacific Ocean'? To do so would have further aroused the ire of the East India Company. Much more politic was the bland commonplace that the convicts had to be shipped out because the jails were full, which was a sentiment the members of parliament could readily agree with. As Earl Camden, the Lord President of the Privy Council, remarked in advising that he would be unable to attend the meeting on Friday 12 January 1787 when Cabinet was to discuss the draft of the King's address, apart from that dealing with the unrest in Ireland, all its advices were 'no more than communications'; that is, they were announcements of decisions to parliament, not discussions of the reasons for them.[29]

2.

The Colony: Society, Law and Governance

THE BOTANY BAY COLONY WAS A very peculiar creation – as the Lord President of the Privy Council observed as it was forming, he was unable to regard this 'embryo' as either a 'settlement or colony'.[1]

Certainly, there was no precedent elsewhere in the British empire at the time. It was not founded, with the Crown's permission, either by religious separatists (as some New England colonies had been), or by merchant adventurers (Virginia). It was not a Crown colony, ruled by a vice-regal representative in conjunction with a nominated council and/or an elected assembly (Jamaica). It was not a conquered colony (New York, Quebec). It was not a commercial enclave within a foreign territory (the East India Company's 'factories' at Bombay, Madras and Calcutta). It was not even a random cluster of Britons employed in gathering raw materials (the 'logwood' settlement in Honduras).

No, Botany Bay was *sui generis*. It was a colony of convicts, administered by a handful of civil officials, and guarded by marines and two small warships. In the beginning, there were no free settlers. And, for the first time in the history of British convict transportation, it was government officials, rather than private merchants and free settlers, who were responsible for organizing the shipping out of the convicts, and their upkeep and employment on the other side of the world.

As I have explained in *Botany Bay: The Real Story* and elsewhere, there was a purpose to this colony quite unrelated to convicts. According to

European notions of international law prevailing at the time, by transferring some of their population and at least a portion of their laws to New South Wales, the British made *actual* the *preliminary* right to possess this territory that they had acquired as a consequence of Cook's having been its first discoverer, and of his having claimed it on behalf of the King.[2]

Rather than examining this situation again, however, let me now consider contemporary ideas of how this colony composed of men and women banished from their homeland for criminal activity might develop.

Society

There is no purposeful statement from August 1786 of how the Pitt administration envisaged the Botany Bay colony developing. The Heads of a Plan and Sydney's letter to the Treasury are concerned only with the symbiotic purposes of ridding the kingdom of felons and making their labour useful to the state, and with mechanisms for establishing the colony. However, there are four other documents that do cast a considerable amount of light on the administration's expectations for it.

The first of these documents is James Matra's addendum to his August 1783 proposal for a free settlement in New South Wales, which he presented to the Home Office in April 1784. Matra considered that sending the convicts thither would combine 'good policy and humanity'. 'Give them a few acres of ground, as soon as they arrive in New South Wales, in *absolute property*,' he urged,

> with what assistance they may want to till them. Let it be here remarked, that they cannot fly from the country; that they have no temptations to theft; and that they must work or starve. I likewise suppose that they are not by any means to be reproached for their former conduct. If these premises be granted me, I may reasonably conclude that it is highly probable they will be useful, [and] that it is very possible they will be moral subjects of society.
>
> Do you wish either by private prudence, or by civil policy, to reclaim offenders? Show by your treatment of them, that you think

their reformation extremely practicable, and do not hold out every moment before their eyes, the hideous and mortifying deformity of their own vices and crimes. A man's intimate and hourly acquaintance with his guilt, and the frowns and severities of the world tend more powerfully even than the immediate effects of his bad habits to make him a determined and incorrigible villain.

By the plan which I have now proposed, a necessity to continue in the place of his destination, and to be industrious is imposed on the criminal. The expense to the nation is absolutely imperceptible, comparatively with what criminals have hitherto cost government; and thus two objects, of most desirable and beautiful union, will be permanently blended: economy to the public and humanity to the individual.[3]

There are indications that this idea that transportation to the distant colony might prove the means of the convicts' redeeming themselves was a significant factor in the administration's thinking. On 23 September 1786, William Pitt reminded his friend William Wilberforce of his offer to find a suitable person to minister to the convicts. On this same day – and it cannot be coincidental – Wilberforce or one of his evangelical friends asked the Reverend Richard Johnson if he were interested in going out. Johnson later stated that the good he might do had been uppermost in his mind when he accepted the position as the colony's chaplain:

From my first hearing that a colony was about to be established … I always understood that it was the intention of government to see whether some reformation might not be affected amongst these unfortunate and abandoned people. [These] motives appear very strong and sufficient reasons for the convicts being carefully instructed in the various and important duties of morality and religion. But, when it is further considered, that convicts, as well as others, are possessed of souls that are immortal and that they must ere long appear before the solemn tribunal of God, there and then to answer for their actions – whoever considers this … must … see and allow, that all possible means should be made use of, to reclaim them from their former wicked course of life.

And Arthur Phillip wrote from the colony that he was 'serving the cause of humanity'.[4]

*

The second document is perhaps the most interesting and informative. This is a long memorandum in which Arthur Phillip presented his views of how he might conduct the voyage, and of the social policies he might pursue in the colony. Partly because it was implicitly mis-dated to March 1787 when published in *Historical Records of New South Wales*,[5] and partly because the 'dumping of convicts' view, which has dominated the historiography for so long, has obliterated all other insights, this memorandum has only rarely received the consideration it deserves. In fact, Phillip wrote it in 1786, soon after he was offered the governorship of the colony – that is, in the period between the end of September and 11 October.[6] My surmise is that he did so at the request of the administration, and after he had been briefed – certainly by Lord Sydney and Evan Nepean, very probably by Sir Joseph Banks, perhaps even by William Pitt himself. If anything is the 'blueprint' for the colony's development, this memorandum is it.

I shall discuss in another chapter what this document tells us about how Phillip thought to manage the voyage out to New South Wales and the necessary first steps in physically establishing the colony. Let me now concentrate on what it and a couple of related ones show of his ideas about the colony's possible social development.

First, Phillip wanted to establish good relations with the 'natives'. Indeed, he hoped to persuade the Aborigines 'to settle near us', giving them 'everything that can tend to civilize them, and to give them a high opinion of their new guests'. To this end, he intended to prohibit the crews of the transports from having any contact with the Aborigines while the ships remained in New South Wales. And he intended to locate the convicts within the settlement so as to prevent their having contact also, 'for if they have, the arms of the natives will be very formidable in their hands, the women abused, and the natives disgusted'. However, Phillip was realistic enough to understand that this ban might not be maintained forever: 'The natives may, it is probable, permit their women to marry and live with the men [i.e., convict men] after a certain time, in which case I should think it necessary to punish with severity the man who used the woman ill.'[7]

It would be necessary to organize and supervise the work of the convicts. Phillip's ideas here were to divide them into gangs according to their skills, and to have the marine officers oversee them, by 'occasionally encourag[ing] such as they observed diligent, and point[ing] out for punishment such as they saw idle or straggling in the woods'.[8]

Considering that some of the women sentenced for theft might retain some personal dignity and sexual morality, Phillip also wanted to isolate them from the men. However, he thought that they should be able to receive male visitors at certain hours, and that when couples wished to marry, 'they should be encouraged if they are industrious, by [being allowed] one day in the week more than the unmarried on their own lots of ground'. As for the rest (the 'most abandoned') of the convict women, he admitted the realities of human nature and suggested that they be allowed to 'receive the visits of the convicts in the limits allotted them at certain hours, and under certain restrictions' – that is, he was willing to sanction prostitution, in the belief that this might reduce social tension.[9]

Phillip had some general strictures. Given that the colony was to be ruled according to British law, he thought slavery should be banned from its very beginning. (What he had seen during his years in Brazil and at the Cape of Good Hope presumably influenced his aversion to slavery as a social institution.) And, 'as I would not wish convicts to lay the foundations of an empire, I think they should ever remain separated from the garrison, and other settlers that may come from Europe, and not be allowed to mix with them, even after the seven years or fourteen years for which they are transported may be expired'.[10] This idea of permanent exclusion seems to sit ill with his opposition to slavery; and in the event, he found it impossible to maintain. Indeed, his five years in New South Wales are marked by an astonishing social inclusion.

Beyond this, Phillip envisaged the emergence of a class of yeoman-farmers. He thought that those convicts 'who behave well' should be rewarded 'by being allowed to work occasionally on the small lots of land set apart for them, and which they will be put in possession of at the expiration of the time for which they are transported'. And he wanted to know 'how far I may permit the seamen and marines of the garrison to cultivate spots of land when the duty of the day is over, and how far I can give them hopes that the grounds they cultivate will be secured to them hereafter; likewise, how far I may permit any of the garrison to remain, when they are ordered home'.[11]

There is in Phillip's memorandum an interesting extension of this idea of a yeoman class. This concerned the women the administration proposed bringing from the Friendly Islands (now Tonga), not only to augment the number of women, but also, I think, to introduce the gathering and gardening skills that had so impressed navigators who had called at these islands. Phillip thought that these women should be 'supported', but also be kept separately, and be given land when they chose to marry 'the soldiers of the garrison'. His distinction between convict women for convict men and Polynesian women for marines is curious, although it does correlate with his more general one between convicts and free people. Presumably, he hoped to encourage the development of a creole class in the colony, something else which would have been familiar to him from Brazil.[12]

The third and fourth documents that convey Phillip's and the administration's ideas about the colony are the draft of his instructions, which the Home Office produced at the beginning of March, and his comments on this draft. The instructions said that he was to 'endeavour by every possible means to open an intercourse with the natives, and to conciliate their affections, enjoining all our subjects to live in amity and kindness with them; and if any of our subjects shall wantonly destroy them, or give them any unnecessary interruption in the exercise of their several occupations, it is our will and pleasure that you do cause such offenders to be brought to punishment according to the degree of the offence'. Phillip went further: 'any man who takes the life of a native will put on his trial the same as if he had killed one of the garrison'.[13]

He was instructed to emancipate convicts who behaved well and showed a willingness to work, and to grant them lands in the following amounts: thirty acres to a single male; twenty more acres if married; and ten acres for each of a couple's children in the colony. These grants were to be free of rents and other charges for ten years. And he might supply such individuals or families with food for twelve months, together with agricultural implements, seeds and animals, if the general stock permitted this.

In case any of the marines should wish to settle in the colony at the end of their term or any private settlers should arrive, he was to report on the colony's soils, and suggest how free settlers might be given land.

He was, as opportunity arose, to bring women from the Pacific Islands, but he was to see that the officers in charge of this 'do not upon any account exercise any compulsive measures, or make use of fallacious pretences'. Excised from the draft of the instructions was the proviso, which Phillip must have known about, that he was 'to exert every means to prevent their living in common with the convicts, but to hold out every indulgence … to promote matrimonial connection'.

There was another excision from these draft instructions, which is both curious and interesting. In the England of the 1780s, the Church of England was the state religion, and while some 'dissenting' groups were tolerated (e.g. Methodists and Baptists), there were severe restrictions on others. Roman Catholics could not openly practise their religion, and were banned from holding public offices and positions in universities. Even in Ireland, Catholics were banned from holding office and from voting, and were forced to pay tithes to the hated English church. Indeed, after the King had forbidden him to grant the Irish some relief from these onerous restrictions, Pitt resigned as Prime Minister in 1801.

The draft of Phillip's instructions contained the proviso that all persons who may hereafter inhabit our said territory of New South Wales, or the islands adjacent within your government, should have full liberty of conscience and the free exercise of all such modes of religious worship as are not prohibited by law, we do therefore hereby require you to permit all persons within your said government to have such liberty, and to exercise such modes of religious worship as are not prohibited by law, provided they be content with a quiet and peaceable enjoyment of the same, not giving offence or scandal to government.

Excised this passage may have been, but it shows how the administration contemplated giving a greater degree of religious freedom to the New South Wales colony than then existed in England.[14]

*

These, then, were Phillip's and the administration's ideas about how the Botany Bay colony might develop as the venture was beginning. We should not suppose that the politicians who took the decision to found it and the civil servants whose task it was to implement this decision thought exactly as the first governor did. However, it is worth reiterating the point I make in *Botany Bay: The Real Story*, that Phillip could not have advanced these ideas if they had differed radically from those held by senior administrators and their advisers – that is, to put it bluntly, he could not have seen the colony as an imperial venture and envisaged the development of a free population in it if he had been told that the government's only intention was to dump the convicts.[15]

Law

When James Matra was asked by a member of the Beauchamp Committee in May 1785 if he thought 'the use of martial law and prompt justice to be necessary' for a colony of convicts, he replied: 'So essentially so that without them they could not be governed'.[16]

Arthur Phillip also suggested that he should at first govern according to military law. He had a particular reason. In order to build up breeding stocks, persons bringing animals to the colony should be allowed to slaughter them only with the governor's express permission: 'This order would only be necessary for a certain time, and I mention it here only to show the necessity of a military government'.[17]

This seems also to have been the Pitt administration's view initially, for in informing the Irish government of the venture towards the end of October 1786, Evan Nepean remarked, 'The form of government is not yet settled, though I rather think it will be a military one, at least whilst the settlement is in an infant state'.[18] In keeping with this intention, the first commissions of the governor and the colony's other officials (lieutenant-governor, deputy judge-advocate, clergyman, surgeon and assistant surgeon), issued on 12 and 24 October 1786, enjoined them to obey orders 'according to the rules and discipline of war'.[19]

But then, a serious complication arose, for the Law Officers pointed out that persons sentenced under one form of law in one jurisdiction were not amenable to being governed under another form of law else-where – i.e., since the convicts had been sentenced under civil law in Britain, they could not be subjected to military law in New South Wales. This advice has seemingly not survived; however, there can be no doubt that it was given, for on 9 November Nepean related to Sydney a conver-sation he had had with Howe:

> I told him that a deputy judge-advocate would be wanted, and that it was probable that he would be appointed also to control the crim-inal and civil courts for the trial of matters which might pass between the convicts ... When I mentioned a civil and criminal court his Lordship seemed rather surprised, as he had understood that the whole was to have been under military law, *convicts* as well as *soldiers*; and though I attempted to convince his Lordship that the former were not amenable to military discipline, he did not appear satisfied, but seemed to think (perhaps without considering well the importance of the subject) that they should be punished according to the discretion and judgment of the governor, even in capital part. How far his Lordship's opinion upon this matter may

be proper to be adopted I will not pretend to say, but I should think that such a discretion would occasion infinite clamour at home.

Nepean concluded this letter to Sydney with the observation: 'However, the matter will be talked over when the Cabinet next meet, and I suppose something conclusive will be done'.[20]

The business was considered further, with Sydney looking at possible analogies. One was what had been done in the former province of Senegal, where: 'Five officers sufficient for a court-martial. Five must concur in this bill to put a man to death. All other sentences [by] a majority. Fixed jury necessary. Rotation impossible'. Another was the practice in Gibraltar, where 'till [1752] everything judged by military law. Since that a jury taking in the military'.[21] One of the Law Officers quickly ruled both these possibilities out:

I do not conceive that the authority given by the commission and instructions to the governor of Senegambia will apply to the settlement at Botany Bay, and the charter for erecting a court of criminal jurisdiction at Gibraltar appears exceptionable, though perhaps not so much so as the former. Lord Thurlow's idea is that it is within the prerogative of the Crown to direct summary 'convictions in capital cases'. The *particular circumstances* that attend this settlement may perhaps make such a regulation the more necessary, and I cannot see, when *those* are considered, any objection can possibly be made against it. It will, however, be necessary to consider what those proceedings in capital cases are to be – who is to preside in the court to be established? whom the person presiding is to call in to his assistance? the mode of proceeding at the trial? how the defence of the criminal is to be made? and what controlling power the governor is to have in cases of punishment, which do not affect the life of the culprit? It may also be proper to consider, whether in the latter case the governor should not have a power of absolute pardon instead of reprieving (supposing that to be in his commission), as otherwise the prisoner must remain in custody till the King's pleasure is known.[22]

While there is no primary record of Cabinet's consideration of this matter, there is an illuminating newspaper report. On 27 November, the *Daily Universal Register* informed readers that the Attorney-General and Solicitor-General had 'attended the [Privy] Council at St James's for the purpose of laying before His Majesty and the Cabinet the new code of laws which they have been drawing up by order of the Cabinet, for the future government of the new intended settlement at Botany Bay, New South Wales'. In an apparent reference to the *mode* of administering the law that would be adopted – i.e., a panel of civil and military or naval officers hearing cases under criminal and civil law according to a summary procedure – the report went on: 'This code is in part military, and in part civil'.[23]

Criminal and civil courts

At the end of January 1787, the administration prepared a bill to provide for a criminal court in the Botany Bay colony, with the Lord President remarking that 'I believe [a summary] jurisdiction in the present state of that embryo (for I can't call it either settlement or colony) is necessary, as the component parts of it are not of the proper stuff to make juries, in capital cases especially'.[24] Earl Camden here alluded to a difficulty which was to beset the colony into the 1820s. It was a fundamental right in British law that accused persons be tried by a jury of their peers; however, with the vast majority of the European population of early New South Wales convicted felons (who strictly had no rights at law), it was not possible to convene juries of free men.

The administration introduced the bill 'to establish a Court of Criminal Judicature on the East Coast of *New South Wales*, and the Parts adjacent' into the House of Commons on 1 February. Among other things, this provided for the governor to convene a court to try all those crimes recognized in Britain, which was to consist of a 'judge-advocate to be appointed in and for such place, together with six officers of His Majesty's forces by sea or land'. It was 'to proceed in a more summary way that is used within this realm' – that is, by calling such offenders respectively before that court, and causing the charge against him, her or them respectively to be read over; which charge shall always be reduced into writing, and shall be exhibited to the said court by the judge-advocate, and by examining witnesses upon oath ... , as well for as against such offenders respectively, and afterwards adjudging, by the opinion of the major part of the persons composing such court, that the party accused is or is not ... guilty of the charge, and by pronouncing judgement therein (as upon a conviction by verdict) of death, if the offence be capital, or of such corporal punishment, not extending to capital punishment, as to the said court shall seem meet.

It required that five members of the courts concur in a death sentence. And it was to be 'a Court of Record, and shall have all such Powers as by the Laws of *England* are incident and belonging to a Court of Record'. After some amendments, this bill passed through parliament and received royal assent on 23 February as 27 Geo. III, c.2.[25]

The civil court established for New South Wales derived its authority from the monarch's personal tribunal, the Court of King's Bench. Originally created to hear both criminal and civil matters, by the late eighteenth century, with the Lord Chief Justice at its head, this court was dealing mostly with a broad range of civil causes. For this reason, it seems, the New South Wales civil court did not need to be established by legislation. It was to comprise the judge-advocate and 'two fit and proper persons' to be appointed by the governor or lieutenant-governor. It was 'to hold plea of, and to hear and determine in a summary way all pleas concerning lands, houses, tenements, and hereditaments, and all manner of interests therein, and all pleas of debt, account, or other contracts, trespasses, and all manner of other personal pleas whatsoever'. It had the power to 'grant probates of wills and administration of the personal estates of intestates dying within the place or settlement'; and to issue summonses and to imprison in civil causes. There was to be appeal from the decision of this court to the governor; and when there was a sum of more that £300 in question, from the governor's decision to the Privy Council. The Privy Council issued Letters-Patent providing for the operation of both the civil and criminal courts on 2 April 1787.[26]

The vice-admiralty court and commission for the trial of pirates

On 26 March 1787, clearly mindful of the potential for escaped convicts to turn pirates, the Home Office advised the Admiralty that the governor of the Botany Bay colony should be given 'such powers as have been usually granted to the governors of His Majesty's colonies in America'. However, as the Lord Commissioners of the Admiralty quickly pointed out, they were empowered to appoint a vice-admiral and 'a judge and other officers requisite for a court of vice-admiralty' only at places where this had previously been done, so that this matter, too, required an explicit decision by the Privy Council.[27]

This the Privy Council gave on 4 April. The Council sent a copy of the requisite commission to the Admiralty on 12 April, and on 18 April, the Admiralty resolved to appoint the colony's governor also vice-admiral of New South Wales, with the commandant of marines one of the vice-admiralty court's judges, the commissary its registrar, and the governor's clerk its marshal. On 30 April, the High Court of Admiralty issued Letters-Patent appointing these officers; and on 5 May it issued a revised charter, now naming the colony's surveyor and the officers of the two Royal Navy ships being sent also as members of the court, along with 'all other captains and commanders of our ships who are or shall be within the Admiralty jurisdiction of the said territory called New South Wales'.[28]

A commission 'for the trial of persons committing offences upon the high seas' – i.e., for the trial of pirates – was a necessary accompaniment to that for a vice-admiralty court. Sydney wrote to the Lord President of the Privy Council requesting this on 26 March. On 4 April, the Council referred it to the Board of Trade, which reported on 13 April that the Law Officers should draw it up; and that the court should be comprised of the officials listed above. The Privy Council accepted this recommendation on 20 April, and issued the commission on 5 May. Phillip acknowledged receipt of it on 10 May.[29]

The governor's civil commission

Once the decision to provide the colony with civil rather than military law had been taken, a different commission for its governor was required. The Privy Council drafted this on 26 March, and it passed the Great Seal on 2 April.[30] It was based on those given to the governors of British colonies in North America, specifically on that for Lord Dorchester as governor-general of the Canadian provinces in 1786.[31] It was, however, necessary to depart from this precedent in one notable way. Whereas Dorchester's commission required him to frame regulations for the provinces in consultation with a nominated council and an elected assembly, as there would be no substantial group of free men in New South Wales to provide the membership of such bodies, Phillip's second commission was silent about them. Indeed, some of the First Fleet officers were taken aback when they learned of the extent of his powers. For example, Arthur Bowes Smyth, the surgeon of the *Lady Penrhyn*, commented that his commission was 'a more unlimited one than was ever before granted to any governor under the British Crown'.[32]

Otherwise, Phillip's commission followed Dorchester's closely. He was enjoined to swear allegiance to, and to maintain, the Protestant succession; to administer civil justice impartially; to enforce the laws relating to trade and plantations; to appoint 'justices of the peace, coroners, constables and other necessary officers and ministers in our said territory and its dependencies for the better administration of justice and putting the law into execution'; to care for idiots and lunatics and administer their estates. He was given the power to pardon, either absolutely or conditionally, according to the seriousness of the crime. He had 'full power and authority to levy, arm, muster and command and employ all persons whatsoever residing within our said territory and its dependencies under your government and as occasion shall serve, to march from one place to another or to embark them for the resisting and withstanding of all enemies, pirates and rebels, both at sea and land'. He might proclaim martial law in war or other emergencies, and 'erect, raise and build ... such and so many forts and platforms, castles, cities, boroughs, towns and fortifications' as he should judge necessary. In wartime, he might appoint and promote naval officers, and exercise his powers as vice-admiral through the court of that office. He might assign lands and establish 'fairs, marts and markets'. His subordinates were to obey him, or those to whom he delegated his authority. He was to pass all legal instruments under the colony's Great Seal.

Subsequent commissions and instructions

It was some years before the Pitt administration issued all the ancillary commissions and instruments needed to underwrite the wide-ranging powers it gave to the Botany Bay colony's first governor. Clearly, officials considered it necessary to complete only those relating to its immediate establishment before the ships sailed. Nonetheless, it is appropriate to describe the later instruments now, so as to indicate the full extent of the colony's governance.

Explicit power for the governor to grant land and details of how he was to do so were conveyed in a set of additional instructions which passed the Privy Council in mid-1789, when the time was approaching for the marines who had sailed out in 1787 to return home. Wishing to encourage numbers of them to settle in the colony, so as to boost its free population and its capacity to defend itself, non-commissioned officers were to be offered one hundred acres and privates fifty acres, 'free of all fees, taxes, quit-rents and other acknowledgements for the space of ten years'. If they were to enrol in the corps that would replace the marines, after five years they would be offered double the amount of land, and be given goods and clothing, seeds and agricultural implements besides. Free persons migrating to the colony were to be given similar grants of land, and convict servants might be assigned to both classes. In allocating land, though, the governor was to reserve areas for towns and the Crown's future needs.[33]

Another commission was needed to permit the governor to remit the convicts' sentences if he saw fit. The administration dealt with this in 1790. I presume it delayed issuing this on the assumption that the convicts in New South Wales remained under sentence. This was generally true, but the terms of some who had been sentenced in the early 1780s had in fact expired by this time. In March 1790, the Solicitor-General advised Evan Nepean that there was a legal problem concerning the pardoning of convicts in New South Wales, as that was not the jurisdiction in which they had been sentenced. But he drafted a bill to provide for this, which conveyed the power to pardon to the governors of all colonies to which felons had been or would be sent. This bill passed through parliament in May and June 1790, and received royal assent on 9 June as 30 Geo. III, c. 47. In November, the Privy Council issued a commission to Phillip conveying this power. Grenville sent this commission, together with additional instructions based upon it, to Phillip a week later.[34]

Similarly, once the governor of New South Wales had been empowered to grant lands and to remit sentences, a Great Seal was needed to give legal effect to the instruments by which he did so. The Privy Council ordered this to be produced in May 1790 and instructed the King's engraver about the design. When finalized, the colony's seal comprised:

One one side: Convicts landed at Botany Bay, their fetters taken off and received by Industry sitting on a bale of goods, with her attributes, the distaff, bee-hive, pick axe and spade, pointing to oxen ploughing, to rising habitations, and a church on a hill at a distance, with a fort for their defence. Motto, *Sic fortis Etruria crevit*; with this inscription round the circumference, *Sigillum Nov. Camb. Aust.**

On the reverse: Your Majesty's arms in a shield, with the supporters, garter and imperial crown with the motto, and round the circumference Your Majesty's titles.

The King gave the seal his final approval in January 1791.[35]

The lack of a currency

One thing that was conspicuously lacking from the arrangements for the Botany Bay colony was money – its governor remarked wistfully in 1788,

---

* 'Thus Etruria grew strong'; 'Seal of New South Wales'.

'this country has no Treasury'.[36] In all the documents, there is simply no mention of its needing a currency. Phillip's being supplied with ducats for purchasing goods in the East Indies indicates that this absence cannot have been an oversight, but what it indicates about official thinking is unclear.

I think there were probably three underlying assumptions, two of which were bluntly practical. If there were money in the colony, the convicts, many of whom were thieves by inclination, would expend their energies in stealing – that is, one of the principal evils that transportation was intended to remove would be perpetuated, with all its attendant violence and social discord. And then, convicts in possession of money would be able to purchase goods from calling ships, or, indeed, passages away from New South Wales, which would negate another purpose of transportation.

More abstractly, the third assumption presumably was that money was unnecessary in a peasant economy. The government would feed and clothe the convicts, who in return would labour in the nation's interest. They would raise herds and crops, which would at first lessen the cost of the colony, then produce a surplus for ships proceeding into or returning from the Pacific Ocean. They would build houses and harbour facilities, so as to consolidate the settlement and increase its role as a place of transportation. They would erect fortifications and harvest naval materials, which, together with its growing population, would make the colony a greater resource in time of war.

Although they did not have a currency available, the colony's officials were not entirely without the means of purchasing goods. The governor and the commissary of stores were authorized to issue bills of exchange (a modern equivalent might be a cross between an open cheque and a bond). Offered to the masters of ships with needed cargoes, or to merchants in foreign ports, these might pass from one person to another before being presented for payment (sometimes years later) to the Treasury in London. (Given the length of time the holder might have to wait before obtaining their sterling value, these bills were usually discounted as they changed hands.)

The paymaster of the marines was the third colonial official able to issue bills of exchange, returnable to the regimental paymaster in England. In the 1790s, the opportunity to have their salaries paid in this way enabled the officers of the New South Wales Corps to band together to import goods from the Cape of Good Hope, India and the East Indies, thus beginning the notorious trade in rum.

The colony

Clearly, all this apparatus of governance far exceeded what was needed for a stark penal outpost. And although the administration initially thought to put the colony under military law, there was always an understanding that it would become a civil settlement. Both Phillip and Nepean indicated that any period of military law would be limited. Once legal imperatives had dictated that it should have civil law, the administration gave it structures of governance which, while truncated, laid a basis for eventual growth in the manner of Crown colonies elsewhere.

Then again, Phillip's conception of how the colony might develop turned on the growth of a body of free settlers who would expand on the beginnings made by the convicts. If he did not share Matra's view that, once reformed, the convicts should be able to return fully to society, neither did he completely reject the idea of their regaining some social ease. His notion of fostering the development of a class of farmers and gardeners – convict, free, and mixed-race – meant not only that the colony would in time become self-supporting, but also that it would be able to offer supplies to calling ships, so that it might become that base south of the equator desired by the Prime Minister as part of the nation's strategic and commercial policies.

Again and again, Phillip alluded to this underlying purpose. He told Nepean that, at the end of his envisaged three-year term, he hoped the colony would not only be self-supporting, but also have become 'of the greatest consequence to this country'. When he had found that splendid waterway – 'the finest harbour in the world, in which a thousand sail-of-the-line may ride in the most perfect security' – and settled his charges about Sydney Cove, he told Lansdowne that 'this country will hereafter be a most valuable acquisition to Great Britain from its situation'. And his design for the permanent township, with its main streets to be 200 feet wide, and with its strategic placement of government buildings so as to offer views down to the North and South Heads, was such as to befit a colony that would become a 'seat of empire', to which 'ships of all nations' would resort.[37]

These were not the meanderings of an impractical visionary. Phillip was an accomplished and hard-headed naval officer. He had participated in the gruesome business of hunting and rendering whales in the Arctic Ocean. He had seen men shorn apart in battle. He had seen them die of scurvy. He had seen the brutality of slavery in Brazil and at the Cape of Good Hope. He had ordered men flogged. In New South Wales he presided over executions. Rather, these were expectations based on what those who decided to establish the colony had said to him. Together, these expectations and the mode of govenance tell us a good deal about the Pitt administration's intentions for the convict colony.

PART TWO:
ASSEMBLING THE FLEET

3.

The People 1: Officials and Officers

IT IS NOT MY INTENTION HERE to give a comprehensive account of the First Fleet colonists. Rather, what I wish to do is to convey a sense of the composition of the various groups; to indicate the roles of and to offer short biographies of some of the more prominent officials; and to indicate those who were sent because they had relevant skills. In this, as in other major aspects of the mounting of the First Fleet, we see both broad and detailed planning, and therefore other signs that the Pitt administration took the business seriously.

The civil establishment

In the sketch of the colony's civil establishment, prepared in mid-August 1786 as an attachment to Heads of a Plan, Nepean allowed for the following appointments and specified their annual salaries:[1]

	£
The naval commander to be appointed governor or superintendent-general	500
The commanding officer of the marines, to be appointed lieutenant-governor or deputy superintendent	250
The commissary of stores and provisions for himself and assistants (to be appointed or named by the contractors for the provisions)	200

Pay of a surgeon	182.10
Ditto of two mates	182.10
Chaplain	182.10
Total	£1497.10

By 10 October, which is the date by which we may consider the civil establishment to have been largely (but not entirely) finalized, he had expanded this list to include:[2]

	£
Allowance to the governor	1000
Lieutenant-governor	250
Deputy judge-advocate	182.10
Commissary	182.10
Provost marshal	91.5
Chaplain	182.10
Surgeon	182.10
Three mates, at £91.5.0 each	273.15
Agent (i.e., for transports)	150
Payment of fees upon the receipt and audit	200
To be paid in advance:	2695

A surveyor was later added to this list.

The governor

The person appointed as the colony's first governor was Captain Arthur Phillip (1738–1814). As a boy, Phillip was educated at Greenwich Hospital School for the sons of poor seamen, and in his youth sailed on whaling voyages to the Arctic Ocean and on trading voyages to the Mediterranean. He joined the Royal Navy in 1755, and in the Seven Years' War (1756–63) saw battle in the Mediterranean and the West Indies.[3]

He married in 1763, to Charlott Denison, a rich widow who was significantly older than he. For a brief period, the couple seem to have resided at Hampton, just to the west of London. By 1766 they had acquired Vernals Farm, on the outskirts of Lyndhurst, in the New Forest. Phillip's enjoyment of the life of a country gentlemen was brief. He seems to have left the district in mid-1768; and in April 1769, after they had lived apart for some time, he and Charlott concluded a formal separation agreement.

In September 1769, Phillip obtained permission from the Admiralty to go to St Omers, in northern France, 'for the benefit of his health'.[4] Given that he and the Home Office later used this reason as a blind, it is probable that this marks the beginning of his career as a spy. In November 1770, at the time of the Falklands Islands crisis, occasioned by Britain's establishing a settlement on these remote islands claimed by Spain, he joined the *Egmont* as 4th lieutenant, but saw only routine service. He left this ship in July 1771, and remained on half-pay until January 1775. In these years, however, he spent two more extended periods in France.

At the end of 1774, with the encouragement of superiors, together with a number of other junior British officers, Phillip joined the Portuguese Navy, serving in Brazilian waters for four years. Portugal was Britain's oldest ally in Europe, and from time to time the Admiralty helped out the much smaller Portuguese Navy. This also gave British officers the opportunity to gather information about harbours and fortifications, particularly in the Spanish colonies.

Britain's American colonies having rebelled in 1776, and France having taken their side, Phillip returned to England at the beginning of October 1778 and was immediately appointed 1st lieutenant of the *Alexander*, a 74-gun line-of-battle ship. In September 1779 he was given the command of the fireship *Basilisk*. Promotion to post-captain of the 24-gun frigate *Ariadne* followed in November 1781. In early 1783, just as the war was ending, in command of the 64-gun *Europe* he sailed as part of a small squadron intended to attack the Spanish settlements in South America. A storm ravaged the ships in the Bay of Biscay and all the captains but Phillip were forced to turn back. Phillip made his way via Rio de Janeiro to India, where he joined the squadron under Admiral Hughes and Sir Richard King, returning to England via the Cape of Good Hope in late April 1784.

There is a considerable mystery concerning some of Phillip's activities in these years. In January 1781, he supplied Lord Sandwich, the First Lord of the Admiralty, with charts of the South American coastline, which showed 'three good harbours, where ships that wanted to wood and water would find only a few settlers'.[5] Then, his name disappears from the records from February to mid-October 1781, with the exception that it continues in the list of half-pay officers – i.e., those who were not presently on active service, but whom the Admiralty wished to retain. If this were really the situation, we should expect that he would have written repeatedly to offer his services, which he did not.

As he was negotiating the terms of his appointment in New South Wales, Phillip made two comments which presumably bear on this silence. The first, to Evan Nepean, was: 'you recollect that in the late war I was deprived of the chance of those advantages every other officer enjoyed, and put to no small expense'. The second, to Lord Sydney, was that 'every officer must naturally wish to meet with some recompense for his labours, and I have hitherto paid for having been anxious to render an essential service to my country'.[6]

Arthur Phillip spoke five European languages: English, German, French, Spanish and Portuguese. The Home Office repeatedly employed him to spy on naval preparations on the Continent; and in the mid-1770s, the Admiralty placed him in the Portuguese Navy so that he might obtain information about coastlines and harbours, ports and their defences in South America. I suspect that the government sent him back to South America in 1781 to prepare the way for a secret expedition it was planning against Spanish settlements there. And if I am right, it is presumably to this hidden period that the following curious story belongs, about which I have been unable to obtain any further details, whether in English archives, or those of Portugal and Brazil:

Captain Phillip, the commander-in-chief of the expedition to Botany Bay, was several years in the Portuguese service, and obtained no small degree of reputation from the following incident. Being employed about five years since to carry out with him near 400 criminals from Lisbon to the Brazils, during the course of the voyage an epidemical disorder broke out on board his ship, which made such havoc that he had not hands sufficient to navigate her. In this dilemma he called up the most spirited of the transports [i.e., convicts], and told them in a few words his situation, and that if they would assist in conducting the vessel and keep their companions in order, he would represent their behaviour to the Court of Lisbon, and, in short, do all in his power to get their sentence mitigated. This speech had the desired effect. The prisoners acted with fidelity, and brought the ship safe to [Rio de Janeiro][7], where they were delivered into the custody of the garrison; and on Captain Phillip's return to Lisbon, and representing the meritorious conduct of the transports, they were not only emancipated from their servitude, but had small portions of land allotted them in that delightful country.[8]

In October 1784, Nepean sent Phillip to spy in France again; and then once more in October 1785. When Phillip returned to England is unknown, but presumably it was about the end of September 1786, for the *Daily Universal Register* announced his appointment on 27 September. When precisely he was first thought of for the governorship of the Botany Bay colony is also unknown. The earliest evidence of this is Howe's dismal comment to Sydney on 3 September 1786, that 'I cannot say the little knowledge I have of Captain Phillip would have led me to select him for a service of this complicated nature'.[9]

But consider. Already by the mid-1780s, Phillip had wide experience of the Atlantic and Indian oceans and of a number of the countries that border them. He had charted coastlines and harbours, and noted their resources. He had made the long voyage out to India, which was the nearest analogy to that to New South Wales. In his espionage, he had shown himself to be just that 'discreet' officer that Nepean had pointed out would be needed in the Heads of a Plan.

And if the story of his having transported convicts to Brazil is true, then he was also qualified for the business in a way in which no other British naval officer was.

There is an additional tantalizing possibility. While it is something about Phillip's life I was never able to elucidate properly, it seems that he had strong connections with the cloth trade. His first wife was previously married to John Denison, a wealthy London cloth and wine merchant. His second wife was Isabella Whitehead, the daughter of Richard Whitehead and Elizabeth Sudell, both of whose families were much involved in the cotton and linen weaving industry.[10] Then, there is the report that one of his midshipmen on the *Europe* in 1783–84 was 'the son of a merchant in the calico printing business in Old Street road, London, at whose table the captain had been kindly entertained'.[11] Phillip's attempts to breed cochineal insects are another indication of this connection, as is his prompting Nepean to obtain cotton seed for New South Wales. So too is Philip Gidley King's advising Nepean in 1791 that he could 'write to a friend of Governor Phillip' to procure cotton seed for Norfolk Island.[12] Given that the Botany Bay colony was part of the Pitt administration's Bounty scheme, an understanding of the business of cotton would have been an additional attribute in the person chosen to govern it.

The lieutenant-governor

Robert Ross (c. 1740–94) joined the marines as a 2nd lieutenant in June 1757; and was reportedly at the siege of Quebec in 1759. He was promoted to captain in March 1773, and may have been at the battle of Bunker Hill in 1775. In 1778 and 1779 he recruited in Ireland, and he served as major on guardships at Plymouth in 1783–84. He was offered the command of the marine companies going to New South Wales in October 1786, and issued with a military commission as lieutenant-governor at the same time. What precisely the everyday duties envisaged for Ross in this second role were is most unclear. His commission is silent about them, and the Admiralty's subsequent directives to him are concerned only with his military duties. Before he sailed, he was also made one of the members of the colony's vice-admiralty court.[13]

Ross gave Phillip no end of trouble in New South Wales. Cantankerous and opinionated, he refused to let the marine officers supervise the convicts in their labour, tried to shield marines who committed crimes from punishment, and insisted on strict adherence to military protocols. He also resented the egalitarian social policies which Phillip pursued, writing at one point: 'Could I have possibly imagined that I was to be served with … no more butter than any one of the convicts (nearly 6 ozs per week), I most certainly would not have left England without supplying myself with that article … or oil for my own use'.[14]

He was soon off-side, not only with Phillip, but also with his officers, whom he wanted to court-martial as a group. In March 1790, so as to have some respite from his complaints and obstinacy, Phillip sent him to Norfolk Island, where, true to form, he administered three different kinds of law – civil, military and a hybrid of his own devising.

In view of Ross's recalcitrant behaviour in New South Wales, it is tempting to think that the administration may have had an inkling of this, and therefore preferred John Hunter (see below) as 'governor-in-waiting'. However, this would be anachronistic. Whereas another naval officer might command the warships, and also appropriately fill the role of governor on a temporary basis, a marine officer might serve as acting governor but not exercise any authority over Royal Navy ships and their officers. Hunter was the appropriate choice to act as governor in Phillip's absence or death.

The deputy judge-advocate

David Collins (1756–1810) sailed with a civil as well as military appointment, for in addition to that he received from the Admiralty to adjudicate at courts-martial, on 24 October 1786 the administration appointed him to head the colony's civil and criminal courts. It is unclear whether Collins's first commission in military form as deputy judge-advocate was ever superseded by one in civil form. In asking for a supply of stationery on 7 February 1787, he referred to his commission 'from His Majesty', but no second commission has ever been found.[15] In the colony, he also served as the governor's official secretary.

The commissary of stores

Andrew Miller (c. 1759–90) had been on the *Basilisk* with Phillip, first as a seaman and then as purser's steward in August 1779. In December 1782 he followed Phillip into the *Europe*. He was offered the position of the colony's commissary (i.e., keeper of the government's stores) before the end of December, when his name appeared in the list published by the *Daily Universal Register*.[16]

The provost marshall

George Alexander was first appointed to this position, but he was not on board when the ships sailed in May 1787; and, indeed, according to Phillip, he 'had not been seen for a considerable time before we sailed'.[17] In his absence, Phillip gave it to his loyal follower Henry Brewer, who had served as his clerk on the *Basilisk*, *Ariadne* and *Europe*, and who joined the *Sirius* in December 1786 as a midshipman. Brewer was also appointed marshal of the vice-admiralty court. One shipmate described him as a person 'of coarse, harsh features, a contracted brow which bespoke him a man soured by disappointment, a forbidding countenance, always muttering as if talking to himself'; but this writer also said that 'if honesty merits heaven, Harry is there'.[18]

The chaplain

At the end of September 1786, a number of people asked the Reverend Richard Johnson if he were interested in going out to New South Wales. Conscious of the inevitable long separation from his extended family and friends that this would involve, of 'the dangers of the sea', and of the disadvantages of life in 'a country wild and uncultivated', where he and his immediate family might be 'exposed to savages, and perhaps to various wild beasts of prey', he was initially very uncertain of the wisdom of doing so. However, he fasted and prayed, and God showed him that he should say yes.[19]

Johnson was recommended by John Newton, former master of slaving ships who had come to detest the trade, and who was the author of 'Amazing Grace'. Newton described Johnson as 'humble and spiritual [... with] no taste or desire for the extensive mode of life so generally prevalent ... a simple man'. He was appointed at the urging of Pitt's friend

William Wilberforce and of Sir Charles Middleton, members of the influential Clapham 'sect', an evangelical group within the Church of England.[20] His commission, in military form, was issued on 24 October 1786. It is also unclear whether this was later superseded by a civilian one.

Two days earlier, on Sunday 22 October, Johnson went down to the hulks to begin his acquaintance with the convicts. Although the Society for the Propagation of the Gospel equipped him lavishly for the daunting task of saving their souls, he had a very hard time of it in New South Wales. Many of his charges showed themselves quite uninterested in religion; the authorities did not hasten to build him a church; and when at last he had one some malicious person burned it down.

Otherwise, Johnson's time in the colony was notable for three things: he fed sick convicts out of his own rations; at the time of the smallpox epidemic in mid-1789, he and his wife took in a young Aboriginal girl; and he proved himself to be one of the best farmers.

The surgeons

John White (c. 1756–1832) was the colony's chief surgeon. Between 1778 and 1786, he served on various Royal Navy ships as surgeon's mate and then as surgeon, before being recommended for Botany Bay by Sir Andrew Snape Hamond.[21] Like other subsidiary officials, he was issued with a military commission on 24 October 1786. Again, it is unclear that this was ever superseded.

White displayed some of the ignorance of his time. He believed, for example, that foul air caused scurvy. However, in general he showed himself to be a very competent medical officer, and the excellent health record of the First Fleet is in large part due to his skill and to his insistence on having proper medical supplies.

White was keenly interested in natural history, and kept an informative journal of his time in New South Wales. He otherwise did not enjoy the colony, though, describing it as 'a country and place so forbidding and so hateful as only to merit execration and curses'.[22]

The assistant surgeons ('surgeon's mates') were Dennis Considen (?–1815); Thomas Arndell (1753–1821); and William Balmain (1762–1803), who had sailed on the *Nautilus* when it explored the southwest coast of Africa.

The agent (for transports)

John Shortland (c. 1739–1803) joined the Navy in 1755, aged fifteen, and was promoted to lieutenant in 1763. Thereafter, he made a career in the Transport Service, taking a convoy to relieve Gibraltar in 1782 and bringing another from North America in 1786. The Navy Board appointed him agent for the First Fleet transports in September 1786. Together with Phillip and White, he was responsible for the success of the voyage. He returned to England in May 1789.

The surveyor

August Alt (1734–1815) trained as an engineer, and was present at the siege of Gibraltar in 1779. In times of peace, he recruited for the army and built roads.

The position of surveyor to the colony was not originally thought of, but it became necessary once the governor was given authority to grant lands. It was included, without the name of the person to hold it, in the list of those to provide members of the panel to try pirates dated 13 April 1787. Alt's name appears in the commissions for this and for the vice-admiralty court issued on 5 May 1787.[23]

The botanist

One of the most persistent criticisms of the Pitt administration's mounting of the First Fleet has been that no botanist was sent. This is true, but things were not exactly as this makes it seem.

The presence of an expert botanist in the colony would have been, if perhaps not quite necessary, certainly advantageous in locating the best soils and in advising on the progress of plantings. He might also have extended that beginning made by Banks and Solander in 1770 in the collection and classification of the unique flora of New South Wales. And the First Fleet officers did sail with the expectation that they would have one, for Tench recorded, 'we flattered ourselves ... that Masson, the

King's botanical gardener, who was employed [at the Cape of Good Hope] in collecting for the royal nursery at Kew, would have joined us'.[24]

Born in 1741 in Aberdeen, Scotland, Francis Masson worked at Kew Gardens as a gardener in the 1760s. When Banks ordered him to collect in southern Africa, James Cook left him at Cape Town in October 1772, where he remained until 1775, in this time sending back some 500 species. In 1776, he collected in the Atlantic islands, but war and a hurricane destroyed his harvests. In 1783 he was in Portugal.

He returned to south Africa in January 1786, and thereafter figured in Banks's plans for the new colony. How strongly in 1786–87 is unclear. In mid-1789, however, as the *Lady Juliana* was preparing, Banks wrote to him that 'I intended about this time to have asked leave of His Majesty to order you to Botany Bay; but, finding from your letter to Mr Aiton that you had an aversion to the place, I have made interest that another person should be sent there, and I hope I shall succeed'.[25] The botanist, gardener and surveyor David Burton sailed out to New South Wales in the *Gorgon*, arriving in September 1791, where he supervised agriculture at Parramatta and collected for Banks.

The second captain of the Sirius

The *Sirius* carried two captains. As the senior naval officer, Phillip would command the Royal Navy ships and conduct the convoy on the way out; but then, since his presence would be required on land, he could not command the ships when they were again at sea. A second officer was needed, but one who must remain under the governor's general direction. The solution that the administration arrived at was to appoint a *second* captain to the *Sirius*, one junior to the governor in naval rank, but senior to the lieutenants of the *Sirius* and *Supply*. Such an arrangement was by no means unknown in the Royal Navy. For example, it was common with the small squadron on the Newfoundland station, which was evidently the model for that in New South Wales;[26] but it had seldom, if ever, been applied to a ship as small as the *Sirius*.

Before the end of October, Phillip had approached Lord Sydney about giving this appointment to John Hunter, who was then assisting him to prepare the *Sirius*.[27] Hunter (1732–1821) was a Scot who joined the Navy in 1754, being promoted to lieutenant in 1760 after service in North American waters, where he served again during the American war. He was appointed second captain in mid-December. Later, he became the colony's second governor, from 1795–1800. Like the other naval officers, Hunter kept a detailed journal, which he published in 1793 as *An Historical Journal of the Transactions at Port Jackson and Norfolk Island … in New South Wales.*

Partly because of Phillip's pride, and partly because of Lord Howe's obduracy, this arrangement caused real trouble. Phillip considered that the appointment of a second captain should entitle him to fly the broad pennant while at sea and when in foreign ports. This pennant indicated the presence of a commodore of a detached squadron sailing on a particular mission, and therefore a status superior to a captain's. Nepean evidently promised Phillip that on this point he would 'go away satisfied', but Howe was opposed to it.[28] I am surmising here, but I think the basis of the First Lord's opposition was that, because as soon as he arrived at New South Wales his business would become 'entirely unconnected with maritime affairs', Phillip would cease to be under the control of the Admiralty, and instead be answerable only to the Secretary of State.[29] In Howe's view, he would not then be entitled to the broad pennant, as he would not be on sea service.

Technically, Howe was in the right. However, I think there may have been other considerations involved. One was that the Admiralty did not have control of the expedition; another was that Phillip had not been Howe's choice to lead it; and a likely third was that Howe suspected that Phillip was seeking this arrangement so that he might obtain status and emoluments he was not genuinely entitled to. Howe could not but have been made more determined in his opposition by a newspaper report on 31 October – that is, while the business was still under discussion and well before anything had been finalized – that Hunter was to be appointed second captain of the *Sirius*, and that Phillip would 'hoist a broad pennant, as soon as his ship comes within sight of [New] South Wales'.[30]

Phillip persisted with his request to this point, but then, in the face of Howe's continuing opposition, backed off, asking Sydney not to pursue the matter: 'My situation would be still more disagreeable if [Hunter] was to be removed, *for somebody must command the ship when I am on shore.* It might, I think, be better if Lord Howe was left to act as he pleases, my dependence being on your office'.[31] But the matter continued to rankle with Phillip, and he did ask again, only for Sydney to tell him in April, as his instructions were being finalized, that 'it is not thought advisable under the present circumstances of the service which you are to perform, that you should be authorized to wear any distinguishing pennant'; but that any officer junior to him arriving in New South Wales would be instructed to follow his orders.[32] In the end, Phillip sailed only with this understanding.

Still, puzzles about this business remain. One of the officers who made the voyage recorded that Phillip 'immediately hoisted his broad pennant as commodore of the squadron'; and midshipman George Raper's painting of the First Fleet ships entering the harbour at Rio de Janeiro shows the red, swallow-tailed pennant flying from the *Sirius*'s mainmast.[33] I do not know what to make of this. Phillip can scarcely have flown this pennant without some approval. It may be that he had a quiet understanding that he might 'wear' it at Rio de Janeiro, as he had served in the Portuguese Navy and a superior naval status would help him in his dealings with the viceroy.

Despite being disappointed in the matter of the broad pennant, Phillip did leave England with Hunter as second captain of the *Sirius*. Because it was unprecedented to have two captains on a 6th-rate (i.e., a warship carrying up to 32 guns, and commanded by a post-captain), the arrangement required Privy Council approval. The Admiralty wrote to the Council on 14 December, which approved the arrangement the next day. The Admiralty informed Phillip on 18 December, and the Navy Board on 22 December. Before the ships sailed, the Privy Council issued Hunter with a dormant commission, empowering him to act as governor in the event of Phillip's absence or death.[34]

Junior naval officers

Among the middle-ranking officers on the *Sirius* were Lieutenants William Bradley (1758–1833) and Phillip Gidley King (1758–1808), one of Phillip's followers, who was to become the colony's third governor (1800–06). Both of these kept detailed and informative journals, with Bradley adding charts and watercolours. So too did George Raper, one of the midshipmen, whose drawings are particularly striking (see the cover). Newton Fowell, another of the midshipmen, described the venture in a long series of letters home.

Lieutenant Henry Lidgbird Ball (1758–1818) commanded the *Supply*.

Marine officers

The commandant of marines was Lieutenant-Governor Ross, who was introduced above. Each of the companies of marines that went out to New South Wales was commanded by one captain and three lieutenants. A number of these fulfilled associated duties: e.g., Lieutenant John Long the adjutant (i.e., administrative assistant to the commandant); and Lieutenant James Furzer the companies' quartermaster.

Three other marine officers deserve more detailed consideration. Watkin Tench (c. 1758–1833) joined the service as 2nd lieutenant in 1776, and volunteered for New South Wales on 25 October 1786.[35] The most literate of the colony's chroniclers, Tench was genuinely interested in the experiment taking place around him, and his two accounts of its early years offer details of agricultural and social development not found elsewhere.

William Dawes (1762–1836) joined the marines as 2nd lieutenant in September 1779, then served on ships in North American waters. He was evidently something of a Renaissance man. One patron recommended him in this way: 'He understands the Spanish and Portuguese languages, as also French and Italian; he has studied botany some considerable time together, with mineralogy; he is a tolerable good astronomer and draws very well'. This recommendation was successful, for on 25 October the Admiralty agreed to his having three weeks leave 'on his private affairs' – i.e., to travel to London to have his scientific expertise assessed.[36]

Dawes attended the Home Office with a recommendation to Brook Watson, the naval stores dealer and friend to the administration, that 'whatever you desire him to do respecting the flax from New Zealand, or any other important article of commerce which that country may produce, his future conduct will prove that his abilities, and application, are worthy your protection'. His major purpose in coming to town, however, was to present himself to Neville Maskelyne, the Astronomer-Royal, in the hope of being appointed astronomer to the expedition. In this he succeeded, for in November the Board of Longitude agreed to supply him with a long list of relevant instruments and books.[37]

Dawes was an upright young man, but an inflexible one. In the colony, he was put in charge of artillery and fortifications; he built an observatory at Dawes Point; and he helped lay out Sydney and Parramatta. However, he and Phillip quarrelled, and he chose to return to England rather than serve another term in the colony. He took with him a notable vocabulary of a local Aboriginal language.

David Collins joined the marines in February 1771. In June 1775 he fought at Bunker Hill, and then afterwards served in Nova Scotia. He was promoted to captain in August 1779, and went on half-pay at the end of the war. On 1 January 1787 the Admiralty appointed him to oversee courts-martial in the colony. He wrote a long account of its beginnings, and subsequently became lieutenant-governor of Van Diemen's Land (Tasmania).

4.

People 2: Ships' Crews, Marines, Convicts, Wives and Children

LET US NOW CONSIDER THOSE who made up the majority of the First Fleet's people: the crews of the various vessels, the marines, the convicts, and the wives and children who travelled with them.

Ships' crews: the Royal Navy

In October 1786, the Admiralty fixed the complement of the *Sirius* at 160, and that of the *Supply* at fifty-five. These complements included marines – twenty-two and twelve respectively.

It was usual for senior naval officers to take boys intending to become officers to sea, so as to begin their training in mathematics, navigation and drawing. These trainees were known as 'Captain's servants'; and post-captains were entitled to bear four on a ship's book. In view of the length of the voyage and nature of the business these ships were embarked on, however, the Admiralty decided not to permit their commanders to take servants with them, decreeing that only 'able seamen' [i.e., those rated 'Able-bodied' or AB] should go. The Admiralty paid the commanders an allowance instead.[1] Reflecting the fact that the Navy was a young man's occupation, most of these crewmen were in their twenties or thirties.

However, some who were not trained sailors also joined the crews. Henry Dodd, who sailed as an AB on the *Sirius*, had reportedly been a farm-hand for Phillip in England. He supervised the labour of the convicts and the establishment of agriculture in the colony. Roger Murley (sometimes spelt Morley) also went out as AB on the *Sirius*. Described by King as 'an adventurer [who] had been a master weaver', he was in the first party sent to Norfolk Island in February 1788. The *Sirius*'s blacksmith also settled in the colony.[2]

Ships' crews: the transports

There is considerable doubt about the number of crewmen on the six convict transports and three storeships, as various sources do not agree about the numbers. In the following table, I give those stated in the passes (certificates) required by the Navigation Act, and those from Philip Gidley King.[3]

	Pass	King
Alexander	19 British, 6 foreign (total 25)	30
Borrowdale	13 British, 4 foreign (total 17)	22
Charlotte	23 British, 7 foreign (total 30)	30
Fishburn	17 British (total 17)	22
Friendship	13 British, 4 foreign (total 17)	25
Golden Grove	15 British, 5 foreign (total 20)	22
Lady Penrhyn	19 British, 6 foreign (total 25)	30
Prince of Wales	17 British, 5 foreign (total 22)	Not recorded
Scarborough	27 British, 8 foreign (total 35)	30
Total	208	211+

Even these totals might be quite inaccurate, however, for the ships may have carried more crew, together perhaps as many as 100.

Marines

The four marine companies sent to New South Wales each comprised one captain, three lieutenants, three sergeants, three corporals, two drummers and forty privates – a total of 208, which became 212 with the addition of the commandant, deputy judge-advocate, adjutant and quartermaster.[4] In view of Botany Bay's distance from England, and of the unusual nature of the service to be undertaken, the Admiralty stressed to the commanding officers of the Portsmouth and Plymouth barracks that in the first instance those enlisted should be volunteers on full pay. Offers of service poured into the Admiralty, many more than were needed. In the end, Tench tells us, all but two of the 212 men in the four companies were volunteers.[5] It is unclear whether the additional thirty-four marines posted to the *Sirius* and *Supply* were also volunteers.

The marine enlistment had naturally been wound back at the end of the war in 1783, so that it was adequate only to 'the requisite demands of parties for [the King's] ships employed in time of peace, and the ordinary duties on shore at the several headquarters'. The decision to send four companies to New South Wales inevitably strained the force's capacity. Accordingly, on 21 November, the Admiralty requested permission to raise four more companies, each to comprise one captain, two 1st and one 2nd lieutenants, three sergeants, three corporals, two drummers and forty-eight privates – a total of sixty personnel each.[6] The Privy Council issued an Order for doing so three days later, which Stephens then conveyed to the Ordnance Board; and the Admiralty instructed the commanders at the Portsmouth and Plymouth barracks each to recruit two new companies.[7]

As subsequent events showed, the private marines who went out to New South Wales were no better and no worse that their peers in society. Some behaved well, others very badly. One was exiled to Norfolk Island for the rape of a little girl. Six were executed for the theft of the precious stores.[8] Indeed, we may suppose that, given education and class, it was probably only luck that many of them travelled free rather than in chains. It is one of the ironies of the colony's first years, and an indication of the strange reversals that occurred there, that, with the governor's approval, the convicts formed a night-watch to prevent assaults and robbery of huts and gardens, and Major Ross argued that errant marines should be immune to arrest by these amateur constables.

Marines' wives and children

In the course of preparations, the Admiralty advised the Home Office that it was usual for some wives to accompany their marine husbands on overseas postings.[9] We may suppose that the basic criterion was that the couples had young, dependent families, though the women would also have fulfilled certain useful domestic duties, such as mending clothes. In all, twenty-eight wives of marines seem to have gone out to New South Wales, together with some twenty-four children. These women were victualled at half the ration of the men, and their children at a quarter.[10]

Convicts

In August 1786, at the time of the decision, the administration intended to send 750 convicts to Botany Bay – 680 men and seventy women. Home Office correspondence with county officials makes clear that the men were to be taken from the hulks in the Thames and at Plymouth. In the weeks before the Fleet sailed, there was some relaxation of this policy, with some convicts being sent also from country jails.

In mid-October, Sir Charles Middleton received a strange letter from an anonymous correspondent, urging him to increase the number of women:

> There appears not now more than *one woman* to five or six men. This can never be right, either as to policy or humanity. *Without* women no colony can thrive. And a *deficient* number will certainly occasion *contentions* and at length *bloodshed*, not to mention *more odious consequences.*

The solution that this writer proposed was that some of the numerous prostitutes who frequented the taverns at Portsmouth should also be shipped out, and once in New South Wales married by lot to the male convicts. Citing as a precedent the method the French Crown had evidently used to populate New Orleans, he observed: 'we do not find that these predetermined weddings turned out worst than the run of marriages commonly do'.[11]

About this time a decision was made to increase the number of women; but precisely when is difficult to establish. Sydney told the Treasury on 22 December that it was 'upon many accounts … advisable' to do so.[12] However, the decision does seem to have been taken significantly earlier, at least informally, for while the *Hampshire Chronicle* reported on 18 September that 'there are 680 men felons and 70 women felons to go' (which is correct in terms of the Home Office's August advice to the Treasury and Admiralty), two weeks later the *Reading Mercury* announced that 'about 700 men and 150 women' were being sent (which is much closer to the final number).[13]

In October and November, the Home Office wrote to the sheriffs of Hampshire, Bristol, Derby, Kent, Worcester, Gloucester, Devon, Wiltshire and other counties, asking for details of any female convicts being held in their jails, and directing that they be sent either to the *Dunkirk* hulk at Plymouth or to the Southwark jail in London, to await embarkation. And arrive the women did – one from Chester, one from Liverpool, one from Durham, two from Brecon, two from Worcester, two from Derby, one from Suffolk, one from Norfolk, one from Reading, three from Norwich, four from Lancaster, one from Durham, four from Bristol, one from Cardiff, three from Salisbury, one from York, two from Worcester. The process continued into 1787.

Alhough the figures are not quite precise, it seems that in the period of embarkation, 586 men and 192 women convicts and wives were taken on board. Seventeen of these died and two were pardoned before the ships sailed on 13 May, so that the actual number who sailed was 568 men and 191 women, for a total of 759.

The ages in 1787 of a sample group of 280 of the convicts were:

Age	No.
1–9	0
10–19	37
20–29	153
30–39	66
40–49	15

| 50–59 | 5 |
| 60+ | 4 |

That is, 68 per cent of the group were aged under thirty, 91 per cent under forty.

The ages of the youngest convicts were (on arrival) thirteen and fourteen, the oldest sixty-seven and sixty-eight, with the great majority aged between twenty and thirty-nine.

Convicts' wives and children

There was a curious group who were supposed to go out with the convicts: relations who asked the administration to send them with their menfolk. As the *London Chronicle* reported in October,

> On Monday applications were made at the Treasury by some females to accompany the convicts to Botany Bay, among whom were the wife and mother of one of the felons now under sentence of transportation. The clerks of the Treasury were for some time at a loss how to act, but on Mr Nepean's coming, and the affair being stated to him, the petitioners were dismissed, with orders to call again in a few days, and a promise that the nature and propriety of their request should be seriously taken into consideration.[14]

These women's plea was successful. The administration made provision for some twenty-five of them to go, clothed and victualled in the same manner as the women convicts.[15] They were to take with them a small number of children. In April, William Richards was still expecting them to come to Portsmouth to be embarked on the *Prince of Wales*, but it seems they never arrived.

Selecting the people

There are two questions to be asked about the First Fleet personnel, which bear on the central one of whether the Pitt administration wished simply to dump the convicts as far away as possible, or whether it also wished to establish a viable colony capable of realizing other purposes. In other words, did it mount the First Fleet in a willy-nilly fashion, or purposefully? These questions are: Was there any selection of those sent? If so, what were the criteria used in selection?

Clearly, as I have indicated in the previous chapter, numbers of the officers were chosen for the particular skills they had – but what of the men and women convicts, and the merchant and Royal Navy seamen and marines?

As a consequence of demographic analysis undertaken in conjunction with Ezra Zebrow,[16] I can now offer the following conclusions, some of which remain tentative:

1. There was no selection of convict women, by age or any other criteria. Particularly once the decision had been taken to increase their number, these women were simply taken from metropolitan and county jails and assembled at Plymouth and London.

2. There was no selection of convict men by age. The age profiles of those sent correlate with those of males in the general population.

3. There may have been a selection of male convicts according to skills. In February 1787, Nepean sent Campbell a list of 120 convicts, asking him to 'select 100' to be put on board the *Scarborough*.[17] Tench said that 'the major part of the prisoners were mechanics and husbandmen, selected on purpose by order of Government'.[18] Ralph Clark says that of the seventy-six men on the *Friendship*, forty-four had 'trades'. His list includes six weavers, two carpenters, three farmers or gardeners, four brickmakers or bricklayers, and one blacksmith.[19] Gillen was able to establish that at least 163 male and sixty-seven female convicts had a trade[20] – but whether these were higher proportions than in the English population at large is unclear.

4. There may have been some selection according to fitness. I know that Phillip's comment in January 1787 that there were several men embarked who 'cannot help themselves' seems to contradict this.[21] However, when delivering convicts for transportation, Duncan Campbell did not include those who were sick or injured. In sending his deputy

lists of the convicts to be put on board the *Alexander* and *Scarborough*, Campbell asked to be informed of their health and whether any had died. In late February, when despatching convicts to the *Scarborough*, Campbell did not send seven from the list of 191 nominated.[22] Subsequently, he asked Erskine to inform him which of the convicts 'who from sickness and other causes were thought unfit to be removed with the other prisoners' were now well enough to follow their confreres.[23]

There is also subsequent vindication of this point. Phillip later reported to Sydney that twenty-six of the seventy-two convict deaths in the colony between January 1788 and February 1790 had been due to 'disorders of long-standing'. However, after the arrival of the Second Fleet in June 1790 he wrote, 'The sending out the disordered and helpless clears the jails, and may ease the parishes from which they are sent; but, Sir, it is obvious that this settlement, instead of being a colony which is to support itself, will, if the practice is continued, remain for years a burden to the mother country'.[24] Together, these comments indicate that there was a selection according to health of the male convicts sent on the First Fleet.

5. Interestingly, there was at least a partial selection according to the seriousness of the crime committed. In nominating in March 1785 first 150, and then 200, men for transportation to Africa, Evan Nepean pointed out to Sir Charles Middleton that these were 'the most abandoned scoundrels in the country selected for this purpose'.[25] It was these men, their numbers altered somewhat by death or release, who formed the bulk of those put on board the *Alexander* in the Thames in December 1786.

6. There evidently was some selection of Navy personnel according to skills that would be useful in the colony. Jacob Nagle, the American sailor on the *Sirius*, recorded that Phillip had 'the privilege of taking any men that turned out from the men-of-war, there was great number turned out, but the captain took his pick, all young men that were called seamen, 160 in number'.[26] This is confirmed by Admiralty correspondence, for as the *Sirius* waited at Portsmouth, and sick sailors were discharged from it, the official in charge asked for volunteers from the guardships, noting their names and trades, and 'as the returns were very numerous and many

handicrafts among them, I had foreborne to complete her complement till Captain Phillip came down, that he might furnish himself with those who occupations he might stand most in need of'.[27]

7. There also seems to have been some selection of the enlisted marines according to relevant skills. Certainly, Nepean called for this in the Heads of a Plan: 'as many … as possible should be artificers, such as carpenters, sawyers, smiths, potters (if possible) and some husband-men'.[28] And in October 1786 Colonel John Hughes advised that from the 200 volunteers at the Plymouth barracks he had chosen 'many of all trades'.[29]

In his return of marines engaged in building works in 1788 Ross listed five masons, ten carpenters, five sawyers, seven shinglers, one miner and one file cutter.[30] The presence in the colony of the represent-atives of the last two categories may have been haphazard, but it seems unlikely that that of those in the first four was.

8. There is also one report that Phillip 'had the peculiar indulgence from government to choose all his own officers'.[31] There does seem to be some truth to this, for there is evidence that, of the commissioned officers, Phillip personally chose at least Hunter and King; and of the warrant officers at least James Lochart (purser), Thomas Brooks (boat-swain) and Peter White (sailmaker); and as well he took his clerk Henry Brewer with him (as midshipman).

9. Finally, the administration may have encouraged tradesmen to join the crews of the transport ships, as another means of providing the colony with the skills it needed. While firm evidence for this is lacking, the *Daily Universal Register* reported at the end of November:

> Almost daily applications have been made at Lord Sydney's office by artificers in different branches, to accompany the felons [to Botany Bay], in order to assist in forming and bringing to maturity the intended new settlement … How far it may be sound policy in government to permit as many as are willing to embark, we will not say, but a limited number of several different professions, we suppose, will of necessity have leave to go.[32]

As well as from the *Sirius* and *Supply*, Phillip did hire some men from the transport ships while they remained at Sydney. It is not impossible that these were men who had come out to work in the colony, but who chose not to stay when they saw the prevailing conditions.[33]

*

Let me end this chapter with two stories which exemplify aspects of the society from which the First Fleet sailed.

James Lochart

James Lochart had been purser on the *Europe* during its voyage to India and back; and he followed Phillip into the *Sirius*. A purser's life was often an uneasy one. He was responsible for dispensing the ship's provisions and clothing ('slops'), for which he did not pay directly, but whose value was charged against his account, to be reconciled at the end of a voyage. To this end, he was required to keep precise records of what he dispensed daily to each officer and man. He was also required himself to pay for 'necessaries' for the ship – such things as wood and coal, oil, candles, hammocks and beds, again for later reconciliation. When in foreign ports, he was able to purchase items, but had to keep strict records, including evidence that he had bought at prevailing market prices. If it happened that these prices were above those in the Navy Board's sched-ules, he was not compensated for the difference. Likewise, if items were lost through shipwreck or enemy action, he was not compensated.

In order for him to have some profit, the purser was entitled to serve food at 14 ounces to the pound rather than 16 ounces, a practice that the seamen naturally resented, as they saw themselves being deprived of proper amounts. And there was always the suspicion that the purser might be further injuring them by dispensing even shorter rations, since the more rations he had left over at the end of a voyage, the more money he could make by selling them back. It was also usual for him to buy stocks of tobacco for private sale to the men. The Navy Board required him to give large sureties, and he was frequently obliged to borrow money from friends and merchants in order to get his business started, with his financial returns being months and even years away. Pursers were thus prime candidates for bankruptcy.

Lochart had ended the *Europe*'s voyage in April 1784 without all of his documentation in order; but on Phillip's testifying on his behalf, on 6 December 1786 the Victualling Board agreed to pass his accounts so that he might go on the *Sirius*.[34]

Then, two weeks later, disaster overwhelmed James Lochart. His two letters to Phillip tell the wrenching story of this demise much more eloquently than I might.

[c. 21 December 1786]

I intended to have seen you yesterday to have thanked you for your good intentions towards me and to have relinquished the *Sirius*. Before you receive this I am left town, therefore apply for a new purser when you think fit. I should think Mr Miller very proper to be recommended. Let me be forgotten. Tomorrow you shall have the particulars relative to the fitting, what I have paid, and what remains due to tradesmen.

The horror of my situation is not to be described and never can be felt by you.

22 December 1786

In my confusion yesterday, I know not what I wrote. Was it possible, I would make every apology for the inconveniences I have put you to, but alas that is as much out of my power as my return to my native country which I am now quitting forever.

Mr Addington, Erle Street, Blackfriars, furnished the *Sirius* with twenty-one cauldrons of coals, for which the purser must pay him. I paid for wood £22, some odd shillings. There is due to Mr Bernard at Deptford £6 for more wood. I paid for candles £7.5.0. And for greens etc. daily expense about £3.3.0. There is due to Mr Eade, ironmonger, Wood Street, Cheapside, for lamps, lanterns etc. an account which I never got from him, but the purser must pay him or return the things. Mr Thomas, coppersmith, King Street, Deptford, has a claim for sundry articles supplied by him. Mr Fisher, tallow chandler, King Street, Deptford, has supplied a box or two of candles and some loose dozens, without being paid and has shipped on board the *Charlotte* three puncheons of tallow, and has all the other candles ready. I have paid him nothing. The purser must settle this.

The steward has distinct accounts of receipts of provisions. The master knows everything has been faithfully stowed away, the three puncheons for the tallow above-mentioned excepted, which return to the ship when she can stow them. When the money that I laid out is recovered from the purser I request that £20 thereof may be given to Lieutenant Maxwell for the honest purpose I have wrote him and the remainder to Mr William Crees, Plymouth.

And now, Sir, I take farewell forever. I was my own master at fourteen years of age, and have experienced wonderful vicissitudes of fortune; have formed some attachments to friends; and have in the end met with disgust and disappointment in them all, yourself, my uncle and two friends in the City excepted. I have had no happiness yet, and now expect none. A miserable existence I shall not long support, and the sneer of mine enemies, or the sympathy of my well-wishers will soon be matter of indifference to me. But I beg pardon for intruding upon your time with reflections that relate only to myself.

Phillip passed on these letters to the Admiralty without comment. It was a hard world, and he needed another purser.[35]

Susanna Holmes and Henry Cabell

There is a very curious story told by John Simpson, the jailor at Norwich, concerning the convicts Susanna Holmes and Henry Cabell (known in the colony as Kable), and their son Henry.

The following narrative, which I believe to be strictly true, having escaped notice though published three weeks ago in the *Norwich Mercury*, I trust will be acceptable to your readers, as it is really a very interesting relation.

In consequence of the late determination of government to send some convicts to Botany Bay, with a design of establishing a colony in New South Wales, an order lately came down to the keeper of Norwich jail to send such female convicts as were then in prison to Plymouth, to be in readiness to go upon that expedition. Three unhappy women, who had been a long while in the castle under sentence of transportation, were accordingly sent, and were committed to the care of Mr Simpson, turnkey of the prison. One of these unfortunate females was the mother of an infant about five months old, a very fine babe, whom she had suckled from its birth. The father of the child was likewise a felon under a similar sentence, and has been in prison more than three years. He had repeatedly expressed a wish to be married to this woman, and though seldom permitted to see the child, he discovered a remarkable fondness for it; and that the mother's only comfort was derived from its smiles, was evident from her peculiarly tender manner of nursing it. When the order came down for her removal the man was much distressed, and very importunate to attend the woman, and application was made to the minister to permit him to go, but so many similar applications having been made, this could not be complied with. The miserable woman was therefore obliged to go without the man, who offered to be her husband, that he might be her companion and protector during a long and melancholy voyage, and in a distant and unknown land. The child, however, was still her property, as the laws of England, which are distinguished by the spirit of humanity which framed them, forbid so cruel an act as that of separating an infant from its mother's breast.

When Mr Simpson arrived at Plymouth with his party, he found that they were to be put on board a hulk which lies there, till the ship which goes to the South Sea is ready to take them. He therefore took a boat, and went to the vessel to deliver up his prisoners. Some forms, which the jailer of Norwich had not been apprized of, having been omitted, the captain of the hulk at first refused to take them, and these miserable creatures were kept three hours in a open boat, before they were received into their new abode of wretchedness. And when they were admitted, the captain finding that one of them had an infant, peremptorily refused to take it on board, saying, that he had no orders to take children; neither the entreaties of Mr Simpson, nor the agonies of the poor wretch, could prevail upon the captain even to permit the babe to remain till instruction could be received from the minister. Simpson was therefore obliged to take the child, and the frantic mother was led to her cell, execrating the cruelty of the man under whose care she was now placed, and vowing to put an end to her life as soon as she could obtain the means. Shocked at the unparalleled brutality of the captain, and his humanity not less affected by the agonies of the poor woman, and the situation of the helpless babe, Mr Simpson resolved still, if possible, to get it restored to her. No way was left but an immediate personal application to Lord Sydney; and having once before been with his Lordship in a business of humanity, he was encouraged to hope he should succeed, could he but have an interview with him. He therefore immediately went back to Plymouth, and set off in the first coach to London, carrying the child all the way on his knee, and feeding it at the different inns he arrived at as well as he could.

When he came of London, he placed the child with a careful woman, and instantly posted to Lord Sydney's. Neither his Lordship nor his secretary were to be spoken to, at least this was told him when he addressed the person in waiting at the office; but humanity will not be restrained by forms. Acting under the influence of a superior power, it moves forward unchecked by the fear of offending any earthly one. Mr Simpson was denied admittance, but in vain, for he pressed forward into one of the offices, and told his story to one of the secretaries, who attended very properly to it, and promised to do all in his power to promote the object of his humane petition, but feared it would be impossible for him to see Lord Sydney for several days. He begged, however, of this gentleman to prepare an order for the restoration of the child, and determined to wait in the hall for the chance of seeing his Lordship pass, that he might prevail on him to sign it. Fortunately, not long after, he saw Lord Sydney descend the stairs. He instantly ran to him; his Lordship very naturally showed an unwillingness at first to attend to an application made to him in so strange and abrupt a manner, but Mr Simpson immediately related the reason of his intrusion, and described, as he felt, the exquisite misery he had lately been a witness to, expressing his fears, lest in the instant he was pleading for her, the unhappy woman, in the wildness of her despair, should have deprived herself of existence. Lord Sydney was greatly affected, and paid much attention to the particular circumstances of his narration, and instantly promised that the child should be restored, commending, at the same time, Mr Simpson's spirit and humanity. Encouraged by this, he made a further appeal to his Lordship's humanity in behalf of the father of the child, which proved equally successful; for his Lordship ordered, that he likewise should be sent to Plymouth to accompany the child and its mother, directing, at the same time, that they should be married before they went on board, and adding that he would himself pay the fees.

One of his Lordship's secretaries wrote immediately to Plymouth, that the woman might be informed of the success of Mr Simpson's application; and he, after visiting the child, and giving directions that it might be taken care of in his absence, set off for Norwich, where he arrived on Wednesday afternoon, and communicated the glad tidings to the unhappy father of the child. The poor man, who is a fine healthy young fellow, seemed very grateful to Lord Sydney and to Mr Simpson, [and] was made very happy by this change of circumstances; and it is hoped he may, notwithstanding his past situation, turn out a useful individual of the new community. He set off Friday night accompanied by Mr Simpson, who, after the fatigues, anxieties, and vexation of his first journey to Plymouth, having travelled three days and nights without sleep, no doubt will be amply recompensed by the satisfaction he must experience, in having thus been the means of rescuing two unhappy people from a situation of distress scarcely to be equalled.

It is proper to observe, that Captain Phillip, who is to go out with the convicts to Botany Bay, is a man of very different disposition to the person alluded to in this narrative, but he, unfortunately, had not power to interfere.

The conclusion of the above relation cannot be more properly given, than in the words of Mr Simpson himself, who wrote the following letter a few days ago to a gentleman in Bath:

Dear Sir,

It is with the utmost pleasure that I inform you of my safe arrival with my little charge at Plymouth; but it would take another pen than mine to describe the joy that the mother received her infant and her intended husband with. Suffice it to say, that their transport, that the tears which flowed from their eyes, with the innocent smiles of the babe, on sight of the mother, who had saved her milk for it, drew tears likewise from my eyes; and it was with the utmost regret that I parted with the child, after having travelled with it on my lap for upwards of 700 miles backwards and forwards. But the blessings I received at the different inns on the road, have amply paid me.

I am, with great respect, your humble servant,
John Simpson.[36]

The young man in question, Henry Cabell, had been convicted of burglary in February 1783 and sentenced to death, then reprieved to fourteen years' transportation to America. Susannah Holmes had been sentenced to death in March 1784 for the theft of clothing, linen and silver, then reprieved to fourteen years' transportation. They met in Norwich Castle, where both were held. Susannah was put on board the *Dunkirk* on 5 November, without her baby, who joined her with her husband-to-be on 15 November after John Simpson's heroic intervention. Initially the family sailed together for New South Wales in the *Friendship*, but Susannah and the baby shifted to the *Charlotte* at Cape Town. The parents married in Sydney on 10 February 1788.

Before they sailed, the publication of their plight and of their devotion to each other resulted in the public subscribing £20 to buy them goods, which was stolen on the *Alexander* during the voyage. In a gesture which would have been impossible in England, where felons were 'atteint' (i.e., dead from the point of view of legal rights), Phillip and Collins allowed Henry to sue the ship's master in the civil court, where he received £15 in damages. Over the next twenty years he and Susannah became prosperous, accumulating land, animals, shops and ships. Their lives were emblematic of the new society that would develop in New South Wales.

5.

The Ships

EVEN THOUGH THE EVIDENCE to gainsay the idea has been available for decades, it has become conventional wisdom that the ships of the First Fleet were clapped-out tubs.[1] It is therefore worthwhile to examine in detail the process by which the Navy Board selected them, for this provides further evidence of the care with which the Pitt administration prepared the expedition.

The Navy Board was the branch of government most concerned with the physical organization of the First Fleet. It was responsible for the Royal Navy's ships, for their upkeep and for the supplies held in the Navy's dockyards at home and abroad. It also was responsible for the appointment of 'warrant officers' (e.g., surgeons, pursers, masters, carpenters, gunners, sailmakers, etc.). The Navy Board was subservient to the Admiralty, which was responsible for the appointment and promotion of commissioned officers and for the deployment of Britain's powerful military marine. At times, relations between these boards could be quite tense, particularly when strong personalities headed them, as was the case in the mid-1780s, when Earl Howe was First Lord Commissioner of the Admiralty and Sir Charles Middleton the Comptroller of the Navy.

Middleton was a remarkable man. Born in 1726, he entered the Navy in 1741, was promoted to lieutenant in 1745 and captain in 1758. During the Seven Years' War he saw service in West Indian waters. He was

325

appointed Comptroller in 1778, and during the next five years was responsible for the maintenance of the fleet during the conflict with the Americans, French, Spanish and Dutch, and assisted Lord Sandwich in the work of strengthening it and obtaining more stores. In the 1780s he oversaw the ambitious building programme that William Pitt insisted on, which by the end of the decade saw the Royal Navy more powerful than it had been in any previous time of peace.[2]

Middleton and the Prime Minister became good friends. Someone who was then a junior official later remembered: 'It was no uncommon thing for Mr Pitt to visit the Navy Office to discuss naval matters with the Comptroller, and to see the returns made from the yards of the progress in building and repairing the ships-of-the-line; he also desired to have a periodical statement from the Comptroller of the state of the fleet, wisely holding that officer responsible personally to him, without any regard to the Board.'[3] Against Howe's opposition, Pitt insisted on Middleton's promotion to rear-admiral in 1787; and, when Middleton was eighty, at a time when Napoleon was threatening to defeat Britain, Pitt appointed him First Lord Commissioner of the Admiralty.

Where the mounting of the First Fleet is concerned, Middleton was one of four administrative focal points. As the Home Office was responsible both for convicts and for colonies at this time (among many other things, of course), it was Evan Nepean's business to inform the Treasury of what measures were needed. One of the two Treasury Secretaries, George Rose or Thomas Steele, would then advise the Navy Board, which would set about hiring and fitting out ships and obtaining goods. Where military matters were involved, the Treasury Secretaries would also advise the Admiralty, usually via its Secretary, Sir Philip Stephens; however, given the nature of the Botany Bay business, these advices were less frequent than those to the Navy Board. The fourth focal point was Arthur Phillip, who knew that he was to be appointed governor of the colony at least by late September, and who thereafter also played a central role in the business, as he let both Middleton and Nepean know how he thought things should be done differently, and what more was needed. As we shall see, although lesser Navy Board officials were irritated by them, Middleton was tolerant of Phillip's demands, and the pair had a respectful relationship. Phillip and Nepean were friends, no doubt owing in part to Nepean's having been Phillip's spymaster when he operated in France.

When either the Treasury or Admiralty or Navy Board had queries or needed more information, the flow of correspondence was reversed. This was a somewhat cumbersome process, but it is because of it that we have such an extensive record of the mounting of the First Fleet. And the procedure itself does not seem to have caused any major delays. (That is, there were delays, but not because of this procedure.) Against the ignorant claims of some historians, it is difficult not to be impressed by these department heads' competence. They worked very long hours and attended to business diligently. Their industry is all the more remarkable when we remember that they wrote everything by hand.

*

The business of initiating and co-ordinating the multitude of arrangements necessary to prepare the ships for the voyage fell to two middle-ranking Navy Board officials: Joshua Thomas, the Board's secretary; and Captain George Teer, its agent for transports. As soon as he was appointed the agent for the First Fleet transports, Lieutenant John Shortland also participated in this detailed work. Shortland's appointment offers a minor illustration of the often-prickly relations between the Admiralty and Navy Board. Shortland had been agent for a transport convoy which had recently arrived from Nova Scotia; and, needing such a person for the First Fleet, the Navy Board offered him the post on 20 September. Belatedly, the Board realized that it should have sought Admiralty approval, which it did on 2 January 1787. The Admiralty replied tartly: 'Their Lordships have no objection to his being employed to superintend those transports, but ... they should have obtained their permission before they appointed him'.[4]

On 26 August, Thomas Steele notified the Navy Board of Sydney's advice about the Botany Bay colonization, and that the Treasury had endorsed it. Accordingly he asked the Navy Board to hire transport vessels for the 680 male and seventy female convicts; and to obtain 'such provisions, necessaries and implements for agriculture as may be requisite for their use after their arrival', including bedding. The provisions were to be for 1000 persons for two years after the voyage, with the women who might come from the Pacific Islands included in this number. The Navy Board was also to obtain 'a quantity of surgeon's instruments, medicines and necessaries for the sick'. These transport ships would be escorted by two Royal Navy vessels; and marines would guard the convicts at sea and on land.[5] Let us see how the business of hiring and equipping the ships then went forward.

Royal Navy ships

Sirius: On 6 September, the Admiralty instructed the Navy Board to prepare the *Berwick* and another vessel of about 200 tons burden for the task of escorting the transports to New South Wales.[6]

The *Berwick* was not, as has so often been said, an old East Indiaman.[7] Rather, it was an 'East Country' ship – that is, built for the Baltic trade. Accordingly, it had a spar deck, so that mast timber might be rolled on board. It is reasonable to speculate that it was chosen because of the service it was to perform at Norfolk Island.

Philip Gidley King, who sailed on it, reported that the *Berwick* had been built in 1780, and, after having burnt to the waterline, been purchased by the Navy Board as an armed storeship.[8] There must be considerable doubt about this, as the Deptford yard officers who inspected it before purchase in 1781 found it to be 'building' in Mr Watson's yard, and made no mention of any fire-damage. In any case, it had not been completed with the 'refuse of the yards', as Barnard Eldershaw claimed; neither was it in 1786 the 'worn-out' vessel that David Mackay represented it to have been. The repairs to it carried out in 1786–87 were to remedy defects that were only to be expected, given its service; and these repairs put it, as Henderson and Stanbury point out, in 'excellent condition'.[9]

The ship the officials saw was 89 feet 8 3/4 inches in length, 32 feet 9 inches in breath. Its depth in the hold was 13 feet, and its burden 511

83/94 tons. The officials recommended a number of alterations. These included enlarging the raft port on the lower deck so that it might accommodate '64- or 74-gun ships' masts', and ports and supports on its middle and upper decks for thirty 9-pounder cannons and four 18-pounder carronades. Altogether, the *Berwick* cost the Navy Board almost £6000.[10] It carried a substantial armament; and being of a 'full, round build' and 'all together a very capacious and convenient vessel',[11] was well-suited to carrying stores, which, again according to King, it did to North America in the last year of the war, and then to the West Indies.[12]

Perhaps not coincidentally, on 23 August the Admiralty Board instructed the Navy Board to prepare the *Berwick* for foreign service, and to report when it would be ready to receive a crew.[13] Upon receiving the formal advice that such a ship was needed for New South Wales, the Admiralty advised the Navy Board that it should be fitted out for this service 'with all possible despatch'. After inspecting it, the Deptford officers recommended a number of repairs and the replacement of some equipment, which they estimated would take forty men twenty-four days, for a total cost of £224.[14]

On 22 September, the Woolwich officers advised that the *Berwick* should be ready to receive men and stores on 16 October, which advice the Navy Board passed on to the Admiralty. But then, a week later, the Deptford officers provided a more extensive list of work to be done, which put back the date.[15]

On 9 and 11 October, the Deptford officers informed the Navy Board that yet more work needed to be done, which would occupy 116 men for ten days and cost £175, and that they wished to work 'two tides' so as to hasten the business.[16] The Board duly informed the Admiralty that this meant there would be a further two weeks' delay before the ship would be ready to receive men.[17]

On 12 October, the Admiralty instructed the Navy Board to register the ship as a 6th rate, by the name of the *Sirius*; that it was to have a complement of 160 men; that it was to be armed with four 6-pounder cannon, six 18-pounder carronades, and eight swivel guns; and that Arthur Phillip was to command it. The Admiralty requested this armament from the Duke of Richmond, the Master-General of the Ordnance, and advised Lord Sydney. King tells us that the ship was renamed after 'the bright star in the southern constellation of the Great Dog' – an unusually poetic gesture by the Admiralty.[18] On 25 October, the Navy Board advised the Admiralty that the ship would be ready in two days. It was commissioned on 1 November, with the Admiralty asking that it be fitted out 'for a voyage to remote parts', and to put twelve months' provisions on board. The same day, it told Phillip he was now in charge of the ship. Manning and provisioning then proceeded. A week later, the Admiralty ordered that both it and its tender receive 'such additional stores and provisions … as [they] can conveniently stow'.[19]

The equipping of the *Sirius* did not conclude at this point, however.

On 31 October, Phillip asked for ten more 6-pounder cannons, and 'the iron work necessary for the carriages', as these extra guns might in future be 'of great use to us, on board or on shore'. The Admiralty agreed to this request, advising the Ordnance Board of it on 1 November.[20] This was a sign that Phillip was thinking beyond the immediate exigencies of a convict colony. Also at this time, the Admiralty ordered that both the *Sirius* and its tender be 'supplied with a camp forge and copper oven, and to have their coppers fitted with Mr Irving's apparatus for rendering salt water fresh, and to furnish them with Lieutenant Orsbridge's machine for rendering stinking water sweet'.[21]

The preparation of the *Sirius* continued through November and December. In mid-November, 20 tons of 'washed and screened shingle ballast' was put in its hold. Then, Phillip requested four more cables, of 15 1/2 inches diameter, to make a total of seven. At the same time, he asked the Board of Longitude for a chronometer, which was granted.[22]

Then there was the matter of ship's boats. On 12 September, the Navy Board ordered a yawl of 27 feet and a launch of 25 feet, with copper fastenings. By mid-November, the *Sirius*'s boats comprised a launch of 27-foot keel, and three cutters, of keels of 25, 22 and 18 feet. Phillip requested that he also be supplied with a 32-foot keeled, 16-oared boat in frame, for use in inshore exploration in New South Wales, which was agreed to. The *Supply* (see below) was also given a boat in frame.

As there was not room for them in the Royal Navy ships, they were loaded into the transports.[23]

Then there were foods and medicines to obtain for both ships. On 1 and 7 November, Phillip asked the Victualling Board for certain provisions, which were granted. On 8 November, it agreed to his request for 2 tons of essence of malt and 'as much sauerkraut as [he] may desire' (both considered to be anti-scorbutics, though in fact the malt contained no vitamin-C, and the pickled cabbage not very much); and one year's supply of 'wheat, sugar and mustard seed'. On 10 November it told him that the bread and other 'dry provisions' would be 'packed in tight casks'. On 14 November, he requested supplies of spirits; and then, another seven days on, four months' supply (7418 lbs) of molasses. Early in December, he asked for bread, wine and ox tongues; and then the *Sirius*'s 1st lieutenant asked for more bread, and beer.[24]

In the same manner, Phillip and the ship's surgeon requested additional medical supplies. George Worgan advised that 'Peruvian bark'[25] would be advantageous, but that 'from the high price of the drug navy surgeons cannot afford the vast quantity required to do justice to the men without wronging themselves'. When the Navy Board said that it did not provide this item, Phillip asked the Admiralty for permission to obtain it.[26]

On 30 December, John Hunter, now appointed second captain, asked for more iron ballast, which he received.[27] Then, Lieutenant Bradley requested more bread and beer. John Palmer, the purser, asked for 'two or three hogsheads' of tobacco for the voyage, but also that these be put into the *Prince of Wales,* as the *Sirius* was now so full. This was done.[28]

Supply: If the choice of the main ship was straightforward, that of its tender gave the Navy Board a great deal of trouble. The Deptford officers first inspected the French-built storeship *Eclipse*, only to find that it had been badly damaged when it had run aground in Ireland, and that 'by her appearance she is not a fit ship to accompany the *Berwick* storeship as a tender'. They next considered the *Rattlesnake*, an American-built sloop that had been offered for sale; but on surveying it they decided that from its age and build it was 'not a fit ship, either in substance or quality' to accompany the *Berwick*.[29]

Then, the Navy Board decided to purchase the *Grantham* packet boat, which its owner, Thomas Hubbert, had advertised for sale on 7 September:

> An extraordinary swift sailer, British-built, for the service of the Post Office; burden 230 tons, more or less; was lengthened about nine years ago, and copper-sheathed to light water mark about four years since; has copper fastenings to her bottom, and is now in extraordinary good condition, fit for immediate employ; has very great plenty of all sorts of stores, and may be sent to sea with the addition of provision only.[30]

It seemed a good buy, but as the Navy Board quickly found out, it was a very tart lemon. On inspection, the Deptford officers found that all its masts and yards were 'defective'; that its planks down to the water's edge were 'all in a decayed state'; that its frame was also decayed; that all its iron fastenings above water were corroded; that the planks underneath the copper sheathing were also decayed; and that the cables were also 'much worn and dry rotten', and, like the rigging, unfit for any 'purpose of government'. It would require 'a great repair' to make it seaworthy, which would employ many workmen for more than two months. And after having stripped it to establish all this, the Deptford officers reported that it would cost more to put it back together than it would then sell for.[31]

Accordingly, the Navy Board proposed using the *Supply*, a small Navy ship then at Portsmouth employed to carry naval stores from one yard to another. The Admiralty agreed to this, and the *Supply* became the *Sirius*'s companion.[32] Built in 1759, it was of 175 tons burden. Hunter said that 'it was a very firm strong little vessel, very flat floored, and roomy'; while King thought that it was 'much too small for so long a voyage'. Both said that it sailed badly, but its rate depended a good deal on weather conditions.[33]

When the *Supply* had arrived from Portsmouth, the Deptford officers surveyed it, and recommended repairs that would take forty men twenty days, and cost £156. At the same time, after consulting Phillip, they proposed that it carry four 18-pounder carronades on the main deck, four 4-pound canon on the quarterdeck, and twelve half-pounder swivel guns.[34]

The matter of the *Supply*'s armament then came in for extended consideration. The Admiralty suggested that it would be better to have four 6-pounder cannon on the main deck. On this suggestion being put to the Deptford officers, they decided that, yes, cannon would be better, but that 6-pounders would be too heavy. They therefore proposed four short 4-pounders.[35]

However, when he assumed command of the ship, Lieutenant Henry Ball advised that even 4-pounders would be too heavy, and recommended 3-pounders instead. This request went the usual path of Admiralty, Navy Board, Ordnance Board and back, and it was agreed to between 12 and 16 December.[36]

On 27 October, the Admiralty instructed the Navy Board that the *Supply* was to carry fifty-five officers and men, and that it was to be fitted out 'for a voyage to remote parts, … [and] victualled to twelve months'. The ship was listed on 28 October, with Lieutenant Henry Ball as its commander.[37]

There was still some work to be carried out on the ship. For example, carronade ports, additional chain plates, and copper sheathing needed to be fitted. Ball also wanted a new fire hearth. Then there were other things – new steering wheels, gratings, shot lockers, wedges for the masts. This work proceeded through November, though the Deptford officers advised that it would be ready to receive men on 11 November.[38]

Like Phillip for the *Sirius*, Ball had a series of requests for the *Supply*. On 11 November, he asked the Navy Board for supplies of ledgers and paper, which were granted. On 11, 13, 18, 22, 23 and 28 November, he asked the Victualling Board for provisions, which he received. On 2 December, in view of the ship's having been 'ordered upon a long and separate service', he asked the Navy Board for a quantity of portable soup, only to be told that this was not something it supplied. Then he asked for some wine, which was granted; but also for a warrant to buy coal, only to be told that the Victualling Board no longer provided this. On 6 December, he asked for 'surgeon's necessaries', upon which the Navy Board agreed to provide an eight-months' supply; and then a few days later, the Victualling Board agreed to provide fresh beef while the ship was in port.[39]

The transports

At the end of August and beginning of September, the Navy Board advertised 'for about 1,500 tons of shipping by the ton, to carry persons and provisions to Botany Bay on the coast of New South Wales', with tenders to close on 12 September.[40]

Turnbull, Macaulay and Gregory's offer, made to Nepean in August, was considered and they were asked to put it into a proper form.[41] Anthony Brough offered a number of 'Archangel-built ships, in the most prefect repair, which have been surveyed by the officers of the East India Company and declared very suitable for the China trade, three years old, and admirably calculated for long voyages'. The Navy Board told him that they would not use Russian ships 'for carrying convicts to New Holland'.[42]

The person who obtained the contract was William Richards Jr, of Walworth. Richards came up with a comprehensive plan, which involved the government's charting ships to carry people and goods out to Botany Bay, where they would be discharged from the government's service, and their going on to Canton, where the East India Company would hire them to bring back tea and other items. In this way, both the government and the Company would make substantial savings. In consultation with Middleton, Pitt and the deputy chairman of the East India Company, Richards developed this scheme over a number of weeks.[43]

On receiving the contract, and with George Rose having prepared the way, Richards offered five ships for the Company's approval: *Britannia*, *Britannia*, *Brothers*, *Scarborough*, *William and Mary*; and another three as storeships to the Navy Board: *Britannia*, *Columbus*, *George*.

The Company agreed to hire the five ships offered to it on 27 September, at £10 per ton, with the provisos that they should reach China by 15 January 1788, and not leave with crews of fewer than eight men and boys per 100 tons.[44]

The Navy Board was more demanding in its requirements and inspections, and in these we again see the care with which the administration approached the business of the First Fleet. The Deptford officers approved of the *Britannia* and *Friendship* as convict transports. They approved of the *George* as a storeship; but thought the *Columbus*, built of American timbers and with 'very indifferent' accommodations, not 'a proper ship'. They disapproved of the second *Britannia* as a storeship, for its copper sheathing had corroded some of its ironwork, and the sheathing itself was very thin. There were other faults, and they could not recommend it 'as fit for a voyage of so remote a nature'.[45] By mid-October, Richards had substituted the *Alexander* as a convict transport, and the *Borrowdale* and *Golden Grove* as storeships.[46]

Let me therefore give details only of those ships that made the voyage. Initially, there were five convict transports. The *Alexander* had been built at Hull, was three years old, and of 452 85/94 tons burden. The *Charlotte* had been built in the Thames, was two years old, and of 345 53/94 tons burden. The *Friendship* had been built at Scarborough, was two years old, and of 278 1/94 tons burden. The *Lady Penrhyn* had been built in the Thames, was less than a year old, and of 338 13/94 tons burden. The *Scarborough* was three and a half years old, and of 418 36/94 tons burden.[47]

In early December, as Teer and Phillip supervised the loading of equipment and provisions into these ships, and they and Middleton and Nepean discussed the dispositions of the people they would carry, it became clear that there simply wasn't enough space for people and things. Accordingly, the administration hired another ship, the *Prince of Wales*. This had been built in the Thames, was one year old, and of 333 67/94 tons burden.[48]

With the exception of the *Prince of Wales*, the owners of these ships completed the fitting-out they were responsible for in early November. The Navy Board then needed to make them capable of securing their human cargoes. It ordered them fitted with cabins and bulkheads 'for

[the] security of the convicts going to Botany Bay'. This work was completed by the end of the month. However, George Teer then suggested that it would be advisable to fit 'strong hatch bars in the between decks and over the gratings on the upper decks … with strong locks as may be thought necessary', which was done.[49] But then, when a marine guard had arrived from Portsmouth, so that the first of the convicts might be put on board the *Alexander*, Lieutenant George Johnston complained that the ship's hatchway 'might with great ease be broke open, having only two cross bars, and them only secured with the common staple and padlock'. He recommended that more bars and bolts be added. He also pointed out that there were 'no loop holes to fire in upon them, supposing any riot or disobedience of orders should take place', and announced that 'under these circumstances I can't be answerable for the security of the convicts'. The Admiralty relayed the lieutenant's complaint to the Home Office, which told the Treasury, which directed the Navy Board to remedy the situation.[50]

Johnston also complained about the handcuffs the Navy Board had provided. The Board had ordered 350 double sets, 'such as are used in securing the convicts on board the hulks at Woolwich', from Mr Cross on 9 November; when they arrived, Teer distributed them among the ships 'agreeable to the number [of convicts] at first intended'. But Johnston found them 'by no means strong enough or calculated for the purpose intended', evidently because they were 'too long'. After some protest, the Board agreed to shorten them.[51]

The storeships

The *Borrowdale* had been built at Sunderland, was one and a half years old, and of 272 26/94 tons burden. The *Fishburn* had been built at Whitby, was six years old, and of 378 26/94 tons burden. The *Golden Grove* had been built at Whitby, was six years old, and of 331 30/94 tons burden.[52] None of these ships was hired by the East India Company. Teer reported on 30 October that the owners had completed their fitting out, and they were ready to receive provisions.[53]

*

There were also a number of arrangements of a different kind which needed to be made for the convict transports and storeships.

The Act 26 Geo. III, c. 60 required that privately owned, British-built ships should have formal permission to sail beyond Europe. The Admiralty sent licenses for the three storeships and four of the convict transports to the Customs Board in November 1786, and those for the others in December and January.[54]

These ships also needed to be licensed by the East India Company to proceed past the Cape of Good Hope. William Richards asked the Navy Board for advice concerning this on 15 December, which resulted in the Board sending a list of the ships to the Company.[55]

Third, in continued pursuit of William Richards's scheme to save the cost of ships returning empty, the government needed to conclude arrangements with the East India Company for those intended to load a cargo at Canton. On 18 October, the Navy Board reminded the Treasury that if the ships would 'reach China by 1 January 1788, they are to be discharged there, and we shall have made a most advantageous bargain for the public; but if unnecessarily detained in Botany Bay so as to be prevented from proceeding in time, we shall be obliged to keep them in pay until their return to Deptford'.[56]

Following standard procedure, George Rose then advised the Home Office and the Admiralty of the need to instruct Phillip accordingly. In mid-December, the East India Company informed its officers in Canton that it had chartered the *Alexander, Charlotte, Lady Penrhyn* and *Scarborough* to bring cargoes home, if they reached China by 15 January 1788. At the end of December, Richards seems to have substituted the *Prince of Wales* for the *Alexander.* In the event, though, only the *Charlotte, Lady Penrhyn* and *Scarborough* went on to China from New South Wales. When it became clear that the ships would not leave England until mid-1787, at the government's request the Company relaxed this deadline.[57]

*

It is clear, then, that the Navy Board did not select any clapped-out old ships that were available to carry the colonists out to Botany Bay.

Despite the faults that gradually revealed themselves, the *Sirius* and *Supply* were in the main sturdy ships, if indifferent sailers. The length of time the *Sirius* took to break up on the reef at Norfolk Island in March 1790 shows its basic strength.

The *Supply* was very much older than the other ships of the First Fleet, having been built in 1759. However, it was in good condition at the time it was chosen – for example, in November 1786 the Deptford officers inspected braces and pintles that had been fitted in April 1785, and found them 'in a perfect state'.[58] From New South Wales, it made a series of voyages – between Sydney and Norfolk Island ten times, and to Lord Howe Island once; to Batavia and back – before returning to England in April 1792. This was sterling service for a small ship, when the average life of a ship was about eight years.

None of the convict transports and storeships was more than six years old. Two were less than a year old; three were two years old; two were three years old; and two six years old. All were in good condition at the time of hiring. These were ships to take the convicts to their destination on the other side of the world, not to founder *en route*. The idea that these were decrepit ships is based on unexamined prejudice or inadequate research.

6.

Equipping the Colonists

The Navy Board followed standard procedure in letting contracts for food and goods for the Botany Bay colonists. However, there was at first a serious flaw in the way officials conceived of the voyage – one which might well have resulted in catastrophic failure. That this did not happen was because Phillip and his surgeons insisted on the need for change, and the Pitt administration agreed. I shall examine in detail what the problem was in Chapter 9. For the moment, let me describe how the Navy Board first went about equipping the colonists.

Food

The administration needed to provide food for two distinct phases of the venture: while the colonists were on board the ships, whether in one or other of the ports of southern England as they waited to sail or during the voyage; and once they were in the colony.

It was the contractor's responsibility to order the items and quantities needed in the first of these phases. The contract which the Navy Board concluded with William Richards on 12 September has seemingly not survived.[1] However, against the unexamined prejudices of some historians, the quality of the foods that Richards provided was high.[2]

As the government was to be the employer of the convicts in New South Wales, the Navy Board was directly responsible for providing them with food there. In his letter of 26 August, Steele asked the Board

339

to order provisions for two years, even though the initial term of appointment of the officers and marines was three years.[3] This was because the administration was assuming that after the first year the colonists would be progressing towards self-sufficiency, so that, combined with local production, one year's provisions from England might be spread over the second and third years.

In return, the Navy Board asked for details of 'the quantity of each a ration is to consist of, distinguishing that for the convicts from [that for] the marines'. Steele sought Nepean's advice, who replied that 'the marines and convicts ... should after their landing be victualled in the same manner as the troops serving in the West India islands, excepting only the allowance of spirits; the women to have 2/3rds of the quantity of provisions supplied to a man'.[4]

As Steele then advised the Navy Board, the weekly ration for a troop in the West Indies was:

7 lbs bread, or in lieu thereof 7 lbs of flour

7 lbs of beef, or in lieu thereof 4 lbs of pork

3 pints of peas

6 ozs of butter (or 1 lb of flour or in lieu thereof 1/2 lb of rice).[5]

There was a good deal of formality to these exchanges, for the Navy Board knew perfectly well what this ration was, but administrative protocols needed to be observed: the Board might not act without explicit directions from the Treasury.

So instructed, the Board proceeded to calculate the weight of this allowance for two years for 1000 people, and the cargo space needed for it – that is, 860 rations for men (officials, marines, convicts), and 140 rations for women (convicts and Polynesians). Between them, the Navy Board and Victualling Board officials worked out that, as stated, the volume would be 1090 tons; but if 'flour is substituted for bread, pork for beef, and rice for flour, the amount will be only 786 3/4 [tons], with the addition of 516 1/2 tons should the bread be packed in casks [i.e., rather than in bags]'.[6]

The Navy Board then advertised for tenders, due on 27 September at 1 p.m.[7] Later correspondence shows that the contracts for the food went to the following firms:[8]

Dawson and Atkinson	butter
Reeve and Greene	flour
Jordaine and Shaw	beef, pork, rice
William Robertson	peas

At the turn of the year, when the administration had increased the number of women convicts to 150 and decided to allow about thirty marines' wives and children and thirty convicts' wives and children to go out, additional quantities of food were ordered.[9]

The quality of these provisions was also high. The flour, for example, was made from 'good sound corn, well-dried and calculated to keep [a] good eighteen months'. And, following the Navy Board's usual practice, Teer took representative casks as they were being loaded into the ships, to keep for twelve months so as then 'to ascertain the warranty' – i.e., to determine whether the contents had kept as they should have. On inspecting them twelve months later, Teer was satisfied, and the contents remained good enough for the contractors to purchase the casks back.[10]

Medicines, surgical instruments, surgeon's necessaries

In his letter to the Treasury announcing the decision, Sydney advised that 'a quantity of surgeon's instruments and medicines and necessaries for the sick will likewise be wanted, and as soon as an estimate can be formed it shall be transmitted to your Lordships'; and Thomas Steele repeated this advice to the Navy Board.[11]

On 24 October, George Rose asked Nepean for the details of the 'surgeon's instruments, medicines and necessaries for the sick for the use of the convicts destined to Botany Bay'. In advance of receiving this list, however, he requested the Navy Board to order a two years' supply. The Board accordingly asked the Apothecaries Company to provide 'a chest of medicines equal to the allowance of a 2nd-rate man-of-war with a complement of 750 men for two years'; and for 'a suitable set of instruments for that quantity of medicines'.[12] Given that the crews of the *Sirius* and *Supply* and the marines would be provided for separately in the way normal to their service, this was an adequate supply for the convicts, whose number at this point was 750.

Robert Adair, the surgeon-general to the Army and the King, and John White, the colony's chief surgeon, then drew up a very extensive list of medicines and surgical instruments and other equipment, including beds, which Nepean passed on to the Treasury on 14 November, whence it went to the Navy Board.[13]

It would require specialist knowledge to assess the competence of this list, which I simply do not have. However, my impression is that it was both much more extensive than might ordinarily have been expected, and was adapted to the needs of a land-based community – an impression presumably confirmed by the fact that in sending it, the Treasury advised the Navy Board that it was to supersede whatever may have been ordered as a consequence of Rose's earlier letter. The Board attended to this. In another sign that the administration saw how important good health was to the success of the venture, Steele also advised that White should oversee the distribution of the medicines and instruments into the various ships.[14]

The supplying of medical items continued into 1787. In January, for example, White asked for two stills, one ream of filtering paper, two pieces of bandage linen, and two sets of amputating and trepanning instruments, which were ordered.[15]

'Surgeon's necessaries' were small items that were then considered efficacious in aiding convalescence. They included almonds, barley, currants, garlic, mace, nutmeg, rice, sago, shalotts, sugar and tamarinds.[16] Later circumstances indicate that supplies of these items were not ordered for the convicts at this time. However wine, also considered a 'necessary', was thought of, with the surgeons recommending it, so that Nepean asked that Phillip be authorized to purchase 'about 30 pipes' of wine at Tenerife, which was done.[17]

Animals

While the records are sparse, some cattle and other animals were loaded on board the ships as they waited at Portsmouth to depart. The surgeon on the *Lady Penrhyn* recorded on 14 July 1787 that 'there were on board sheep, hogs, goats, puppies, kids, turkeys, geese, ducks, chickens, rabbits, pigeons, cats'. While some of these animals may have been loaded at Tenerife, at which the ships had called in early June, I think it likely that many of them were taken on board at Portsmouth.[18] However this may have been, the difficulties of preventing penned animals from being injured in pitching seas and of providing fodder for them on a very long voyage meant that it was sound policy to take the majority of the colony's animals on board at ports *en route*. The Treasury therefore gave Phillip permission to purchase 'live stock, seed etc. for the new settlement' at the Cape Verde Islands (thought of before Phillip had decided it would be better to call at Rio de Janeiro) and the Cape of Good Hope, but with the caution that he was to keep a proper account of his expenditure.[19]

When the ships were about to depart, Phillip announced that dogs were to be off-loaded. Banks's contemporareous advice to him and to the gardener who was to look after the breadfruit plants tells us that this was because of these animals' habit of burying their excrement, which might be most injurious to the plants being carried out in tubs. However, it is clear that not everyone obeyed this edict, including Phillip himself, who took some greyhounds with him for hunting game in the colony.[20]

Plants and seeds

Although the details are now lost, Phillip clearly consulted Sir Joseph Banks soon after he was appointed, for in his memorandum concerning the voyage and the colony, he remarked: 'such fruit trees and cuttings that will bear removing should be added to the seeds carried from England, as likewise roots that will bear keeping that length of time out of the ground'; and a few weeks later, he advised Nepean that the kitchen-garden seeds should be packed in 'very small parcels'. This was because they might then be distributed among the ships, so that if one ship went down, others would bring these precious items to their destination. This was done.[21]

Only some of the plants were obtained in England. Among those sent as nurslings or engrafted were peaches, nectarines, apricots, apples, pears, plums, cherries, pomegranates, oranges, lemons, limes, shaddocks, walnuts, almonds, figs, olives. There were strawberries, gooseberries, raspberries, filberts (hazelberries), vines, currants, mulberries. Among the common herbs were sage, mint, chives, tarragon, marjoram; and among the root garnishes horseradish, artichoke, garlic and shallot.[22]

Most of the seeds for the First Fleet, though by no means all, were taken from England. Under the direction of Sir Joseph Banks, these, vast in both variety and quantity, were obtained from James Dickson, the nurseryman with whom Banks habitually dealt. They were packed in camphor to stop them spoiling from heat and salt on the voyage, and roughly parallel assortments were loaded into different ships.

The list is very extensive. Among the cereals were spring wheat, winter wheat, barley, rye and oats. Of vegetables there were dwarf marrow peas, field peas, long orange carrot, early York cabbage, onions, leeks, kidney beans, asparagus, red and white beet, cauliflower, broccoli and parsnips. There were mustard, cress, nasturtium, spinach, parsley, fennel, thyme, basil, hyssop and balm. Among the pastures were lucerne, sainfoin, and red and white clover.

That is, a remarkable number of those grains, fruits, vegetables and herbs that Europeans had long cultivated, from the shores of the Mediterranean Sea north to England, Germany and Scandinavia, were sent on the First Fleet. We might see Banks's approach as something of a blunderbuss one; however, he was providing, as it were, a blanket insurance: if one variety of carrot or cabbage did not find the Botany Bay environment to its taste, another presumably would. If all – or even most – of the plants and vegetables that went out on the First Fleet were to flourish, then the New South Wales colonists would have a much greater range of food stuffs than was then available in any single English county.

It is worth pointing out that this was what in fact happened. In the first three years, when the colonists had to locate the areas of good soil and to learn about the environment, and when the long drought set them back in their efforts, the business of establishing horticulture and agriculture in New South Wales was certainly retarded. However, by about 1800, the colonists having had the benefit of additional shipments of animals, plants and seeds, the Cumberland Plain behind Sydney had become a prolific garden, spread over by fields of grain, fruit groves, vines, vegetable gardens and pastures. For example, one modern grower has estimated that there may have been as many as 160,000 peach trees by about 1802; so prolific were their yields that farmers fed their pigs upon them.[23] And behind Lieutenant-Governor Paterson's Sydney house was a 'vast garden', with a 'great number of useful vegetables ... which have been procured from every part of the world'.[24]

The colony's progress with grain cultivation and animal husbandry was equally impressive. By 1805, there were 12,700 acres under cereals; and on the native and introduced pastures grazed 517 horses, 4325 cattle, 20,617 sheep, 5123 goats and 23,050 pigs, as well as innumerable chickens, ducks and geese. François Péron, who arrived with the Baudin expedition in 1802 and visited Samuel Marsden's estate at Parramatta, wrote in awe: 'no longer ago than 1794, the whole of this spot was covered with immense and useless forests of Eucalyptus. This residence ... is ... isolated, in a manner, in the midst of woods; and it was over a very excellent road, in a very elegant chaise, that Mr Marsden drove me to it. What pains, what exertions must have been taken to open such communications! And these communications, these pastures, these fields, these harvests, these orchards, these flocks, are the work of eight years.'[25]

By the turn of the nineteenth century, that is, the New South Wales colonists had established that biota that had sustained Western Europeans for millennia (and added some exotics to it as well). And, benefiting from a better food supply, a benign climate, and free of the usual childhood illnesses, the first generation of native-born colonists grew up to six inches taller than their parents.[26]

Shelter

It was of course necessary for the colonists to have some shelter while they built their huts. For the ordinary marines and the convicts, the administration took tents out of the Ordnance store at Portsmouth.[27] In his letter of 26 August, Thomas Steele asked the Navy Board to obtain clothing and bedding for the colony's convicts, marines and officials. On 11 September, the Board called in Mr Simms, who agreed to deliver 750 beds for the convicts. These were ready about two weeks later.[28]

Providing for the officials and the marine officers proved more complicated. At the end of October, Phillip asked for some marquees for these two groups, and Nepean told Middleton privately in early December that twenty-two were required. The Treasury made this request official a week later, but the Navy Board advised that they could not be obtained in less than three weeks. Phillip then suggested that soldiers' tents be substituted, and volunteered to set an example to the others by using one himself, a move which would save something over £600. On 22 December Major Ross presented an extensive list of camp equipment needed for the marine officers, including forty-one tents and marquees, with Phillip annotating that these items were also 'wanted in addition for the governor, and eight officers of the staff'.[29]

The Admiralty then ordered Lieutenant Furzer, the marines' quartermaster, to Portsmouth, to see if items in store there left over from the American war might do. However, these had evidently become unserviceable, for on 4 January 1787 Middleton advised Nepean that the Navy Board was now ordering the tents, marquees, canteens and kettles. These were ready at the end of the month.[30]

There was also the matter of a temporary house for the governor, to serve while a permanent dwelling was being erected. On 8 November, the Navy Board ordered Mr Smith of Knightsbridge to make a prefabricated house of timber and canvas 45 feet long, 17 feet 6 inches wide, 8 feet high, with five windows on each side. While this dwelling did not provide as much comfort as Phillip hoped for – he wrote dismally from Sydney that it was 'neither wind nor water proof' – at least, it was better than nothing, as he waited for his permanent house to be completed.[31]

Clothing

The clothing ordered for the male convicts accorded with the list attached by Evan Nepean to Heads of a Plan, *viz.*, for one year:[32]

    2 jackets
    3 frocks
    3 pairs trousers
    4 woollen drawers
    3 shirts
    1 hat
    4 pairs worsted stockings
    3 pairs shoes

Nepean provided no such list of clothing for the female convicts, simply noting that 'the expense of clothing female convicts may be computed to amount to the same sum [as allowed for the men]. A proportion for two years to be provided'.[33] However, the Navy Board minute of 7 September 1786 and the list of items ordered in December for an additional thirty female convicts indicate that the yearly allowance for women was:[34]

    4 white shifts
    1 grey cotton jacket
    1 white cotton jacket
    2 check cotton jackets
    2 linsey cotton jackets
    2 canvas petticoats
    [2 linsey woolsey petticoats][35]
    1 serge petticoat
    3 handkerchiefs
    2 caps
    1 hat
    4 pairs yarn stockings
    3 pairs shoes

The Navy Board ordered a two-years' supply of the men's and women's items on 7 September. The contracts were awarded to:

Mr Darby	woollen jackets and drawers
James Wadham	13 tons of 'slop' clothing[36]
W. and R. Borrowdale	1 ton of hats
John Yerbury	1/2 ton of stockings
Peter Pope	1/2 ton of stockings
William Goodman	2 1/2 tons of shoes[37]

When Nepean advised that there would be an extra thirty female convicts shipped from Newgate, the Navy Board ordered supplies of the same items for them.[38]

Tools and other implements

In his letter of 26 August 1786, Steele also asked the Navy Board to order 'tools and implements of agriculture' for the convicts and marines.[39] On 13 September, the Board asked the firm of Harrison, Gordon and Stanley to provide a long list of utensils, tools, implements and hardware.

Each of the male convicts and the marines was to have:

1 spade
1 shovel
1 grubbing hoe
1 West India hoe
1 garden hoe
1 felling axe
1 hatchet
1 knife
gimblets
wooden bowls, platters and spoons

Included in the list of communal tools, implements and hardware were: saws, adzes, broad axes, augers, chisels, planes, files, forges, bellows and anvils, grindstones, wheelbarrows, iron mills, ploughs, cooper's tools, nails, hinges, locks, bar iron, steel, glass, fishing lines, etc. But Sir Charles Middleton then had second thoughts about what was really needed, and drew up another list, telling Nepean that 'in the first list many things were wanting and other ill-sorted. I will take care that nothing superfluous is sent nor anything material omitted'.[40]

The items in the additional list are interesting, and give the lie to a number of hoary chestnuts, of which the most prominent is that no ploughs were sent. Plough and cart harnesses for six horses and six oxen were requested; a flax-dressing mill, together with 'the necessary articles for dressing flax'; mills for grinding cassava; canvas to make 250 beds for the colony's hospital; wheelbarrows; wheels on axles 'for the moving of timber, etc.'; bricks for chimneys and a kiln; 500 tin plates; coppers; stone mason's tools; scythes. The next day, the Board also asked for 'small shot of [different] sorts, 2 cwt from no. 1 downwards, with moulds for it'. On 31 October, at Phillip's request, the Board added an order for five dozen razors, and large and small combs. These items were ready for loading in mid-November.[41]

On 29 December, the Navy Board ordered 'a further quantity of 2 cwt of buck shot, 6 scythes and 5 dozen of razors'. Phillip considered these quantities 'very insufficient', and asked for an additional '20 scythes, 12 dozen of razors (at 12s a dozen) and 5 cwt of small shot, chiefly buck'. The Navy Board ordered another 6 cwt of small shot.[42]

Ordnance

Another of the matters that Phillip gave thought to soon after his appointment was the colony's defences.

In something I have never been able to get to the bottom of, at some point Phillip evidently trained as a soldier as well, for he had a specialized knowledge of artillery. This training is reflected in his remark in his memorandum about the colony that 'it will be necessary to throw up a slight work, as a defence against the natives ... and against the convicts ... For this my own little knowledge as a field engineer will be sufficient'; and a portrait done in London somewhere about this time shows him holding a plan of a pentangle redoubt.[43]

By the end of October, Phillip had asked for eight 12-pounder cannon to arm this fort, which the Duke of Richmond, the Master-General of the Ordnance, then reduced to four 12-pounders and four 6-pounders. Subsequently, this was changed again, to two iron 12-pounders 9 feet in length, two 12-pounders of 7 1/2 feet, and two 6-pounders of 8 feet, and two light brass 6-pounders of 4 1/2 feet.[44]

The Ordnance Board also gave him all the paraphernalia needed to keep these guns in good order, and to work them, including carriages, powder and shot, cartridges, handspikes, matches, sponges and rammer heads, fuses, hand grenades, blunderbusses, harness, lead aprons, ropes, laboratory knives, lanterns, tarpaulins, etc. As the muskets and cutlasses in the Portsmouth and Plymouth barracks stores were worn, the marines going to New South Wales were issued with 200 new ones, with the muskets to have steel rammers and bayonets, and with the attendant flints, locks, swivels and loops. As already indicated, quantities of ammunition were also provided.[45]

Bricks

On 26 October, the Navy Board ordered the Deptford officers to load 5000 bricks into the transports, to be used for building chimneys and kilns. This number was evidently later doubled, and brick moulds were also shipped. Under the supervision of the convict James Bloodworth, the kilns built at the brickfield about a mile to the southwest of the camp at Sydney, produced bricks that were used in the governor's permanent house.[46]

Implements for manufacturing cloth

From late Tudor times, southeastern Lancaster, in the English midlands, was a centre of cloth manufacture. With this development aided by easy river access to the major port of Liverpool, by the later eighteenth century proto-factories had been established in centres such as Preston, Blackburn, Bolton, Wigan and Stockport, with Manchester as the most important, and with a myriad individual spinners and weavers in the adjacent rural areas supplying them with yarn and cloth. The cloths ('fustian' or 'calico'[47]) were often a mixture of flax and cotton, with the flax coming from Ireland and the cotton from the Levant or the West Indies.

The market for linen and cotton cloths expanded in the eighteenth century, with demand for brightly coloured pieces in Africa, America and the West Indies, and with a growing domestic preference for women's dresses to be made of these materials.

And what, you may well ask, does this digression have to do with New South Wales? Well, as I explain in *Botany Bay: The Real Story*, one of the Pitt administration's reasons for establishing the colony was to obtain supplies of New Zealand flax (*Phormium tenax*), both to provide cloth with which to make clothes for the convicts and free settlers who might later arrive, and canvas and cordage for the warships stationed in Indian waters, but also for more general distribution – as Evan Nepean remarked in late October 1786, the colony's 'most considerable object' (i.e., apart from sending the convicts out of the kingdom) was 'the cultivation of the flax plant ... [which] has been found in that neighbourhood in the most luxuriant state, and small quantities have been brought to Europe and manufactured, and, from its superior quality, it will, it is hoped, soon become an article of commerce from that country'. The administration instructed Phillip that he was to attend to the cultivation and harvesting of this fibre plant,

> as it has been humbly represented unto us that advantages may be derived from the flax plant which is found in the islands not far distant from the intended settlement, not only as a means of acquiring clothing for the convicts and other person who may become settlers, but from its superior excellence for a variety of maritime purposes, and as it may ultimately become an article of export.

He was also to 'send home by every opportunity which may offer, samples of that article, in order that a judgement may be formed whether it may not be necessary to instruct you further upon this subject'.[48]

Therefore, it was necessary for the administration to provide Phillip with the means of doing so. In October, Nepean made contact with William Sharrow and John Singleton. William and George Sharrow (who may have been brothers) had first had a linen-manufacturing business in Ireland, which they then expanded into England, to Yorkshire and then to Birmingham, and with strong links to Manchester. Stating that, 'after much study and application, and at a great expense', they had 'invented a simple and easy process for dressing backings or hirds, being the common refuse of tow, dressed from flax, so as to answer the same end in several manufactures as cotton, particularly in the manufacture of checks, stripes and low-priced fustians; and also for candle wick and lamps, where real cotton is used', in February 1783 the Sharrows petitioned parliament for a financial reward, in return for which they offered to make their process generally available to linen and cotton manufacturers, which would 'be the means of a great saving in the imports of a foreign article of commerce'.[49]

Nepean's surviving correspondence with William Sharrow is not complete. Sharrow evidently wrote to him on 24 October, pointing out that the New Zealand flax might present problems of importation. Nepean replied on 27 October, thanking Sharrow, and asking for details of how he thought the fibre might be managed, 'so as to serve as an instruction to the people who may be employed in its cultivation, and tend to remove those objections to its importation which you suggest'. Sharrow answered three days later, that, 'on arrival of the convicts', the cultivation of it would 'employ men, women and children'. He asked for a sample of it, so that he might 'do everything in my power to communicate the improvement of the flax plant, [so as] to make it eligible for importation, which certainly is a great national object, as the manufacturers of this country will reap a considerable advantage from it (far more so than is yet seen)'. A week later, he asked if it would be too late for him to present his 'report and instructions … the middle of next month' (i.e., December), as he would then be in London.[50] These documents have not been found. My assumption is that they were given to Phillip without being copied, for him to pass them on to those whom he sent to Norfolk Island.

Simultaneously, and at Phillip's urging, Nepean sought advice from John Singleton, a Wigan check manufacturer, about the cultivation of cotton in New South Wales. Saying that he had talked to 'a West India merchant who tells me he is sure cotton will thrive in [the] South Seas', Singleton offered to send seeds of different varieties, adding that 'it is very possible the profit in [the] end may be considerable to this country'.[51] As the following quote shows, Singleton provided seeds. Phillip subsequently took on more seeds, and plants, at Rio de Janeiro. King sowed cotton immediately on landing at Norfolk Island; but this planting evidently did not succeed, for Phillip later reported that 'of the cotton seed brought from England very little vegetated'.[52]

Given the intermingling of flax and cotton in cloth manufacturing then, these conversations must have been linked. Indeed, it is possible that the Sharrows and Singleton made a joint approach to the administration; but whether or not this was so, officials duly provided for the refinement of fibres and the manufacture of cloth in the colony, when they shipped 'twenty-four spinning whorls, forty-eight spinning brasses, nine hackles for flax, nine hackle pins, three flax dresser's brushes, 127 dozen combs, [and] one machine for dressing flax, with iron work and brushes'; and a 'loom for weaving canvas, complete'.[53]

There were many other small items that the administration needed to provide, many of them necessary for the various officers to be able to fulfil their duties – e.g., in January 1787 Andrew Miller, the commissary, spent £20.11.0 on stationery 'for the business of his department'.[54] Often, these items were so routine that they were provided without record. And on 4 December, at Phillip's request, the Navy Board ordered sets of weights and measures – weights from 1/4 cwt down to 1 lb; and 1/2 bushel and smaller measures according to the Winchester standard.[55]

Trade goods

The administration also thought that, in line with Matra's suggestion, the colony might obtain animals at places closer to New South Wales than Europe or the Cape of Good Hope – for instance, from Savu in the Molucca Islands and from the Pacific Islands.

Accordingly, at the end of October, Phillip asked Nepean what items had been ordered as 'presents' for the natives; and suggested some additions. Nepean then asked the Treasury to obtain £50-worth of ducats and 'two or three cask of beer' to bribe the Dutch at Savu; and 200 muskets and cutlasses to induce the local inhabitants to pass over their 'black cattle, goats and hogs'. He asked also for £150-worth of 'small hatchets, some of them made in the Tahiti fashion, glass beads, chiefly white, pocket looking glasses [i.e., mirrors], nails and gimlets, and a few *real* red feathers' to trade with the Society islanders. The Treasury ordered these from Brook Watson's firm, Rashleigh and Company. They were ready four weeks later. (One newspaper reported also that 'an immense number of toys are to be sent … for the natives'; but this may only be a garbled version of the above.)[56]

Equipping the marines

As we have seen, both the marines and convicts going out to New South Wales were victualled in the manner of troops sent to the West Indies, with the qualification that the convicts were not allowed spirits. However, because they were part of the regular peacetime naval establishment, the marines were otherwise equipped separately from the convicts, and by the Admiralty and Navy Board rather than by the Home Office.

Clothing and Goods: In November, Phillip Stephens told the marine storekeeper at Portsmouth that it was intended that the troops should be supplied with clothing in the colony; and on 5 December, he ordered a long list of 'necessaries', including shirts, stockings, shoes, ribbons, knapsacks, kitchen utensils, shears, needles and threads, combs and razors. The majority of these items were ready by the end of the month.[57]

Wine and Spirits: At the beginning of November, the Navy Board queried the Treasury's earlier advice that the marines were not to be provided with spirits at Botany Bay, to be told that this was indeed so.[58] In keeping with this intention, the administration also did not make any provision for spirits or wine (except, as mentioned, what would be required for the sick). Curiously, a merchant firm offered to supply the marines with Tenerife wine 'at 20 shillings per gallon delivered on board at the island of Santa Cruz, in stout pipes with a proper quantity of hoops'. Treasury referred this offer to the Navy Board, which replied 'that by the orders we have received for providing the rations of provisions for them, there is not any mention of wine or spirits'.[59]

Officials had a foreboding about the trouble these exemptions would cause for months before it became a tumult. Phillip put it to the Navy Board that the marines should be supplied with spirits in New South Wales, to be told that he must approach the Treasury. He then asked Nepean to do so, saying that he feared 'much discontent in the garrison if there is no allowance of wine or spirits (to which they have ever been accustomed)'; and that he could take on wine at either Tenerife or the Cape of Good Hope.[60] At this time, however, he received no satisfaction on this point.

Equipping the colony for science

Lieutenant William Dawes was included in the marine officers going to New South Wales because of his scientific expertise. He came to London for consultations at the end of October 1786. On 14 November, Neville Maskelyne, the Astronomer Royal, told Board members that Dawes was interested in making 'useful nautical and astronomical observations in his passage [to Botany Bay], and during his stay there', and had asked the Board to lend him instruments and manuals; and that he 'was capable of making proper use of them'.[61]

Dawes had earlier presented the Royal Society with a long list of instruments he wished to have, but this was now reduced according to what the Board of Longitude had available. These included an astronomical quadrant; a sextant; an acromatic telescope with a micrometer; various clocks and watches; barometers and thermometers; tables of logarithms; and nautical almanacs. However, believing that the governor would be in a position to take better care of them than Dawes, the Board stipulated that the 'said instruments and books should be ... delivered into the charge of Captain Phillip'. The Board also added a Kendall chronometer for Phillip, 'he giving a receipt for the same and promising to return it at the expiration of his voyage'.[62]

Long afterwards, Dawes received £100 from the Board 'as an allowance for my observations made in New South Wales'.[63]

Providing for the soul

As well as to their physical needs, authorities thought to attend to the spiritual welfare of the convicts. Following a request from the Archbishop of Canterbury, the Society for the Propagation of the Gospel provided the Reverend Richard Johnson with large numbers of bibles, prayer books, catechisms and improving tracts, including *Religion Made Easy, Great Importance of a Religious Life, Christian Soldier, Offices for the Penitent, Admonitions* – and more to the point, perhaps, *Plain Exhortations to Prisoners, Dissuasive from Stealing, Caution of Profane Swearers* and *Exhortations to Chastity*.[64]

We may wonder how many of the convicts were suitably appreciative of these presents.

Providing for commerce

In the list of seeds sent in the *Sirius*, Banks included a category for 'commerce' – i.e., for trade with passing ships or for export: hemp, flax, rhubarb, tobacco, potato seed and oats.[65]

At first glance, this is a curious mixture, but it has a not-immediately-obvious significance. As just discussed, one of the reasons for establishing the colony was to manufacture the New Zealand flax; and if *Phormium tenax* flourished in the islands of the southwest Pacific Ocean, so too might the European fibre plants. Rhubarb was then widely used in medicine as a laxative. Tobacco was a common return cargo for ships visiting the southern American colonies. Light and able to be compressed, it was a convenient item to carry. It was also a staple of a sailor's life. Oatmeal was an integral part of the ration on Royal Navy ships, being served on three days out of seven. Brought from America after Columbus's voyages, the potato was being widely cultivated in Europe by the end of the eighteenth century, when it had become a common food for the poor (most famously in Ireland). It was also a common substitute in the naval ration for bread, with the established proportions being 2 lbs of potato for 1 lb bread.[66]

These examples show how such items were relevant to ships doing business in the great ocean. In 1793–4, James Colnett undertook a voyage into the Pacific Ocean, which was to have been an official one but which, after the outbreak of war with France, went forward privately, although Colnett continued to see himself as fulfilling Admiralty intentions. Its purpose was to search for places where Southern whalers might refresh, and Colnett planted 'garden seeds, of every kind, for the benefit and comfort of those who might come after us'. Similarly, early in the nineteenth century, reflecting their contact with Euopeans and their acumen, Maori at the Bay of Islands had extensive fields of wheat and beds of turnips, potatoes and sweet potatoes, which they traded to visiting ships.[67]

The items that Banks annotated 'For Commerce', then, were all such as ships would require – not only those ships which would carry convicts out in the future, but also those which would pursue trade independently – a development in line with Phillip's expectation that in time 'ships of all nations' would come to the colony.

7.

Loading the Ships and Embarking the People

THERE WAS A MYRIAD arrangements to be made, and items to be shipped. What I offer here is an indicative description only, not a comprehensive analysis. Also, the chronology of steps was in reality more convoluted than I make it seem. For example, while a certain number of officers went on board the ships as soon as they were fitted out, so as to begin preparing them for the voyage, others who were either appointed subsequently or who needed to make extensive preparations for their particular roles in the colony embarked much later. Among this latter group were the governor, the chief surgeon and some of his deputies, the surveyor, the commandant of marines, the quartermaster and the astronomer.

Fitting out and loading the ships
On 25 October 1786, the Admiralty advised the Navy Board that Arthur Phillip would command the *Sirius*, which should carry a crew of 160 (including twenty-two marines), and 'be fitted out for a voyage to remote parts, … victualled to twelve months of all species of provisions at whole allowance and stored to a proper proportion for foreign service'.[1] The same day the Deptford officers advised the Navy Board that the *Sirius* would be ready to receive its crew on 27 October. A skeleton crew began rigging it on 28 October. This work continued for some weeks, as the number of crew increased. On 9 November, the ship shifted down to

358

Long Reach to take on its cannon and other ordnance stores. During this time, officers and crew were accommodated on the *Flora,* so as 'to keep them clear of the artificers'. John Hunter assumed day-to-day command of the ship on 5 December.[2]

On 27 October, the Admiralty similarly advised the Navy Board that Lieutenant Henry Ball would command the *Supply,* which was to have a crew of fifty-five (including twelve marines), and be fitted out and provisioned for a voyage to remote parts in the same manner as the *Sirius.*[3] On 1 November, the Deptford officers proposed further works on it; and on 6 November, they advised that it would be ready to receive its crew on 11 November.[4] It took on provisions in the second half of November, and its guns in December.

Since they were needed to work them, the crews of the transport ships also went on board at an early stage.

*

Captain George Teer was the Navy Board official responsible for overseeing the fitting out and the loading of the transport ships, after their owners had done some basic work on them. On 30 October, he told the Board that the storeships – *Borrowdale, Fishburn* and *Golden Grove* – were ready to receive stores, which was done through November.[5] Soon after, the first of the convict transports, the *Lady Penrhyn,* was ready to receive stores. On 4 November, for example, it took on board five barrels of tar and two of pitch, two casks of rosin, eight dozen brooms, two gallons of oil, one horse hide, eight casks of oakum 'and other small stores for [the] ship's use'.[6]

On 20 November, the Navy Board advised the Treasury that the *Alexander, Charlotte, Friendship* and *Scarborough* were also ready to receive stores. They were then loaded, with the *Alexander,* for example, taking on 'government stores' on 23 November, 'four cases of hats' on 27 November, and 'sundry' articles and stores on 30 November and 1 and 2 December.[7]

The stowing of eighteenth-century sailing ships was a complicated business, what with the need to carry ballast, cables, sails, water, fuel (timber or coal), food and goods, and still to leave room for people. Various items (e.g., butter, beef, wine, spirits, water) were packed in different-sized casks, which created further difficulties. And the loading of the First Fleet ships was even more complicated than was normal, given that they were to carry criminals, and implements, animals, a two-years' supply of provisions for the colony, and the knocked-down boats for the *Sirius* and *Supply*. The business required a great deal of expertise, which might only be born of experience. This George Teer certainly had; but Arthur Phillip thought he had it too, so there was soon tension between the two. On some points, Phillip was right – for example, the gunpowder on board the *Alexander* certainly could not be put where the convicts might get their hands on it.[8] But Phillip's 'advice', suggesting as it did faults in Teer's management, clearly riled the Navy Board official.

After Phillip wrote to the Navy Board on 4 December with several criticisms about how items were being stowed, Teer exploded with frustration:

> I beg leave to acquaint you that Captain Phillip has from time to time so increased the orders for stores, and implements for Botany Bay, and increased the number of marines from 74 up to 160 – I believe I may venture to assure you, they will occupy amongst all the ships upwards of three hundred tons space – each day and week continuing to add more, that I was obliged to put a stop to his wishes still to add more.

The Board replied that if there were space after all the stores ordered by the Treasury had been stowed, he was to meet Phillip's requests.[9]

Phillip wrote again on 7 December, with additional comments about how the beds were arranged, the need for fresh air in the holds, and the amount of water being carried. Teer replied at length, which must have been an unwelcome distraction from his work. He had recommended scuttles rather than hatchways, he said, since these would better deliver fresh air into the holds where the convicts would be held. Since some of the ships were to carry few convicts, he did not see the need for barricades on them. The beds were placed 'in the best manner they possibly can be'. He conceded there was a need for night-time toilet 'tubs'; but Phillip had made a mistake about the size of the water casks (70 gallons in a Navy ship, but 126 gallons in a merchant one), so that in fact the transports would carry sufficient water. He concluded: 'the convicts' ships are *completely fitted*, their provisions and accommodations are better than any set of transports I have ever had any directions in, as they have more water and provisions on board than any of those that went to India with Commodore Johnstone's fleet'.[10]

Already acute, this problem of lack of space was exacerbated by the Home Office's decision to increase the number of female convicts to 150 and to permit a certain number of convicts' wives and children to go out, decisions which meant, not only were there more people to ship, but also the clothes, food and water for them.[11] After considering the various possibilities, Middleton came up with an arrangement to distribute the female convicts among three ships, two of them also carrying men. This was contrary to the earlier decision of the Treasury, that the women should be accommodated together on one ship, 'so as to keep them separate from the men'.[12] When Nepean very diffidently proposed an alternative arrangement, Middleton himself grew testy, telling the Under-Secretary that 'it is absolutely impracticable to arrange the transports in any other manner than we have done without unloading and new fitting all the ships, and which would require at least three weeks from this time'. He also pointed out that 'the women cannot be more crowded than they are, having only 1 1/2 tons allowed to each, and which is as little as possible for so long a voyage'. He concluded by saying that he would 'be very happy in following any mode that can be pointed out for putting an end to this disagreeable and troublesome business'.[13]

Despite these problems, the loading of the five convict transports was largely completed by 6 December, when the Navy Board informed the Admiralty and Treasury that they would be ready to leave Deptford (i.e., to receive people) after they had been fitted with beds for the marines who were to go on them.[14] But once people were on board, it became clear that more items were needed. Four chests of arms for the marines were put into the *Charlotte* in mid-December, for example, and ordnance from the Tower into various of the ships. In mid-January, arms and accoutrement chests were ordered for the *Friendship*, and 200 sets of new muskets and cutlasses were loaded onto the *Sirius* for carriage to Portsmouth.[15]

Then, in early January, the marines on board the transports found that they were not provided with all the things they needed – that is, while the detachments going on normal sea service into the *Sirius* and *Supply* would be equipped in the usual manner, the contractor and masters were not obliged to supply certain items for the marines on the transports. Telling him that he would be recompensed, the Navy Board asked Richards to provide candles on 8 January.[16] Six days later, Captain Tench complained that 'camp utensils' were also lacking, and that, when asked about them, the master of his ship had said that 'as he had no allowance of necessary money from the Navy Board, he did not consider himself bound in any state to furnish us with these indispensable requisites'. Ross took up the complaint with the Admiralty, which referred it to the Navy Board, which asked Richards to supply those items that were allowed on the King's ships.[17]

There was a set of colours needed for the marines to parade with, and drums, drumsticks and fifes. Then, two years' supply of light clothing needed to be loaded for those who were to serve in New South Wales, and one year's supply for those on the *Sirius* and *Supply*. It was also thought proper to order 150 new 'check' shirts for the troops.[18]

On 21 January, John Shortland complained that the kitchen coppers on the *Alexander* were much too small, which necessitated two preparations of food. Expressing 'surprize' at this, the Navy Board directed Richards to replace them.[19]

*

Well before this, however – by 7 December in fact – it had become apparent that another ship was needed. In what was clearly a concerted move, Phillip suggested this to Nepean on 12 December, saying 'I do not see that it is possible to put all the marines and the number of women allowed to go with their husbands on board the transports intended to carry the convicts; and by the quantity of provisions and stores put on board the storeships, none can be received in those ships'. Nepean so advised the Treasury, which told the Navy Board to 'hasten the equipment of the *Prince of Wales* transport' – that is, before the Treasury had formally agreed to the request, and before William Richards had offered this ship to the Board (27 December 1786) and the Deptford officers had inspected it (29 December 1786).[20]

The *Prince of Wales* was fitted and loaded in January 1787. On board it were put (among other items) the 18 tons of camp equipment Major Ross considered indispensable for the marines; the tobacco for the sailors and marines on the *Sirius*; additional clothing and provisions for the extra women and children; and also provisions to be taken round to Portsmouth to replace those which were first intended for the voyage but which were now being consumed as the ships waited.[21]

*

In loading the ships, there were also a number of routine legal requirements to be met. These included Customs and Excise approvals for the technical exportation of some of the goods. On 6 November, Messrs Harrison, Gordon and Stanley asked the Navy Board to obtain exemptions from the Customs Board to permit those they had supplied 'to be shipped free of duties and fees'. The Board referred this request to the Treasury, for George Rose to ask for 'a list of the several articles and the name of the ship or ships on board of which they are intended to be sent, in order that the same may accompany the warrant for permitting the exportation of the same duty free'. Subsequently, the Board approached Customs for 'free cockets and bills [of health] for the transports ... hired to carry convicts to Botany Bay'.[22]

Then, William Richards requested the Navy Board to obtain exemption from excise charges for the rum he was loading for the marines going to Botany Bay (i.e., for the voyage, not for after landing).

The Navy Board approached the Treasury, which approached the Excise Board, which gave approval. Subsequently, the Navy Board and Treasury also requested exemptions for the rum loaded into the *Prince of Wales*.[23]

There was one such request that the Commissioners of Customs and Excise refused to grant, however. Phillip was intending to take a considerable amount of goods out with him, including two pipes and 104 dozen bottles of port; two puncheons of rum; twelve barrels of porter (a dark, bitter beer); twenty hundredweight of sugar; thirty-four dozen glasses; and forty decanters. Considering that he ran the risk of 'losing half those articles' if they were sent in a transport, he asked that the *Sirius* be included in the list of ships which qualified for the 'drawback' – i.e., the reimbursement of any duties which had previously been paid on the goods being shipped out. Nepean approached the Treasury on his behalf, which asked Customs, to be told that this was legally impossible, since the goods were to be carried on a Royal Navy ship and not a merchantman.[24]

Marines and convicts

Putting the various groups of colonists on board the ships of the First Fleet also proved an intricate and protracted business, with four steps – three legal and one practical – needing to be taken in order to embark the convicts.

The first of the legal steps was an order for transportation. As discussed in *Botany Bay: The Real Story*, the comprehensive Transportation Act of August 1784 (24 Geo. III, c. 56) had provided for the King-in-Council's fixing the place to which felons sentenced to transportation would be sent. The places identified for those so sentenced into the mid-1780s had been America or Africa, or the more general 'part or parts beyond the seas'. Therefore, New South Wales had now to be specified as the place for each of those intended to be sent there. On 1 December, asking that this be done, Sydney sent the Lord President of the Privy Council lists of those so destined. In a series of Orders-in-Council and warrants the Privy Council identified their new destination as 'the

eastern coast of New South Wales extending from the latitude of 10°37'
to the latitude of 43°39' south, or some one or other of the islands lying
between those latitudes to the Eastward of the said coast of New South
Wales within the southern Pacific Ocean'.[25]

The Orders are as follow. On 6 December, one containing the names
of 321 persons sentenced to transportation 'beyond the seas'; and one
containing the names of fifty persons sentenced to transportation to
America or Africa. On 22 December, one containing the names of four
women sentenced to transportation to America, and of fifteen sentenced
to Africa; and another containing the names of eighty-one women sentenced to 'beyond the seas'. On 12 February 1787, one containing the
names of thirty-three persons sentenced to 'beyond the seas'; and another
containing the names of four persons sentenced to America or Africa. On
20 April, one containing the names of twenty-seven persons sentenced to
'beyond the seas'; and one containing the names of one person sentenced
to America, and two to Africa.[26] When these Orders did not quite fill up
the intended complement of 750 convicts, the Privy Council and the
Home Office began issuing Orders identifying New South Wales as the
place for individuals or small groups recently sentenced to death, but
reprieved on condition of transportation.[27]

The second step was the drawing up of warrants authorizing the
keepers of convicts to deliver them over for transportation. Those for
Duncan Campbell, for example, were issued on 3 and 20 January and
24 February 1787; and that for Henry Bradley at Plymouth on 5 March.[28]
Others for convicts held in county jails followed – e.g., for the Kingston-
upon-Thames jailor on 10 March, and for the High Sheriff of Leicester
on 11 April.

The third step was that those taking 'jail delivery' of the convicts
needed to sign contracts and post bonds for receiving them and delivering them to their destination. The concluding of these certificates was a
tedious business, as it had to be done with representatives of the courts
which had sentenced the prisoners. Nepean pointed out this need to
Middleton on 9 December, saying that 'the owners as well as the masters
and mates [of the ships] must enter into the bonds which the acts of

parliament require, for the safe custody of the convicts whilst on board the transports. If that has not been done new difficulties will arise, for the courts will not vest them with the custody of the convicts without it.' Middleton replied that he could see 'a real difficulty unless the King's authority can supersede the usual practice of the courts in dispensing with [the requirement]', because, unlike as with earlier transportation to North America, those concluding the bonds would have no vested interest in delivering the convicts safely.[29]

Nepean circulated the forms to be completed for the convicts to go on board the *Alexander* to the clerks of the various assize circuits on 13 December, and announced that William Richards and Duncan Sinclair, its master, would be at the Home Office in the morning of Friday, 15 December, in order to sign them. When some of the clerks queried the need to conclude contracts, Sydney sought the Law Officers' opinion, which was that 'in order to comply with the requisites of the acts relative to the transportation of offenders, that the persons agreeing to transport the offenders should contract for the due performance of such transportation with two justices of [the] peace appointed by the court before whom the prisoners were respectively tried, or by a subsequent court held with the like authority'.[30]

These contracts were then drawn up for each of the convicts transported. Curiously, although there were once more than 750 of these, it seems only a few are now extant, including one made on 27 January 1787 by the magistrates of the town of Kingston-upon-Thames to deliver Mary Mitchell to Richards and William Sever for embarkation on the *Lady Penrhyn* and transportation 'to the eastern coast of New South Wales or some one or other of the islands adjacent in pursuance of His Majesty's Order-in-Council lately made in that behalf by virtue of the statute'.[31]

*

The practical step was to place the marine guards on board the transports before they received their convicts – or at least, on those that were to receive male convicts, for the women were put on board the *Lady Penrhyn* ahead of a marine detachment.

Only two of the six transports, the *Alexander* and the *Lady Penrhyn*, loaded their convicts in London. As those dangerous rogues who had earlier been selected for transportation to Africa went in the *Alexander*, it was particularly important that there be a strong guard for them. Under the command of Lieutenant George Johnston, thirty-seven marines marched overland from Portsmouth, reaching London on 6 December. They went on board the ship on 14 December, but Johnston soon reported that the security arrangements for the convicts were inadequate, so that these had to be increased.[32] On 6 January 1787, 184 convicts went from the hulks into the *Alexander* – 101 from the *Ceres*, fifty-one from the *Justitia* and thirty-two from the *Censor*. On 15 January (five days ahead of the relevant warrant being issued), another twenty-five convicts went into this ship, bringing its number very close to the planned 210.[33]

The women from Newgate and Southwark jail were also put on board the *Lady Penrhyn* through January – fifty-six on 6 January, 'victualled … the same day agreeable to Mr Richards's plan'; six women and three children on 9 January; sixteen women and one child on 26 January; and twenty-two women on 31 January.[34]

The Admiralty began directing parties of marines to board the other ships in mid-January. The *Sirius* and *Supply* received their complement on reaching Portsmouth on 24 February.[35] Lieutenant William Collins went on board the *Lady Penrhyn* on 17 March, and his servant three days later. Captain James Campbell and his nephew joined them on 3 May.[36]

On 20 and 24 February, the Home Office sent Campbell lists containing the names of some 191 convicts, of whom 184 were to be sent on board the *Scarborough*, and others on the *Alexander*.[37] It was now necessary to send these overland. Nepean arranged for six wagons to carry them, for a cavalry guard to escort them, for the marine guard to go on board the *Scarborough* (which it did on 27 February), and for Portsmouth authorities to provide lighters, etc., to take them from shore to ship.[38]

This caravan left London on 27 February, and reached Portsmouth on 2 March. One young naval officer later remembered:

> All the ship windows and doors of Portsmouth [were] closed on this
> occasion, and the streets were lined with troops, while the wagons …
> passed to Point Beach, where the boats were ready to receive them; as
> soon as they were embarked, they gave three tremendous cheers.[39]

However, the weather had turned so bad that it was impossible to ferry the convicts out at the Mother Bank. Instead, they were temporarily put on board the *Gorgon*, and fed out of the Navy's stores, until 4 March, when the weather moderated enough for them to be embarked on their proper ships.[40]

On 5 March, the Home Office directed Henry Bradley, the keeper of the *Dunkirk* hulk at Plymouth, that he was to put eighty male and twenty-two female convicts on board the *Friendship*, and ninety-nine men and twenty-two women on board the *Charlotte*; and another twenty-six male convicts, who were to be transferred to the *Scarborough* on arrival at Portsmouth. John White, the colony's chief surgeon, travelled west to oversee the business. The marine guards went on board these ships on 9 and 10 March, but gales made it impossible to load the prisoners until 11 March. The men were shackled, but not the women.[41]

A number of disparate groups went on board the *Prince of Wales* at Portsmouth. There were single marines; the married ones who had received permission to take their wives and children with them; and some late additions to the number of female convicts. On 7 March, twenty-nine marines and four wives were embarked; two female convicts from Chester a week later; and four female convicts and one child on 28 March. A warrant for jail delivery having been issued on 27 April, at the beginning of May, a second convoy of two wagons took two men, thirty-seven women and one child to Portsmouth, most of whom were put on board the *Prince of Wales*.[42] There were also transfers to and from other ships. All in all, when it sailed it carried some (it is impossible to give precise figures) thirty marines, twenty-eight marines' wives, twenty-five female convicts, and some children.

*

As the ships waited at Portsmouth to sail, there were various additions and alterations to the numbers of people on them. Some of the crewmen of the *Sirius* and *Supply* and some of the marines died or were invalided ashore, and were replaced by others. Lieutenant Long and Lieutenant Furzer were ordered on board the *Sirius* on 21 February; Major Ross and Captain Collins (together with one sergeant, three drummers and six privates) on 2 March; and Andrew Miller, the colony's commissary of stores, on 30 April.[43] Phillip was the last official to embark on the flagship, arriving from London on 7 May.

The situation was similar with the convicts. In March and April, in order to complete complements, or as some of those on board were released or died, more convicts were sent to the ships. Two women were transferred from the *Friendship* to the *Lady Penrhyn* after arriving from Plymouth. Three women and two children went on board the *Friendship* on 17 April.[44]

On 26 April and 6 and 8 May, the convict transports seem (because lists vary slightly) to have been carrying:[45]

	Men		Women		Children	
	26 April	6/8 May	26 April	6/8 May	26 April	6/8 May
Alexander	197	195				
Scarborough	205	205				
Charlotte	86	86	20	20	2	2
Friendship	76	76	21	21	5	4
Lady Penrhyn[46]	1	1	101	101	5	5
Prince of Wales		2	10	47	1	2
Totals	565	561	152	189	13	13

At the beginning of June, when the First Fleet reached Tenerife, these totals were: 558 male convicts, 192 female convicts and wives, thirteen convicts' children; together with twenty-eight marines' wives and seventeen children. The ages of the children ranged from infants up to fifteen years.[48]

Together with the officials and marines, these were the people who would found the New South Wales colony. Theirs was a strange destiny. As children in their villages and towns, and as feckless or desperate adults who transgressed their society's rules, they could have had no inkling of the voyage they were going on, or of what awaited them at its end.

PART THREE:
PREPARING TO SAIL

8.

At Portsmouth

In the event, the First Fleet sailed some six months after administration officials thought it would.

On 5 September 1786, the Navy Board advised the Treasury that 'the shipping for carrying the convicts may be got ready in about six weeks'. In mid-October, the Home Office advised various county officials that the ships would sail at the end of the month, or the beginning of November.[1] Various newspapers then announced that they would depart in mid-November, then late December, then mid-January.

In January 1787, as the ships gathered at Portsmouth, Evan Nepean began a memorandum concerning their route to Botany Bay with: 'In case of no unforeseen accident, it is expected that the instructions will be ready, the convicts be embarked, and the convoy prepared in all respects for their departure by the first or second week in March'.[2] At the end of February, the *General Evening Post* reported that the Fleet would sail 'in two or three days'. On 7 March, General Collins, commandant of the Portsmouth Barracks, ordered that the equipping of the marine companies be completed as soon as possible, so that they might be ready to embark 'at an hour's notice'.[3]

But still weeks went by. On 17 April, Newton Fowell wrote to his father that he did not expect to sail 'this month'. On Wednesday 18 April, Nepean told Middleton that, as Phillip's commissions were to be approved by the Privy Council on Friday, he hoped the governor would leave London for Portsmouth on Saturday. In the event, however, the Privy Council did not approve the commission and instructions until 25 April, and the Admiralty did not issue the last of the legal instruments until 5 May. Phillip reached Portsmouth on 7 May, and the ships sailed six days later.[4]

There were a number of causes of this delay. First, it took William Richards and the Navy Board longer than they expected to select the transport ships, what with a number of those first proposed proving unsatisfactory, and owners evidently withdrawing others. Then, following the administration's decision to double the number of female convicts and to allow some convicts' wives and children to go out, another ship had to be added, fitted out and loaded. This decision also meant that the additional women had to be brought from jails about England to London and Plymouth. Both these things took time. Then there were the outbreaks of 'jail fever' and dysentery on the *Alexander*, which made it necessary to clear and disinfect that ship when it reached Portsmouth.

A greater factor, however, was the administration's realization in November 1786 that the colony needed to be governed under civil law. This required the pursuit of complicated administrative processes and the issuing of lengthy legal instruments, neither of which could be done overnight. For example, the administration could not introduce the bill providing for a criminal court in New South Wales before parliament resumed at the end of January 1787. And of course, Botany Bay was not the only extensive business government departments had to deal with between August 1786 and May 1787.

Nonetheless, there was a significant elapse of time between decision and departure. Fundamentally, there are two ways to view this 'delay'. The first is that taken by the traditionalist historians: that it shows the Pitt administration's incompetence. Manning Clark wrote that 'an indescribable hopelessness and confusion dominated the [Portsmouth] scene'. A.G.L. Shaw concluded that the government was 'rather inefficient and did not seriously consider the needs of a new settlement, penal or otherwise'. Robert Hughes wrote that 'the late winter and spring of

1787 went by in a stream of blunders and delays'. James Thomas said that 'the First Fleet's hallmark proved to be endless delay'.[5]

It is striking that these historians did not offer any example of an equivalent expedition that was more efficiently mounted, so as to establish a valid comparison. How long did it take to prepare for expeditions of 1500 soldiers to the East Indies, for example – two months, three months, four months? But then, such expeditions required no innovations in administrative and legal arrangements. Were there any real analogies for what the administration was attempting with the First Fleet? If so, how long did it take to send them off? The traditionalist historians have never asked these questions. They concluded that the mounting of the First Fleet was a shambles, and assumed that this judgment does not require any proof.

The second way to view the 'delay' between the decision to establish a convict colony at Botany Bay and the sailing of the First Fleet is that the sheer intricacy and extent of the preparations needed only became apparent as the business proceeded; that, as they realized what was needed, officials worked diligently to ensure that the venture would succeed; and that this took more time than they initially expected.

Rendezvous at Portsmouth

The Home Office, Treasury and Admiralty began assembling the First Fleet from 7 December, once the Navy Board had all but completed the fitting out of the ships and the loading of goods into them. Progressively, they were ordered to rendezvous at Portsmouth.[6] The *Scarborough*, *Fishburn*, *Golden Grove* and *Borrowdale* left the Thames on 15 December. The *Scarborough* reached Spithead on 21 December, followed by the *Fishburn* two days later. The *Golden Grove* came in on 24 December, and the *Borrowdale* arrived on 28 December. The *Sirius* met the *Alexander* and *Lady Penrhyn* at Gravesend on 31 January, and the three went on to the Nore, where they were joined by the *Supply*. The *Lady Penrhyn* then went ahead, reaching Portsmouth on 10 February. Gales forced the others to anchor in the Downs, on the southeast coast of Kent, from 4 to 19 February, when they proceeded into the English Channel, joining the *Scarborough*, *Lady Penrhyn*, *Prince of Wales*, *Borrowdale*, *Fishburn* and *Golden Grove* at the Mother Bank on 21 and 22 February. The *Friendship* and *Charlotte* left for Plymouth on 15 and 16 December, with the *Friendship* arriving on 21 December 1786, and the *Charlotte* on 7 January 1787. The *Charlotte* and *Friendship* came into Portsmouth from Plymouth on 15 and 16 March.[7]

In mid-January 1787, at the request of the Home Office and the Treasury, the Admiralty and Navy Board began ordering the masters of the transports to put themselves under Phillip's orders. Once the ships were all assembled at the Mother Bank, the Admiralty formally ordered Phillip to take charge of them 'and give them such orders for their further proceedings as you may judge necessary'. As Phillip remained in London until early May completing administrative arrangements, in practice this meant that John Hunter had immediate charge of the ships in February, March and April.[8]

*

Inevitably, there were many adjustments to the ships and goods during this time. A number of the ships needed further repairs and adjustments to their fittings. Because the *Sirius* was dragging its anchors in strong winds, Phillip asked for larger anchors to be fitted, and for another cable, both of which were granted. It emerged that the ship also needed further work, for water was getting into the sail room, a bulkhead needed to be moved, the hawse holes were damaging the cables, two eye bolts were missing from the main topmast, and the gun room ports were faulty. Then, rotten planks were found on the gun deck. The Navy Board ordered that these defects be fixed. The work took a week, and the Admiralty asked the Board to explain how the ship had been let out of the Deptford yard 'without being thoroughly inspected'. At the end of March 1787, Phillip asked for a set of magnetic bars (used to minimize the deflection of the compass needle caused by the ship's iron fittings), which he received.[9]

The situation was similar with the *Supply*. As it was about to leave the Thames, two ships collided with it, which necessitated replacing its bowsprit and repairing other damage, which was done by 11 January. By the time it reached Portsmouth, however, it had become clear that the new bowsprit needed to be refitted.[10]

Phillip asked for additional crewmen for the *Sirius*. There were also deficiencies of stores to be made up and extra items to be ordered.[11] Ball also asked for boatswain's and carpenter's stores, which he received. Then, he suggested that the ship's ballast be lessened by five tons, which was done.[12] Phillip asked for 200 lbs of portable soup in addition to the 50 lbs already supplied, 'as it is probable that the ship's company will be on salt provisions for some months after they arrive on the coast of New South Wales', which he received.[13]

There were problems to remedy on the transports, too. John Shortland asked for some flags and old canvas, which he received. He asked for 'junk' – shredded cable used to caulk the deck planks, a task which was often the responsibility of a ship's crew rather than of dockyard artificers. He received several hundredweight, and also paint for his cutter and a new windsail (used to introduce fresh air into the hold) for the *Alexander*.[14]

Adjustments to the transport ships' accommodations continued. For greater security, all the others were altered as the *Alexander* had been, with Phillip pointing out the need to do so before the convicts to be sent there overland were embarked. Towards the end of January, the marine officers on the *Charlotte*, who were then at Plymouth waiting to load its convicts, complained that the arrangement of the troops' and convicts' sleeping quarters was 'such that very serious consequences may be apprehended in case of an insurrection'. The Navy Board asked the commissioner at Plymouth to change things as he saw fit. The *Friendship*'s master and commanding marine officer then asked that its accommodation be similarly altered, which was done.[15] The grating on the *Prince of Wales* was closed, so as to prevent 'any communication in conversation' between the marines and the female convicts. The Navy Board also ordered thirty more sets of handcuffs and 'a dozen heavy irons for such of the convicts as are refractory'.[16]

Then, Major Ross suggested that the way the marines were berthed in the *Alexander* might have contributed to the spread of illness: they were 'excluded from all air but what passes through the hatchway leading from the seamen's berth, which must in some degree render it putrid before it reaches the others'. The ship's accommodation was consequently altered, though it is unclear whether Hunter's suggestion of a round house on the upper deck was followed.[17]

John White asked for, and received, sick kettles for the ships. Two cots, for the senior marine officers, were put into the *Scarborough* and *Prince of Wales*. Those on the *Friendship* and *Charlotte* then asked for the same favour. Soon all the marine officers and surgeons on the transports asked for cots to take ashore with them on reaching New South Wales, which they got. Phillip asked for extra hammocks, which he did not get, because there were not enough in store. Hunter wanted twelve leather hides for the *Sirius*, which he got.[18]

Then there was the need to keep replenishing provisions and stores used up as the ships waited to depart. As mentioned, Phillip and Ball each asked for more stores at the end of February, which necessitated the Navy Board authorizing them to be issued at Portsmouth (though in fact, Captain Marshall had already ordered this by the time he received this official notice). As the cost of these additional supplies could not be met out of the regular funding of the Portsmouth and Plymouth yards, the Board asked the officers there to keep separate accounts of the cost of items provided to the First Fleet ships. At intervals, the Board also directed William Richards to keep up the provisions on the transports to eight months' supply, the expected duration of the voyage.[19]

More clothing was also needed for the marines and the convicts. At the end of February, the Admiralty ordered the Portsmouth storekeeper to put supplies of 'light clothing' on board the *Alexander*, *Scarborough* and *Prince of Wales*, which was done. The Plymouth storekeeper likewise put light clothing on board the *Charlotte* and *Friendship,* and also 200 'check' shirts. The marines also needed extra ammunition. The problem was that in peacetime the barracks commandants ordered only enough supplies from the Ordnance to meet routine needs. When Ross pointed out that his companies might require greater amounts than normal to put down a convict insurrection, whether at Portsmouth or during the voyage, the Admiralty Secretary instructed Generals Smith and Collins accordingly. The Navy Board also put chests on board each of the convict transports 'for securing the ammunition for the marine guard'. In the event, the Botany Bay marines seem not to have received sufficient extra supplies; nor, evidently, were they provided with additional amounts of cartridge paper and sets of armourer's tools.[20]

There was also the question of how the wives of the marines and convicts who had been given permission to go on the voyage, and their children, were to be fed. No allowance for people in these categories had been made in the original contracts with William Richards, and now they were deprived. Ross wrote of one case on the *Alexander* where a marine, his wife and their two children were trying to live on 1 1/2 rations. Prompted by the Home Office, Treasury and Admiralty, the Navy Board fixed the rations at 1/2 for a marine's wife and 1/4 for a child, which had the curious consequence of a convict's wife (3/4) and child (1/2) being better fed than a marine's. Before this, however, Richards had been providing food for these women and children, in the expectation that the matter would be dealt with.[21]

Then there was the need to send Phillip the beer and ducats he was to use to obtain stock from the Molucca Islands.[22] And there was the need to pay Jonathan Altree, the young surgeon who had been ministering on a temporary basis to the women on the *Lady Penrhyn*. Phillip pleaded his case, and the Navy Board granted him £30.[23]

In short, there was a myriad day-to-day arrangements that needed to be made. Mostly, these were conveyed by notes passed between Hunter, Shortland, the masters of the transports, and the naval and marine officers. There must have been hundreds, if not thousands, of these notes, but they were ephemeral, and only a handful now remain. Two examples give their flavour. On 23 April, Ralph Clark told Richard Johnson that a newborn convict baby on the *Friendship* was dying and needed to be baptized. The next day, Clark asked Shortland to send a boat to take one of the officers to see Hunter on the *Sirius*.[24]

Disgruntlements

At Portsmouth a number of problems arose from the vagaries of human nature, and the pressure of incompatible people being confined together for extended times.

In mid-March, the master and the surgeon of the *Supply* complained to the Navy Board that Lieutenant Ball had altered their mess accommodation for the worse. The Admiralty directed him to restore the space to what it had been when the ship left Deptford. Hunter investigated the complaint, to find that Ball had not made any alteration to the ship. The Admiralty directed Hunter to 'reprimand the master and surgeon for making so groundless a charge'.[25]

No sooner had Ball dealt with this complaint than the master made another against him, more serious because it bore on the interest of the whole crew. On 18 March, Christopher Holmes showed Ball a letter which he said he intended to send to the Admiralty, complaining that he was stinting the crew of their proper rations. Nine days later, having heard nothing further, Ball demanded a formal enquiry. The Admiralty asked Samuel Marshall, the senior officer at Portsmouth, to put together a group of captains to investigate. These found that the crew 'never had made a complaint, or ever thought of so doing', and advised the Admiralty that 'we all are fully satisfied with the propriety of Lieutenant Ball's conduct'. The Admiralty directed the Navy Board to dismiss Holmes, and to appoint another in his place.[26]

John White, the surgeon, thought it unfair that, while the Admiralty had denied him a servant, the Reverend Richard Johnson was taking one out with him. White argued: 'without a servant my situation must be truly uncomfortable, … not only on the passage but after landing. I have applied to Captain Phillip, who has no objection, and admits the propriety (if not necessity) of it.' He was given a servant.[27]

Newton Fowell, midshipman on the *Sirius*, took a keen interest in his prospects of promotion, and fretted about when it might happen.[28]

Because their lives were otherwise in turmoil, or because the reality of service in far-distant New South Wales was drawing closer, some young marine officers found that they preferred not to go. Lieutenant

James Morrison was first absent from the Portsmouth barracks without leave in February 1787. When he returned apologetically in March, his commandant interceded successfully with the Admiralty on his behalf. He was reprimanded and his pay restored, and he went on board the *Scarborough*. But then, two weeks later, he disappeared again, and was replaced by Lieutenant Maxwell.[29]

Lieutenant Ralph Clark might well have done the same. As the time to departure shortened, he grew increasingly anxious about the coming long separation from his wife. Repeatedly, and against the advice of his friends, he implored the authorities for permission to take her and their son with him, even offering to pay the cost himself. It was to no avail. Phillip clarified the situation with the Home Office, and told him firmly, No. He asked a second time, to get the same answer. He asked Lord Howe, again to be told, No. Then, he asked for ten days' leave to see his family at Plymouth. Phillip told him he should have applied via Ross, but that in any case the answer would have been No, as they were soon to sail.[30]

Clark's discontent continued. He was appalled by the coarse and violent behaviour of some of the convict women during the voyage. In June, when four whom he had put in irons for fighting were released, he commented: 'there was never three great[er] whores living than they are, the four of them that went through the bulkhead while we lay at the Mother Bank. I am convinced they will not be long out of them, they are a disgrace to their whole sex, bitches that they are. I wish all the women were out of the ship.' When the women were put into another ship at Cape Town to make way for sheep, he thought that these would prove more congenial companions. During the voyage to the colony and once he was there, he dreamed repeatedly of sexual congress with his 'beloved' Betsey Alicia.[31] Mind you, these sentiments did not prevent him from taking a convict woman as his mistress.

There was also tension between the marines and sailors in the *Alexander*. When Ross asked for the marines' accommodation to be changed in a way that would have disadvantaged the crew, the sailors promptly said they would not go.[32]

At Portsmouth, all the ordinary marines grew most disgruntled when they learned that they would not be given spirits in New South Wales. There were two reasons for their unhappiness. The first was that they felt betrayed. In his initial advice to the Admiralty, Sydney had stated that they would be 'properly victualled by a commissary immediately after their landing', and the Admiralty Secretary had repeated this when he wrote to the recruiting officers at the barracks at Portsmouth and Plymouth. So too did Major Ross.[33] To the ordinary troops, being 'properly victualled by a commissary' meant that they would be supplied with spirits, or at least with wine, as per established practice. The second reason for their unhappiness was that they realized that while they would not have 'this principal necessary of life' in the colony, their brothers-in-arms on the *Sirius* and *Supply* would, since those marines would continue in sea service.

From early April, the marines on the transports petitioned their officers to change the situation. The *Alexander*'s detachment felt themselves 'much injured'. They were committed to using 'their utmost endeavours in defending the just rights of their King and country'; however, in view of the hardship being imposed on them, they – all of them volunteers – would prefer not to go. Those on the *Prince of Wales* pleaded, 'as the allowance of liquor is a great support to nature it will be an utter disappointment to the whole detachment as we all embarked with the idea that we should have been victualled as on board any of His Majesty's ships'. Those on the *Scarborough* held that a 'moderate distribution' of spirituous liquor or wine was 'indispensably requisite for the preservation of our lives, which change of climate and the extreme fatigue we shall be necessarily exposed to may probably endanger'. 'In the most respectful and dutiful manner', those on board the *Charlotte* pointed out the hardships 'which being thus deprived of our grog will subject us to from our being placed on an island where nothing of the kind can by any other means be procured, and the necessity of it to soldiers whose duty will be active and unremitting; … besides which we believe it is extended to all garrisons abroad'. Ross and Phillip took up the matter again with the Admiralty and the Home Office.[34]

Before this, however, Middleton and Sydney had discussed the situation, and decided to give way. Just before the ships sailed, the London officials told Phillip and Ross that Phillip had approval to purchase *en route* 'such a quantity of spirits and wine for [the marines'] use as he can for £200'. The letters made clear, however, that this indulgence would not be continued after the initial three years.[35] In this ruling, I think, lie the origins of the colony's notorious rum trade of the 1790s.

Finally, there were the convicts. It is difficult now to know what these thought of the business. Many of them were illiterate, and for all they knew about New South Wales they might as well have been going to China or the moon. However, some of them did write to friends on shore. At the end of April, Ross ordered the marine officers to inspect their letters. Tench described this duty as 'not one of the least tiresome and disagreeable'. However, he was also often surprised at the contents. These 'varied according to the dispositions of the writers', he said; 'but their constant language was, an apprehension of the impracticability of returning home, the dread of a sickly passage, and the fearful prospect of a distant and barbarous country'. Tench saw pretence too, however, for he considered that the gloomy sentiments were often 'an artifice to awaken compassion, and call forth relief; the correspondence invariably ending in a petition for money and tobacco'.[36]

*

While these were largely mundane matters, and most of them were slight, the attending to them meant the First Fleet sailed better prepared that it otherwise would have been. However, there were other things of crucial importance to the success of the voyage that were addressed at Portsmouth, which I shall now describe.

9.

Preparing Bodies for the Voyage

Happily, the vast majority of the First Fleet convicts survived the long and arduous voyage. However, it was not inevitable that they should have done so.

We should consider that there were three major phases in the process of ensuring the good health necessary to their doing so: first the Navy Board's laying an adequate basis, by ordering good-quality supplies for the voyage; second, detailed preparations in the months and weeks before departure; and third, the management of the voyage itself. In the event, it was the second of these phases that was the most important, for it was at Portsmouth, as a consequence of the surgeons' agitations and Phillip's insistence, that the colonists' health was raised to a different level. These Portsmouth preparations had a number of facets, some specific, others more general.

Clothing the women

The fact that a full supply of women's clothing was not loaded has become a notorious sign of the supposed general negligence that afflicted the First Fleet. In addition to Manning Clark's lurid, unhistorical description of the women lolling semi-naked on the decks of the transports (discussed in the Introduction), there is Shaw's catalogue of woes: 'there were … not enough clothing, no anti-scorbutics, insufficient surgical supplies … Perhaps no more can be deduced from this than that

384

the government was rather inefficient and did not seriously consider the needs of a new settlement, penal or otherwise'. Mackay, Hughes and Hill each highlighted how Phillip complained. Mackay: 'In the course of the preparations, Phillip had cause to complain about the inadequacy of the medical supplies, agricultural implements, ordnance stores, victualling (particularly the meat, bread and flour), the convicts' clothing, the anti-scorbutics and the wine'. Hughes: 'The pale, ragged, lousy prisoners, thin as wading birds from their jail diet, were herded on board and spent the next several months below; orders forbade them to exercise on deck until the flotilla was out of sight of land. The condition of the women provoked Phillip to a furious outburst: "The situation in which the magistrates sent the women on board ... stamps them with infamy – tho' almost naked, and so very filthy ...".'. Hill: 'When the Fleet eventually sailed from Portsmouth ... it left without enough clothing for the women'.[1]

What we have in these writers' accounts is a history only of the illness, not of its cure. None of them recognized that Phillip was complaining (as he put it) about 'evils [that] may be redressed', nor acknowledged that (with one partial exception), this was in fact done. Let us see what the real story was.

In the first place, this shortage in the supply of women's clothing arose because of the acute need to clothe the female convicts sent from Newgate and Southwark jails in the depth of winter. It was to these that Phillip referred when he indignantly said, 'the situation in which the magistrates sent the women on board the *Lady Penrhyn* stamps them [i.e., the magistrates] with infamy – though almost naked, and so very filthy, that nothing but clothing them could have prevented them from perishing, and which could not be done in time to prevent a fever, that is still on board that ship'.[2] In order to succour these women immediately, the ships' agent and surgeon drew on the slop clothing supplied for life in the colony.

In the second place, the shortage arose because the number of women was doubled. The Navy Board did order extra supplies of clothing in December, which were put into the *Prince of Wales* for transshipment to Portsmouth.[3] Before these arrived, however, on 20 January the Navy Board directed Shortland to send

> a list of the convict women on board the *Lady Penrhyn* without loss of time and to demand of the storekeeper at Portsmouth the beds and slops that are to be left there by Gustavus Vasa, to replace what may be ordered to be issued here, reporting to us if there is any deficiency that it may be provided for and sent in the *Prince of Wales*, observing that he is not to make any difficulty in supply[ing] the women with men's clothing if there is not a sufficiency for the women.[4]

This expedient was evidently a temporary one, for on 14 March Shortland asked the Navy Board that the deficiencies be 'made up', and the Board ordered that this be done. But then, the problem was exacerbated by the arrival of the *Charlotte* and *Friendship* from Plymouth with more women – as Phillip told Nepean on 18 March,

> the giving clothes to those convicts who have been embarked at Plymouth is so very necessary that I have ordered it to be done, and presume the Navy Board will replace the clothing, but as there are more convicts to be sent on board the different ships, unless orders are given for their being washed and clothed on their leaving the prison or the hulks, all that we may do will be to no purpose.

These new arrivals were clothed too, but by once more drawing on the supplies that had been ordered for issue in the colony – as Nepean subsequently told Middleton,

> I find from Captain Phillip that some of the convicts are almost destitute of clothing, and that it will be necessary to supply them with such articles as are needful immediately. Captain Hunter and Lieutenant Shortland have been desired to inquire into their wants and to supply them, and Lord Sydney will be glad if the quantity which they may issue out of the general stock be replaced.[5]

Shortland continued to issue these women with clothing from the 'general stock' into April, but this stock was also evidently insufficient. The Board authorized further purchases on 20 April, which either did not happen or were again insufficient.[6] When Shortland and Phillip pointed this out to the officials in London, the Treasury authorized the Navy Board to purchase additional quantities on 10 May. The next day, the Board sent a directive for this to be done at Portsmouth, but the authority did not reach Phillip before he sailed. Simultaneously, the Board asked six London contractors to send supplies to Portsmouth 'with the greatest despatch possible', only to have to cancel these requests three days later on receiving news that the ships had sailed.[7] It may be that we are justified in finding some inefficiency here, but given the many arrangements necessary to send the ships off, it is hardly surprising that there should have been some mistakes. In any case, what is the more significant is that the shortage arose not from a callous disregard of, but from a humane concern for, the women's welfare; and that it was progressively, if not completely, redressed.

Containing illness

'Jail fever' or 'jail distemper' was an ever-present reality where the convicts were concerned. This was a blanket term for either typhus or typhoid fever, which were undifferentiated at the time. Its prevalence arose from the exceptionally poor conditions of the prisons; and it was frequently brought into the hulks by infected persons arriving from metropolitan and country jails.

Consider the following collection of observations on the conditions of English jails made by the reformer John Howard in the 1770s and 1780s. During his extended tours, Howard found that, often, prisoners were kept in small, dark, dank and very unhygienic conditions, without beds, or even straw; without water or toilet facilities; without infirmaries; and usually without adequate food. In 1773, eleven prisoners in the Oxford jail died of smallpox, and the illness continued for the next two years, with five dying of it in mid-1775. Howard commented: 'No infirmary: no bath: no straw: the prisoners lie in their clothes on mats.

The men's dungeon swarms with vermin'. The keeper of the Petworth Bridewell told him in 1774 that 'all his prisoners upon discharge, were much weakened by the close confinement, and small allowance [of food]'; and in January 1776 three men died there of privation. In the spring of 1779 at Cambridge he found seventeen women confined in a room about 6 metres square, which had no fireplace or sewer. 'This made it extremely offensive, and occasioned a fever or sickness among them … Two or three died within a few days'. At Maidstone Bridewell, he saw 'two prisoners with the smallpox, lying on loose straw, and their only covering was common mats'. At St George's Fields, Southwark, he found 'several sick on the floors: the county allows no bedding nor straw … A woman sick on the floor. The rooms were dirty: in two or three of them were fowls'. In January 1783 at the Clerkenwell Bridewell in London, he saw in the male infirmary five sick and one dying, 'with little or no covering. In another room one was dead. In the women's sick ward twelve were lying in the clothes on the barrack-bedstead and floor, without any bedding.' When he visited the New Jail in Southwark in October 1783, he found many prisoners 'sick on the dirty floors; one of the turnkeys had lately died of a fever'. Howard explained, 'I had seen on board the hulks a few days before, several sickly objects, who told me they had lately come from this and other jails; which, by the looks of those convicts, I was persuaded must be in a bad state'.[8] It was from the Southwark jail that some women went to the *Lady Penrhyn*.

There was illness on two of the First Fleet transports during embarkation. The surgeons seem to have controlled the fever on the *Lady Penrhyn* quickly but that and the 'fluxes' (dysentry or cholera) that swept through the marines and convicts on board the *Alexander* were a good deal more virulent. These appeared in January and February, while the ship was still in the Downs. After reaching Portsmouth, it was evacuated, cleaned with vinegar, and 'smoked' (dried out). By the end of April, when the infections were at last contained, eleven convicts and an unknown number of marines and sailors had died. (The uncertainty arises because many sick marines were taken on shore and replaced by new recruits.) But at least the ships sailed free of infection.[9]

The scourge of scurvy

Until the end of the eighteenth century, scurvy was the bane of those undertaking long voyages. Resulting from a deficiency of vitamin C, in its extreme state scurvy caused dizziness, swelling of limbs and gums, loose teeth, foetid breath, haemorrhages (ulcers and old wounds re-opening) and loss of energy; death followed the emergence of these symptoms within days, or even hours. Modern clinical studies have established that, without any replenishment, the body loses its store of vitamin C in sixty-eight to ninety days; and that labour in wet and cold conditions, lack of hygiene, and high intakes of salt and alcohol increase the rate of loss.

It is now also known that a very small daily intake of 15–28 milligrams of vitamin C is sufficient to maintain health – hence the seemingly miraculous recovery of scurvy patients once put ashore and given a diet of fresh food, including fruits and vegetables. Take the case of the crew of the *Sirius* as it sailed to Cape Town at the end of 1788:

> Going round the Horn this passage, the ship's company was taken with the scurvy till we had but thirteen in the watch with the carpenter's crew. I was carried below three times in one night, but I done my duty the next day. Some died in sight of the Cape of Good Hope, or Table Bay … The doctor went to town and brought a quantity of fruit on board to be served out to both sick and well, for even those that were doing their duty, when biting an apple, pear, or peach, the blood would run out of our mouth from our gums with the scurvy. The next day we run up to Table Bay and moored ship. By Captain Hunter's orders and at the insistance of the doctor, we were supplied with the best of provisions the Cape could afford. Mutton and vegetables was the most suitable for the scurvy, and the captain allowed us to send for as much wine as we thought fit to make use of, the ship's company recovering daily, till we were all well and hearty.[10]

For hundreds of years, scurvy wreaked a fearsome havoc at sea. Naval squadrons leaving England in the first months of the year were particularly prone to epidemics, as the crews had not had the benefit of early spring vegetables (such as brussels sprouts) and summer fruits. So, too, were those whose crews were not in good health in the first place. In 1740 Lord Anson sailed from England with eight ships and 1955 men, many of them old or ill, to attack the Spanish settlements on the west coasts of the Americas. By the time the squadron entered the Pacific, there had been hundreds of deaths from malaria, dysentery and scurvy. In all, 1415 of the original complements died, 997 of them of scurvy.[11] In 1780, after a six weeks' cruise, there were 2400 cases of scurvy among the crews of the Channel squadron.

The true cause of scurvy remained unknown until the turn of the twentieth century, when vitamins were identified and their dietary roles established. Before this, some far-fetched theories of its causes were entertained, including that of foul air in the holds of ships. However, experienced naval commanders knew that scurvy appeared during prolonged voyages when people fed on salt provisions; that it was important that people should keep themselves clean and their clothing and bedding dry; that they should have fresh air and exercise regularly; that they should be provided with anti-scorbutics; and that they should revert to a diet of fresh foods wherever possible.

Some astute people understood more. In 1593, for example, Sir John Hawkins praised the efficacy of oranges and lemons in curing the disease: 'This is a wonderful secret of the power and wisdom of God, that hath hidden so great and unknown virtue in this fruit, to be a certain remedy for this infirmity.'[12] Indeed, in 1747, in a clinical experiment, the naval surgeon James Lind proved conclusively the value of these citrus fruits; but the official view lost sight of this knowledge for fifty years, partly as a consequence of James Cook's unfortunate preference for sauerkraut and wort of malt. Despite this lack of official recognition, there is evidence that belief in the virtue of citrus fruits continued amongst those experienced in long voyages. When he showed signs of scurvy on the *Endeavour* voyage, for example, Joseph Banks drank some of the lemon juice he had brought with him.[13]

Like most naval officers, Arthur Phillip had had first-hand experience of scurvy. As a boy, he had sailed on the squadron which Admiral Byng had taken out from Portsmouth on 6 April 1756, some of whose sailors were afflicted by the time it reached Gibraltar in early May. Later, he had commanded a ship in the squadron of twelve which Sir Richard King took out from Madras on 2 October 1783. When they reached the Cape of Good Hope on 9 December, they had 1800 cases of scurvy, and many more sailors had died on the passage. And if the story of Phillip's having taken 400 Portuguese convicts to Brazil is true, he had additional close experience of the disease.

So Phillip knew only too well the danger that scurvy would pose during the First Fleet's voyage. When he drew up his memorandum concerning the colony at the beginning of October 1786, he noted that 'sickness must be the consequence in so long a voyage' and that 'scurvy must make a great ravage amongst people naturally indolent and not cleanly'. As he had become aware of how the Navy Board officials were treating the voyage as one to America rather than to 'the extremity of the globe', his apprehension increased. He feared, he told Sydney in mid-March, 'that it may be said hereafter the officer who took charge of the expedition should have known that it was more than probable he [would lose] half the garrison and convicts, crowded and victualled in such a manner for so long a voyage'.[14]

Given what we now know about the etiology of scurvy, the underlying health of the colonists as the ships gathered at Portsmouth becomes a pertinent question. Since they were fed the usual naval rations and had medical care, the crews of the *Sirius* and *Supply* would probably have been in reasonable health but, given the season, their bodily stores of vitamins would likely have been at lower levels than modern science recommends. The situation of the marines would have been similar, though perhaps not quite so good. That of the convicts who came from the Thames hulks may have been, if anything, somewhat superior to that of the marines, for these had been required to wash, they had had medical attention, and they had been adequately clothed and fed. The situation of those convicts from the country jails who gathered at Plymouth and in London, and that of those who went directly to Portsmouth, was manifestly the worst of all, for these had been poorly clothed, were ill-fed, and had had little or no medical care. It was no doubt these whom Collins had in mind when he recorded that many convicts 'were embarked in a very sickly state' (where 'embarked' means when they were put aboard the ships, not when they sailed).[15]

As the ships were assembling at Portsmouth, Phillip and his officers campaigned to improve the health of all. William Balmain, the *Alexander*'s surgeon, was convinced that serving fresh food was an essential measure if the illness on that ship was to be contained, as he told Shortland on 17 February:

> As some of the marines are much impaired in health from fever and a number of the convicts severely afflicted with fluxes, I think it my duty to acquaint you that I am of opinion if an allowance of fresh provision (from which broth and other nutritious aliment might be extracted) could be procured in the room of salt it would greatly assist in restoring the sick to health and strength, and if during our stay in England fresh food could be conveniently got for the whole it might in a great measure prevent the growth of disease. A small quantity of wine would also be a powerful restorative to the sick.

Shortland passed this request to the Navy Board, which sought the Treasury's opinion, which replied (no doubt after consulting the Home Office) that it should be acceded to. Accordingly, the Board told Richards that he was to provide fresh meat. It told Shortland that he was to see 'that no more is provided for than the surgeons think actually necessary'; and that in any case he was to limit expenditure on fresh provisions to 1s per person per day.[16]

The difficult point here was that the Navy Board had long since concluded with Richards a contract for feeding the convicts and marines that did not include fresh provisions. Any alteration to it would constitute an additional charge, not against the contractor but against the government, so that the Treasury's approval was needed. At the end of the month, Phillip increased the pressure for this, when he asked Sydney 'that orders may be given for the supplying both marines and convicts with fresh meat and vegetables while they remain at Spithead, and that a small quantity of wine may be allowed for the sick'. Warning that the surgeons attending the marines and convicts were 'decidedly of opinion that unless they are supplied with fresh meat, vegetables and other refreshments a great mortality amongst them may be expected', Nepean passed on this request to Middleton on the same day, who replied: 'In consequence of a letter lately received from the Treasury, the contractor proceeded to Portsmouth on Saturday to furnish the sick with fresh provisions and vegetables, and which may be extended to the convicts and marines in general if an order is sent from the Treasury for that purpose.'[17]

There clearly was some delay in the Home Office's arranging this, for on 6 March the Navy Board told Shortland that 'we have no directions to allow fresh provisions etc. to any but the sick convicts and marines'.[18] Phillip pressed the point again on 18 March, stating that 'fresh meat for all the convicts and wine for the sick I was informed had been ordered in consequence of the representation I made as soon as the ships got round to Portsmouth, *but the sick only* have fresh meat'. Now he had his way. On 21 March the Navy Board told Richards 'to cause all the marines and convicts to be victualled with fresh provisions on the same terms already fixed on for the sick during their continuance at Portsmouth, and with wine for the sick according to the discretion of the surgeons, and to provide 1 ton weight of essence of malt'. Thereafter, Tench says, fresh foods were given 'indiscriminately' to the marines and convicts, well and sick.[19]

Preparing for illness on the voyage

For Phillip, a larger issue underlay that of feeding the people with fresh foods while they were at Portsmouth, important as this undoubtedly was.

There is no question but that in the beginning the Navy Board officials and the contractor did not conceptualize the voyage adequately. As Middleton told Nepean at the end of February 1787,

the Navy Board, in contracting for the victualling of the convicts on their passage, have observed the same rule that has been always followed with soldiers on board of transports – that is, 2/3rds of what is allowed to the troops serving in the West Indies, spirits excepted.[20]

Although it is yet to be found, ancillary correspondence makes clear that the contract which the Board concluded with William Richards on 12 September was indeed drawn up according to this model.

Middleton defended this decision on the ground that since they would not have the opportunity of much exercise during the passage, the convicts did not need more food. From Middleton's perspective, this may have been a justifiable view. As well, however, the model allowed rice to be substituted for the flour usual in the Royal Navy ration, and did not provide for either anti-scorbutics or 'necessaries' for the sick. A naval officer experienced in very long voyages, one aware of the health record on Anson's 1740–44 circumnavigation, of Lind's subsequent clinical trial and of Cook's regimen, might only see the model's limitation – as Phillip told Sydney:

> I have repeatedly pointed out the consequences that must be expected from the men being crowded on board such small ships, and from victualling the marines according to the contract, which allows no flour, as is customary in the Navy. This must be fatal to many, and the more so as no anti-scorbutics are allowed on board the transports for either marine or convict. In fact, my Lord, the garrison and convicts are sent to the extremity of the globe as they would be sent to America – a six-weeks' passage.[21]

It is important to note here that Phillip's complaint was not that not enough food was being provided, but rather that certain items needed for a very long voyage were not – i.e., that the voyage needed to be conceptualized as one of eight months, during which scurvy would inevitably appear, rather than one of six weeks, when it perhaps would not.

Since he was convinced that 'if salt meat is issued, without any proportion of flour – the scurvy must prove fatal to the greatest part' of the marines and convicts, Phillip pursued the matter for a number of months, asking for the rations to be altered, and also that he be able to provide fresh provisions for all when in port *en route*. Initially, the Admiralty told him that it could give him no directions on these points, and the Navy Board told him that it could not agree to alterations to the contract, as to do so would increase the cost of the voyage.[22]

Phillip turned to the Home Office, asking Sydney 'whether it may not be advisable to make some alteration in the provisions, by allowing the marines *a proportion of flour* in lieu of a certain proportion of salt meat; and some addition to the provisions served to the convicts: at present a convict has only, for forty-two days, 16 lbs of bread'. He added: 'The contractor's having a power of substituting a 1/2 lb of rice in lieu of 1 lb of flour will be very severely felt by the convicts'. When Nepean referred these requests on, Middleton gave a little ground, telling Nepean that 'if flour is preferred to rice, Captain Phillip may direct a preference on the passage, and repay it out of the storeships on their arrival'. However, at the same time he cautioned that 'the substitute of rice for flour is agreeable to the army contract, and so paid by the Treasury'.[23]

Phillip wanted still greater latitude. Pointing out that 'the contracts for the garrison and convicts were made before I ever saw the Navy Board on this business', he asked again for those things the army-type contract lacked – flour, anti-scorbutics and fresh foods *en route*. The Board explained wearily to him on 25 April that

> not having received any orders from the Treasury to direct the contractor to purchase fresh meat etc. for the marines and convicts at such places as the ships may stop at, or wine and spirits for the marines and officers of the garrison so long as they shall be victualled by him, we have not given him any directions thereon;

that

> it was consented to that the contractor might make such alteration in the provisions as Captain Phillip desired, provided the expense

should not be increased to the public, but we have no authority to make any alteration that would require additional tonnage without orders from the Treasury;

and that

> his apprehensions of the consequence that may attend the not allowing the usual quantity of flour and not allowing more bread instead of salt provisions for the convicts will be more properly represented to the Treasury, as the ration provided is in consequence of their orders and therefore we conclude has been properly considered.[24]

Even as the Navy Board restated this position, however, it was being subverted, for on this same day (25 April) the Privy Council issued Phillip's instructions, which included an authority to purchase provisions *en route*; and Nepean wrote to William Richards concerning this need. Before he sailed, Phillip took on board quantities of 'good, though coarse' bread for the convicts.[25]

Purser's and surgeon's necessaries

Other deficiencies were remedied while the ships were at Portsmouth. In the late eighteenth century, two classes of 'necessaries' were carried on Royal Navy ships – 'purser's necessaries', including the (supposed) anti-scorbutics, sauerkraut and wort of malt; and 'surgeon's necessaries', small foodstuffs for the sick, which, as explained in Chapter 6, included almonds, barley, currants, garlic, mace and nutmeg, rice, sago, shallots, sugar and tamarinds. Oatmeal, for making gruel, was sometimes included under the one heading, sometimes under the other.[26]

The nature of the Navy Board's contract with William Richards meant that these items had also not been supplied for the marines and convicts for the voyage. On 7 February, John White told Phillip of this. Pointing out that these people were 'equally subject to the diseases incident to men embarked on board the King's ships', he asked that these items be provided 'in the usual manner of the Navy'. Phillip told Nepean and Stephens, with the latter telling the Navy Board on 10 February. The Board instructed its commissioners at Portsmouth and Plymouth to 'cause such a quantity to be put on board – as shall be a proper proportion for the number of marines and convicts on board each ship during the passage'. It turned out that there were insufficient stocks on hand at these ports, so on 28 February the Board asked George Cawthorne to supply 'necessaries for the number of marines and convicts embarked on board each transport in the same proportion as for the King's ships for six months'. On 12 March, following a request from White, now at Plymouth, the Navy Board ordered necessaries for the *Charlotte* and *Friendship* to be sent from London to Portsmouth, the ships' next destination.[27]

Phillip continued to pursue this business. Pointing out that it was his 'duty to repeat complaints *that may be redressed*', on 18 March he asked for wine for the sick, among other things. The Navy Board ordered two pipes the next day, along with 1 ton of essence of malt for distribution among the transport ships.[28]

At the beginning of April, as the time till departure shortened, White asked for the supplies of necessaries to be completed to eight months, the expected duration of the voyage. The Navy Board minuted that 'the deficiency may be sent on board a few days before they sail', and asked Cawthorne to make up quantities 'to the period that the other species of provisions are'. A week later, Phillip asked for more portable soup and sauerkraut. Another week on, Nepean asked for casks of oatmeal to be put on board to make gruel for the sick, which were to be considered 'as surgeon's necessaries'. The Navy Board ordered two casks for each ship. Then, on 23 April, White asked for another pipe of wine, which was supplied. The additional supplies of necessaries reached Portsmouth on 10 May, and were loaded onto the ships.[29]

The surgeon of the *Lady Penrhyn* recorded receiving 1 lb almonds, 6 lbs currants, 40 lbs (moist) sugar, 6 lbs sage, 100 lbs 'fine' rice, a 'large quantity' of French barley and smaller quantities of mace and cinnamon, 'some portable soup, tea, lump sugar', two kegs of 'fine essence of malt', and 10 gallons of 'red port wine'. We may assume that these quantities are indicative of what all the transport ships received.[30]

A hospital ship

Arthur Phillip also knew that if there were epidemics during the course of the voyage, he would need to isolate the sick – as David Collins observed, 'prior to our departure it was generally conjectured, that before we should have been a month at sea one of the transports would have been converted into a hospital ship'.[31] Accordingly, Phillip asked for permission to use a ship for this purpose, which the Navy Board gave. When the illness spread in the *Alexander* at Portsmouth, he thought to convert the *Friendship*, but the need abated, and never arose again.[32]

*

In April 1787, in its usual dismissive fashion, the *Bath Chronicle* observed, 'from the mortality that has already taken place on board the transports, it is supposed that not more than one in five [of the convicts] will survive the voyage'.[33] It's a pity that today's practice of newspapers printing 'Corrections' or 'Retractions' did not exist then. For, against this dire prediction, the voyage of the First Fleet was a striking success. From the time of the ships' leaving England to that of their arrival at Botany Bay, only twenty male and three female convicts and five of their children died. Among the marines and their families there were only three deaths (one man, one woman, one child). This health record speaks for itself; but if we remember Collins's caveat that many of the convicts 'were embarked in a very sickly state', it speaks with even more purpose, and eloquently refutes the charge that the First Fleet colonists were ill-prepared for the voyage to New South Wales.[34]

While the story of the First Fleet's extraordinary health record is told mostly in these mortality figures, it is also told in another way, one that turns on a profound difference between our perceptions of good health and those held by late eighteenth-century people.

In September 1785, when Lieutenant Henry Pemberton extolled the virtues of the southern coast of Africa near the Krome River as a site for a convict settlement, he pointed out how the Dutch settlers in the vicinity 'are remarkably healthy and live to a great age'; and to the women, 'whose prodigious stature and florid complexion announced the most perfect state of health'. In October 1792, from Norfolk Island, Charles Grimes wrote home that 'I have been very ill on the voyage here, and [for] some time prior to my leaving the Cape, but I am now much better and fatter than when I left England'. In September 1802, when Mary Hutchinson married Dorothy Wordsworth's brother William, Dorothy wrote that her sister-in-law 'looked so fat and well that we were made very happy by the sight of her'.[35] To these people, plumpness indicated good health.

So it was on the First Fleet. When the ships reached Rio de Janeiro, Phillip remarked that the convicts were 'much healthier than when we left England'. What he meant was that they were *fatter*. From Cape Town, David Collins wrote home that 'my brother William as well as myself have enjoyed our healths perfectly since we sailed. William is grown so tall and stout withal you would hardly know him'.[36]

Now, it is hardly surprising that the people on the First Fleet should have gained weight during the voyage. It has been estimated that the male convict's preserved ration 'had a daily energy value of between 4000 and 5500 k cals, far in excess of the 3,350 k cals required by the average 65-kilogram man employed on heavy labour'; and when in port, they were given what are to us very large quantities of food – at Rio de Janeiro, for example, 20 ounces (c. 560 grams) of meat daily.[37] They were certainly not burning these calories on the ships, for they were not labouring and had only very limited opportunities to exercise. However, they would not have grown plumper without the basis of good health they were given at Portsmouth.

*

It is true that, at first, the Navy Board's following of established ways was an obstacle to achieving this success; but the more significant point is that in the end, rather than rigidly adhering to these ways, those planning the voyage circumvented or abandoned them. Roger Knight makes the good point that, since the business was undertaken in peacetime, the officials were able to attend to it in a detailed, thorough manner.[38]

Indeed, in the preparations at Portsmouth for the First Fleet's voyage, what we see is a group of officials progressively recognizing that they needed to do things differently from how they were accustomed to if the venture were to succeed. They did – and it did.

As described at the beginning of Chapter 8, traditionalist historians have seen the ships' long sojourn at Portsmouth as yet another sign of the Pitt administration's incompetence. It is certainly true that officials did not manage to send the First Fleet off nearly as quickly as they initially expected. But the delay had a particular benefit, for it enabled Phillip and his surgeons and, indeed, the contractor William Richards too, to prepare the people as well as they knew how to for such a long voyage. Their insistence on clothing the people adequately and on cleanliness; on containing illness; on having ample supplies of anti-scorbutics and necessaries; and on providing fresh foods while they waited to sail meant that the twelve weeks from late February to 12 May were crucial to the success of the voyage, for the colonists left with their illnesses cured and their bodily stores of vitamins replenished.

Rather than continuing to gaze at the mirage of the Pitt administration's callous disregard of the convicts' welfare, we should attend to the real story.

PART FOUR:
THE VOYAGE

10.

Leaving the World

ONCE – DECADES AGO NOW – I boarded a long-haul flight in Melbourne bound for England, in order to continue my research into the British colonization of New South Wales. This particular flight path took us to Bombay, then over southern Iran, Turkey and Europe to London.

As it happened, I had previously walked among the Hittite ruins in Central Anatolia and visited the Persian cities of southern Iran – Isfahan with its great madan and stunning Blue Mosque; Shiraz with its rose gardens; and Persepolis, its austere ruins splendid in the arid air. At Isfahan, I had stayed at a converted caravanserai, where drivers and their camels would rest before beginning the long trek through present Iran, Irak and Turkey to Constantinople. In the old days, this trek would take six months, leaving the beasts – as T.S. Eliot put it memorably – 'galled, sore-footed, refractory', and the men 'wanting their liquor and women'. In my aircraft, we covered the distance in six hours. Of course we did not have to endure the annoyances of land travel through sand and snow and over rocky mountains; but then, neither did we have the experience of olden-time passage across the great earth.

In the early twenty-first century, when we have become accomplished international travellers as a consequence of fast jet aircraft, it is all too easy for us to forget the realities of travel in earlier ages. Then, long sea voyages were no less arduous than land treks – perhaps more so, if for different reasons. Before the mid-nineteenth century, when steel hulls

403

powered by steam engines began to render passages independent of the tyrannies of oceanic winds and currents, and to make voyages much less hazardous to health (because safer and faster), sea travellers often had a very hard time of it. The tedium of voyages was legendary, the mortality from scurvy terrible.

In the early decades of the fifteenth century, Prince Henry of Portugal ('the Navigator') sent ships from Portugal to reconnoitre the islands in the Atlantic Ocean and the western coasts of Africa. In 1488, Bartolomeu Dias reached the Cape of Good Hope, thus showing there was a sea route to India; and in 1498 Vasco da Gama rounded it to reach India. In 1500, sailing further west than these predecessors, Cabral discovered Brazil on his way to the East.

These voyages established the basic routes that Europeans pursued for three centuries in their quest for the eastern spices, cloths and porcelains that they so much desired, and that they had previously been able to obtain only from the Arab traders who had brought them overland by camel train, or by boat up the Red Sea. The routes were determined by the prevailing winds and currents of the Atlantic and Indian oceans. From western Europe, ships would proceed down the Atlantic more or less parallel to the African coast to Madeira, the Canary, Azores and Cape Verde islands; but then they needed to sail south and west towards Brazil, which led to the growth of Rio de Janeiro as an important port of supply.

From Brazil, they made a broad sweep though the southern Atlantic Ocean until, with the winds and currents of the 'Roaring Forties' at their back, they turned east for the Indian Ocean. Once round southern Africa they turned north or northeast for India or the East Indies. Early, the Portuguese established ports of refreshment and supply in Moçambique; later, the Dutch did so at the Cape of Good Hope, and the French at Mauritius. All but one of the major European maritime trading nations established bases in India or the East Indies; and some did also in China and Japan. Spain was the exception. The papal division of the non-European world between Portugal and Spain by the Treaty of Tordesillas in 1493 meant that Spanish navigators were required to approach Asia by rounding South America and crossing the Pacific Ocean, so that Spain's bases were in Argentina, Chile, Peru, on the west coasts of Central America and in the Philippines.

By the 1780s, centuries of voyaging had made these basic routes to and from the East familiar to Europeans, and they naturally provided some analogy for that to New South Wales – hence the appearance of the East India Company's shipping official Charles Coggan before the House of Commons Committee enquiring into transportation in 1785.[1] But this analogy could not be a complete one. Once past the Cape of Good Hope, East India Company ships and Royal Navy warships and transports proceeding to India had well-established routes whose hazards (winds and currents, shoals) were known, and on or adjacent to which were places where ships in need might stop – Madagascar, the Coromo Islands, Mauritius, Ceylon, the coasts of India, the many islands of the East Indies. This was not the case of the First Fleet ships intended for Botany Bay. Once they would leave the Cape of Good Hope, they would head into a largely unknown ocean which offered no places of refreshment until Van Diemen's Land.

In fact, in 1786 there were only three precedents for the voyage of the First Fleet. These were that by Abel Tasman in 1642, when he had sailed west from Batavia to Mauritius, then south and east to Van Diemen's Land, before crossing to New Zealand and returning to Batavia by going north of New Guinea; James Cook's second voyage, when he went from the Cape of Good Hope through the southern Indian Ocean to the south island of New Zealand; and Cook's third voyage, when, after leaving Cape Town, he took the *Resolution* across to New Zealand, and his companion Charles Clarke in the *Discovery* called at Van Diemen's Land on the way to New Zealand. Moreover, a voyage through unknown seas by a discovery ship specially equipped for the purpose, and carrying an appropriate crew, was one thing; that by a group of transports carrying convicts was another.

There are many accounts of the voyage of the First Fleet. I do not intend to deal with it in all its aspects here. Rather, I shall concentrate on the commanders' continuing efforts to make it a success, and to obtain additional items that the colony would need.

Planning the voyage

In planning the voyage of the First Fleet, Arthur Phillip drew not only on accumulated European experience but also on his own deriving from his voyages to Brazil and India.[2]

He saw the ships stopping at Tenerife in the Azores, at the Cape Verde Islands and perhaps at Rio de Janeiro, in order to replenish water, and to obtain fresh foods and certain other items, such as wine. At Cape Town, the ships would take on a large amount of additional supplies, particularly animals. From Cape Town, he would go on ahead, for:

> By arriving at the settlement two or three months before the transports, many and very great advantages would be gained. Huts would be ready to receive those convicts who were sick, and they would find vegetables, or which it may naturally be supposed they will stand in great need, as scurvy must make a great ravage amongst people naturally indolent, and not cleanly. Huts would be ready for the women, the stores would be properly lodged, and defended from the convicts in such a manner as to prevent their making any attempt on them. The cattle and stock would be likewise properly secured; and the ground marked out for the convicts.

He and the lieutenant-governor should go in separate ships; and the goods and animals should also be distributed among the various ships, so that at least part of them would arrive. As he would reach Botany Bay first, he should take with him some of 'the articles of husbandry, stores, corn, seeds, and of the articles for traffic [i.e., trade]'. And he would need to provide the people with fresh foods when in port *en route*, so as to keep them healthy.[3]

So was the basic outline of the voyage fixed. About the beginning of 1787, when officials thought departure was eight to ten weeks off, Evan Nepean wrote:

> The convoy will probably arrive at Tenerife in three weeks, which will bring it to the last week in March or first in April.

The passage from thence to the Cape of Good Hope direct may be about seven weeks at most. But it is imagined that it may be of advantage to touch at Rio de Janeiro, where there is a certainty of obtaining supplies, and which is not to be depended upon at the Cape. The passage will of course be lengthened, and will most likely delay their arrival at the Cape till the latter end of July or the beginning of August.

The passage from the Cape of Good Hope to Botany Bay will most likely be effected in two months, which will bring it up to the latter end of October or beginning of November, the spring of that country.

It will be a winter passage from the Cape to Botany Bay, but if the favourable season was to be preferred, it would occasion a considerable delay and the convoy would arrive at a time when the settlers ought to be employed in gathering their crop.[4]

Nepean's estimate of an eight-months' duration proved accurate, even if, in the event, the Fleet didn't sail until mid-May.

Fuelled by such descriptions as George Worgan's of the failure of the initial plantings of vegetables –

The spots of ground that we have cultivated for gardens, have brought forth most of the seeds that we put in soon after our arrival here … but whether from any unfriendly, deleterious quality of the soil or the season, nothing seems to flourish vigorously long, but they shoot up suddenly after being put into the ground, look green and luxuriant for a little time, blossom early, fructify slowly and weakly, and ripen before they come to their proper size

– it has been one of the most hoary of old chestnuts in the historiography of the Botany Bay colonization that the British were so inept they didn't even know that the seasons were reversed in the Antipodes. Nepean's estimate that the ships would likely arrive at 'the latter end of October or beginning of November, the spring of that country' should immolate this baseless idea forever. The colonists planted vegetables at Sydney in February 1788 because they needed them to cure the sick of scurvy, not because they didn't know that it was autumn in the southern hemisphere. The failure that occurred was only to be expected – as Worgan himself observed, 'this circumstance must be considered, they were sown [at] the very worst season'.[5]

In its various instructions to Phillip, the administration provided for the voyage to proceed as he and Nepean outlined. In those issued on 25 April 1787, he was given permission 'to call with the ships and vessels under your convoy at the island of Tenerife, at the Rio de Janeiro, and also at the Cape of Good Hope, for supplies of water, and other refreshments for the voyage'. He might buy wine at Tenerife; and at any or all of these places, seed grain and 'any number of black cattle, sheep, goats, or hogs which you can procure', and 'any fresh provisions which it may be requisite to procure' for the marines and convicts.[6]

At the beginning of May, Nepean arranged with Middleton that, should the fresh provisions *en route* cost more that the dry ones contracted for, then Richards would be paid the difference.[7] And the Home Office arranged with the Admiralty that, after leaving the Cape of Good Hope, Phillip might, 'if he thinks fit, [proceed] to the said coast of New South Wales in the *Supply* tender, leaving the convoy to be escorted by the *Sirius* to the rendezvous which he may fix upon'.[8]

This is precisely how the voyage went forward. After leaving Portsmouth, Phillip went down the Atlantic Ocean to Tenerife; then crossed southwestwards to Rio de Janeiro, then southeastwards to Cape Town. After Cape Town, he went aboard the *Supply*, and, together with the *Alexander*, *Friendship* and *Scarborough*, set out ahead of the rest of the convoy for New South Wales. To Phillip's enemies in the First Fleet (for already by this time there were some), this was another example of his wilful incapacity – as the surgeon of the *Lady Penrhyn* wrote: 'Had he conceived the idea, and put it in practice at leaving Rio de Janeiro, it might have succeeded in some measure, but as it was now produced it was a mere abortion of the brain, a whim which struck him at the time'.[9] But all this comment really shows is that, like some of the later historians of the venture, Smyth didn't know what he was talking about. As we have just seen, Phillip's going ahead was envisaged from the first, and was part of the administration's careful planning.

The voyage

All business in London having been effectively concluded, Arthur Phillip reached Portsmouth on 7 May, bringing with him the chronometer and sextant from the Board of Longitude. He gave the chronometer to William Bayly, the astronomer who had sailed with Cook and who was now headmaster of the Portsmouth Naval Academy, to determine its accuracy precisely. This is another sign of the care with which the administration equipped the expedition. The use of the chronometer in navigation was a recent development. On his first voyage, Cook had calculated longitude using direct observation and lunar tables; on the second and third voyages, he used chronometers, which allowed him and his astronomers to determine the difference in time between Greenwich and whatever was their present position. In 1785, the India Board recommended that the East India Company issue chronometers to the officers it was to send to survey the ocean between India and Africa. Now, one was given to Phillip for the First Fleet, and another to Bligh for the breadfruit voyage.[10] These are signs, less immediately obvious than some others, but telling nevertheless, that the administration wanted these expeditions to succeed.

On 10 May, Phillip signalled the ships gathered at the Mother Bank to prepare to put to sea. He paid the crews of the *Sirius* and *Supply* two months' advance on 12 May, and the *Hyaena* arrived, to help guard against any mutiny by the convicts while the transports were within reach of England.

Several new difficulties appeared. Quantities of clothes ordered for the women convicts did not arrive, and the marines did not take on enough musket balls and armourer's tools. And, protesting that their ships' masters had not advanced them wages to purchase goods for the voyage, the crews of the transports declined to put to sea. The lack of the clothing and musket balls did not bother Phillip greatly, for he knew that he might either obtain them at a port *en route*, or that they might follow in the *Bounty* or another ship.[11] But the difficulty with the sailors was another matter, and he spent the day rectifying it.

On 13 May, at daybreak, with the wind from the southeast, the *Sirius* weighed anchor 'and made sail to the westward within the Isle of Wight, in company His Majesty's ship *Hyaena*, armed tender *Supply* with six transports and three storeships under convoy'.[12] At 9 a.m. they passed through the Needles into the English Channel. Forty-eight years old, and a traveller of goodly states and kingdoms and wide oceans, Arthur Phillip was on his way out of the world. So too were the 1200 colonists in his charge.

The voyage began auspiciously. Whereas on the last occasion Phillip had sailed from Europe, winter storms had shattered the squadron in the Bay of Biscay and he had had to proceed alone, now he sailed in 'fine' weather with a 'good breeze' at east southeast.[13] Five hundred kilometres out from Portsmouth, he farewelled the *Hyaena* and headed his ships southwest into the Atlantic.

Sailing down the route that thousands of voyages had made second nature to European navigators, the First Fleet reached for the Canaries. The weather continued good. Preparing for the tasks of colonization, Phillip gathered details of the convicts' 'different trades and occupations'; and with him and his surgeons paying particular attention to diet and hygiene, the general level of health far exceeded expectation. Especially was this true of the convicts. After three weeks, not only were they 'not so sickly as when we sailed', but all the ships were 'remarkably healthy'.[14] And already, in their behaviour, they showed the benefit of a change of circumstance. There was a brief worry with some rogues on the *Scarborough*, but the officers quickly put paid to their intended mutiny. Indeed, Phillip found so little cause for concern that he gave permission for the males to be unfettered, and for all to be allowed above deck at intervals. He reported from Tenerife, 'in general, the convicts have behaved well … they are quiet and contented'.[15]

The Fleet reached the Canaries in the first days of June. The position of these islands across southerly winds and currents meant that they were ideally situated to be a place of refreshment for ships sailing to the West Indies, South America, Africa and India. After settling them in the fifteenth century, the Spanish colonists had quickly provided for this demand, raising animals and poultry, vegetables and fruit. In time, they also produced goods for the European mainland – first sugar, then wines. By the 1780s, Santa Cruz, the chief town on Tenerife, had become the group's central port, and had a population of more than 6000. To it came a great variety of European goods – beef, pork, butter, fish, candles, wheat, maize, rice, timber, cloths. From it went wines, silk and orchilla.

Having sighted the famous Peak of Tenerife the previous day, the ships reached Santa Cruz on 3 June, and the governor received Phillip helpfully. In the next week, Phillip obtained fresh food, considering this 'absolutely necessary' for the colonists' present and future wellbeing. The marines and their wives received 1 lb of fresh beef per day, together with rice, wine, and what vegetables and fruit were available. The convicts had 3/4 lb of beef and 3/4 lb of bread daily, and vegetables. Phillip also took the opportunity to replenish the ships' supplies of water.[16]

During these days, the officers inspected Santa Cruz and its surrounding districts. They found the town to be 'very irregular and ill-built', but nonetheless to have some 'spacious' and 'convenient' houses; and they were shocked at the 'restless importunity' of the beggars and the brazen behaviour of the prostitutes. Beyond the port and Laguna, the island's capital, they found 'fertile' valleys and 'a romantic pleasant country'.[17] Nevertheless, the First Fleet people did not see the Canaries at their best. Vegetables were scarce, and few fruits were in season. Still, in the solidity of the town's buildings, the fertility of its environs, the production of wines, dye, cotton and silk, and the establishment of a regular government over the mixed population, they saw enough to gain a sense of how a small-scale European colonization might succeed. Tenerife was the first in a series of such experiences during the voyage to prepare them for the business they were about.

Phillip took the ships to sea again on 10 June. A week later, when at the Cape Verde Islands, he decided the voyage was going well enough for him not to need to stop, so he pressed on for Brazil. Despite some tropical heat and storms, the weather continued favourable, and the people's health good. The waters swarmed with fish, with which the colonists supplemented their diet.

When they reached Brazil early in August, they had lost only fifteen convicts and one marine's child; and most of these had been on embarkation 'such objects as could not have been supposed would have lived, had they remained in England'.[18]

The arrival at Rio de Janeiro was something of a homecoming for Phillip, who brought his convoy through the heads with flags flying and cannon sounding. His friend the Marquis of Lavradio was no longer viceroy; but the new ruler, Luis de Vasconcelos e Souza, greeted him as an equal, returning his salute, providing him with accommodation on shore, and ordering the palace guard to receive him formally whenever he landed. Phillip found the soldiers' attention a hindrance to the efficient conduct of his business, and sometimes sought to avoid it by landing where they were not expecting him – which led to the comical sight of desperate soldiers running to meet him and hastily drawing themselves up on parade. Inconvenient as this attention was, Phillip had for the most part to accept it, for he needed the help that went with it. The viceroy made the country's resources freely available; and, in a rare gesture, he permitted the British officers to move without military escort about the city and its environs. This was in sharp contrast to the obstacles that Lavradio had placed in Cook's way in 1769, and it reflected Vasconcelos's awareness of his nation's debt to Phillip.

As I have explained, the basis of the First Fleet colonists' good health was laid during the months at Portsmouth. It was brought to another peak during the stay at Rio de Janeiro. The day after the ships came to anchor, canoes swarmed round them, with the Negro crews selling oranges at two dozen and then four dozen for 6d. And when the officers toured ashore, they found themselves besieged with offers of fresh fruits. Ralph Clark recorded how on one trip into the country, 'we stepped into a grove of oranges when the gentleman asked us if we would walk in and offered us knives and go and eat oranges in the grove. He sent his servant with us to pull them off of the trees for us where we eat as many as we could and stuffed our pockets full and he would take nothing for them.' Smyth recorded of another walk, 'an old gentleman ... seeing us pass his garden, by signs invited us in and treated us in the most friendly manner, insisting upon our eating of every fruit his garden afforded, viz.: oranges of many sorts, sweet and sour lemons, pineapples, bananas, guavas. He also loaded us home with presents of each.'[19] Many of these fruits are very rich in vitamin C: a medium-sized orange contains from 25 to 50 milligrams, a tangerine 31, a persimmon 40, a guava an astonishing 200.

It was not only officers whose health benefited from Rio de Janeiro's bounty. Smyth recorded how on 8 August the *Lady Penrhyn*'s captain 'went early on shore and brought off great plenty of vegetables, fruits, etc. The canoes alongside brought prodigious quantities of oranges of two sorts, one very small, of a dark red colour; very sweet and rich flavoured; and the other remarkable large. The officer of the guard boat brought a bucketful as a present, of the largest I ever saw, which measured a foot in circumference, with the stalks and leaves adhering to them.'[20]

And so too did the convicts benefit. As before, Phillip's concern was the health of all in his charge. Immediately on arrival, he obtained 'great plenty' of vegetables, fruits, and fresh beef; and he saw that all persons continued to have supplies throughout their stay. These foods were cheap, and Phillip ordered very generous allowances – more than 1 1/4 lbs of beef per adult per day; 1 lb of rice; yams, plantains, radishes, cabbages, lettuce and endive; and large quantities of oranges, limes, guavas and bananas. (John Easty recorded serving the marines and convicts on the *Scarborough* ten oranges each on 12 August.) He landed the sick at the Ilha das Cobras; and the fresh air and fresh foods 'soon removed every symptom of the scurvy prevalent among them'. By the time the ships sailed from Rio de Janeiro, the convicts were 'much healthier than when we left England'.[21]

As he attended to immediate needs, Phillip also looked ahead, purchasing items that they would need either during the rest of the voyage or in New South Wales: 115 pipes of rum and 15 of wine; 100 sacks of the bread substitute cassava; 10,000 musket balls.[22] He gathered plants and seeds, too – some rare varieties to send back to Sir Joseph Banks, and others he expected would flourish in New South Wales – fruits, vines, coffee, cocoa, indigo, cotton and some cochineal. David Collins enlarged this list to include coffee (both seed and plant), cocoa (in the nut), cotton (seed), banana (plant), oranges (various sorts, seed and plant), lemon (seed and plant), guava (seed), tamarind, prickly pear plant (with the cochineal on it) and Eugenia or *pomme rose*.[23]

While Phillip forwent the pleasures of the city, the officers, to whom it was unfamiliar, walked about it. Some, like John White and William Dawes, discussed professional matters with their Portuguese counterparts. Others were simply tourists, and wandered to admire the imposing civic square, the towering aqueduct and the churches. Many joined the throngs at the colourful festivals, enjoyed the displays of fireworks, and sought out 'tender' attachments. As those who have travelled since to this romantic city have found, while it offered great contrasts of wealth and poverty, it also offered an abundant sense of life.

To the officers, it was a welcome interlude between tedious wastes of ocean; and it showed them how European colonization might succeed on a grand scale. They might have enjoyed it less, however, had they understood as Phillip did the difficulties that lay ahead.

*

The company refreshed, the ships reprovisioned and bearing more of what the party would need in New South Wales, Phillip sailed from Rio de Janeiro for the Cape of Good Hope on 4 September. The good fortune continued. Despite the weather being rougher than before, there were no serious incidents; and while some were sick with scurvy and dysentery by the time they sighted the Cape on 13 October, in general the expedition remained unusually healthy.

At Cape Town, Phillip followed a similar procedure to that at Rio de Janeiro. He saluted the fort as the ships entered Table Bay and, after the port master had ascertained that the ships carried no contagious illnesses, he paid his compliments to the governor and requested permission to purchase food and livestock. At first, the Dutch authorities restricted the amounts of bread and flour, citing the failure of crops two years before. The Dutch merchants' charging double or treble their usual prices was another annoyance, but as he could not manage without their supplies, there was little Phillip could do about this. He must have found the situation all too familiar; and the difficulties entirely justified his and Nepean's decision that he should first call at Rio de Janeiro, and not sail ahead of the Fleet until they had left Cape Town.

Despite the initial difficulties he encountered, Phillip persisted with his requests, and his persistence paid dividends. After repeated applications and explanations, he received permission to buy most of what he wanted, and the people once more benefited from daily fresh food, with the convicts, 'men, women, and children [having] the same allowance as the troops, except wine' – '1 1/2 lbs of soft bread, and an equal amount of beef or mutton daily' together with 'a liberal allowance of vegetables'. In this circumstance he found it unnecessary to land the few sick, who were 'perfectly re-established in three or four days'.[24] On the face of things, there was little reason for the party not to be confident. The voyage was going well, far better than might reasonably have been expected.

Phillip and some of the officers lodged ashore. As always, he was more concerned with business than pleasure; John White, for example, was moved to speak of his 'sagacity and industrious zeal for the service';[25] but his juniors again looked interestedly about a place that was strange to most of them.

They noticed the township's regularity and neatness, and its avenues of oak. Predictably, they were most struck by the Dutch East India Company's garden, by its fertility, its cool passages and its menagerie, which put a number in mind of St James's Park; and Governor Graaf added to their pleasure by entertaining them at his residence. As it had done in Brazil, the experience suggested they might expect a happy outcome to their own venture. 'The Cape is situated in a fine climate,' one wrote, 'and yields most of the necessaries of life, and some of its luxuries. We have good hopes of Botany Bay, it being in nearly the same latitude.'[26]

But a distinct sobering of outlook also attended their arrival at the Cape; officers' writings from this time reveal a loss of optimism, and the growth of a sense of menace. The Cape colony itself occasioned the first manifestations of this sense. Though prosperous enough, Cape Town was no Rio de Janeiro; however much they enjoyed it, the officers found that the Dutch settlement 'certainly suffer[ed]' in comparison. Here there were no 'picturesque and beautiful' environs 'abounding with the most luxuriant flowers and aromatic shrubs', but rather the forbidding Table Mountain, on whose bleak rocks renegade slaves took refuge.[27] Here there were no taverns for the officers to lodge at, provisions were dear, and the governor was reluctant to allow the British access to them. The regularity with which the township was laid out, and the regulation of its inhabitants' lives bespoke the Calvinism of the Dutch. Here were no exuberant festivals. Here ladies did not let passionate glances slip past enticing veils, throw nosegays from balconies, gather at the gates of convents to encourage assignations, or mingle with the festival crowds to achieve them. Rather, they sat demurely in the middle of austere churches, with the men about the walls so as to surround them. Wearing black, couples married only on Sundays. Slaves moved about the streets in fear, not in celebration.

To some extent, the change in their mood resulted directly from what the British officers saw at the Cape; but there were other causes, one quite practical. Knowing that they were destined for a region 'that does not furnish any of the necessaries of life', Phillip acted to take on as many of these as he possibly could. He shifted persons from one ship to another, crowding them together to make room for the stalls which he filled with animals: 'bulls, cows, horses, mares, colts, sheep, hogs, goats, fowls and other living creatures by pairs'. Hunter said that the government stock consisted of: one stallion, three mares, three colts, two bulls, six cows, forty-four sheep, four goats and twenty-eight pigs; and then there were fowls of all kinds. Phillip spent some £2000 on livestock. Some of the officers also bought stock for the small farms they intended to establish in the colony, but found themselves constrained by the high cost of feed.[28]

Taking advice from the botanist Francis Masson, who was collecting at the Cape of Good Hope for Banks for the second time, and from Colonel Gordon, the commander of the Dutch troops, Phillip likewise gathered 'a vast number of plants, seeds and other garden articles, such as orange, lime, lemon, quince apple, pear tree – in a word, every vegetable production that the Cape afforded'. These also included fig trees, sugarcane, vines, strawberries, oak and myrtle.[29] And the company at large now felt the urgency of the need. 'This is the last port we touch at in our way to the new settlement,' a junior officer wrote, '[and it] has been a time of constant bustle – indeed it is right to take every advantage of it, for the leaving behind of any of the many articles that are requisite, and necessary, would be now irreparable.'[30]

There was a deeper, less tangible cause. Instinctively, the officers knew that when they left the Cape of Good Hope for the southern Indian Ocean they would leave the known world. As Cook had written from the Cape to his old master and friend John Walker in November 1772, 'having nothing new to communicate I should hardly have troubled you with a letter was it not customary for men to take leave of their friends before they go out of the world, for I can hardly think myself in it so long as I am deprived from having any connections with the civilized part of it, and this will soon be my case for two years at least'. Now, those on the First Fleet faced this reality. 'The land behind us was the abode of a civilized people,' David Collins observed as they prepared to sail, 'that before us was the residence of savages. When, if ever, we might again enjoy the commerce of the world, was doubtful and uncertain'.[31]

In this atmosphere, the voyagers clutched at the intangibles of their world. Some of them had received letters just before they sailed, and as the ships moved away from the Cape, they encountered the *Kent* whaler: 'On our first discovering her, as she seemed desirous of joining or speaking to the Fleet, we were in hopes of her being from England, probably to us, or at least that we might get letters by her; but our suspense on these points, a suspense only to be conceived by persons on long voyages, was soon put an end to by hearing she had been so many months out.'

The disappointment gave finality to the move from the Cape. 'We weighed anchor,' Tench wrote, 'and soon left far behind every scene of civilization and humanized manners.'[32]

With each ship like 'another Noah's ark', crowded with cattle, sheep, pigs, horses and poultry, and loaded deep with food and extra water for these beasts and the plants, with his own cabin 'like a small green house', Phillip sailed again on 11 November.[33] He did so without Masson, whom some had expected to join the expedition.[34]

Phillip now decided finally to go on ahead. Shifting into the *Supply*, and taking trusted junior officers and some convict artificers with him, he set off with three of the faster sailers. This advance party lost sight of the body of the convoy on 27 November, and proceeded eastward through a 'great number' of black and blue petrels and albatrosses and a 'prodigious quantity of whales', as well as frequent squalls and high seas. On 24 December, for example, the squalls were 'very violent', with 'great quantities of rain, sleet and large hail stones'. Phillip described how the wind was 'seldom more than twenty-four hours in one quarter, veering regularly from the northward to the westward where it seldom stood more than a few hours, … [and was] seldom to the eastward and then for a few hours only'. Interspersed were days of 'very pleasant and serene weather'. The *Supply* sighted the South Cape of Van Diemen's Land on 3 January, and entered Botany Bay in the afternoon of 18 January 1788, to be followed by the three transports the next day.[35]

Meanwhile, Phillip's departure had increased the psychic dislocation amongst the main party. Hunter, now responsible for seven ships and about 1000 persons, became excessively cautious. Put out by Phillip's not consulting him about his decision to sail ahead, Major Ross grew bitter. The convicts fell back into old patterns of behaviour, and became fractious. In December, the passage grew distinctly worse. The ships wallowed constantly in the great swell, and encountered fogs and gales. So as to preserve the water for the animals and plants, Hunter put the colonists on 3 1/2 pints a day. Illness increased, and there were frequent injuries from the ships' equipment shifting in the gales and seas. As they entered the longitudes of New Holland, the officers pored over the charts deriving from Cook's voyages, so as to know when theirs would end. At Christmas, nostalgia for country and friends half a world away engulfed them.

In this final stage of the voyage, accidents, disease and cold damaged the plants and caused great mortality among the animals, whose food grew short. The master of the *Fishburn* reported that he had lost many sheep and 'three dozen fowls out of four dozen'; that of the *Golden Grove* that he had also lost 'the greatest part of his fowls'; that of the *Prince of Wales* reported that he too had lost 'almost the whole of his fowls'. On the night of 31 December, when the sea was 'mountains high', the chicken coups on the *Lady Penrhyn* 'gave way and came with such violence against the side as to drive the goat house all in pieces and lamed the goat and kid'. Nine days later, there was only one day's supply of hay left on this last ship, and in 'a greater swell than at any other period ... the tubs in the cabin with the banana plants, grape vines etc. broke from their fastenings and were thrown out of the tubs and much hurt'.[36]

Then came those portents the voyagers were longing for. Some of the plants from Rio de Janeiro began to bloom, and on 6 January 1788 they sighted the southern coast of Van Diemen's Land. Cook's charts allowed them to identify their position, and the captains distributed wine. They swung away from land again, but more briefly now they knew, to have a clear run up to their destination. On 19 January, they came upon the coast of New South Wales just south of Botany Bay. The wind was 'fair', the sky 'serene, though a little hazy', the temperature 'delightfully pleasant', the coastline as Cook and Banks had described it. The next day, they entered Botany Bay, to find the ships which had gone ahead.[37]

As the ships of the second division arrived so quickly after him, Phillip was not able to prepare beforehand as he had intended. However, this was the only blemish in an achievement remarkable on a number of counts. To have eleven indifferently-sailing ships follow a route that only Tasman and Cook had previously taken, through 'a long track of ocean ... totally unknown' to their masters,[38] and arrive within two days of each other, was a remarkable feat of navigation, which says much for Phillip's and Hunter's technical competence. To pass such a long voyage without any serious incidents on the ships, too, reflects the alert care with which the commanders supervised the venture. While there were several plots laid on the *Scarborough* and *Alexander*, these were quickly discovered, and the murmurs of rebellion easily silenced. When we consider what happened among the shipwrecked people of the *Batavia* 160 years earlier we may see how easily it might have been otherwise.

Collins caught the magnitude of the achievement best:

Thus, under the blessing of God, was happily completed, in eight months and one week, a voyage which, before it was undertaken, the mind hardly dared venture to contemplate, and on which it was impossible to reflect without some apprehensions as to its termination. … In the above space of time we had sailed 5021 leagues; had touched at the American and African Continents; and had at last rested within a few days sail of the antipodes of our native country, without meeting any accident in a fleet of eleven sail, nine of which were merchantmen that had never before sailed in that distant and imperfectly explored ocean: and when it is considered, that there was on board a large body of convicts, many of whom were embarked in a very sickly state, we might be deemed peculiarly fortunate, that of the whole number of all descriptions of persons coming to form the new settlement, only thirty-two had died since their leaving England, among whom were to be included one or two deaths by accidents; although previous to our departure it was generally conjectured, that before we should have been a month at sea one of the transports would have been converted into a hospital ship.[39]

This was an extraordinary accomplishment; and it was made possible by the care with which the voyage was planned, the skill of the people who conducted it, and the foods that the colonists were given.

*

Arthur Phillip quickly decided that Botany Bay was not a suitable site for a large settlement and, after investigating the splendid Port Jackson, established the colony about Sydney Cove.

Having unloaded most of the stores and stock, and landed the convicts, on 7 February 1788 Phillip formally established the colony. At ten in the morning he had assembled all the colonists at the marines' parade ground on the west side of the cove. When the convicts had been gathered together and ordered to sit, the marines entered, led by their band and with their colours flying, to form an encircling guard. Phillip stood bare-headed in the centre, in company with his principal officers. David Collins, the deputy judge-advocate, read Phillip's commission and the Letters-Patent establishing the colony's courts. At intervals, the marines fired volleys of muskets and the band played bars of 'God Save the King'.

Empowered as the giver of law and dispenser of mercy, Phillip addressed the convicts – in a 'short speech, extremely well adapted to the people he had to govern', according to one officer who heard it; in a 'mild and humane manner', said another; in an 'excellently adapted speech, accompanied with many judicious exhortations', said a third. From the records of these observers, we can reconstruct a good deal of what Phillip said at this, the colony's formal beginning. He praised those who had behaved well during the voyage, and pointed out how he had been lenient towards those who had not. He was convinced, he said, that there were many fundamentally good persons amongst them, who had succumbed to vice in moments of misfortune, or drunkenness, or under the influence of bad companions. But he also feared that 'there were some men and women among them, so thoroughly abandoned in their wickedness, as to have lost every good principle'. He urged all 'to forget the habits of vice and indolence in which too many of them had hitherto lived; and exhorted them to be honest amongst themselves, obedient to their overseers, and attentive to the several works in which they were about to be employed'. He pointed out that only 200 of the 600 men had done the work in the past days, while the others had 'skulked' in the woods. Henceforth, those who would not work would not eat, for the *good* men ... should not be slaves for the *bad*'. He forbade the theft and slaughter of the colony's livestock, and assured his audience that all transgressions would be punished with the utmost severity, no matter how 'it might distress his feelings'. He said the sentries would fire on any men trying to enter the women's tents at night, and he urged the convicts to form regular relationships by marrying. He told the convicts that it was 'entirely in their power to atone to their country for the wrongs done at home, that nothing but a new repetition of their former demerits could draw down upon them the severity of those laws of which he was invested with the dispensation'. He would ever be ready, he said, 'to show approbation and encouragement to those who proved themselves worthy of them by good conduct and attention to orders; while on the other hand, such as were determined to act in opposition to propriety, and observe a contrary conduct, would inevitably meet with the punishment which they deserved'. He extolled the humanity of the law which they had transgressed and, citing the absence of temptation in their new situation, pointed out how this offered the opportunity, not only 'to expiate their offences', but also 'to become good, and even opulent men, as many of the first settlers in the western world had been convicts like themselves.' 'Nor,' said he, 'could shame be imputed to such as reformed and became useful members of society.' He concluded by wishing them 'reformation, happiness, and prosperity, in this new country' – and by giving them the day free from labour.[40]

These officers, marines and convicts were European Australia's first colonists, and the new world was all before them.

PART FIVE:
THE COST

11.

No Cheaper Mode?

A RECURRING CLAIM IN THE historiography of the Botany Bay decision is that the Pitt administration was seeking an inexpensive solution to a pressing problem. 'The Government of Pitt chose New South Wales as a prison, commodious, conveniently distant, and, it was hoped, cheap', wrote Hancock in 1930. Fifty years later, Mackay said: 'From the moment the decision was announced (and attacks on it began) the planners of the First Fleet, and its commander, were enjoined to economy. Everything was done to reduce the cost of the enterprise. The stores were cheap and shoddy. The equipment level was low.' In arguing that the existence of any other motive for the venture was 'only speculation', Shaw cited Pitt's remarks to the House of Commons in February 1791: '"No cheaper mode of disposing of the convicts could be found"', declared Pitt, 'and that has to be explained by those who urge that other reasons were more important'.[1] *No cheaper mode of disposing of the convicts could be found*? But did the politicians really think that New South Wales would be a cheap solution to the convict problem? On the assumption that this is what Pitt and his advisers believed, the historians have found them sadly wanting. Let us see what the story really is.

In the mid-1780s the administration was paying Campbell approximately £28 per annum to keep a convict on a hulk,[2] and in 1778 the House of Commons Committee had accepted that the value of his labour

425

constituted a return of about one-third of this cost. If the ministers thought that transporting convicts halfway around the globe would cost less than £18 per person, then clearly common sense had deserted them. On the other hand, the ministers were obviously incompetent if, knowing how costly it was likely to prove, they decided to transport convicts to Botany Bay because they simply could not think of another way to dispose of them. As Molony wrote:

> In England some critics thought that the settlement in New South Wales was absurd, impractical and grossly expensive. Half a million pounds had been spent up until the end of 1792, but Pitt was convinced that no cheaper method could be devised of disposing of the Kingdom's worst criminals who, at home, would help to corrupt others.[3]

The business of estimating in detail the cost of carrying convicts to New South Wales began in 1785, with the Beauchamp Committee. Members heard from Charles Coggan, the East India Company's chief shipping official, that it cost £25.2.9 to send a soldier from England to India, when the Company had to meet the expense of the outward section of the voyage only. The Committee also interviewed Duncan Campbell, whom they asked, 'If you were to carry convicts a voyage of probably six months to a place where no kind of trade is carried on, how much per man would you contract for?' Campbell answered that if the ship were of 700 or 800 tons with a crew of seventy to eighty men, and the round voyage of fifteen months duration, then the cost might be £30 per person for 300 convicts, or £40 per person for 200.[4]

In January 1786 Nepean took the question up again. Starting from the idea that the expedition would comprise a 40-gun warship, a tender and two transports, he asked Campbell to estimate the cost of sending out 260 or 270 male convicts per transport, together with surgeons and a guard of thirty marines, and maintaining them for one year in New South Wales. It is worth looking at these estimates in detail.

Nepean: What would be demanded for the conveyance of 260 or 270 male convicts to New South Wales, together with any provisions and stores that the ship can conveniently stow? (The contractors to furnish the convicts with provisions during their passage.)

Campbell: The vessel being hired and fitted for the sole purpose of carrying out the convicts: I apprehend the cost, and charges of wages and provisions during the voyage, less what she may be supposed to sell for on her return, will be the expense of sending out 270 convicts. See the calculation of the expense, which amounts to £50. 8.2 per man.

Nepean: The ship must also be of sufficient size to take about thirty marines as guards. What would be the charge of their victualling to New South Wales, and of the surgeon* and a mate or two*, in addition to the above?

[*Campbell's annotation*: These are provided for in the calculation for the ship's company.]

Campbell: The ship being of a size sufficient for this purpose, the only charge for these will be victualling, which I suppose may be done for 1s per diem each. Government to find water casks.

Nepean: What is supposed to be the annual expense of a year's clothing for a convict?

Campbell: £2.2.0 in a warm climate.

Nepean: Each convict must have a bed and hammock: what is the price of each?

Campbell: Perhaps a better mode than a hammock may be adopted and the expense included in the allowance of 10d per diem mentioned in the calculation.

Nepean: What is it supposed an allowance of beef or pork for one year would amount to for the support of 600 convicts on shore, with a proportion of flour and any other species of provisions that may be requisite for their use in addition thereto, to be sent from this country? NB: In this we suppose that the quantities, whatever they may be, may be sent out in the 40-gun ship, the tender and the two convict ships, so that no freight can be charged.

Campbell: Allowing 4 lbs for six men per day and five days in the week would require 520 barrels [of] beef and pork. Bread and flour, allowing 1 lb of either per day to each man, will require 109,500 lb bread, and also of flour 109,500 lbs. To hold the first will require 240 sugar barrels; and to hold the last will require 291 barrels or sack casks. Allowing 3 pints per mess of six men of peas and barley or oatmeal for their soup on meat and bargoo days, will require as per calculation 10,355 bushels or 217 barrels for every six men. A cheese two days in the week will require 10 tons of cheese. The provisions for the country expenditure for twelve months will amount to £3567.

Nepean: What sort of tools and utensils for building and implements for agriculture are proper for the use of the convicts; and what would the assortment amount to for 600 convicts and the marine guards consisting of three companies?

Campbell: Stores and implements £958

Added to the £3567 allowed for provisions, Campbell noted, this made for a sum of £4525. Concerning his estimate of £50.8.2 for transportation, Campbell pointed out: 'But if this calculation is right government must pay considerably more, because no man can be expected to undertake such a contract but with considerable prospect of gain.' However, he qualified this caution with: 'Should the ship be permitted to take in a load at China for Britain, in that case the contractor might be able to obtain a handsome profit by the voyage, and of course to relax in their terms.'[5]

Sometime about the beginning of August 1786, after T.B. Thompson's unfavourable report concerning Das Voltas Bay had led the administration to concentrate on Botany Bay, officials again pursued the question. An estimate, probably drawn up by the Navy Board, states:[6]

By Mr Campbell's estimate:

The charge of taking the convicts to New South Wales will amount to £50.8.2 per man. But it is to be observed that in forming this estimate, he includes, 1st, their provision and clothing for eight months; 2nd, the provision for thirty marines during that time at 1s per day; 3rd, the ship to be navigated by seventy men, and their provision charged at £1.15.0 per month, although by the answers from the Admiralty Office it appears that the public expense of victualling seamen and marines amounts but to 10 67/100 d each per day.

This charge may therefore be considerably reduced by government's undertaking to victual the ship's crew, marines and convicts, and by the reducing the ship's crew from seventy to fifty men, for the latter number is equal to the mere purpose of navigating her, and thirty marines joined to the crew will be a sufficient guard.

Upon this foundation the *whole estimate* will stand nearly as follows:

	£
A 40-gun ship, every charge included, per annum	4392
A tender of 200 ton if freighted	1400
The annual pay of two companies of marines	2451
Victualling the same	...
Clothing 600 convicts per annum	1260
Victualling 600 convicts per year, no liquor included*	3567
Annual charge not including the victualling of the marines	13,070
Tools etc., necessary for 600 convicts if bought	1000
Victualling the crew of the convict ships, 100 men for eight months	1117
Freight of 600 convicts at £40 each	24,000
	26,117
Total	39,187

* As the convicts when on shore will be victualled but for one year at most, the annual expense after the first year will be reduced [by] £3567.

Neither Campbell's estimate nor this one contained any provision for a civil establishment. This was added by Nepean in the next calculation in the series, in which he also increased the number of marines to three companies and the amount to be allowed for tools, and included provision for purchasing stock and seeds:[7]

	£
[Annual charge of warship and tender]	5792
Annual pay of three companies of marines (say 180)	3676
Victualling of ditto	2874
Annual clothing [for] 600 convicts	1260
Victualling 600, no liquor allowed	3567
Annual pay of the superintendent	500
	17,669

It is presumed that after the first year one half of the victualling of the marines and convicts may be saved, so that instead of £17,669 per annum it will be reduced to £14,449.10.0; and that the service of the tender after the second year or even the 40-gun ship will not be necessary, so that the expense of the establishment at the end of three years will probably not exceed £7000 per year.

Freight of 600 convicts, including all the expenses of the crew of the two ships which convey them, including their victualling for eight months and the pay and victuals of the crew etc., calculated upon a supposition that the ships may be absent fifteen months, [at] £45 each	27,000
Tools to be purchased	1000
Stock to be purchased and seeds	1300
	46,969

Before his next revision, Nepean estimated the cost of an enlarged staff establishment:[8]

Yearly salary

The naval commander to be appointed governor or superintendent-general	500
The commanding officer of the marines, to be appointed lieutenant-governor or deputy-superintendent	250
The commissary of stores and provisions, for himself and assistants (to be appointed or named by the contractors for the provisions)	200
Pay of a surgeon	182.10.0
Ditto of two mates	182.10.0
Chaplain	182.10.0
	1497.10.00

He then incorporated this figure into an extended estimate:[9]

Annual expense of a ship equal in size to one of 40-gun according to the Navy Board's calculation, supposing no unusual accidents to happen	1500
Annual pay of her officers and men, supposing her crew to consist of eighty	1600
Annual expense of victualling her crew, including the water casks, necessary money, etc.	1292
Annual expense of a tender of 200 tons, including her crew, provisions, etc.	1400
Annual pay of three companies of marines, supposed to consist of 180	3676
Annual expense of victualling them	2874
Annual expense of clothing 600 convicts	1260
Ditto of victualling them, no liquor allowed	3567
Annual pay of superintendent and staff establishment	1500
Total	18,669

It is presumed that after the first year, one half of the expense of victualling the convicts and marines may be saved, so that instead of an annual charge of £18,669 it will be reduced to £15,449.10.0. That after the second year the service of the tender will be unnecessary, and after the third, or possibly the second, the 40-gun ship may return home. So that the annual expense of the whole establishment will probably not exceed £7000 per annum:

Freight of 600 convicts, including all the expenses
    of the two ships and the victualling of the convicts
    during their passage, which it is presumed may
    be about eight months, calculated at £45 per man   27,000
Tools to be purchased and implements for agriculture, etc.   1000
Stock and seeds for the settlement   1300
                       29,300

That is, Nepean came to the conclusion that it would cost £48.10.0 to transport a convict to New South Wales, and to equip him for his tasks; and that the cost of maintaining 600 convicts there, a marine guard of 180 men, and a civil establishment would drop from £18,669 to about £7000 per annum over three years, as the colony grew towards self-sufficiency – or roughly £23 per annum per convict. It was on this basis that in August 1786 the Pitt administration found it financially feasible to establish a convict colony at Botany Bay.

*

However, as soon as the administration moved to implement this decision, there began that 'blow out' so familiar in modern government budgets and contracts. One reason for this was that the intricacy of the business of establishing a colony of convicts in a place so far away, where local resources were slender and points of succour remote, only emerged as it was pursued. As it did, the administration increased the quantity of some items and added others. Another reason was that new aspects were added to the scheme – for example, bringing Polynesian women to the settlement, and sending one of the transports to New Zealand for the flax plant, and to the Friendly Islands [Tonga] to obtain breadfruit plants for the West Indies. By December, when, at Pitt's request, Nepean asked Sir Charles Middleton for an estimate of the 'expenses which it is supposed will be incurred under the direction of the Navy Board for the providing of provisions, clothing, implements, etc. for the convicts, and sending them out to Botany Bay, including the expenses incurred for the detachment of marines', Middleton replied with the following figures:[10]

Freight of convicts, no. 750	6734
Freight of provisions	7840
Expenses of extra etc.	460
Provisions [for] convicts for two years	15,758
Victualling convicts and marines in their passage	6169
Slops and beds for convicts	3042
Medicines for garrison	1500
Implements, necessaries, etc.	3000
Agent	220
	44,723

He added: 'NB: If this embarkation is detained so as to prevent the convict ships from reaching China by January 1788, £10,000 more must be added to the freight'.

At this point, Middleton implicitly saw that the remaining period of embarkation and the voyage would constitute twelve months, so that his estimates covered a three-year period. The above figures did not include all the costs, however. To be added were those for:[11]

The Navy ships, the *Sirius* and *Supply*	31,663
The annual pay and clothing of the marine establishment for three years	14,089
The cost of the civil establishment	8632
Ordnance	2435
	56,819

Therefore, on a still very incomplete reckoning, by mid-December 1786 the members of the Pitt administration knew that it was going to cost in the vicinity of £100,000 over a three-year period to establish a colony of 750 convicts in New South Wales, or some £45 per convict per annum – and more if the transports did not obtain a return cargo.

In April 1787, four weeks before the First Fleet sailed, Middleton drew up a more nearly complete account:[12]

Freight of convicts	19,464
Freight of provisions	7840
Provisions for the convicts for two years	15,578
Victualling convicts and marines on the passage	8000
Slops and beds for convicts and medicines for garrison	4600
Implements and necessaries	3000
Agent and extra expenses	700
Expense of *Sirius* and *Supply* tender, including stores, wages, provisions and wear and tear for three years	34,375
Marine establishment, including officers and victualling for two years	12,220
	105,777

Missing from this account are those costs that did not fall within Middleton's purview:

Civil establishment for three years	8632
Ordnance	2435
	11,067

So that, by mid-April 1787, the administration's estimate of the cost of the colony over a three-year period had risen to some £116,000, or to £52 per convict per year.

*

When the final accounts came in, the cost was still higher. According to the returns that Nepean and Middleton prepared for the Treasury in February 1790,[13] over the three-year period from January 1787 to the end of 1789, the costs of the New South Wales venture had variously been:

Preparations in England

Clothing Bedding etc. purchased by the Navy Board for the
    supply of 680 male and 70[14] female convicts who composed
    the first embarkation, supposed to be sufficient for their
    use during the passage to New South Wales and for two
    years after their arrival   5156

Tools and implements of husbandry, for erecting
    public edifices, including nails, glass etc.   3056

Medicines, surgeon's instruments, necessaries of
    different sorts, etc., for the hospitals   1202

Seed grain   286

Handcuffs and irons for securing the convicts   42

Marquees for the governor, the civil and marine officers   389

Old canvas supplied from Portsmouth dockyard for tents,
    etc. for the convicts, until huts could be erected   69

Portable house for the governor[15]   130

Stationery for the commissary of stores and provisions   20

Provisions for two years for the settlement
    [1000 rations per year]   16,205

Mr Richards, for provisions supplied the marine guard and
    convicts from the time of their embarkation to the time
    of their sailing from Spithead, including a quantity of
    wine, essence of malt and other necessaries of that nature
    purchased by him   4705

Fees paid upon Governor Phillip's commission and for that
    of establishing courts of justice   627

Expenses incurred in conveying convicts from the Old Bailey
    to Portsmouth to embark on board the transports   84

The Reverend Mr Johnson to enable him to provide necessaries
for the voyage   50
Travelling expenses of Captain Norman and other persons
charged with despatches from Governor Phillip and other
trifling expenses   79
Fees on the above payments   57
Subtotal   32,157

On the Voyage
Mr Richards, for freight of transport ships[16]   40,993
Ditto for provisions etc. supplied the above-mentioned marines
and convicts from the time of their sailing to the time of
their disembarkation in New South Wales including 2 1/8
per cent discount on Navy bills   7612
Lieutenant Shortland, agent for transports, his pay and
disbursements during the passage   881
Commissioner Miller's bills for wine, fresh provisions, etc.,
purchased at Tenerife   76
Governor Phillip's bills from Rio de Janeiro for supplies   135
Commissioner Miller's bills for fresh provisions, etc., at
Rio de Janeiro   2303
Ditto for fresh provisions, cattle and seed and grain purchased
at the Cape of Good Hope   1966
Subtotal   53,966

In New South Wales
[Mr Richards] for surplus salt beef provided by him for the supply
of the above marines and convicts landed as per agreement
in New South Wales, for which he obtained bills upon the
Treasury   436
Pay of the artificers belonging to the *Sirius* and *Supply* employed
on the public works at Port Jackson, for which bills have been
drawn upon the Treasury   172

Flour, grain and surgeon's necessaries purchased by Captain Hunter of the *Sirius* at the Cape of Good Hope, to which place he was sent by Governor Phillip after the establishment had been made at Port Jackson	128
Subtotal	736

To this list we need to add:

Cost of the *Sirius* and *Supply* for three years (as per estimate)[17]	39,209
Civil establishment for three years	8632
Marine establishment for three years	14,088
Ordnance	2435
Compensation made to Mr William Richards, Jr, for [the] value of the *Friendship*[18] transport, which was scuttled and sunk on her passage home	1972
Value of casks, etc. supplied by him to the settlement, and for some other articles lost in the *Friendship* transport	350
	66,686
Total	153,545

That is, the cost as the administration knew it in February 1790 of the colony in its first three and a quarter years was £153,544, or £63 per convict per year, so that sending the convicts to New South Wales had cost about 2.25 times what it would have cost to keep them on hulks in the Thames. This ignores the simple benefit of the hulk convicts' labour. If we take this into account but on the other hand assume that, in this early period, there was little equivalent benefit to be had from the labour of the convicts sent to New South Wales, the differential increases still further. The initial cost of maintaining a convict in New South Wales, then, was approximately 2.25 to 3.5 times as great as that of keeping him on a hulk.

These ratios increase sharply when the cost of the *Guardian*'s voyage is taken into some account. Partly because one-quarter of the items ordered for it went on the *Lady Juliana*, and partly because some of the supplies it carried did reach the colony eventually, it is impossible to calculate this cost precisely. However, the sources give us the following partial list:[19]

Expenses attending the equipment of His Majesty's ship *Guardian* employed in carrying out provisions and stores etc.	7710
Expense of victualling twenty-five convicts (artificers) and eight superintendents	209
Pay of her commander and crew, provisions, ordnance, wear and tear	6756
Clothing sent out in the *Lady Juliana* and *Guardian*	3962
Hospital stores ditto	4767
Implements for husbandry etc.	2656
Sundry stores	810
Provisions sent out in the above ships	12,034
Bill drawn by Lt Riou of the *Guardian* for wine purchased at Tenerife	220
	39,124

This calculation does not include Riou's claim that the *Guardian* carried £70,000 worth of food and stores, nor the cost of the wrecked ship. If, however, for the sake of a rough comparison, we say that the *Guardian*'s voyage took the cost of the New South Wales colony between October 1786 and the end of 1789 past £200,000, then the raw cost per convict per year was £82, or between 2.5 and 4.5 times the cost of keeping them at home.

*

Major Robert Ross's contemporary claim that it would have been cheaper to have fed 'the convicts on turtle and venison at the London Tavern', then, was a valid, if caustic, one; or, in Blainey's less emotive assessment, 'the settling of eastern Australia was a startlingly costly solution to the crowded British prisons'.[20] Indeed it was – and the Pitt administration knew this at the time. Why then did the ministers decide to do so?

Because they were incompetent – or because they saw that it would serve a number of purposes?

If in February 1791 Pitt claimed that 'no cheaper mode of disposing of the convicts … could be found' than to dump them at Botany Bay, then he was either lying or tacitly admitted to massive incompetence – but was this really what he said? Shaw has misrepresented Pitt's speech, the contemporary report of which is:

Mr *Pitt* said, he had no objection to the motion; on the contrary, he was glad it had been made, because, if reports prevailed that the settlement at Botany Bay was disastrous, and contrary to the purpose intended, it was most desirable that the public should be relieved from the prejudices which such opinions necessarily created, by having the real situation of the colony explained, and stated upon grounds of authority. Government, he said, were convinced that the reverse was the fact, and that there was no reason whatever for any such apprehensions as had been hinted at.

With regard to what the learned gentleman [Sir *Charles Bunbury*] had said, relative to the suspension of the sailing of the vessels now going with convicts abroad, he should betray his trust, as a minister of the Crown, if he were to advise a moment's delay, in despatching those vessels to the place of their destination. What good purpose did the learned gentleman suppose could be answered by it, granting, for the sake of argument, that Botany Bay had proved improper for such a colony? Were the convicts now embarked to be detained till some new place of settlement was explored, and all the first expense again encountered? Or, if it was thought better to distribute them in penitentiary houses, were they to wait until proper houses were erected? In what way were they to be disposed of in the interim?

If Botany Bay was not capable of receiving them, he would freely acknowledge, that ministers were highly reprehensible for sending out so many as were now on the point of going there; but government had no reason to suppose it to be the case. In point of expense, no cheaper mode of disposing of the convicts, he was satisfied, could be found. The chief expense of the establishment of the colony was already passed and paid. Why, then, were they, unless strong reasons indeed operated to enforce the measure, to begin *de novo*, and make a new colony? And where it could be made to more advantage he was really a stranger.[21]

Rather than to the whole Botany Bay venture, as Shaw supposes, I think these comments refer to the convicts on the Third Fleet ships. That is, what Pitt effectively said was: 'Now that the government has met the initial costs of establishing the colony in New South Wales, no cheaper mode of disposing of convicts sentenced to transportation is to be found.' The wording of the motion put by Bunbury, to which Pitt was responding, confirms this reading: 'That there be laid before this House, an account of the number of convicts which had been shipped from England for New South Wales, *and of the number intended to be sent in the ships now under orders for that service*' (my emphasis).

And if, in February 1791, Pitt was making a specific point about costs, it is inconceivable that he did not also have specific returns on investment in mind when he said that he did not know where else a colony might be founded to more advantage. The report of his speech (which evidently is not a complete one) does not indicate what he then considered these to be. However, we do not have far to look to find them. In February and March 1791 the administration was negotiating with the East India Company to obtain three major trading innovations in the East. As I describe in *Botany Bay: The Real Story*,[22] Pitt, Dundas and Hawkesbury wanted the Southern whalers and the Nootka Sound fur traders to be able to operate without licences; to be able to operate anywhere in the Pacific Ocean east of the latitude of Canton (113°E) – that is, to be able to trade not only among the Pacific Islands and to Korea and Japan, but also to the Philippines, among the Molucca Islands, and along the coasts of New Guinea and New Holland; and, 'when they come into the seas of the East Indies', they wanted them to be considered as 'country' (i.e., local) traders, and to be free to operate accordingly.[23]

No, Pitt evidently did not at this time enlarge publicly on how Britain would benefit from the new colony's being built about splendid Port Jackson, which lay adjacent to one of the only three feasible routes into the Pacific Ocean. But the next year, writing to Phillip in New South Wales, the Prime Minister's confidant Henry Dundas, who had now become Home Secretary, pointed to the advantages 'which must always be derived from a port so capacious and secure as Port Jackson'[24] – advantages which helped to justify the colony's huge cost.

Conclusion

A GREAT DEAL OF VERY poor history has been written about the First
Fleet. Clark's comment about the near-naked women convicts 'lolling'
on the decks at Portsmouth, and Wilson's about the venal incompetence
of the civil servants are on a par, really, for lurid error. Such comments –
wilful because unexamined – arise from entrenched assumptions.
These writers *know* what the members of the Pitt administration and
the departmental officials thought of the convicts and how they dealt
with the First Fleet; and they don't need to examine the sources carefully to know what they know. Coming to the questions with their opinions already well-developed, they attend only to those fragments of the
very extensive historical record that seem to confirm their prejudices.

The evidence I have presented makes it abundantly clear how wrong
such claims are. More invidious – because at first glance less obviously
faulty – are the many statements which agree with one hundred years
and more of historiography, but which do not take account of the
countervailing evidence. I have pointed to some of these statements in
the Introduction and the body of this work. Let me now give you two
more examples. Mackay claims that 'the despatch of the First Fleet to
Botany Bay was a reckless act on the part of a desperate ministry. The
intended site for the settlement was insufficiently known; the expedition
itself was poorly organized and badly equipped'.[1] But he offers no
extended analysis of the third and fourth of these points, which, as this

full-length study shows, the historical record simply doesn't support. Neither does he establish any comparisons with similar ventures, which might give some weight to his views. Rather, he simply asserts these views categorically, so as to make his even more sweeping first claim seem unquestionable.

Then, in volume 1 of *The Europeans in Australia*, Alan Atkinson several times states that in 1786–87, as the Pitt administration was mounting the expedition to establish a colony at Botany Bay, officials were not necessarily thinking that there would be a second one. 'To gentlemen in Downing Street it seemed likely to begin with that the First Fleet ... would also be the last to New South Wales', he says; and continues that it was 'doubtful' whether any more convicts might follow this first lot: 'There was no certain vision of a Second Fleet, a Third Fleet and so on indefinitely ... During the months of planning even Captain Phillip once seemed doubtful whether, as he put it, "ships may arrive in Botany Bay in future"'. And again: 'Nowhere was there any boasting about a permanent answer to the problem which had vexed the government and its critics for the last ten years. This was because there was no certainty at all that Botany Bay would be a permanent answer. Though expensive, it was a simple scheme with no clear future'. In her recent book, Emma Christopher has blithely endorsed these views.[2]

The idea that Botany Bay was likely to be a 'one-off' venture has lead traditional historians to various other suppositions. But what evidence is there that this is how ministers and officials were thinking in 1786–87? Atkinson offers only two pieces, which on close examination prove illusory. First, the relevant paragraph makes clear that when Phillip remarked that 'ships may arrive at Botany Bay in future' he meant trading vessels, for he continued: 'On account of the convicts, the orders of the port for no boats landing in particular places, coming on shore and returning to the ships at stated hours, must be strictly enforced.'[3] Atkinson's second supposed piece of evidence is that when the King announced the Botany Bay decision in his speech at the opening of parliament on 23 January 1787, he did not mention any future extension of it. As I showed in Chapter 1, this is an unwarranted construction.[4]

On the other hand, while it is true that there is no explicit statement from August 1786 to this effect, there is abundant evidence from the period 1785–88 that the Pitt administration did intend a new convict colony to be a permanent solution to the convict problem.

First, when he suggested that the convicts be sent to Cape Coast Castle, John Roberts said that 200 might be sent 'annually'. Then, in proposing Lemain Island as an alternative destination, John Barnes and his colleagues stated that, 'after the first year, the island would be of course in a more cultivated state, and would consequently grow more healthy, and a regular succession of convicts might be sent out annually', and that 'in a very few years they would become planters, and take those who might be sent out hereafter into their service'.[5]

And then, there is the overt evidence that the Pitt administration always intended such a colony to endure. First, we have Evan Nepean's statement that, by mid-1786, William Pitt had taken control of the convict business, and that he had decided that they should be used to establish a new settlement south of the equator.[6] As I explain in *Botany Bay: The Real Story*, the only possible context of this decision was the need for a base adjacent to the major shipping routes from Europe to the great world beyond.[7] This was the clear rationale for the administration's interest in Das Voltas Bay, on the southwest coast of Africa, which it had sent a ship to survey the previous September, a rationale that would not be realized if the colony were not a permanent one.

In mid-1786, as they waited for the *Nautilus* to return, the Prime Minister moved to placate two of parliament's most vocal critics of his administration's failure to resume transportation, writing to John Rolle:

Though I am not at this moment able to state to you the place to which any number of the convicts will be sent, I am able to assure you that measures are taken for procuring the quantity of shipping necessary for conveying above a thousand of them. And I have every reason to suppose that all the steps necessary for the removal of at least that number may be completed in about a month. The plan may, I am in hopes, afterwards be extended to whatever farther number may be found requisite.

PS: I will beg the favour of you to communicate the contents of this letter to Mr Bastard.[8]

The plan may, I am in hopes, afterwards be extended to whatever farther number may be found requisite! Yes, Pitt wrote this in the expectation that the convict colony would be established at Das Voltas Bay; but if we claim on this ground that the expectation was not then transferred to Botany Bay, we are postulating an abrupt chasm in official thinking, a sudden abandonment of an earlier view, a decision indeed taken in 'a fit of absence of mind'. This did not happen.

Then, there is William Richards's request to Pitt on 28 September 1786, when he had secured the First Fleet contract: 'As the convicts will, I suppose, go out annually, I hope that as I have been the first promoter of this plan of economy in transporting them, you will be kind enough to let this be secured to me in future'.[9]

From the time of his appointment, Arthur Phillip also clearly understood that the administration intended the colony to endure. There are his October 1786 comments that 'as I would not wish convicts to lay the foundations of an empire, I think they should ever remain separated from the garrison, and other settlers that may come from Europe, and not be allowed to mix with them, even after the seven or fourteen years for which they are transported may be expired'; and: 'the laws of this country will of course be introduced in [New] South Wales, and there is one that I would wish to take place from the moment His Majesty's forces take possession of the country – that there can be no slavery in a free land and consequently no slaves'.[10] Then, at the end of October, when he asked to be allowed a commodore's pennant, he told Nepean: 'I shall not, I hope, leave the colony till it is in such a state as to repay government the annual expense, as well as to be of the greatest consequence to this country. In such a state, I presume, it will be in every respect as advantageous to the officer who supercedes me, as the Newfoundland station is.' He repeated this point to Sydney a few days later:

By putting this service on the same footing as the Newfoundland station, the appointment will be adequate to the expenses, which no commanding officers will find so great hereafter, and as there's some *désagrément* thought to attend this particular service, it will then be effectually done away. To me, my Lord, the difference of the appointment is considerable, to the nation it cannot be an object, and still less as I presume, though the rough task is mine, no commanding officer will be sent out hereafter without the honourable distinction I solicit.

In April 1787, in telling Ralph Clark that he might not take his wife with him, Phillip said: 'When the settlement is made I make no doubt but government will provide for the passage of those officers' wives who wish to join the garrison'.[11] These statements contradict the view that in 1786–87 officials expected the colony's existence to be short.

Phillip repeated these sentiments in his early letters home from New South Wales, which, as he had then received no new despatches from England, could only reflect understandings he had been given before sailing. He told Lansdowne: 'Perhaps no country in the world affords less assistance to first settlers. Still, my Lord, I think that perseverance will answer every purpose proposed by government, and that this country will hereafter be a most valuable acquisition to Great Britain from its situation'. To Sydney he wrote: 'The additional force which I presume your Lordship will see it is necessary to send out, [and] a few families and proper people to superintend the convicts, will change the face of this country, a country that from its situation will, I doubt not, be hereafter a valuable acquisition to Great Britain'. And to Middleton: 'The rough survey [of Port Jackson] which I enclose will show that hereafter, when this colony is the seat of empire, there is room for ships of all nations'.[12]

In the mind of its first governor, then, the colony was to be no fly-by-night venture. Numbers of the administrative arrangements made for the colony reflect the same view. There is the Home Office's advice to the Admiralty that, in the first instance, the marines going out to the colony should be volunteers, encouraged to do so either by 'bounty, or promise of discharge should they desire it upon their return, or at the expiration of three years, to be computed from the time of their landing at the new intended settlement should they prefer the remaining in that country'.[13] Then, there are Phillip's comments that he needed to know:

> How far I may permit the seamen and marines of the garrison to cultivate spots of land when the duty of the day is over, and how far I can give them hopes that the grounds they cultivate will be secured to them hereafter; likewise how far I may permit any of the garrison to remain, when they are ordered home in consequence of a relief;

and that he envisaged rewarding well-behaved convicts by allowing them 'to work occasionally on the small lots of land set apart for them, and which they will be put in possession of at the expiration of the time for which they are transported'.[14]

Then, there is Phillip's comment, on a draft of his instructions, that he needed to have 'the tenor by which lands are to be granted, [to be] pointed out by the article which gives me the power of granting lands'; and the inclusion of precise advice in the amended instructions issued on 25 April 1787.[15] Then, there is the way in which, over the next two years, the administration reinforced the governor's ability to grant lands and to emancipate by legislation and through additional instructions.[16]

Now, of course it is true that only in the last of these documents are transportations other than that of the First Fleet alluded to; but together they show that, from the first, the administration intended that the colony should be a permanent one, not one to wither quickly. Why would the officials have gone to so much effort, if they thought that it would soon disappear, or that they would not be sending more criminals to it?

Moreover, with all the replacement women's clothing not having arrived before they sailed, and having learnt that the marines lacked sufficient supplies of ammunition, cartridge paper and sets of armourer's tools, Philip wrote to Sydney and Nepean from Tenerife, asking that these items 'be sent out by the first ship'. He repeated this request from Rio de Janeiro. Phillip understood that the first British ship sent into the Pacific Ocean after those of the First Fleet would be that sent to collect breadfruit (i.e., the *Bounty*). Nonetheless, his use of the term 'first' indicates that he expected more.[17]

The plain fact is that Arthur Phillip left England knowing that other convict voyages would follow. This was because the officials who sent him told him it would be so. Indeed, he had helped them plan for it. In mid-1787, echoing what Nepean had written to Sackville Hamilton the previous October, he had told the Home Office 'it certainly will not be advisable to send out any more convicts till my situation is known, and the strength of the garrison must always be in proportion to the numbers of convicts, *till the garrison is of a certain force*'.[18]

The administration pursued this sensible policy. In December 1787, after Newton Fowell's mother had asked about sending items out to him, Evan Nepean replied:

> There is not the least probability of our sending out to Botany Bay until we receive accounts of Governor Phillip of his arrival and the situation in which he finds matters to be with regard to the inhabitants and the probability of supplying the convicts already sent out.[19]

And in October 1788 Sydney advised the Treasury:

> Not having received any accounts of Governor Phillip's arrival in New South Wales, I am unwilling to recommend the sending any more convicts thither immediately, but if the advices which I imagine I shall shortly receive from him answer my expectations, I shall certainly propose that the female convicts [in Newgate] should be sent to the same place.[20]

Thinking to delay a second embarkation, however, is by no means the same thing as not having one in mind. There were a number of reports in the press that it was always the government's intention to send out further shipments of convicts. For example, the *Reading Mercury and Oxford Gazette* reported in early November 1786 that 'ships are to proceed annually to Botany Bay with convicts from the several jails in the kingdom'. Then, at the beginning of April 1787, the *Hampshire Chronicle* reported:

> It is the intention of government, as soon as the settlement in Botany Bay is fully formed, and Commodore Phillips has sent home his despatches (which cannot however be expected for twelve months at least from the time of his sailing) to send out two ships every year with convicts for the complete peopling of the colony, and getting rid of a set of people whom this over-cloyed country vomits forth.

Given that, then as now, government and opposition politicians were wont to play out their antagonisms in the press, we should normally be wary of accepting such reports as accurate; but these so closely mirror the advice that Nepean gave Mrs Fowell in December 1787 and Sydney gave the Treasury in 1788 that we may be confident about their accuracy. Atkinson's claims fly in the face of a large body of evidence: the old newspapers knew better than the modern historian.[21]

*

If Atkinson's idea can be refuted on empirical grounds, it can also be denied on logical ones.

From the autumn of 1786 into the spring of 1787, as the First Fleet was mounting, there were several moments when an administration whose fundamental interest lay in getting the convicts out of England quickly and at the least possible cost might have clearly revealed these aims. In late August, the Navy Board advertised for 1500 tons of shipping. By November, the volume contracted for had risen to 2800 tons; and in December, when it had become clear that even this increased total would not accommodate all the people and goods being sent, it engaged another ship, so that the total exceeded 3100 tons. Doubling the tonnage meant doubling the expense of hiring it; but the administration never said: 'Enough is enough. We shall spend no more money. The convicts aren't worth it.'

Next, in March 1787, as the ships waited at Portsmouth, Phillip argued fiercely for fresh foods and more supplies, so that the venture might succeed. He had his way. The fresh foods given to the marines, crews and convicts in March and April, the medicine chests, surgeon's necessaries, anti-scorbutics and wine put on board the ships, the extra clothing and the supplies for the voyage all cost more money. But again the administration spent rather than cut corners.

So was it too with Phillip's request that he be allowed to provide the colonists with fresh foods at the ports *en route*. Once more, the administration accepted the cost of doing so.

Similarly, the administration would have saved significant effort and expense had it provided only a minimal governance structure for the new colony. But it did not; rather, it created an elaborate mechanism of government, one not to be justified for a one-off landing of 1000 people, but one, of course, eminently justified and prudent for a settlement it intended to develop into a fully fledged colony.

And then, when Phillip reported the colony's initial difficulties, the Pitt administration did not decide to abandon it. Rather, it sent out a Royal Navy frigate, the *Guardian*, carrying fifteen agricultural supervisors and twenty-five skilled convicts, and loaded 1003 tons of supplies which cost £70,000. Lieutenant Riou loaded more supplies at the Cape of Good Hope, including seven horses, eighteen cattle, twenty-two sheep, pigs, rabbits and poultry of all kinds. The plants and trees loaded in England and at the Cape numbered 150. The ship was within six weeks of reaching Sydney when it struck an iceberg.[22]

By the end of 1789, the colony had cost something over £250,000, or over £100 per convict per annum. This made it, as Blainey pointed out, a very expensive solution to a penal problem if the intention was only to dump the convicts.[23] Other objectives, however, might justify such expense.

*

In March 1787, Arthur Phillip became insistent that the people of the First Fleet had to be better fed and otherwise better provided for. First, he told Sydney: 'I fear, my Lord, that it may be said hereafter, the officer who took charge of the expedition should have known, that it was more than probable he lost half the garrison and convicts, crowded and victualled in such a manner, for so long a voyage'. Then, he told Nepean: '*At present* the evils complained of may be redressed, and the intentions of government by this expedition answered'.[24]

This latter statement is at once opaque and translucent. It conceals, because Phillip did not state explicitly what he understood the 'intentions of government' to be. But it also reveals that there were indeed intentions, intentions which he would be unable to realize if his colonists were reduced by poor diet, illness and death. Logic and the evidence I give in *Botany Bay: The Real Story* suggest that among these intentions were:

- A viable colony
- And therefore a place of future convict transportation
- A settlement able to defend itself
- A port able to resupply ships operating in the Pacific Ocean
- A source of naval materials.

*

As I have pointed out in *Botany Bay: The Real Story* and elsewhere, the striking innovation in Britain's transportation of convicts to New South Wales when compared to its earlier transportation of criminals to North America was that the central government became the provider for and regulator of the convicts and (in the first years) the employer of their labour.

With this salient difference in mind, it is worth considering how else the Botany Bay venture differed from earlier ones, both undertaken and proposed.

The labour of those convicts shipped across the Atlantic Ocean to Virginia and Maryland was sold to merchants and planters for a maximum period of seven years, with these private individuals becoming responsible for the convicts' maintenance during their servitude.

If they did not go enlisted in the Army or Navy, convicts sent to West Africa were simply landed, and left to their own devices. As the governor of Cape Coast Castle described it:

Since that time I have paid a deal of attention to what I humbly conceive to be the views of government in sending those wretches to this country, and the evident defect there is in the mode of transporting them. One motive is no doubt to save their lives, of which I conclude the major part have been forfeited to the laws of their own country; but the grand consideration seems to be, *to get them out of Europe at all events;* without ever once adverting to the evil consequences that must attend this mode, a few of which I shall beg leave to lay before you.

The governor and council are directed to receive a certain number of convicts. No provision whatever is made for them; neither are we directed to receive them as soldiers: from which it is natural to infer that government understands it is just simply landing these people in Africa, to let them shift for themselves, and get their bread in the best manner they can. In some other parts of the world they might by their industry maintain themselves, but here it is impossible. We have no employment for them but that of soldiers … The natives have none. How then are they to be maintained? They are landed as it were naked and diseased on the sandy shore. The more hardy of them probably will plunder for a living for a few days until the climate stops their progress, and then, shocking to humanity, loaded with the additional diseases incident to the country, these poor wretches are to be seen dying upon the rocks, or upon the sandy beach, under the scorching heat of the sun, without the means of support or the least relief afforded them.[25]

This was a 'dumping of convicts' scheme, as was the proposal intended to supplant it, that of sending the convicts to the island of

Lemain, 400 miles up the River Gambia, where they were again to be left to their own devices, with whatever governance they themselves chose to establish. The slavers who proposed this scheme explained: 'It is natural to suppose that upon the first settlement a great many of the convicts would die from the change of climate ... After the first year, the island would be of course in a more cultivated state, and would consequently grow more healthy.'[26]

And when the Irish government resumed transportation to North America in the late 1780s, often those to whom it contracted the business simply 'dumped' the convicts in Newfoundland or Nova Scotia or thereabouts. Consider the voyage of the *Providence* towards the end of 1788. This ship loaded 103 male and twenty-three female convicts, forty-six of whom (36 per cent) died during the four weeks' passage. In view of the onset of winter, Captain Debenham elected simply to land his charges on the almost uninhabited northeast coast of Cape Breton Island, where snow had already fallen: 'the seamen were armed with pistols, cutlasses and swords, and when the boat reached the shore, they tumbled these people headlong from the boat into the surf among the rocks, and one man was killed by being thrown against a rock'.

These poor people were lightly clothed (some in rags only), seven had no shoes, and Debenham gave them no food. Through the night, local fishermen tried to succour them. They found between thirty and forty persons straggling about, without knowing which way to go'; six of the seven without shoes died of exposure. Eventually, a fisherman took the survivors to Sydney, the main settlement in Nova Scotia.[27]

The next year, there was another such disastrous voyage. In June, Richard Harrison took 113 male and fourteen female convicts off from Dublin in the *Leinster*. He reached Newfoundland on 15 July, and landed the convicts at two points on the southeast coast. He gave some food to the first group, but 'the strongest beat the weak, and over a cask of rank butter or beef, there was for a time as severe fighting as if a kingdom had been at stake'. When a majority of the convicts reached St John's, they stole from shops and houses, and attempted to burn down the town. Sixty-three of the men, many of them ill with typhus fever, were held in a large house and fed by the town's inhabitants, while the women were left to prostitute themselves. The illness spread into the population – as the local priest wrote, 'we've had a most malignant jail fever imported to us by some unhappy convicts landed here …, of which no less than 200 people already died in this harbour, which is as yet an entire hospital'. When Admiral Milbanke arrived for his annual patrol at the beginning of September, he commended the magistrates for their handling of the situation: 'I think you acted very prudently in complying with the desire of the inhabitants and thereby prevented many irregularities in the fishery, which would have been the consequence of suffering such a Banditti to go at large about the island'. Milbanke organized for the surviving convicts to be shipped back, but this well-intentioned action led to a very serious situation, as it put him and the master of the ship they went on in danger of prosecution for aiding felons to return illegally.[28]

*

Consider how very different was the Botany Bay venture.

As soon as the convicts came under the control of the agents of central government they were cleaned, clothed, fed and had their ailments treated.

The ships they were embarked in were, according to Navy Board official George Teer, '*completely fitted*, their provisions and accommodations are better than any set of transports I have ever had any directions in'.[29] For two months at Portsmouth, they and the marines were given fresh foods in abundance, and the surgeons obtained adequate medical supplies (at a cost of some £1200). The issuing of fresh food continued at the ports *en route*. While at sea, the colonists were fed superior standard provisions: 'I believe few marines or soldiers going out on a foreign service under government were ever better, if so well provided for as these convicts are', Smyth said; and Collins wrote of 'the excellent quality of the provisions with which we were supplied by Mr Richards Junior, the contractor'.[30] And when landed, the convicts lived within established social and legal structures, which reduced violence and gave them good prospects, not just of survival, but of eventual freedom and some prosperity.

*

This central point – that Botany Bay was *not* a 'dumping of convicts' scheme – is also to be made via another comparison.

The victory of the rebellious American colonists meant that large numbers of Loyalists were dispossessed and displaced – numbers are uncertain, but the best estimate seems to be 60–80,000. About 7000 of them fled to England, there to live in much reduced circumstances, if not in outright penury. Take the case of Mrs Magra. Her husband, Dr Magra, had been a very wealthy New Yorker, with large business and property holdings; but the family lost just about everything in the revolution. Their son James (Matra) later declared that, 'exclusive' of his father's property, he 'had out in that country £6275 [sterling]. This money was formally tendered to my agent, in Congress bills, and while a law existed which declared such a tender, if refused, a legal discharge of the debt' – in other words, he lost the lot.[31]

Recognizing the inevitability of the family's financial ruin, his aged mother emigrated to England at the end of 1779. In her memorial for compensation, she stated that she 'was an inhabitant of New York, and since the commencement of the rebellion in America, she has been deprived of her whole property, and reduced to a dependence on her two sons, who are in His Majesty's service; but they having also suffered from the same cause, her support is rendered painful and precarious'. She continued, that from 'her great distresses, and the difficulty and uncertainty of her support …, at a very advanced time of life', she had found it necessary 'to relinquish every hope of recovering the smallest part of her property, and come to England'. The commissioners appointed to investigate Loyalist claims granted her a pension of £60 per year.[32]

Or take the case of Thomas Danforth. His memorial to the commission reads in part:

Having devoted his whole life, at the age of near thirty, in preparing himself for future usefulness, ten useless years have [closed] the account; and he now finds himself near his fortieth year, banished under pain of death, to a distant country, where he has not the most remote family connection, nor scarcely an acquaintance, who is not in the same circumstances – cut off from his profession – from every hope of importance in life, and in a great degree from social enjoyments. And where, unknowing and unknown, he finds, that after having expended the little, he hopes to receive, as above related, that he shall be unable, while he may be said only to wait for death, to procure common comforts and conveniences, in a station much inferior to that of a menial servant, without the assistance of government.[33]

Large numbers of the Loyalists – perhaps as many 30,000 – chose instead to migrate north to the Canadian provinces, where they set about building new lives for themselves. And 'building' is the operative term – in a region notorious for the harshness of its winters, they had to start again from scratch, finding shelter, grafting livings as farmers or merchants or in their former professions or occupations.

Now, these were people – landowners, government officials, doctors and lawyers, merchants, and ordinary men and women (and their children) – who had supported their country and upheld its laws, and who as a consequence had fallen on very hard times. They had suffered the loss of family members in fighting, had lost their money and possessions, had had friendship and business networks shattered; so that, in middle or advanced age, they were faced with beginning again, in arduous circumstances and with slender means, for, apart from some assistance in the form of land, food and tools, the government was applying strict criteria in assessing claims for compensation, and paying only a proportion of losses.

By comparison, how were those men and women who had transgressed their country's laws being treated? These too were going into exile. However, the government was providing them with food; with shelter (yes, I know, tents at first, but no one was going to freeze to death in Botany Bay's winter); with medical care; and with social controls. True, they would need to work in their new situation; but had they eschewed a life of crime, they would have needed to work in England too. In some ways, to be a convict at Botany Bay was to be better circumstanced than a displaced and dispossessed Loyalist. Given that late eighteenth-century British society did not share our belief in the need for social welfare and broad reform programs, it is striking just how well the Pitt administration provided for the convicts sent to form the new colony.

*

I do not claim that none of the arrangements which the administration made for the colony might have been better done. The First Fleet did sail without a three-years' supply of women's clothing; the marines also lacked some equipment; animals and plants perished in the heavy seas; and some seeds became barren in the course of the voyage. Also, experience soon showed that some antipodean circumstances (e.g., areas of thin soil overlaying stone and hardwoods) called for sturdier tools than those which sufficed in England. However, the wonder is, not that a few of the hundreds upon hundreds of arrangements were flawed, but that so many were in fact satisfactory.

It is also true that a number of other factors combined to hinder the New South Wales colony's progress once it was established about the shores of Port Jackson. There was first the marine officers' churlish refusal to supervise the convicts in their work; then there was the long, *el niño*-induced drought, from July 1790 until October 1791; then the losses of the *Guardian* and the *Sirius*. But as Phillip told Grenville in June 1790, 'from the day of our landing to the present hour, [the colony] has laboured under every possible disadvantage, and many obstacles have been met with which could not have been guarded against, as they never could have been expected', so that it was rather 'a matter of surprise that a regular settlement exists than that it is not in a more flourishing state'.[34]

Even so, however, when Phillip left Sydney at the end of 1792, it was clear that the colony would survive – but more than this, that it was beginning to flourish. That is, it was showing signs of the future that the Pitt administration always intended it should have.

*

Twenty years ago, in analysing the mounting of the First Fleet, Roger Knight rightly pointed out that 'it is doubtful that in the late 1780s any other European power could have achieved a similar level of success in an expedition of this nature'.[35]

In this business, the Pitt administration deployed Britain's superior administrative capability, and its accumulative experience of sending large expeditions into distant seas. It also drew on the nation's considerable financial resources. The First Fleet was a very expensive venture. But just as it spent to see that its plan to bring the breadfruit from the Pacific Ocean to the West Indies succeeded (when the first voyage failed, it mounted an even more expensive second one), so too did the Pitt administration spend largely to make the New South Wales colony succeed.

It did so because it saw that a colony in the southwest Pacific Ocean would be clearly in the nation's interest, not only because it would provide a solution to a troubling penal problem, *but also* because (as the Heads of a Plan indicated) it would achieve other objects – most immediately a base and a source of naval materials, and more generally as a point of interchange for an intended vast trading network.

A variety of circumstances combined to mean that these other objects were not immediately realized; but this does not mean that they were not envisaged. History, whether in its course or in its retelling, is rarely a straightforward business. But most of the historians of the decision to colonize New South Wales and of the mounting of the First Fleet have greatly distorted ours by attending only to the fact of the convicts in Britain, and by comprehensively misrepresenting the scale and competence of the preparations to send them to distant New South Wales. They have assessed intentions in the past according to outcomes known to us in the present – since the scheme to obtain naval materials from the islands of the southwestern Pacific Ocean came to nothing, they reason, it must always have been a harebrained fantasy; and therefore, in founding the Botany Bay colony, the British wished only to dump their convicts as far away as possible.

With this premise established, they have assumed that they needed to take account only of the evidence that seemed to validate it – principally, the many complaints from country officials about the presence of transport convicts in their jails. Accordingly, they have not considered that they needed to establish the precise extent of the documentary record; as the matter was clear, this was unnecessary: looking further would not lead to new insights. Nor have they seen fit to relate the decision to other matters of national concern – specifically, the shortages of naval materials, the political situation in Europe and India, and trading ambitions in the East.

Lacking a proper understanding of the range of Pitt's concerns and the seriousness of his intent, and of his administration's very detailed preparations for the First Fleet, these historians have characterized the founding of the convict colony as a shambles – which of course has only helped to confirm the premise they started from. Later writers have accepted the assumptions of earlier ones, and repeated their mistakes.

The historians of the beginning of modern Australia have given us less than half a history. The real story is much more intricate – and much more interesting.

Acknowledgments

All reasonable efforts have been made to locate copyright holders. Where they have held the copyright, the directors and/or governing bodies of the institutions listed in the bibliography have kindly given permission to cite and to quote from original sources.

I have specifically to thank: The Direcção-Geral de Arquivos, Lisboa; the Curator, Early Modern and Osborn Collections, Beinecke Rare Book and Manuscript Library, Yale University; the Keeper of Special Collections, Bodleian Library, University of Oxford; the Trustees of the British Library, London; the UK Science and Technology Facilities Council and the Syndics of Cambridge University Library; the Director, William L. Clements Library, University of Michigan; the Director, National Library of Australia; the Archive and Manuscripts Manager, National Maritime Museum, London; the Trustees of the Natural History Museum, London; the Director, Perkins Library, Duke University; the Keeper of the Public Records, Public Records Office, National Archives, Kew; the Trustees of the Royal Botanic Gardens, Kew; the Librarian and Director of the John Rylands University Library, University of Manchester; the State Librarian and Chief Executive, State Library of New South Wales, Sydney; the Director of the Sutro Library, the San Francisco branch of the California State Library; the National Librarian, National Library of New Zealand: Te Puna Mātauranga o Aotearoa, Wellington.

Some sections of this work were first published (in somewhat different form) in *Convicts and Empire: A Naval Question, 1776–1811* (Oxford University Press, Melbourne, 1980), *Arthur Phillip, 1738–1814: His Voyaging* (Oxford University Press, Melbourne, 1987) and *Botany Bay Mirages: Illusions of Australia's Convict Beginnings* (Melbourne University Press, Melbourne, 1994). The publishers have kindly agreed to my including them here.

*

During a long career – and mine now comprehends fifty years – an academic writer learns from many people and accumulates many debts, some obvious, but others obscure. It would be an impossibility for me now to list all of those – friends and opponents (in an intellectual sense) – to whom I am indebted for numbers of the insights I offer here. However, there are some people whom I do wish to thank explicitly.

Geoffrey Blainey has steadily encouraged me to develop my views, and I also benefited from discussing them with Geoffrey Bolton. Extended conversations with Bernard Bailyn have enabled me the better to place the Botany Bay decision in the context of the Atlantic world of the 1780s. Isabel Moutinho has helped me to uncover the Portuguese dimension of British thinking about what to do with the convicts. Michelle Novacco facilitated research in England. I have had significant help from Gary Sturgess, who also possesses very extensive knowledge of the documentary record, and who has freely shared his knowledge, both by extended conversations about meanings and significance, and by locating and providing materials I did not know about. Briony Sturgess has also helped in this last task. Advice from Gary Sturgess and Michael Flynn has enabled me to correct some mistakes in the first printing.

The generous encouragement and hospitality that Glyndwr Williams and Sarah Palmer have offered over many years have made my periods of research in England so much more pleasurable than they otherwise would have been. I am grateful, too, for the extended friendship and encouragement of John Salmond, Inga Clendinnen and Roger Wales, now sadly 'all gone into the world of light'.

Natasha Weir undertook the bulk of the laborious task of transcribing and editing the c. 2500 drafts, original papers and letters and copies on which these studies are based. This electronic database is now available at the State Library of New South Wales.

I have also warmly to thank the editorial and production staff at Black Inc., in particular Chris Feik, Denise O'Dea and Lauren Carta.

*

I have been in the curious situation of being a historian of Australia who has had to travel repeatedly to overseas archives to study the circumstances of our beginnings. These research trips would have been impossible without financial support from La Trobe University and the Australian Research Council, and the writing up of results would have been even more protracted without periods of leave from teaching given by La Trobe University. I thank both organisations warmly.

Even in being grateful for the substantial help I have had, however, I must also express my deep regret about how the university world has changed in recent decades. It would now be virtually impossible to commence a research project such as this, which has taken thirty-five years to complete. Universities and external funding bodies would require results within two to three years; and the concomitant regimens of grant applications and reporting requirements would mean that you would have to present your findings without the benefit of the leisure to reflect on them and on what you might still look for. And without efficient 'performance', you would find it progressively more difficult to obtain the further research grants you would need to complete the project. Universities – and scholarly pursuits more generally – are not businesses or government departments, and they shouldn't be regulated as though they are. In measure as they are, so is our intellectual life diminished.

Endnotes

Abbreviations

1. Archives and Files

AHN: Archivo Historico Nacional (Madrid)
    Estado
AJCP: Australian Joint Copying Project
    Microfilms at the National Library of Australia and the State Library of
    New South Wales
ANTT: Arquivo Nacional da Torre do Tombo (Lisbon)
    MNE: Ministério dos Negócios Estrangeiros
Beinecke: Beinecke Rare Book and Manuscript Library, Yale University
    Osborn: James Marshall and Marie-Louise Osborn Collection
BL: The British Library
    Add. MS: Additional Manuscripts
    Egerton: Egerton Manuscripts
    OIOC: Oriental and India Office Collections
        B: Minutes of the Court of Directors
        D: Committee of Correspondence
        E: General Correspondence
        F: Board of Control Records
        G: Factory Records
        H: Home Miscellaneous Series
        I: Europeans in India
        L/MAR: Marine Records
        L/PS: Political and Secret Department Records
Brotherton: Brotherton Library, University of Leeds
    Sydney: Sydney Papers
Clements: William L. Clements Library, University of Michigan (Ann Arbor)
    Nepean: Nepean Papers
    Shelburne: Shelburne Papers
    Sydney: Sydney Papers
CUL: Cambridge University Library (Cambridge)
    RGO: Records of the Royal Greenwich Observatory
Kew: Kew Gardens Herbarium
    JBK: Banks Papers
    KBP: Banks papers
Kingston: Kingston-upon-Thames Record Office

NAS: National Archives of Scotland
    GD: Gifts and Deposits
NH: The Natural History Museum (London)
    DTC: Dawson Turner transcripts of Banks Papers
NLA: National Library of Australia (Canberra)
    MS: Manuscript
NLNZ: National Library of New Zealand (Wellington)
    Turnbull: Alexander Turnbull MS
NMM: National Maritime Museum (London)
    ADM/A, B, BP, C, OT: Navy Board Papers
    HOW: Howe Papers
    MID: Middleton Papers
    SAN: Sandwich Papers
    THM: Thompson Papers
Perkins: William Perkins Library, Duke University (Durham, NC)
    Dundas: Dundas Papers
    Grenville: Grenville Papers
    Pitt: Pitt Papers
PRO: Public Record Office, The National Archives (London)
    ADM: Admiralty
    AO: Audit Office
    BT: Board of Trade
    CO: Colonial Office
    FO: Foreign Office
    HCA: High Court of Admiralty
    HO: Home Office
    PC: Privy Council
    PR: Patent Rolls
    PRO: Public Record Office
    SP: State Papers
    T: Treasury Papers
    WO: War Office
RMM: Royal Marines Museum (Southsea)
    Archive
RS: The Royal Society (London)
Rylands: The John Rylands University Library, University of Manchester
    English: English MSS
SLNSW: State Library of New South Wales (Sydney)
    Bonwick: Bonwick transcripts
    Dixson: Dixson Library
    Mitchell: Mitchell Library
SRNSW: State Records of New South Wales (Sydney)
Sutro: Sutro Library, California State Library (San Franscisco)
    Banks: Banks Papers
    EN: Entomology
USNA: The National Archives of the United States (Washington, DC)
Record Group: Miscellaneous records

2. *Printed Sources*

Authentic Journal: [An Officer], *An Authentic Journal of the Expedition under Commodore Phillips to Botany Bay* (London, 1789).

Authentic Narrative: [An Officer], *An Authentic and Interesting Narrative of the late Expedition to Botany Bay* (Aberdeen, 1789).

Banks: *The 'Endeavour' Journal of Joseph Banks*, ed. J.C. Beaglehole, 2 vols (Angus and Robertson, Sydney, 1963).

Bligh: William Bligh, *A Voyage to the South Sea* (London, 1792).

Clark: *The Journal and Letters of Lt Ralph Clark, 1787–1792*, eds Paul G. Fidlon and R.J. Ryan (Australian Documents Library, Sydney, 1981).

Colenbrander: H.T. Colenbrander, ed., *De Patriottentijd, vol. 3: Appendix* (Martinus Nijhoff, [n.p.], 1899).

Collins: David Collins, *An Account of the English Colony in New South Wales*, ed. B. H. Fletcher (A.H. and A.W. Reed, Sydney, 1975 [1798]).

Colnett: James Colnett, *A Voyage to the South Atlantic and round Cape Horn into the Pacific Ocean* (London, 1798).

Cook: *The Journals of Captain James Cook on his Voyages of Discovery*, ed. J.C. Beaglehole, 3 vols in 4 parts (Hakluyt Society, Cambridge, 1955–68).

Cornwallis: *Correspondence of Charles, First Marquis Cornwallis*, ed. Charles Ross, 3 vols (John Murray, London, 1859).

Despatches Despatches from Paris, 1784–1790, vol. 1: 1784–1787, ed. O Browning (Camden Society, 3rd series, vol. 16: London, 1909).

Dropmore: *Report on the Manuscripts of J.B. Fortescue, Esq., Preserved at Dropmore*, 10 vols (Historical Manuscript Commission, London, 1892–1927).

Easty: John Easty, *Memorandum of the Transactions of a Voyage from England to Botany Bay, 1787–1793* (Angus & Robertson, Sydney, 1965).

Eden: [William Eden], *Principles of Penal Law* (London, 1771).

Fielding: Henry Fielding, *An Enquiry into the Causes of the Late Increase of Robbers and Related Writings*, ed. Malvin R. Zirker (Clarendon Press, Oxford, 1988 [1751]).

Fowell: Newton Fowell, *The Sirius Letters: The Complete Letters of Newton Fowell, midshipman and lieutenant aboard the* Sirius, ed. Nance Irvine (The Fairfax Library, Sydney, 1988).

George III: Correspondence: The Correspondence of George III, ed. Sir John Fortescue, 6 vols (Frank Cass, London, 1967 [1927–8]).

George III: Later Correspondence: The Later Correspondence of George III, ed. A. Aspinall, 5 vols. (Cambridge University Press, Cambridge, 1966–70).

Hawkesworth: John Hawkesworth, comp., *An Account of the Voyages undertaken by the Order of His Present Majesty for making Discoveries in the Southern Hemisphere, and successively performed by Commodore Byron, Captain Wallis, Captain Carteret, and Captain Cook*, 3 vols (London, 1773).

Howard: John Howard, *Prisons and Lazarettos, vol. 1: The State of the Prisons in England and Wales*, 4th ed. (Patterson Smith, Montclair, NJ, 1973 [1792]). (This is a reprint of the 4th edition of Howard's work.)

HRA: *Historical Records of Australia*, 4 series (Commonwealth Parliament, Sydney, 1914–1925).

HRNSW: *Historical Records of New South Wales*, 7 vols (Government Printer, Sydney, 1892–1901).

Hunter: John Hunter, *An Historical Journal, 1787–1792*, ed. John Bach (Angus and Robertson, Sydney, 1968 [1793]).

Instructions: *British Diplomatic Instructions, vol. 7: France, vol. 4: 1745–1789*, ed. L.G.W. Legg (Camden Society, 3rd series, vol. 49, London, 1934).

Janssen: Stephen Janssen, *This Sheet Contains Three Tables, from 1749 to 1771* (London, 1772).

JHC: *Journals of the House of Commons*

JRAHS: *Journal of the Royal Australian Historical Society*

King: *The Journal of Philip Gidley King: Lieutenant, RN, 1787–1790*, ed. P.G. Fildon and R.J. Ryan (Australian Documents Library, Sydney, 1980).

Lapérouse: Jean-François Galaup de la Pérouse, *A Voyage Round the World*, ed. L.A. Milet-Mureau., 2 vols (London, 1799).

Martin: *Letters and Papers of Admiral of the Fleet Sir Thomas Byam Martin*, ed. Sir Richard Vesey Hamilton (London, 1898–1903).

Nagle: *The Nagle Journal: A Diary of the Life of Jacob Nagle, Sailor, from the year 1775 to 1841*, ed. J.C. Dann (Weidenfeld and Nicolson, New York, 1988).

Péron: M.F. Péron, *A Voyage of Discovery to the Southern Hemisphere* (London, 1809).

Phillip: *The Voyage of Governor Phillip to Botany Bay* (1789), ed. J.J. Auchmuty (Angus & Robertson, Sydney, 1970).

PH: *Parliamentary History*

PR: *Parliamentary Register*

Sandwich: *The Private Papers of John, Earl of Sandwich: First Lord of the Admiralty, 1771–1782*, ed. G.R. Barnes and J.H. Owen, 4 vols (Navy Records Society, London, 1932–8).

Smith: Adam Smith, *An Enquiry into the Nature and Causes of the Wealth of Nations*, ed. R.H. Campbell and A.S. Skinner, 2 vols (Clarendon Press, Oxford, 1976 [1776]).

William Smith: *The Diary and Selected Papers of Chief Justice William Smith, 1784–1793*, ed. L.F.S. Upton, 2 vols (Champlain Society, Toronto, 1963).

Smyth (1): Arthur Bowes Smyth, Journal extracts, *HRNSW*, vol. 2, pp. 387–14.

Smyth (2): *The Journal of Arthur Bowes Smyth, Surgeon, Lady Penrhyn, 1787–1789*, eds P.G. Fildon and R.J. Ryan (Australian Documents Library, Sydney, 1979).

Statutes at Large: *Great Britain: Statutes at Large* (London, 1763–).

Tench: Watkin Tench, *A Narrative of the Expedition to Botany Bay* (1789), in *Sydney's First Four Years*, ed. L.F. Fitzhardinge (Library of Australian History, Sydney, 1979 [1789]).

White: John White, *Journal of a Voyage to New South Wales*, ed. A.H. Chisholm (Angus and Robertson, Sydney, 1962 [1790]).

Wilberforce: *The Private Papers of William Wilberforce*, ed. A.W. Wilberforce (London, 1897).

Winslow: [Edward Winslow], *Winslow Papers, AD 1776–1826*, ed. W.O. Raymond (New Brunswick Historical Society, St John, 1901)

Wordsworth: *Journals of Dorothy Wordsworth*, ed. Mary Moorman (Oxford University Press, Oxford, 1971).

Worgan: George Worgan, *Journal of a first Fleet Surgeon* (Library of Australian History, Sydney, 1978).

Botany Bay

Introduction

1. Barrington, pp. 5–7.
2. Lang, p. 23.
3. Flanagan, vol. 1, pp. 20–22.
4. Sutherland, p. 14.
5. Blair, p. 91.
6. 'The Day We Were Lagged', *Bulletin*, 21 January 1888, p. 4.
7. The Bonwick Transcripts now constitute one of the treasures of the State Library of New South Wales.
8. Hancock, p. 11.
9. O'Brien (1937), pp. 159, 179.
10. Crawford, pp. 34–5.
11. Crowley, pp. 1–3.
12. Shaw (1966), p. 49.
13. Clark, p. 69.
14. Seeley, p. 8.
15. Clark, p. 70.
16. Rusden, vol. 1, pp. 14, 17.
17. Gonner, pp. 629, 632.
18. Barton, vol. 1, pp. 1–9.
19. Rutter, p. 14.
20. Hancock, p. 11.
21. Dallas, pp. 4–12.
22. Blainey (1966), pp. 16–37.
23. See Shaw (1968), Bolton (1968, 1969), and Blainey (1968(1) and (2)). Many of the contributions to the debate were summarized or reprinted in Martin (1978).
24. Anna Seward, *Elegy on Captain Cook*, 1st ed. (London, 1780), pp. 11–12.
25. F.W. Martyn, *The Geographical Magazine*, 2nd ed. (London, 1785–7), vol. 1, p. 578.
26. See the various essays in Martin; and Gillen (1982), Mackay, and Frost (1985).

1. Eighteenth-Century England: Crime

1. Edmund Burke, *Reflections on the Revolution in France* (1790), in *The Writings and Speeches of Edmund Burke, Vol. 8*, ed. L.G. Mitchell (Clarendon Press, Oxford, 1989), pp. 146–8.
2. *Fielding*, pp. 143–44.
3. *Boswell's Life of Johnson*, ed. G.B. Hill, rev. L.F. Powell (Clarendon Press, Oxford, 1971 [1934]), vol. 3, p. 178.
4. Wordsworth, *The Prelude* (1805 version), Book 7, ll. 184–310.
5. Diary entry, 27 December 1784, *William Smith*, vol. 1, p. 176.
6. Chambers and Mingay, pp. 3, 15, 34–5.
7. William Cobbett, in the *Political Register*, 15 March 1806, cols 361–2.
8. Ibid., 12 July 1817, col. 463.
9. Briggs, pp. 18, 23.
10. Rodger, p. 206.

11. Nagle, p. 209.
12. Malcolmson, p. 85.
13. Ibid., pp. 85-127.
14. William Paley, *The Principles of Moral and Political Philosophy* (London, 1785), quoted in Beattie, p. 148.
15. 'The Felon's Muster Roll', *Edinburgh Magazine*, vol. 2 (1785), pp. 42–3.
16. Quoted in Beattie, pp. 157–8.
17. Quoted ibid., p. 156; and *Bath Chronicle*, 18 January 1787.
18. *Bath Chronicle*, 11 January 1787.
19. Beattie, p. 152.
20 Thompson (1971); Thompson (1975).
21. *PH*, vol. 19 (for 1777–8), col. 970.
22. Quoted in Beattie, p. 138.
23. Quoted ibid., p. 151.
24. *Bath Chronicle*, 8 January 1784, 18 January 1787.
25. Thompson (1975), pp. 225–7.
26. P. Cromp to Sydney, 17 January 1785, HO 42/6, fos 31–2.
27. Janssen, as quoted in Langbein, p. 110 and Beattie, p. 22.
28. Cited by Beattie, pp. 227–8.
29. *Salisbury Journal*, 6 October 1783 (quoted in Beattie, p. 228).
30. *Fielding*, p. 75.
31. E.g., [Anon.], *An Account of the Endeavours that have been used to Suppress Gaming-Houses* (London, 1722), p. 20.
32. Camplin to [Germaine], quoted in Beattie, p. 138; Thomas Robertson to [Sydney], 30 November and 10 December 1782, HO 42/1, fos 360, 379; quoted in Malcolmson, p. 87; quoted in Reece, p. 182.

2. Eighteenth-Century England: Punishment

1. Langbein, pp. 96, 118.
2. Quoted in Beattie, p. 467.
3. See Ekirch (1987), pp. 17–18, 70–71.
4. Campbell's memorandum, in C.R. Freire to Sá e Mello, 7 September 1784, ANTT, NME caixa 706, no. 66.
5. Suffolk, Warrant, 28 December 1775, SP 44/91, pp. 446–7.
6. Sydney to Shortland, 8 May 1787, HO 13/5, p. 185.
7. *JHC*, vol. 40 (1784–5), pp. 1161–2.
8. *William Smith*, vol. 1, p. 173. (9 Geo. 1, c. 22, passed in 1723, became known as the 'Black Act'.)
9. See Beattie, pp. 183, 333, 426.
10. For Ryder, see Langbein, pp. 98, 111–3.
11. Ibid., p. 112.
12. Ibid., pp. 111–2.
13. Janssen (as cited in Langbein, p. 110).
14. Rochford to the Norfolk Justices, 23 September 1772, SP 44/92, pp. 52–3.
15. Sydney to the Oxford Justices, 12 April 1787, HO 13/5, pp. 130–3.
16. See below, pp. 51–52.
17. Nepean to Sydney, 9 November 1786, SLNSW, Mitchell MS An 53/1.
18. Nepean to Astley, 9 October 1786, HO 13/4, p. 231.

19. Arnold and others to Moore, and Moore to Nepean, 24 April 1784, HO 42/4, fos 163–4.
20. See Beattie, passim.
21. The Proceedings of the Old Bailey (Online), T 1783 0430-64; Gillen (1989), p. 131.
22. Ibid., T 1786 1213-35; Gillen (1989), pp. 148–9.
23. Ibid., T 1785 0511-3; Gillen (1989), p. 150.
24. Ibid., T 1782 0109-8; Gillen (1989), pp. 155–6.
25. Ibid., T 1782 1204-68; Gillen (1989), p. 155.
26. Ibid., T 1783 0910-50; Gillen (1989), pp. 221–2.

3. *Dealing with the Convict Problem*

1. This evocative phrasing is from the prologue supposedly spoken at the first play performed at Sydney. See Geoffrey Ingleton, ed., *True Patriots All* (Angus and Robertson, Sydney, 1952), p. viii.
2. William Eddis, *Letters from America*, ed. A.C. Land (Belknap Press, Cambridge, Mass., 1969), p. 36.
3. Morgan, pp. 201–27; Ekirch (1987), pp. 97–132.
4. *JHC*, vol. 36 (1776–8), p. 927.
5. This analysis is based on Campbell's letterbooks in SLNSW, Mitchell MSS ZA 3225–3232, and on his returns and related correspondence in the HO 42 and T 1 and T 54 series.
6. Campbell to Eden, [mid-1776?], SLNSW, Mitchell MS ZA 3231, p. 3.
7. Campbell to Cooper, 14 February 1782, SLNSW, Mitchell MS ZA 3231, pt 2, p. 51; to Rose, 12 January 1785, T 1/622, no. 210.
8. Campbell to Iain Campbell, 14 February 1767, SLNSW, Mitchell MS ZA 3231, pt 1, p. 13.
9. Eden to the Recorder of London, 29 November 1775, SP 44/91, p. 437.
10. Eden to [Weymouth?], 16 June 1776, BL Add. MS 34413, fos 11–12; and see Oldham, pp. 33–4.
11. Eden to Campbell, 12 December 1776, SP 44/93, pp. 126–7; Campbell to Robinson, 19 December 1776, Mitchell MS ZA 3226, pp. 2–3.
12. Scott, p. 39.
13. Crawford, p. 33.
14. Crowley, p. 4.
15. Clark, pp. 64, 69.
16. Shaw (1966), p. 43.
17. Conway, p. 50.
18. Hughes, p. 62; Molony, pp. 2–3; Mackay, pp. 13, 16.
19. Quoted in Bain Attwood, *Possession: Batman's Treaty and the Matter of History* (The Miegunyah Press, Melbourne, 2009), p. 168.
20. [William Eden], *Principles of Penal Law* (London, 1771), pp. 28–9.
21. Campbell to Eden, [mid-1776?], SLNSW, Mitchell MS ZA 3231, pt 2, pp. 3–5.
22. Campbell, Testimony, April 1778, JHC, vol. 36 (1776–8), p. 926; Campbell to Treasury, 11 March 1777, T 1/529; to Eden, 17 March 1777, SLNSW, Mitchell MS ZA 3226, pp. 34-5, and JHC, vol. 36 (1776–8), p. 927; Campbell to Akerman, 8 March, to Eden, 4 June 1777, SLNSW, Mitchell MS ZA 3226, pp. 38, 55–6; Campbell and Treasury, Agreement, 2 February 1778, T 54/42, pp. 442–7; and JHC, vol. 36 (1776–8), p. 927.

23. Campbell to Fraser, 24 July 1778, SLNSW, Mitchell MS ZA 3226, pp. 218–9; to Treasury, c. 27 July 1778, T 1/539, fo. 242.

24. Bunbury, Report, 1 April 1779, *JHC*, vol. 37 (1778–80), pp. 306–14.

25. Campbell and Treasury, Agreement, 5 November 1779, T 54/43, pp. 143–9.

26. 'An Account of the whole Number of Convicts on board the several Hulks … in each Year from 12 July 1780 to the 31 December 1790', [undated], CO 201/5, fo. 339.

27. Report, 15 April 1778, *JHC*, vol. 36 (1776–8), pp. 927–9.

28. Ibid., pp. 926–9.

29. Ibid.; and Campbell to Hill, 20 February 1786, SLNSW, Mitchell MS ZA 3229, p. 128.

30. Report, *JHC*, vol. 36 (1776–78), pp. 929–30. Bentham's report is printed in an abridged form in Oldham, pp. 201–2.

31. Ibid.

32. Report, *JHC*, vol. 37 (1778–80), pp. 308–9; Campbell to Bunbury, 21 April 1779, SLNSW, Mitchell MS ZA 3226, p. 306; and Campbell's Returns, variously in T 1/539, 548, 564, 578, 594.

33. Campbell's Returns, variously in T 1/619, 622, 626, 630, 634, 637.

34. E.g., Campbell to Clayton, 21 August 1777, SLNSW, Mitchell MS ZA 3226, p. 77.

35. Campbell to Rose, 12 January 1785, T 1/622, fo. 210.

36. Campbell to Robinson, 6 July 1778, SLNSW, Mitchell MS ZA 3226, p. 216.

37. Campbell to Eden, 15 October 1776, SLNSW, Mitchell MS ZA 3225, pp. 494–5.

38. Campbell to Eden, 26 October 1776, ibid., p. 544.

39. Campbell to Treasury, [c. 27 July 1778], T 1/539, fo. 242.

40. Quoted in W.B. Johnson, *The English Prison Hulks*, 2nd ed. (Phillimore, London, 1970), p. 5.

41. Report, *JHC*, vol. 36 (1776–8), pp. 927, 932; Campbell, Return, 11 January 1779, T 1/539, pt 2, fo. 310.

42. Campbell to Hill, 20 February 1786, SLNSW, Mitchell MS ZA 3229, p. 127.

43. Quoted in Johnson, p. 5.

44. Report, *JHC*, vol. 36 (1776–8), p. 928; Campbell to Suffolk, 1 October 1778, SLNSW, Mitchell MS ZA 3226, pp. 248–50; Report, *JHC*, vol. 37 (1778–80), p. 309.

45. Reports, *JHC*, vol. 36 (1776–8), pp. 928, 932, and vol. 37 (1778–80), pp. 309, 313; Campbell, Return, 3 December 1778, T 1/539.

46. Nepean, Memoranda, 1789, CO 201/4, fos 154, 183, 192.

47. Campbell to Eden, 4 June 1777, to Fraser, 8 and 25 May and 6 July 1778, to the Ordnance Board, 24 September 1778, Mitchell MS ZA 3226, pp. 55–6, 201–2, 205, 214–15, 248.

48. Campbell, 'Observations on the Act for punishing Convicts by Labour on the Thames', with Campbell to Eden, 12 January 1778, SLNSW, Mitchell MS ZA 3231, pt 2, p. 13; Reports, JHC, vol. 36 (1776–8), p. 928, and vol. 37 (1778–80), p. 309.

49. See O'Brien (1937), p. 133; Shaw (1966), p. 42.

50. Reports, *JHC*, vol. 36 (1776–8), p. 928, and vol. 37 (1778–80), p. 309.

51. Campbell to Eden, 12 January 1778, SLNSW, Mitchell MS ZA 3231, pt 2, pp. 13–15; Johnson, p. 5.

52. Reports, *JHC*, vol. 36 (1776–8), p. 928, and vol. 37 (1778–80), p. 309; Campbell to Eden, 5 December 1777, SLNSW, Mitchell MS ZA 3226, p. 126.

53. See, e.g., 'State of Bounties and Clothing . . .', July 1785–July 1786, T 1/637.

54. Campbell to Fraser, 24 July and 17 December 1778, SLNSW, Mitchell MS ZA 3226, pp. 218, 302; Suffolk, Warrants, 31 July and 26 December 1778, SP 44/93, pp. 277, 313–4.
55. Campbell to Lance, 13 August 1778, and to Eden, 6 October 1779, SLNSW, Mitchell MSS ZA 3226, p. 236, ZA 3227, p. 6.
56. Campbell to Porten, 1 June, to Fraser 23 and 24 August and 16 December 1780, SLNSW, Mitchell MS ZA 3227, pp. 143–4, 167, 244.
57. Campbell to Philips and Nash, 26 November 1781, SLNSW, Mitchell MS ZA 3227, p. 372; Return, 9 October 1781, T 1/564, fo. 334; to Fraser, 27 December 1781 and 4 February 1782, SLNSW, Mitchell MS ZA 3227, pp. 389, 415; Stormont, Warrants, 8 January and 12 February 1782, SP 44/96, pp. 187–8, 195–6; Campbell to Buller, [June 1782], SLNSW, Mitchell MS ZA 3228, p. 50.
58. Reports, *JHC*, vol. 37 (1778–80), p. 309, and vol. 40 (1784–8), p. 1161.
59. Weymouth, Warrant, 18 December 1770, SP 94/91, p. 27, and Warrant, 16 January 1776, SP 44/93, pp. 3–4.
60. Campbell to Eden, 10 February 1777, SLNSW, MS ZA 3226, p. 27; Campbell to Fraser, 6 July, 7 September and 14 October 1780, to Porten, 8 November 1779 and 31 October 1780, to Stormont, 5 and 6 June 1781, SLNSW, Mitchell MS ZA 3227, pp. 33, 156–7, 179, 192, 222, 304, 307.
61. Brown to Amherst, 13 March 1779, WO 1/1137.
62. See Conway.
63. John Roberts to Gilbert Ross, [c. January 1785], HO 42/5, fo. 465.
64. Buller to Shelburne, 1 July 1782, Clements, Shelburne, vol. 152, no. 40.
65. Rose to Nepean, 3 January 1783, HO 35/4; North to Campbell, 24 August 1783, Sydney to Campbell, 23 January 1784, HO 13/1, pp. 173–4, 316–7.
66. The 1778 House of Commons committee stated that: 'The Yearly Average of the Felons, who were ordered for Transportation during a Period of Six Years and an Half, from the 1st of November 1769 to the 1st of May 1776, amounts to 960, of which a Fourth being deduced for Women, which is nearly the Proportion that appears from the Accounts given to your Committee of Persons transported in the said Six Years and an Half, there remain 720 Males liable to the Punishment of hard Labour on the River Thames.' JHC, vol. 36 (1776–8), p. 932.
67. Report of the Debate, 11 March 1784, *PH*, vol. 24 (for 1783–8), col. 756.

4. The Atlantic World and Beyond

1. Bailyn, pp. 31, 55.
2. The literature concerning the Atlantic slave trade is vast. Some recent studies are Falola and Roberts (2008), and Richardson (2009). Then there is the massive electronic resource, www.slavevoyages.org, of which Yale University Press published a paperback version in 2015.
3. Anderson to North, 20 November 1783, HO 42/3, fo. 176; Bouverie to Nepean, 4 December 1783, HO 12/3, fo. 266; Bailey to [Nepean], 26 January 1784, HO 42/4, fos 44–5; Carter to Sydney, 20 May 1784, HO 42/4, fo. 235; Lygon to Sydney, 10 June 1784, HO 42/4, fo. 279; Kent to Sydney, 2 November 1784, Simpson to Sydney, 8 November 1784, HO 44/40, pp. 101, 103.
4. Sydney to Spencer, 18 December 1784, HO 42/5, fo. 375.
5. Wallis to Sydney, 29 December 1784, HO 42/5, fo. 384; Sedley to [Nepean], 6 February 1785, HO 42/6, fo. 64; Higgins to [Nepean], 9 February 1785, HO 42/6,

fo. 68; White to [Nepean], 12 April 1785, HO 42/6, fo. 189; More to Sydney, 20 April 1785, HO 42/6, fo. 205.

6. Hurford to Shelburne, 27 July 1782, Clements, Shelburne, vol. 152, no. 44.

7. For instance, Wright to [Nepean], 24 August 1782, HO 42/1, fos 290–3, and Robertson to Sydney, 30 November and 10 December 1782, HO 42/1, fos 360, 429–30.

8. Lewes to [?], [c. May 1785], HO 42/7, fos 28–33.

9. [?] to [?], [undated], HO 42/7, fos 40–5.

10. Report, 1 April 1779, *JHC*, vol. 37 (1778–80), p. 312.

11. Shelburne, Memorandum, c. July 1782, Brotherton, Sydney R 8.

12. Buller to Shelburne, 2 April 1782, Clements, Shelburne vol. 152, no. 39.

13. African, Committee Minutes, 28 September and 2 October 1782, T 70/145, pp. 153, 154; to Nepean, 28 September 1782, T 70/69, p. 307; to Sydney, 2 October and to Miles, 6 November 1782, T 70/69, pp. 307, 309.

14. African Committee, Minute, 6 November 1782, T 70/145, p. 159.

15. Miles to African Committee, 1 February 1783, T 70/33, pp. 53–5.

16. Ibid.

17. African Committee, Minute, 22 December 1784, T 70/145, pp. 253–4; to Sydney, 22 December 1784, T 70/69, p. 330.

18. W.H. to [Nepean?], c. 27 December 1782, and Campbell to [Nepean], 27 December 1782, T 1/581, nos 92a and b.

19. Privy Council, Order-in-Council, 27 April 1785, PC 2/130, pp. 156–7.

20. North to the King, 11 July 1783, the King to North, 12 July 1783, *George III: Correspondence*, vol. 6, pp. 415, 416.

21. North to the King, 18 July 1783, ibid., p. 418; North, Warrant for transportation, 12 August 1783, HO 13/1, pp. 173–4; to Governor Parr, 12 August 1783, CO 218/25, pp. 430–1.

22. Hurford to Campbell, c. 22 June 1782, Clements, Shelburne vol. 152, no. 41; Campbell to Buller, 28 June 1782, SLNSW, Mitchell MS ZA 3228, p. 63; Shelburne, Memorandum, [undated], Brotherton, Sydney R 8; Buller to Shelburne, 1 July 1782, Clements, Shelburne vol. 152, no. 40.

23. Pinto de Sousa to Sá e Mello, 3 October, Sá e Mello to Pinto de Sousa, 26 October 1782 (draft), ANTT, MNE caixa 705, no. 561, and livro 129.

24. Thompson to Shelburne, 9 October 1782, Clements, Shelburne vol. 152, no. 27.

25. Thompson to Rose, 1 August, to Sydney, 8 August 1784, NMM, THM 6.

26. Houghton to Sydney, 24 February 1783, CO 267/20, fos 349–56.

27. Morse to North, 6 March 1783, CO 267/7.

28. 23 Geo. III, c. 65.

29. North to Admiralty, [c. 15 September 1783], SP 42/66, fos 420–2; African Committee to Nepean, 16 September 1783, CO 267/20, fo. 245.

30. Morse to Sydney, 23 June 1784, CO 267/8.

31. Thompson, Description of St Thomas, and to Rose, 1 August 1784, NMM, THM 6.

32. Clarke to Pitt, 17 March 1785, PRO 30/8/363, fos 56–66.

33. Bindley to [Sydney], 16 September 1782, HO 42/1, fos 334–5.

34. Matra to [North], 23 August 1782, CO 201/1, fos 57–61.

35. See Ehrman, pp. 140–1.

36. Report of the Debate, 2 March 1784, *JHC*, vol. 39 (1782–4), p. 968.

37. Matra to Sydney, Supplement, 6 April 1784, CO 201/2, fos 64–5.

38. Attorney-General to Sydney, [c. 11 August 1784], HO 42/6, p. 56; Memorandum, [c. 11 August 1784], Clements, Sydney vol. 11.
39. Matra to Fox, 7 August 1784, BL, Add. MS 47568, fos 240–6.
40. Call to [Sydney], [c. 1 September 1784], HO 42/7, fos 49–57. I have given this approximate date for this paper, because Call wrote to Warren Hastings on 3 September 1784: 'I have lately suggested to the ministry the sending of our criminals to an establishment on New South Wales, or on New Zealand.' BL, Add. MS 29166, fo. 27
41. Young to Pitt, [c. 1 September 1784], PRO 30/8/342, fos 283–4.
42. Matra to Nepean, [1November 1784], CO 201/1, fo. 65.
43. Young, Revised proposal, [before 13 January 1785], Arden to Sydney, 13 January 1785, Matra to Nepean, [13 January 1785?], CO 201/1, fos 51, 53, 66.
44. Matra to Nepean, 1 [November] 1784, CO 201/1, fo. 65.
45. C.R. Freire to Sá e Mello, 31 August and 7 September 1784, Sá e Mello to Freire, 2 October 1784 (draft), ANTT, MNE caixa 706, nos 65, 66, and livro 125, fo. 46.
46. Holdsworth to Milbanke, 14 April 1784, HO 28/4, fo. 130.
47. Daniel Hill, Deposition, 4 July 1788, CO 123/11, pp. 319–30.
48. Sydney to Clarke, 5 October 1784, CO 137/84, fo. 147.
49. What Shaw quoted was: 'The more I consider the matter, the greater difficulty I see in disposing of those people.' Shaw (1966), p. 45.
50. 24 Geo. III, c. 56.
51. [Roberts] to Ross, [c.1 January 1785], HO 42/5, fos 465–9.
52. Sydney to African Committee, 5 January 1785, CO 267/21, fos 1–2; Ross to Nepean, 5 January 1785, HO 42/6, fos 23–4.
53. Barnes to [Nepean], 4 February 1785, HO 35/1.
54. Howe to Pitt, 25 December 1784, PRO 30/8/146, fos 209–10; to Sydney, 26 December 1784, HO 28/4, fo. 386.
55. [Nepean], 'Memo. of matters to be brought before Cabinet', [undated, but c. 27 December 1784], SLNSW, Dixson MS Q 522.
56. The *General Advertiser* for 28 December 1784 recorded that Cabinet had met the previous day at Lord Gower's house; and Nepean to Nichol, 29 December 1784, HO 42/5, fo. 461.

5. The Lemain Fiasco of 1785

1. Nepean to Nichol, 29 December 1784, HO 42/5, fo. 460.
2. Bradley to Nepean, [c. 1 January 1785], HO 42/1, no. 26.
3. Thompson, Journal entry, 3 January 1785, BL, Add. MS 46120, fos 45–6; to Nepean, 10 January 1785, CO 267/9.
4. Thompson, Journal entry, 31 July 1783, BL Add. MS 46120, fo. 7.
5. [Dalrymple], 'Memorandum communicated to the Chairman of the India Company in January 1782', and 'Heads of Instructions given by the Secret Committee to the Captain of the *Swallow*, September 1783', CO 77/25, fos 119–22, 123–5.
6. Thompson, 'Some account of the Country on the West Coast of Africa between 20° and 30° of South latitude …', 9 March 1785, CO 267/9; Thompson, Journal entries, 20 February and 21 March 1785, BL, Add. MS 46120, fos 55, 62.
7. Wilson to Nepean, 31 January 1785, CO 267/21, fos 6–8.
8. These documents went as enclosures to Sydney's letter to the Treasury Board, 9 February 1785, T 1/614, no. 335. There is a copy of this letter in HO 35/1.

9. Sydney to the Treasury Board, 9 and 12 February 1785, T 1/614, nos 335, 339a; Rose to Navy Board, 23 February 1785, T 27/37; Navy Board to Rose, 28 February 1785, T 1/616, no. 447a.

10. Sydney to the Lord President of the Privy Council, 3 March 1785, HO 43/2, pp. 17–18; Privy Council, Orders-in-Council, 11 March 1785, PC 2/130, pp. 75–80.

11. Campbell to Nepean, 5 March 1785, T 1/619; Sydney to Treasury, 20 March 1785, T 1/619, no. 856a.

12. Report of the Debate, 16 March 1785, *PH*, vol. 25 (1785–6), cols 391–2.

13. Report of the Debate, 11 April 1785, ibid., cols 430–1.

14. Ibid.

15. Beauchamp Committee, Minutes, HO 7/1, from which I have taken the witnesses' order of appearance. The quotations, however, are from the Report printed in *JHC*, vol. 40 (1784–5), pp. 954-60. I have modernized spelling, punctuation and capitalization. Details not in the printed report are from the minutes.

16. Beauchamp, Report, 9 May 1785, *JHC*, vol. 40 (1784–5), pp. 954–60.

17. Beauchamp Committee, Minutes, HO 7/1.

18. There is a copy of this printed version at CO 201/8, fos 152–3.

19. Memorandum, [undated], HO 42/6, pp. 53–4.

20. This letter is evidently lost.

21. Report of the Debate, 29 June 1785, *PH*, vol. 25 (1786–8), col. 906.

22. Nepean, Memorandum, [undated], HO 42/1, p. 462.

23. Sydney to Cavendish, 20 May 1785, Beinecke, Osborn no. 14753 (1).

24. Privy Council, Orders-in-Council, 13 May 1785, PC 2/130, pp. 219–21, 221–2.

25. See above, pp. 97–8, 110. It may be that Call did not present the committee with the complete text of his proposal.

26. The manuscript copy in HO 42/6, fos 449–67 was annotated by Pitt, 'June 1785', and by another person '21 June 1785'. The printed version, from which the following quotations are taken, was presented to the House of Commons on 28 July 1785. JHC, vol. 40 (1784–5), pp. 1161–4. There are no substantive differences between the texts.

27. Sydney to Admiralty, 22 August 1785, HO 28/5, fos 118–20.

28. Thompson to Howe, 29 December 1784, NMM, THM 6.

29. Admiralty to Thompson, Instructions and Secret Instructions, 15 September 1785, ADM 2/1342.

30. Blagden to Banks, 3, 10 and 15 September 1785, Kew, JBK nos 201, 203, 204; Banks, 'Heads of Instructions to be given by Captain Thompson … to Mr Hove', [c.15 September 1785], ADM 2/1342.

31. Pemberton to Dundas, [c. 15 September 1785], BL, OIOC G/9/1, pp. 18–25.

32. Diana Dalrymple to Devaynes, [c. 17 September 1785], PRO 30/8/128, fos 64–5.

33. Devaynes to Dundas, 17 September 1785, NAS, GD 51/3/17, fos 1–3; William Dalrymple to Dundas, 2 October 1785, T 1/624, fos 93–4; Pitt to Grenville, 2 October 1785, Dropmore, vol. 1, p. 257.

6. *Thinking about the Whole Globe*

1. Baugh, p. 341.

2. Newcastle to Holdernesse, 25 July 1758, BL, Add. MS 32882, fo. 65.

3. See, e.g., Pocock to Clevland, 7 December 1758, ADM 1/161, fo. 292; Cornish to Clevland, 24 June 1761 and 5 April 1762, ADM 1/162, pt 1, fo. 129, pt 2, fos 17–18; Harland to Stephens, 20 September 1773, ADM 1/163, fo. 240.
4. See H.M. Scott.
5. *Sandwich*, vol. 3, p. 170
6. Hughes to the Bombay Council, EIC, 27 January 1784, BL, OIOC H 178, p. 917; to Stephens, 10 September 1784, HO 28/5, fo. 30.
7. The characterizations of Gower and Camden are Ehrman's, p. 184. The others are by W. W. Grenville, 'Commentaries on my own Political Life and of Public Transactions connected with it', Perkins, Grenville book 6, pp. 3–6.
8. Sydney to Pitt, 24 September 1784, PRO 30/8/181, fo. 261; Dundas to Cornwallis, 29 July 1787, *Cornwallis*, vol. 1, p. 321; *William Smith*, Diary entry, 5 July 1786, vol. 2, p. 124.
9. Quoted in Ehrman, p. 303.
10. India Board, Secret minute, 26 August 1786, BL, OIOC L/P&S/2/1, no. 14; Dundas to Hawkesbury, 16 September 1786, BL, Add. MS 38192, fo. 44; Dundas to Eden, 28 September 1786, BL, Add. MS 34466, pp. 353–5; Pitt to Carmarthen, 16 September 1786, Bodleian, English Letters d. 122, fo. 146.
11. Dundas to Lowther, 25 July 1806, quoted in C. Matheson, *The Life of Henry Dundas* (Constable, London, 1933), p. 375.
12. Chairmen, EIC, to Hillsborough, 25 October 1781, BL, OIOC H 154, pp. 119–20.
13. Hughes to Bombay Council, EIC, 27 January 1784, BL, OIOC H 178, pp. 916–7.
14. For Suffrein's views on Acheen, see George Smith to Dundas, 27 January 1785, BL, OIOC H 434, pp. 49–54; Carmarthen to Hailes, 23 December 1784, BL, Egerton MS 3499, pp. 75–6.
15. Dundas to Sydney, 2 November 1784, PRO 30/8/157, fo. 6.
16. Howe to Pitt, 25 December 1784, PRO 30/8/146, fos. 209–10; to Sydney, 26 December 1784, HO 28/4, fo. 386.
17. India Board, Secret minute, 9 April 1785, BL, OIOC L/P&S/2/1, no. 3; and Draft of secret despatch, 9 April 1785, BL, OIOC L/P&S/5/583.
18. HO 42/6, fos 462, [468].
19. India Board, Secret minute, 27 June 1785, BL, OIOC L/P & S/2/1, no. 6; Draft of secret despatch, 27 June 1785, BL, OIOC I/1/13.
20. Clark, p. 69; Bolton (1968), p. 15; and particularly Atkinson (1997).
21. Barnes, Testimony, 2 May 1785, HO 7/1.
22. Nepean to Middleton, 12 December 1786, CO 201/2, fo. 53; Middleton to Nepean, 13 December 1786, CO 201/2, fo. 54; Middleton to Pitt, 13 December 1786, (privately owned); Stephens to Middleton, 14 December 1786, NMM, MID 1/177; Rogers to Nepean, 21 December 1786, CO 201/2, fos 66–7; Stephens to Nepean, 28 December 1786, CO 201/2, fos 41, 43.
23. Phillip to Sydney, 1 March 1787, CO 201/2, fo. 114.
24. Banks to Barrow, 12 August 1815, NHM, DTC vol. 19, pp. 174–8; to Nepean, 9 September 1787, HO 42/12, no. 115.
25. Turnbull, Macaulay and Gregory to Nepean, 10 May, Calvert to Nepean, 1 June, Nepean to Steele, 10 June 1786, T 1/632, fos 35–40.
26. India Board, Draft of Cathcart's instructions, undated but before 30 November 1787 (the date of the finalized version), BL, OIOC G/12/18, pp. 121–34.
27. *Smith*, vol. 2, p. 631.

28. Ibid.
29. E.g., Rough Minutes, [June 1786?], BT 6/226; and Minutes, 14 November 1786, BT 5/4, pp. 75–7.
30. See Frost (2003), pp. 168–9.
31. Nepean to Sackville Hamilton, Draft, 24 October 1786, HO 100/18, fos 372–3.
32. India Board, Memorandum, 25 May 1787, PRO 30/8/360, fos 108–14.
33. Banks to Dundas, 15 June 1787, PRO 30/8/361, fos 33–5.
34. For details of the Nootka Sound alarm, see Frost (2003), ch. 9.
35. Board of Trade, Minutes, 20 January 1791, BT 6/95, pp. 391–2, and BL, Add. MS 38390, fos 9–10.
36. Board of Trade, Minutes, 21 January 1791, BT 5/7, pp. 21–3; and Southern Whalers to Fawkner, 24 January 1791, BT 6/95, p. 395.
37. Grenville to Westmoreland, 13 January 1791, *Dropmore*, vol. 2, p. 14.
38. Board of Trade, 'Confidential Paper', 14 February 1791, BT 6/227, and Minutes, 14 February 1791, BT 5/7, p. 52–4, and BL, Add MS 38393, fos 26–7.
39. Select Committee, EIC, Memorandum, 17 March 1791, BT 6/227.
40. Lushington to Cottrell, 17 March, Cottrell to Dundas, 18 March 1791, BL, OIOC G/32/164; Memorandum, undated, but c. 21 March 1791, BT 6/227.
41. Writing in July 1804, Dundas recalled that 'it is almost twenty years since I first had occasion to consider that subject, and I had much conversation with Sir Charles Middleton upon it when he was comptroller of the navy'. Dundas to Wellesley, 4 July 1804, BL Add. MS 37275, fo. 260.
42. India Board, 'Observations on the Account of Materials that may be procured in India for Ships of any Size', 15 January 1788, PRO 30/8/360, fos 116–18.
43. See Frost (2003), Ch. 11.
44. Report of the Debate, 14 December 1790, *PH*, vol. 28 (1789–91), col. 979.
45. Phillip to Sydney, 15 May 1788, CO 201/3, fos 6–7; to Lansdowne, 3 July 1788, SLNSW, Mitchell MS 7241, p. 3; to Middleton, 6 July 1788, [privately owned].

7. Voices Prophesizing War

1. Secret Committee, EIC, to Bengal Council, 9 and 19 September 1783, BL, OIOC L/P & S/1/9, fos 223–33, 234–47, 253–66.
2. Carmarthen to Storer, 1 January 1784, FO 27/11, pp. 1–2.
3. Pitt to Carmarthen, 10 April, Howe to Carmarthen, 11 April 1784, BL, Egerton MS 3498, fos 30, 178.
4. Hailes to Carmarthen, 2 June and 21 July 1785, BL, Egerton MS 3499, fos 116, 128–9; 4 August and 1 December 1785, FO 27/17, pp. 782, 930.
5. Carmarthen to Hailes, 28 May 1784, FO 148/4, no. 12.
6. Dorset to Carmarthen, 1 July 1784, FO 27/12, p. 768.
7. Hailes to Carmarthen, 2 September, Dorset to Carmarthen, 7 October 1784, *Despatches*, pp. 19, 23; Carmarthen to Dorset, 19 October 1784, FO 27/13, pp. 1158–9.
8. Phillip to Stephens, 14 October 1784, ADM 1/2307, and Register of Officers on leave abroad, ADM 6/207, fo. 8; Nepean, Entry, 11 November 1784, Clements, Nepean, Secret Service Ledger ; Phillip to Nepean, January 1785, FO 95/4/6, pp. 499–500.
9. Hailes to Carmarthen, 28 April 1784, FO 27/11, p. 597; Dorset to Carmarthen, 22 July 1784, *Despatches,* pp. 4–5, 16; Dorset to Carmarthen, 30 June 1785, FO 27/16, pp. 672–3; Keith to Carmarthen, 7 December 1785, FO 7/11, pp. 631–2.
10. [Baldwin], 'Speculations on the Situation and Resources of Egypt, 1773–1785',

[3 May 1785], BL, Add. MS 38346, fos 256–7.

11. 'Heads of [a] Conversation between Mr Dundas and Mr Baldwin in February 1784', PRO 30/8/360, fos 287–91; Mulgrave, Memorandum on the transmission of despatches via Suez, [undated], PRO 30/8/360, fos 338–45; India Board to Carmarthen, and Draft of Instructions for Baldwin, 19 May 1786, BL OIOC F/2/11, pp. 74–119; Baldwin to Carmarthen, 24 June 1786, BL, OIOC G/17/6, fo. 20.

12. Dundas to Sydney, 2 November 1784, PRO 30/8/157, fo. 6.

13. For Suffren's views, see George Smith to Dundas, 27 January 1785, BL, OIOC H 434, pp. 53–4.

14. Carmarthen to Dorset, 23 December 1784, FO 27/13, pp. 1368–70; to Hailes, 23 December 1784, BL, Egerton MS 3499, fos 75–6.

15. Dorset to Carmarthen, 28 December 1784, FO 27/13, pp. 1398–9; Hailes to Carmarthen, 13 January 1785, BL, Egerton MS 3499, fo. 85.

16. Carmarthen to Dorset, 15 February 1784, BL, Add. MS 28060, fos 99–100, 16 February 1784, FO 27/11, pp. 249–51, 2 July 1784, FO 27/12, pp. 758–60, 1 October 1784, FO 27/13, p. 1068; Carmarthen to Dorset, 1 November, and Dorset to Carmarthen, 2 December 1784, FO 27/13 (after pp. 1211 and 1331).

17. Carmarthen to Hailes, 4 June 1784, Hailes to Carmarthen, 10 June 1784, FO 27/12, pp. 689–92, 715–7; Carmarthen to Harris, 14 January 1785, Harris to Carmarthen, 4 March 1785, FO 37/6.

18. Hailes to Carmarthen, 10 June 1784, FO 27/12, pp. 715–7; Carmarthen to Dorset, 27 July 1784, *Instructions*, p. 251; Dorset to Carmarthen, 8 and 22 July, 19 and 26 August 1784, *Despatches*, pp. 18, 19.

19. Harris to Carmarthen, 19 August 1785, FO 37/7, no. 42.

20. Harris to Carmarthen, 23 September 1785, FO 37/8, no. 60; Pitt to Grenville, 4 October 1785, *Dropmore*, vol. 1, p. 257.

21. Harris to Carmarthen, 9 and 16 September 1785, FO 37/8, nos 52, 55; 8 November 1785, FO 37/9.

22. Grimoard to Vergennes, 18 and 30 September 1785, and Castries, 'Observations relative à la Hollande', 8 October 1785, *Colenbrander*, pp. 10–16.

23. Carmarthen to Dorset, 17 February, Vergennes to Dorset, 1 April 1786, FO 27/18; Carmarthen to Harris, 24 February 1786, FO 37/10.

24. This account is based on the documents in *Colenbrander*, pp. 1–34.

25. [   ], Memorandum, 15 May 1785, BL, Add. MS 28060, fo. 342.

26. Harris to Carmarthen, 3 February 1786, BL, Add. MS 28061, fo. 21.

27. Macpherson to the Secret Committee, EIC, 23 September and 27 October 1785, BL, OIOC L/P & S/1/9, fo. 140, and H 555, pp. 283–9; Hailes to Carmarthen, 22 June 1786, FO 27/18.

28. Article 13, Treaty of Versailles, 3 September 1783, FO 93/33/2.

29. Bengal Council to the Secret Committee, EIC, 10 and 27 January and 4 February 1786, BL, OIOC L/P & S/5/20, nos 8, 9, 10; and Secret Committee, Minutes, 23 June 1786, BL, OIOC L/P & S/1/9, fos 144–5.

30. Bengal Council to the Secret Committee, EIC, 10 January 1786, L/P&S/5/20, no. 8.

31. Harris to Carmarthen, 1, 4 and 8 August 1786, FO 37/11, nos 68, 70, 72.

32. Sydney to the King, and the King's reply, 16 August 1786, *George III: Later Correspondence*, vol. 1, p. 244.

33. 'Private Instructions …', 'Plan of the Voyage', 'Extract from the general instructions', and 'Memoir drawn up by the Academy of Sciences', in *Lapérouse*,

    vol. 1, pp. 11–43, 119–35.

34. Dorset to Carmarthen, 5 May and 9 June 1785, FO 27/16, pp. 553, 605–6; Dalrymple to Carmarthen, 8 June 1785, BL, Egerton MS 3501, fo. 39.
35. Carmarthen to Fitz-Herbert, 23 June 1785, FO 97/340.
36. Bolton (1968), p. 6.
37. Fitz-Herbert to Carmarthen, 17 January 1786, FO 97/340.
38. Fitz-Herbert to Carmarthen, 18 February 1786, ibid; Carmarthen to Fitz-Herbert, 17 November 1786, FO 97/341.
39. William Richardson to Hawkesbury, 8 September 1786, BL, Add. MS 38220, fos 11-14.
40. [   ], *The Public Advertiser*, 19 August 1786.
41. Forster and Thornton, Testimony, 24 August 1786, BT 5/4, fos 2-4.
42. Board of Trade, Minute, 25 August 1786, BT 5/4, fo. 9; Navy Board, 'An Account of the Average Prices . . .', 21 March 1787, ADM BP/7.
43. Middleton to Pitt, 29 August and 5 September 1786, PRO 30/8/111, fos 129, 132.
44. Mitchell to Hawkesbury, 21 September 1786, BL, Add. MS 38220, fos 81-2.
45. See above, ch. 6, pp. 142–3.
46. Sydney to the Chairmen, EIC, 15 September 1786, BL, OIOC E/1/79, no. 187.
47. George III, Instructions to Phillip, 25 April 1787, CO 201/2, fo. 35.

8. An Overseas Convict Colony: Investment and Return

1. Letter, 11 February 2010.
2. Eden, pp. 28–9.
3. See above, ch. 4.
4. Pitt to Grenville, 2 October 1785, *Dropmore*, vol. 1, p. 257.
5. Thompson, 'Some account of the Country on the West Coast of Africa ...', 9 March 1785, CO 267/9.
6. Report, *JHC*, vol. 40 (1784–5), p. 1164.
7. [Nepean], Heads of a Plan, [c.15 August 1786], T 1/639, no. 2176.
8. Blainey (1966), p. 28.
9. Sandwich, Memorandum, c. 31 December 1781, *Sandwich*, vol. 4, p. 282.
10. Palliser, Memorandum, ibid., p. 308.
11. These details are taken from the voluminous Navy Board records in the ADM 106 series, with the figures for the mid-1780s coming from Navy Board to Admiralty, 21 April 1804, BL, Add. MS 37275, fos 302–3. For other details, see Frost (2003), chs 4 and 11.
12. 'Account of Masts made 1780, 1781, 1782, 1783', [1784], ADM 106/3321, fo. 30.
13. Jervis, Reasons for Peace, [1783], Clements, Shelburne vol. 72, no. 91.
14. Durno to Stormont, 13 January 1780, FO 64/1; Stormont to the Admiralty, 24 January 1782, Admiralty to Stormont, 11 March 1782, FO 64/3; Middleton to Pitt, 29 August 1786, PRO 30/8/111, fo. 129.
15. Hughes to Stephens, 23 April 1780, ADM 1/164, fo. 187.
16. Hughes to Stephens, 20 March 1781, ibid., fo. 222.
17. Most of the following details are from Hughes's Letterbooks, ADM 7/733, 734.
18. Richmond, pp. 253, 258–9.
19. Hughes to Stephens, 12 August 1782, ADM 1/164, fo. 347.
20. Hughes to the Bombay Council, EIC, 27 January 1784, BL, OIOC H 178, fo. 917; to Stephens, 10 September 1784, HO 28/5, fo. 30.

21. Deptford Officers to Navy Board, 20 August 1788, ADM 106/3322, fo. 17.
22. Navy Board, Minute, 1 August 1786, ADM 106/2621.
23. Young to Pitt, [c. 1 September 1784], PRO 30/8/342, fo. 284.
24. Hughes to Stephens, 10 September 1784, HO 28/5, fo. 30.
25. Young and Call, Memorial, 21 June 1785, BL OIOC E/1/76. no. 213.
26. EIC to Bengal Council, 6 May 1791, BT 6/101.
27. Matra, Proposal, 23 August 1783, CO 201/2, fo. 60.
28. Young to [Pitt], [c. 1 September 1784], PRO 30/8/342, fo. 283.
29. Beauchamp Committee, Report, 28 July 1785, JHC, vol. 40 (1784–5), p. 1164.
30. Morris to Banks, 19 April 1772, BL, Add. MS 33977, fo. 18.
31. Banks, Instructions to Hove, [ ] March and 3 April 1787, BT 6/246. 'Nankeen', named after Nankin, the southern capital of Kiangsu province, was made of yellowish cotton.
32. Banks to Hawkesbury, 28 August and 16 November 1789, BT 6/246.
33. Matra, Proposal, 23 August 1783, CO 201/1, fo. 57.
34. Smith to Dundas, 27 January 1785, BL, OIOC H 434, fos 43–54.
35. Banks to Yonge, 15 May 1787, PRO 30/11/13, fos 322–7.
36. Admiralty, Instructions to Bligh, 20 November 1787, in *Bligh*, pp. 5–8; Nepean to Fraser, 17 June 1787, FO 27/21, fo. 430.
37. Matra, Proposal, 23 August 1783, CO 201/1, fos 59–60.

9. *Towards a Decision: August 1786*

1. *Annual Register*, vol. 28 (1786), pp. 233–4.
2. The King to Hertford, 7 August 1786, *George III: Later Correspondence*, vol. 1, p. 242; Sydney to Lansdowne, 12 August 1786, Clements, Sydney vol. 13.
3. Thompson, Log of the *Nautilus* voyage, 8 April and 17 May 1786, ADM 55/92; to Stephens, 15 August 1786, ADM 1/2594.
4. Mackay, p. 57.
5. Shaw (1966), p. 45.
6. *Edinburgh Magazine*, vol. 3 (June 1786), p. 473.
7. Pinto de Souza to Mello e Castro, 8 August 1786, ANTT, MNE caixa 706, no. 698.
8. Blankett to Howe, 6 and 16 August 1786, NMM, HOW 3; to Nepean, 10 August 1786, HO 42/9, fo. 94.
9. Blankett, Memorandum, [undated, but August 1786], NMM, HOW 3.
10. Howe to Blankett (draft), 19 August 1786, NMM HOW 3.
11. Memorandum, 17 June 1789, CO 77/25, fos 127–8; Grenville to Admiralty Board, and Heads of Instructions, 3 October 1790, ADM 1/4154, no. 43, and ADM 1/4155, after no. 59.
12. 'Madagascar might become highly advantageous, but it is probable the India Company would make obstacles to such an establishment': to Howe, 6 August 1786, NMM, HOW 3.
13. The following details are from, variously, *Cook*, vol. 1, pp. 304–13; *Banks*, vol. 2, pp. 53–61; Banks's testimony to the 1779 and 1785 House of Commons committees, HO 42/5, fos 111-13 and HO 7/1; Matra's proposal, 23 August 1783, CO 201/2, fos 59-61, and his testimony to the 1785 House of Commons committee, HO 7/1.
14. *White*, p. 110; L.A. Gilbert, 'Plants, politics and personalities in Colonial New South Wales', in *People and Plants in Australia*, ed. D.J. and S.G.M. Carr

(Academic Press, Sydney, 1981), pp. 220–21.

15. *Banks*, Testimony to the 1785 House of Commons committee, HO 7/1; and *Banks*, vol. 2, p. 128.

16. For an extended analysis, see Frost (1994), pp. 176–89.

17. Matra, Proposal sent to Fox, 7 August 1784, BL Add. MS 47568, fo. 245.

18. Young, Proposal, [c. 1 September 1784], PRO 30/8/342, fo. 283.

19. Pitt, Memorandum, 17 September 1804, PRO 30/8/196, fo. 88.

20. White to Skill, 17 April 1790, *HRNSW*, vol. 1, pt 2, p. 333.

21. *Cook*, vol. 1, p. 206; *Banks*, vol. 1, p. 436.

22. *Banks*, vol. 2, p. 10.

23. *Cook*, vol. 2, pp. 565–6, 868–9.

24. Sandwich to the King, 16 July 1774, George III: *Correspondence*, vol. 3, p. 118.

25. Stephens to Cook, 20 July 1776, in *Cook*, vol. 3, p. 1513.

26. *Gentleman's Magazine*, vol. 41 (1771), p. 425.

27. Ibid., vol. 44 (1774), p. 21.

28. Ibid., vol. 46 (1776), p. 119.

29. Middleton, *A New and Complete System of Geography* (London, 1777–8), vol. 2, p. 519.

30. G.H. Millar, *The New, Complete, Authentic, and Universal System of Geography* (London, 1782), p. 206.

31 Watson to Winslow, 6 March 1785, *Winslow Papers*, ed. W.O. Raymond (New Brunswick Historical Society, St John, 1901), p. 274.

32. Shaw (1968), p. 202.

33. *Morning Chronicle*, 13 October 1786; *London Chronicle*, 14 October 1786.

34. Mackay (1985), p. 65.

35. *Fielding*, p. 100.

36. *Howard*, passim.

37. *JHC*, vol. 37 (1778–80), pp. 307, 310, 314. (My emphasis.)

38. Lewes to [Sydney?], [mid-1785], HO 42/7, fos 28–9, 32–3.

39. Board of Trade, Minutes, 23 August 1786, BT 5/4, p. 1.

40. Fawkener to Hawkesbury, 16 and 17 August 1786, BL, Add. MS 38219, fos 349–51; BT, Minutes, 18 August 1786, BL, Add. MS 38389, fo. 262. Dorchester had been appointed governor of the Canadian provinces.

41. 'Heads of Instructions given by the Secret Committee to the Captain of the *Swallow*, September 1783', CO 77/25, fo. 123; Thompson, 'Some account of the Country on the West Coast of Africa …', 9 March 1785, CO 267/9; Admiralty, Secret Instructions to Thompson, 15 September 1785, ADM 2/1342, and Tripp to Stephens, 24 March 1786, HO 28/5, fo. 228; Dalrymple to Devaynes, c. 17 September 1785, PRO 30/8/128, fo. 65; Devaynes to Dundas, 17 September 1785, T 1/624.

42. *Morning Herald*, 6 December 1786. (I am grateful to Gary Sturgess for this reference.)

43. Nepean/Sydney to Admiralty, 31 August 1786, ADM 1/4152, no. 25, [p. 2].

44. For an extended account of Phillip's career, see Frost (1987).

45. Collins to General Collins, 19 August 1787, SLNSW, Mitchell MS 700, no. 8.

46. Ross to Stephens, 10 July 1788, ADM 1/3824, fo. 48; Campbell to Ducie, 12 July 1788, SLNSW, Mitchell MS AC 145, p. 3.

47. Campbell to Ducie, [November 1788], SLNSW, Mitchell MS AC 145, pp. 3–4 (of this letter).

10. *The Decision for Botany Bay*

1. Botany Bay's precise co-ordinates are 33°58'S lat., 151°13'E long. However, as 33°S is what appears in the documents, I shall use it as a shorthand form.

2. These undated estimates, which were drawn up before 18 August 1786, are in HO 42/7, fos 23–4, CO 201/2, fos 15–21, and HO 42/10, pp. 426–7. Concerning the annual cost of keeping a convict on a hulk at this time: according to the returns in T 1/626, 630, 634, 637, in 1786 Campbell received a total of £13,732 for the 490 convicts he had contracted to keep on the Justitia and Censor hulks in the Thames, or £28 per man per annum.

3. There are seven copies of 'Heads of a Plan' extant. That in CO 201/2, fos 11–13 seems the earliest – though it is worth noting that none of these copies is a draft.

4. See above, pp. 168–70, 173–5, 194.

5. Sydney to the Treasury Board, 18 [21] August 1786, HO 35/7 and T 1/639, no. 2176; Treasury Board, Minutes, 18 [21] August 1786, T 29/58, pp. 22–4.

6. Blainey (1968 (1)), p. 204; Dallas, pp. 4–5.

7. Howe to Sydney, 26 December 1784, HO 28/4, fo. 386.

8. [Nepean/Sydney] to the Treasury Board, 21/18 August 1786, T 1/639, no. 2176.

9. [Nepean], Heads of a Plan, [c.15 August 1786], CO 201/2, fo. 11.

10. Ibid., fo. 13.

11. Clark saw that 'in a perfunctory, slapdash way, some of the commercial arguments for New Holland were tacked on to the Botany Bay solution for the evil of the over-crowded jails': p. 69. Bolton explained the presence of these paragraphs as the work of a Home office clerk 'confronted with the task of putting together a memorandum to justify the choice of New South Wales as a convict colony': (1968), p. 10. Shaw found it 'curious that Sydney should have placed these paragraphs, if they are so important, at the end rather than in the forefront of a lengthy document, and that he omitted them altogether from the detailed letter which he wrote to the Treasury explaining his "plan"': (1968), p. 195. Blainey characterized this generic approach as seeing the paragraphs only as 'quaint displays of window-dressing': (1966), p. 27.

12. E.g., when Thomas Robertson send his 'Abstract … of [a] plan for employing the convicts in His Majesty's Royal Navy', to Sydney at the end of 1782, he referred to 'the heads of my plan' (HO 42/1, fos 28–31). In September 1785, Banks drew up the 'Heads of Instructions to be given by Captain Thompson … to Mr Antoni Pantaleon Hove' (ADM 2/1342). In 1787, Mulgrave composed a 'Sketch of the Heads of a Treaty of Defensive Alliance …', PRO 30/8/360, fos 199–212. About June 1786, the Board of Trade drew up the 'Heads of a Plan for opening Free Ports in the Island of Bermuda and in the Bahama Islands' (BT 6/226). When Pitt sent a draft to Carmarthen concerning commercial negotiations in Paris in September 1786, he termed it 'Heads of a Despatch' (Bodleian, English Letters, d. 122, fo. 146). On 30 January 1787, *The Daily Universal Register* reported that Pitt had presented to the House of Commons 'a small packet of papers, relative to the convicts intended for Botany Bay. The general heads of those papers being read …'. In October 1789, the Admiralty Board drew up 'Heads of Instructions to be given to the Commander of the Vessel to be appointed to examine Isla Grande, Tristran da Cunha, etc.' (ADM 1/4155, after no. 59).

13. Eden to [Weymouth?], 16 January 1776, BL, Add. MS 34413, fo. 11.

14. Rose to Nepean, 3 January 1783, HO 35/4.

15. Sydney to the Treasury, 10 November 1785, T 1/616.
16. Nepean to Sharrow, 27 October 1786, HO 43/2, fo. 175; Sharrow to Nepean, 30 October 1786 and undated, HO 42/9, fo. 92, HO 42/8, no. 12.
17. Thomas, 'Additional Tools and Utensils …', USNA, Record group 45/446, fo. 143a; 'Articles sent by the First Fleet to Botany Bay', *HRNSW*, vol. 2, p. 388; Sever, Log of the *Lady Penrhyn*, ibid, p. 407.
18. Twiss to Watson, 29 October 1786; Watson to Nepean, 2 November 1786, HO 42/10, fos 393–4. Hunter identified Murley as a 'weaver': *Hunter*, p. 201. King, who took him to Norfolk Island, described him as 'an adventurer, [who] had been a master weaver': *King*, p. 40. Murley served as an AB on the *Sirius* (entered 8 December 1786) during the voyage out.
19. Nepean to Sackville Hamilton, Draft, 24 October 1786, HO 100/18, fos 369–72. Nepean annotated: 'This clause [i.e., paragraph] left out in the letter written to Mr Hamilton'. I don't think that its omission from the version sent lessens in the slightest degree its significance, for what it gives is the considered view of the administration official most involved in the Botany Bay decision and the mounting of the First Fleet. It may be that, on reflection, Nepean thought he should not advertise some of the venture's motives; but his omitting it does not reduce its importance as a statement of his understanding of the business. (Michael Roe (1952) first drew attention to this draft letter, and pointed out its significance.)
20. See above, ch. 6, pp. 154–8
21. Clark, p. 69.
22. Phillip to Nepean, 1 March 1787, CO 201/2, fo. 115.
23. Privy Council, Instructions to Phillip, 25 April 1787, CO 201/2, fos 35–6.
24. *King*, p. 37; Phillip to King, Instructions, 12 February 1788, CO 201/3, fo. 27.
25. *Tench*, p. 74.
26. Phillip to Nepean, 30 October 1786, HO 42/10, fo. 301; Singleton to Nepean, 5 November 1786, HO 42/10, fo. 383; Phillip to Banks, 2 September 1787, SLNSW, Mitchell MS C 213, p. 5; Phillip, Instructions to King, 12 February 1788, CO 201/3, fo. 27; *King*, pp. 56, 106; Phillip to Nepean, 17 November 1788, CO 201/3, fo. 166.
27. Phillip, Journal, Clements, Sydney vol. 17.
28. See Frost (1993).

Conclusion

1. *Eden*, pp. 28–9.
2. Beauchamp Committee, Report, 28 July 1785, *JHC*, vol. 40 (1784–5), p. 1164.
3. Report of the Debate, 7 February 1786, *PR*, vol. 19 (1787), p. 54.
4. Report of the Debate, 7 February 1786, *Gentleman's Magazine*, vol. 56 (1786), p. 168.
5. *Cook*, vol. 1, p. 278; *Banks*, vol. 2, p. 4.
6. Dallas, p. 5; Blainey (1968 (2)), p. 204.
7. Yeats, 'The Circus Animals' Desertion'.
8. I am providing details in *The First Fleet: The Real Story*.
9. Report of the Debate, 9 February 1791, *PH*, vol. 28 (1789–91), cols 1223–4.
10. Shaw (1984), p. 90.
11. Here, I acknowledge that A.G.L. Shaw did make an extensive examination of hemp and flax papers and references in the Board of Trade collections. My point is rather than he and others didn't look at commodores' reports and Navy Board statistics to ascertain the need for naval materials and the quantities actually in store.

12. Atkinson (1997), pp. 58, 72, 213. It is also telling that Atkinson does not include the subheadings 'flax' and 'timber' in his 'Norfolk Island' entry in the index.
13. Keneally, pp. 43–4.
14. Shaw (1968), pp. 196, 199.
15. Hughes, p. 70; Molony, p. 1.
16. Bolton (1969), p. 70.
17. Lawson.
18. In 1787, Dundas told Lord Cornwallis, the governor-general of India, that Pitt intended to reconstitute the India board, so as to make him 'not only in reality but declaredly ... the Cabinet minister for India' – Dundas to Cornwallis, 27 July 1787, *Cornwallis*, vol. 1, p. 245.
19. Dundas to Sydney, 2 November 1784, PRO 30/8/157, fo. 6; Report of the Debate, 14 December 1790, *PH*, vol. 28 (1789–91), col. 979.
20. Phillip to Banks, 26 July 1790 and 2 April 1792, SLNSW, Mitchell MS C 213, pp. 58–9, 87–8.
21. Grose to Nepean, 2 April 1792, *HRNSW*, vol. 1, part 2, p. 613.

THE FIRST FLEET

Introduction

1. Clark, p. 77.
2. Shaw (1966), p. 54.
3. King (1982), p. 31.
4. Mackay, p. 57.
5. Hughes, pp. 74–5.
6. Molony, p. 1.
7. Gillen (1989), pp. xxiii, xxxiii, xxxvi.
8. Wilson, p. 32.
9. Clark, p. 77.
10. Phillip to Nepean, 18 March 1787, CO 201/2, fo. 123.
11. Hughes, p. 70.
12. *Botany Bay: The Real Story*, pp. 55–76.
13. *Smyth (2)*, p. 47; *Tench*, p. 32; *Collins*, pp. 1–2.
14. Shaw (1966), pp. 53–4.
15. See Gillen (1989), p. 445. There is some uncertainty about these figures, as the number of seamen on the transport ships cannot be known accurately, which means that there may have been as many as 100 more.
16. 15,000 nautical miles; 17,500 miles; 28,000 kilometres.
17. *Collins*, p. 1.
18. Campbell, Testimony to the House of Commons Committee, [April 1778], *JHC*, vol. 36 (1776–8), p. 927.
19. Barnard Eldershaw, p. 34.
20. Frost (1980), p. 137. The error was repeated by Jonathan King (1982), p. 17, and by John Moore (1987), p. 24.
21. *King*, p. 19; Henderson and Stanbury, p. 39; Hill, p. 48.
22. Campbell, pp. 264–6.
23. Barnard Eldershaw, p. 25.

24. Clark, p. 73; *Phillip*, pp. 343–4; Moore, p. 25.
25. Hill, p. 37; Keneally, p. 42. (At least Keneally got Rose's position right.)
26. See Frost (1987), pp. 49–55.
27. See ibid., pp. 105–25, 129–33.
28. *Fowell*, pp. 23, 26.
29. Frost (1980), p. 218.
30. For example, the vast bulk of the Earl of Shelburne's papers went to the William L. Clements Library at the University of Michigan. Papers relating to Australia from the collections of Sir Joseph Banks and Lord Sydney came first to the remarkable collectors David Scott Mitchell and Sir William Dixson, and then to the State Library of New South Wales. Others found their way to the Sutro Library in San Francisco. Some of Pitt's and Dundas's papers went to the Duke University Library, others to the William L. Clements Library.
31. This very brief summary is based on the studies by Edward Hughes (1934) and Brewer.
32. Dorset to Carmarthen, 5 May and 9 June 1785, FO 27/16; Dalrymple to Carmarthen, 8 June 1785, BL, Egerton 3501, fo. 39.
33. For details, see Frost (1987), pp. 129–33.
34. Various intelligence reports sent to Nepean, and his ledgers, are in FO 95/7/3, 4.
35. Middleton to Nepean, 11 December 1786, and 20 March 1787, CO 201/2, fos 51–2, 243.

1. Announcing the Decision

1. The earliest version of this letter is in Nepean's hand, and is dated 21 August 1786, with 21 then cancelled and 18 substituted (HO 35/7).
2. This letter is another indication of the true date of the decision and the administrative steps that followed it.
3. Sydney to Treasury, 18 August 1786, T 1/639, no. 2176.
4. Though the titles are different, they were the joint heads of the Treasury Department, and therefore Nepean's equivalents.
5. Treasury, Minutes, 18 and 19 August and 26 October 1786, T 29/58, pp. 22–4, 28–9.
6. Sydney to Admiralty, 31 August 1786, ADM 1/4152, no. 25.
7. Sydney to Chairmen, EIC, 15 September 1786, BL, OIOC E/1/79, no. 187; Court of Directors, Minutes, 19 September 1786, OIOC B/103, p. 570, and 21 September 1786, D/1.
8. Richards to Pitt, 6 October 1786, PRO 30/8/171, fos 31–2; *Daily Universal Register*, 12 October 1786.
9. There had been earlier information, when the Navy Board had advertised for shipping and supplies at the beginning of September (e.g., in *Morning Herald* and *Whitehall Evening Post* on 1 September). However, these were specialist notices intended for ship-brokers and commercial firms.
10. *Public Advertiser*, 19 September 1786; *Hawkesworth*, vol. 3, pp. 495–506.
11. Other, briefer, descriptions of Botany Bay/New South Wales appeared in the *Morning Chronicle*, 30 September 1786, and the *Public Advertiser*, 30 September 1786.
12. *Daily Universal Register*, 27 September 1786.
13. *Birmingham Daily Gazette*, 25 September 1786.

14. *Morning Chronicle*, 13 October 1786; the *London Chronicle*, 14–17 October 1786. Since the quoting is so direct, the papers either had these details from Matra, or from the Home Office.
15. *London Chronicle*, 4 December 1786; and see *Botany Bay: The Real Story*, pp. 190–2.
16. *St James's Chronicle*, 5–7 December 1786; *Daily Universal Register*, 8 and 18 December 1786 and 4 January 1787.
17. *Morning Chronicle*, 3 October 1786.
18. *Public Advertiser*, 13 October 1786.
19. *St James's Chronicle*, 16 January 1787; *London Chronicle*, 16–18 January 1787.
20. *Daily Universal Register*, 21 and 23 November 1786.
21. *Daily Universal Register*, 4 December 1786.
22. *Gentleman's Magazine*, vol. 56 (1786), pp. 806–7.
23. *Bath Chronicle*, 11 January 1787.
24. Pinto de Souza to Mello e Castro, 19 September 1786, ANTT, MNE caixa 706, no. 705.
25. Robert J. King, p. 17 (citing Campo de Alange to Florida Blanca, 13 October 1786, AHN, Estado legajo 4250/1).
26. 'Mercator', in the *Public Advertiser*, 6 October 1786; *Hampshire Chronicle*, 16 October 1786; *Dublin Evening Herald*, 30 October 1786; *Reading Mercury and Oxford Gazette*, 30 October 1786; *Hampshire Chronicle*, 1 January 1787.
27. *Daily Universal Register*, 23 January 1787; *JHC*, vol. 42 (1787), pp. 3–4; *PH*, vol. 26 (1787), col. 214.
28. E.g., Clark cited this paragraph in the context of his assertion that 'everyone associated with the execution of the decision named the overcrowding in the jails as the only motive' (p. 69).
29. Camden to Sydney, 11 January 1787, Clements, Sydney vol. 14. In the event, the reference to troubles in Ireland was removed from the address.

2. *The Colony: Society, Law and Governance*

1. Camden to Pitt, 29 January 1787, PRO 30/8/119, fo. 131.
2. See *Botany Bay: The Real Story*, p. 201; and 'Our Original Aggression? New South Wales as *terra nullius*', in Frost (1994), pp. 176–89.
3. Matra, 'Supplement', 6 April 1784, CO 201/1, fos 64–5.
4. Pitt to Wilberforce, 23 September 1786, *Wilberforce*, pp. 16–17; quoted in Thomas, p. 19; Phillip to Sydney, July 1788, *HRNSW*, vol. 1, part 2, p. 179.
5. 'Phillip's Views on the Conduct of the Expedition and the Treatment of Convicts', *HRNSW*, vol. 1, part 2, pp. 50–4.
6. Phillip, Memorandum, [c. 1 October 1786], CO 201/2, fos 88–93. Phillip's reference to his ship as the *Berwick* fixes the latest date of composition of this document as 11 October, since it was renamed the *Sirius* the next day (Admiralty to Navy Board, 12 October 1786, ADM A/2816). As for the earliest date: while Phillip's appointment was mooted at the beginning of September (Howe to Sydney, 3 September 1786, CO 201/2, fo. 31), it was first publicly announced on 27 September (Daily Universal Register, 27 September 1786). It therefore seems likely that Phillip returned to London only about this time, a supposition reinforced by his afterwards remarking of the victualling contracts for the First Fleet which the Navy Board concluded on 12 September, that these 'were made before I ever saw the Navy Board on this business' (Phillip to Sydney, 12 March 1787, CO 201/2, fo. 120).

7. Phillip, Memorandum, [c. 1 October 1786], CO 201/2, fos 90–1.

8. Ibid.; and Phillip to Sydney, 16 May 1788, *HRNSW*, vol. 1, part 2, p. 138.

9. Phillip, Memorandum, [c. 1 October 1786], CO 201/2, fo. 91.

10. Ibid.

11. Ibid., fos 90, 92.

12. Ibid., fo. 92.

13. [Home Office], Draft of Instructions, [c. 1 March 1787], CO 201/2, fos 29–40; Phillip, Comments on his Instructions, 11 April 1787, CO 201/2, fo. 130.

14. Privy Council, Amendments to draft Instructions, 25 April 1787, CO 201/1, fos 36–7, 38.

15. *Botany Bay: The Real Story*, pp. 155–6.

16. Matra, Testimony, 9 May 1785, HO 7/1.

17. Phillip, Memorandum, [c. 1 October 1786], CO 201/2, fo. 91.

18. Nepean to Hamilton, 24 October 1786, HO 100/18, fo. 372.

19. These commissions are printed in *HRNSW*, vol. 1, part 2, pp. 24–7. I have been unable to locate the originals.

20. Nepean to Sydney, 9 November 1786, SLNSW, Mitchell MS An 53/1.

21. [Sydney], ['Notes relative to Act to settle N. S. Wales'], [undated, but c. 9–27 November 1786], SLNSW, Dixson Add. MS Q 522. (It is not entirely clear that this title is a contemporary annotation, though.)

22. [Attorney-General or Solicitor-General] to [Sydney or Nepean], [undated, but c. 9–27 November 1786], HO 48/1B, p. 565.

23. *Daily Universal Register*, 27 November 1786; and cf. *Hampshire Chronicle*, 4 December 1786.

24. Camden to Pitt, 29 January 1787, PRO 30/8/119, fo. 131.

25. *JHC*, vol. 42 (for 1787: London, 1803), pp. 288, 305, 367, 376, 378, 381, 402, 404; 27 Geo. III, c. 2, *Statutes at Large* vol. 15 (London, 1789), pp. 254–5.

26. Privy Council, 'Charter for Establishing Courts of Civil and Criminal Jurisdiction on the Eastern Coast of New South Wales', 2 April 1787, PR, C 66/3834, part 5, no. 10.

27. Sydney to Admiralty, 26 March 1787, ADM 1/4152, no. 58; Admiralty, Minute, 27 March 1787, ADM 3/102, and to Privy Council, 27 March 1787, PC 1/62/16.

28. Privy Council, Order, 4 April 1787, PC 2/132, pp. 135–6, and to Admiralty, 12 April 1787, HCA 50/13, fos 136–7; Admiralty, Minute, 18 April 1787, ADM 3/103, and to Marriott, 18 April 1787, ADM 2/1062, pp. 314–5; HCA, Letters-Patent, 30 April 1787, HCA 50/13, fos 138–45, 146–9, 152–3; HCA, Letters-Patent, 5 May 1787, *HRNSW*, vol. 1, part 2, pp. 95–100.

29. Sydney to Lord President, 26 March 1787, HO 43/2, pp. 218–19; Privy Council, Minute, 4 April 1787, PC 2/132, p. 136; Board of Trade, Minute, 13 April 1787, BT 5/4, p. 239, and Report, BT 6/180, pp. 45–6; Privy Council, Order, 20 April 1787, PC 2/132, pp. 156–7, and Commission, 5 May 1787, HCA 50/13, fos 153–8; Phillip to Stephens, 10 May 1787, ADM 1/2308.

30. Privy Council, Commission, 26 March 1787, CO 202/5, fos 7–16. This is annotated: 'NB: The above commission passed the Great Seal the 2nd April 1787.'

31. For this precedent, see Macdonald to Nepean, 25 March 1787, HO 48/1B, fo. 119.

32. *Smyth (2)*, p. 68; cf. *Tench*, p. 42.

33. Privy Council, Minute, 23 June 1789, PC 2/134, pp. 125–6; Additional Instructions, draft, 23 June 1789, HO 31/1, and final version, 8 August 1789, PC 2/134, pp. 188–92; Grenville to Phillip, 24 August 1789, CO 201/4, fo. 28.

34. Macdonald to Nepean, 30 March 1790, HO 48/1B, p. 351; JHC, vol. 45 (for January–June 1790: London, 1803), pp. 410, 484, 486, 493, 496, 506, 522, 543; Statutes at Large, vol. 16 (London, 1794), p. 57; Attorney-General, Draft warrant, 8 November 1790, HO 48/1B, pp. 345–50; Grenville to Phillip, 13 and 15 November 1790, CO 201/5, fos 211, 218; Privy Council, Additional instructions, 15 November 1790, HRNSW, vol. 1, part 2, pp. 413–4.
35. Privy Council, Minute, 21 May 1790, PC 2/135, p. 76; Board of Trade, Minute, [c. 3 August 1790], BL, Add. MS 38392, fo. 122, and Report, 3 August 1790, BT 6/182, pp. 251–2; Privy Council, Minute, 4 August 1790, HO 31/1; Privy Council, Minute, 21 January 1791, PC 2/135, p. 378.
36. Phillip to Nepean, 28 September 1788, *HRNSW*, vol. 1, part 2, p. 183.
37. Phillip to Nepean, 28 October 1786, HO 42/9, fo. 84, and to Sydney, 15 May 1788, fos 6–7; to Lansdowne, 3 July 1788, SLNSW, Mitchell MS 7241; to Middleton, 6 July 1788, [privately owned].

3. *The People 1: Officials and Officers*

1. [Nepean], 'Staff Establishment for the Settlement at New South Wales', [c. 15 August 1786], T 1/639, no. 2176.
2. [Nepean], 'Estimate for defraying the Establishments in New South Wales from the 10 October 1786 to 10 October 1787', 10 October 1786, BT 6/263. (I have corrected the total, which Nepean incorrectly gave as £2705.)
3. For an extended account, see Frost (1987).
4. Phillip to Admiralty, 25 September 1769, ADM 106/2972.
5. Phillip to Sandwich, 17 January 1781, NMM, SAN F/26/23.
6. Phillip to Nepean, 28 October 1786, HO 42/9, fo. 83, and to Sydney, 3 December 1786, HO 42/10, fo. 304.
7. The editor wrote 'Buenos Aires', but as that was a Spanish town, whose authorities would scarcely have been willing to take charge of Portuguese criminals, it is much more likely that Phillip landed the convicts in Brazil.
8. *St James's Chronicle*, 2 February 1787.
9. Howe to Sydney, 3 September 1786, CO 201/2, fo. 31.
10. See Frost (1987), pp. 49–50, 225.
11. Edward Spain, Journal, SLNSW, Mitchell MS C 266, pp. 65–6.
12. King to Nepean, 14 February 1791, *HRNSW*, vol. 1, part 2, p. 455.
13. Privy Council, Ross's Commission, 24 October 1786, *HRNSW*, vol. 1, part 2, p. 26; Admiralty to Ross, 2 March 1787, ADM 2/1178, pp. 167–70.
14. Ross to Stephens, 10 July 1788, ADM 1/3824, fo. 52.
15. Admiralty to Collins, 29 November 1786, ADM 2/1178, p. 17; to Stewart, 23 December 1786, ADM 2/1178, pp. 64–5; Collins to Sydney, 7 February 1787, CO 201/2, fo. 211. (There is another puzzle concerning Collins's commissioning. The version of 24 October 1786 printed in HRNSW (vol. 1, part 2, pp. 26–7) is clearly a Privy Council document; however, the Admiralty subsequently said that he had been appointed 'by warrant from the Right Honourable the Lords Commissioners of His Majesty's Treasury dated 24 October last' – Admiralty to Steward, 6 March 1787, ADM 2/1178, p. 177.)
16. *Daily Universal Register*, 30 December 1786.
17. Phillip to Nepean, 20 May 1787, CO 201/2, fo. 156.
18. Edward Spain, Journal, SLNSW, Mitchell MS C 266, pp. 67–70.

19. Quoted in Thomas, p. 19.
20. Newton to Middleton, 30 October 1786, [privately owned].
21. Hamond to Nepean, 16 October 1786, CO 201/1, fo. 45.
22. White to Skill, 17 April 1790, *HRNSW*, vol. 1, part 2, p. 333.
23. Board of Trade, Report, 13 April 1787, BT 6/180, pp. 45–6; Commissions, 5 May 1787, HCA 50/13, fo. 154, and *HRNSW*, vol. 1, part 2, p. 96.
24. *Tench*, p. 66.
25. Banks to Masson, 3 June 1789, NHM, DTC vol. 5, pp. 173–4.
26. Phillip to Sydney, 3 December 1786, HO 42/10, fos 303–4.
27. Phillip to Nepean, 28 October 1786, HO 42/9, fos 83–4.
28. Ibid.; Phillip to Nepean, [c. 28 October 1786], CO 201/2, fo. 84, and to Sydney, 1 November 1786, SLNSW, Dixson MS Q 162, pp. 1–2.
29. Sydney to Admiralty, 30 August 1786, ADM 1/4152, no. 25.
30. *Daily Universal Register*, 31 October 1786.
31. Phillip to Nepean, [c. 1 November 1786], CO 201/2, fo. 86.
32. Phillip, Comments on his Instructions, 11 April 1787, CO 201/2, fos 129–30; Sydney to Phillip, 20 April 1787, CO 201/2, fo. 27.
33. *Authentic Narrative*, p. v; and see the cover illustration.
34. Admiralty, Minute, 14 December 1786, ADM 3/102, and to Privy Council, 14 December 1786, PC 1/61/15; Order-in-Council, 15 December 1786, ADM 1/5177; Admiralty to Phillip, 18 December 1786, ADM 2/117, p. 269, and to Navy Board, 22 December 1786, ADM A/2816; Sydney to Phillip, 28 April 1787, CO 201/2, fo. 144. (The dormant commission has not been found.)
35. Stephens to Tench, 27 October 1786, ADM 2/1177, p. 525, to Collins, 14 December 1786, ADM 2/1178, p. 42.
36. Bayly to Banks, 8 [September] 1786, Kew, KBP vol. 1, no. 237; Stephens to Smith, ADM 2/1177, p. 521; Twiss to Watson, 29 October 1786, HO 42/10, fo. 394.
37. See below, Ch. 6, pp. 111–2.

4. People 2: Ships' Crews, Marines, Convicts, Wives and Children

1. Admiralty, Minute, 1 November 1786, ADM 3/102, and to Phillip and Ball, 1 November 1786, ADM 2/117, p. 213; to Navy Board, 1 November 1786, ADM 2/262, p. 495.
2. King, p. 40; Phillip to Nepean, 28 September 1788, *HRNSW*, vol. 1, part 2, p. 185.
3. The passes are recorded in ADM 7/104, 106. (I am grateful to Gary Sturgess for these references.) *King*, p. 6.
4. Stephens to Tupper and Hughes, 8 October 1786, ADM 2/1177, pp. 491–3.
5. *Tench*, p. 13.
6. Admiralty to Privy Council, 21 November 1786, ADM 2/1178, pp. 2–3.
7. Stephens to Ordnance Board and Generals Smith and Collins, 14 December, and Admiralty to Smith and Collins, 20 December 1786, ADM 2/1178, pp. 42, 43, 55–6.
8. See *Collins*, pp. 48–9, 66.
9. Admiralty to Sydney, 21 November 1786, CO 201/2, fo. 39.
10. Nepean to Rose, 22 December 1786, T 1/639, no. 2985; Thomas to Nepean, 24 December 1786, HO 28/61, fo. 120; Navy Board, Minute, 20 April 1787, ADM 106/2623; Phillip, 'State of the Garrison and Convicts …', 10 June 1787, CO 201/2, fo. 172.
11. [   ] to Middleton, 13 October 1786, [privately owned].

12. Sydney to Treasury, 22 December 1786, T 1/639, no. 2984.
13. *Hampshire Chronicle*, 18 September 1786; *Reading Mercury and Oxford Gazette*, 2 October 1786.
14. *London Chronicle*, 17–19 October 1786.
15. Middleton to Nepean, 18 January 1787, CO 201/2, fo. 201; Teer to Navy Board, 29 January 1787, ADM 106/243.
16. We conducted this analysis during Professor Zebrow's time as a Fellow of the Institute for Advanced Study, La Trobe University. It has not been published.
17. Nepean to Campbell, 20 February 1787, HO 13/5, p. 58; Campbell to Erskine, [c. 20 February 1787], SLNSW, Mitchell MS ZA 3229, p. 270. As Nepean's list has evidently not survived, we cannot know what principle of selection Campbell followed.
18. *Tench*, p. 13.
19. *Clark*, pp. 2–6.
20. Gillen (1989), p. 446.
21. Phillip to Nepean, 11 January 1787, CO 201/2, fo. 105.
22. Campbell to Erskine, 30 January 1787, SLNSW, Mitchell MS ZA 3229, p. 262; Campbell's annotations to the list, 24 February 1787, HO 13/5, pp. 65–8.
23. [Campbell] to Erskine, 27 March 1787, SLNSW, Mitchell MS ZA 3229, p. 283.
24. Phillip to Sydney, 12 February 1790, and to Grenville, 17 July 1790, *HRNSW*, vol. 1, part 2, pp. 298, 361–2.
25. Nepean to Middleton, 8 March 1785, NMM, MID 1/131.
26. *Nagle*, p. 77.
27. Marshall to Stephens, 18 March 1787, ADM 1/989.
28. [Nepean], Heads of a Plan, [c. 15 August 1786], CO 201/2, fo. 11.
29. Hughes to Stephens, 14 October 1786, RMM, Archive 11/51/1, no. 345.
30. Ross, 'Artificers belonging to the Marine Detachment, employed from the 17th May to the 30th September 1788', *HRA*, series 1, vol. 1, p. 81; cf. Ross, 'Return of Artificers belonging to the Detachment, employed from the 30th of September 1788, to the 31st December 1789', CO 201/5, fo. 89.
31. *Authentic Narrative*, pp. v–vi.
32. *Daily Universal Register*, 30 November 1786.
33. Phillip to Nepean, 28 September 1788, *HRNSW*, vol. 1, part 2, p. 183.
34. Victualling Board to Phillip, 29 November 1786, and Minute, 6 December 1786, ADM 111/108.
35. Lochart to Phillip, [c. 21] and 22 December 1786, Phillip to Stephens, 23 December 1786, ADM 1/2308.
36. 'Humanitas', the *London Chronicle*, 2–5 December 1786.

5. The Ships

1. See Bateson, pp. 94–6, and Knight.
2. See Webb.
3. *Martin*, vol. 3, p. 381.
4. Navy Board, Minutes, 20 September 1786 and 2 January 1787, ADM 106/2622; Admiralty, Minute, 4 January 1787, ADM 3/102.
5. Steele to Navy Board, 26 August 1786, HO 35/7.
6. Admiralty, Minute, 6 September 1786, ADM 3/102, and to Navy Board, 6 September 1786, ADM 2/262, pp. 418–9.
7. See Introduction, p. 4.

8. *King*, p. 5.

9. Barnard Eldershaw, p. 34; Mackay, p. 59; Henderson and Stanbury, p. 61.

10. Deptford Officers to Navy Board, 12 November and 6 December 1781, ADM 106/3320, fos 30–31, 34.

11. *Hunter*, p. 1.

12. *King*, p. 5.

13. Admiralty to Navy Board, 23 August 1786, ADM 2/262, p. 393; Navy Board, Minute, 25 August 1786, ADM 106/2622.

14. Deptford Officers to Navy Board, 6 September 1786, ADM 106/3321, fo. 87.

15. Navy Board, Minute, 22 September 1786, ADM 106/2622, and to Stephens, 22 September 1786, ADM 106/2213, p. 432; Deptford Officers to Navy Board, 27 September 1786, ADM 106/3321, fos 84–5.

16. A 'tide' was an overtime unit of 1.5 hours.

17. Navy Board, Minutes, 9 and 11 October 1786, ADM 106/2622, and to Stephens, 9 October 1786, ADM 106/2213, p. 437; Deptford Officers to Navy Board, 11 October 1786, ADM 106/3321, fo. 91.

18. Admiralty, Minute, 12 October 1786, ADM 3/102, and to Navy Board, 12 October 1786, ADM A/2816; to Sydney, 12 October 1786, ADM 2/374, pp. 135–6, and to Richmond, 12 October 1786, ADM 2/262, pp. 468–9; *King*, p. 5.

19. Navy Board to Stephens, 25 October 1786, ADM 106/2213, p. 456; Admiralty to Navy Board, 25 October 1786, ADM 2/262, fos 485–6, and to Phillip, 25 October 1786, ADM 2/117; to Navy Board, 1 November 1786, ADM A/2816, and to Phillip and Ball, 1 November 1786, ADM 2/117, pp. 213–4; Navy Board to Victualling Board, 2 November 1786, ADM C/664.

20. Phillip to Stephens, 31 October 1786, ADM 1/2308; Admiralty to Richmond, 1 November 1786, ADM 2/262, pp. 496–7, and to Navy Board, 1 November 1786, ADM A/2816; Navy Board, Minute, 3 November 1786, ADM 106/2622.

21. Admiralty, Minute, 1 November 1786, ADM 3/102, and to Navy Board, 1 November 1786, ADM A/2816.

22. Deptford Officers to Navy Board, 13 November 1786, ADM 106/3364, fo. 80; Navy Board, Minute, 21 November 1786, ADM 106/2622; Parker to Phillip, 21 November 1786, CUL, RGO series 14, vol. 9, fo. 33.

23. Navy Board, Minutes, 12 September, 14, 15 and 16 November 1786, ADM 106/2622; Phillip to Admiralty, 27 October 1786, ADM 1/2308; Admiralty to Navy Board, 8 November 1786, ADM A/2816; Navy Board to Teer, 1 December 1786, ADM 106/2347, p. 166.

24. Victualling Board, Minutes, 1, 7, 8, 10, 14, 21, 22 and 28 November, 5 and 12 December 1786, ADM 111/108.

25. The bark of the cinchona tree, considered efficacious in treating fevers, neuralgia and debility.

26. Worgan to Phillip, 21 November 1786, Phillip to Stephens, 30 November 1786, ADM 1/2308.

27. Navy Board, Minutes, 1 and 3 January 1787, ADM 106/2623; Deptford Officers to Navy Board, 3 and 5 January 1787, ADM 106/3364, fo. 93.

28. Victualling Board, Minute, [c. 10 January 1787], ADM 111/108; Palmer to Navy Board, 20 January 1787, ADM 106/1291; Navy Board to Teer, 24 January 1787, ADM 106/2347, p. 188.

29. Deptford Officers to Navy Board, 9 September 1786, ADM 106/3321, fo. 87; Navy Board, Minute, 11 September 1786, ADM 106/2622; Deptford Officers to Navy Board, 12 September 1786, ADM 106/3321, fo. 89.

30. *Daily Universal Register*, 7 September 1786.

31. Navy Board, Minute, 22 September 1786, ADM 106/2622, and to Stephens, 22 September 1786, ADM 106/2213, p. 432; Deptford Officers to Navy Board, 27 and 28 September 1786, ADM 106/3321, fo. 85 and ADM 106/3364, fos 73–4.

32. Navy Board, Minute, 27 September 1786, ADM 106/2622, and to Stephens, [28] September 1786, ADM 106/2213, p. 435; Admiralty to Navy Board, 12 October 1786, ADM 2/262, pp. 469–70.

33. *Hunter*, pp. 1–2; *King*, pp. 5–6.

34. Deptford Officers to Navy Board, 18 October 1786, ADM 106/3321, fos 93–4.

35. Stephens to Navy Board, 20 October 1786, ADM 2/587, p. 98; Deptford Officers to Navy Board, 24 October 1786, ADM 106/3321, fo. 96; Navy Board, Minute, 24 October 1786, ADM 106/2622, and to Stephens, 24 October 1786, ADM 106/2213, p. 454.

36. Stephens to Navy Board, 12 December 1786, ADM A/2816; Navy Board, Minute, 13 December 1786, ADM 106/2622, and to Stephens, 13 December 1786, ADM 106/2213, p. 506; Admiralty, Minute, 14 December 1786, ADM 3/102, to Richmond, 14 December 1786, ADM 2/262, p. 556, and to Navy Board, 14 December 1786, ADM A/2816; Navy Board, Minute, 16 December 1786, ADM 106/2622.

37. Admiralty to Navy Board, 27 October 1786, ADM 2/262, p. 490, and to Ball, 27 October 1786, ADM 2/117, pp. 210–11; Navy Board, Minute, 28 October 1786, ADM 106/2622.

38. Deptford Officers to Navy Board, 1 and 6 November 1786, ADM 106/3321, fos 97–9; Navy Board, Minute, 8 November 1786, ADM 106/2622; Deptford Officers to Navy Board, 15 November 1786, ADM 106/3321, fo. 99.

39. Ball to Navy Board, 11 November 1786, ADM 106/1286; Navy Board, Minute, 16 November 1786, ADM 106/2622; Victualling Board, Minutes, 14, 21, 22, 23, and 28 November, 5 and 12 December 1786, ADM 111/108; Ball to Navy Board, 2 and 6 December 1786, ADM 106/1286; Navy Board, Minutes, 5 and 8 December 1786, ADM 106/2622.

40. Navy Board, Minute, 29 August 1786, ADM 106/2622, and Draft advertisement, [29 August 1786], [privately owned]; *Morning Herald*, 1 September 1786; *Whitehall Evening Post*, 1, 4 and 8 September 1786.

41. Navy Board, Minute, 6 September 1786, ADM 106/2622.

42. Brough to Navy Board, 9 September 1786, ADM 106/1286; Navy Board to Brough, 11 September 1786, ADM 106/2347, p. 160.

43. Richards to Pitt, 9 and 28 September and 6 October 1786, PRO 30/8/171, fos 17, 29–30, 31–2.

44. Rose to Chairmen, EIC, 15 September 1786, BL, OIOC E/1/79, no. 184; Richards to EIC, 19 September, OIOC E/1/79, fo. 193; EIC, Minutes, 19 and 27 September 1786, OIOC B 103, pp. 570, 588–9.

45. Deptford Officers to Navy Board, 28, 29 and 30 September 1786, ADM 106/3364, fos 73–4.

46. See Deptford Officers to Navy Board, 12 October 2786, ADM 106/3321, fo. 92.

47. Deptford Officers to Navy Board, 2, 16, 18, 20 and 24 October, 3 and 10 November 1786, ADM 106/3321, fos 92–8.

48. Deptford Officers to Navy Board, 29 December 1786, ADM 106/3407, p. 34.

49. Deptford Officers to Navy Board, 1 November 1786, ADM 106/3321, fo. 97; Teer to Navy Board, 29 November 1786, ADM 106/243.

50. Johnston to Stephens, 18 December 1786, ADM OT; Stephens to Nepean, 18 December 1786, HO 28/5, p. 358; Nepean to Rose, 18 December 1786, T 1/639, no. 2927b; Rose to Navy Board, 18 December 1786, ADM OT; Navy Board, Minutes, 19 and 20 December 1786, ADM 106/2622.

51. Navy Board, Minutes, 9 November and 19 and 20 December 1786, ADM 106/2622; Teer to Navy Board, 13 December 1786, ADM 106/243.

52. Deptford Officers to Navy Board, 18 and 24 October 1786, ADM 106/3321, fos 94, 96.

53. Navy Board, Minute, 31 October 1786, ADM 106/2622.

54. See, e.g., Stephens to Stiles, 29 November 1786, ADM 2/587, p. 179. There are copies of the licences in ADM 7/104, 106. (I am grateful to Gary Sturgess for this information.)

55. Navy Board, Minute, 15 December 1786, ADM 106/2622, and Thomas to Morton, 15 December 1786, USNA, Record group 45/446.

56. Navy Board, Minute, 18 October 1786, ADM 106/2622.

57. Rose to Navy Board, 20 October 1786, ADM OT; Rose to Nepean, 21 October 1786, HO 35/7, and to Stephens, 21 October 1786, T 27/38, fo. 375; EIC to Canton Supercargoes, 13 December 1786, BL, OIOC R/10/33; Navy Board, Minutes, 15 and 28 December 1786, ADM 106/2622.

58. Deptford Officers to Navy Board, 8 November 1786, ADM 106/3321, fo. 98.

6. Equipping the Colonists

1. For the date, see Navy Board, Minute, 27 November 1786, ADM 106/2622.

2. See above, Introduction, pp. 2–3.

3. Steele to Navy Board, 26 August 1786, ADM OT.

4. Navy Board, Minute, 29 August 1786, ADM 106/2622, and to Steele, 29 August 1786, T 1/639, no. 2218; Steele to Nepean, 30 August 1786, HO 35/7; Nepean to Steele, 4 September 1786, T 1/639, no. 2269.

5. Steele to Navy Board, 9 September 1786, ADM A/2816.

6. Thomas to Watts, 12 and 14 September 1786, Watts to Thomas, 14 September 1786, ADM C/663.

7. *Morning Herald*, 18 and 23 September 1786.

8. Navy Board, Minute, 26 December 1786, ADM 106/2622; Thomas to Dawson and Atkinson, 26 December 1786, USNA, Record group 45/446.

9. Navy Board, Minute, 22 January 1787, ADM 106/2623.

10. Fell to Teer, 4 December 1786; Teer to Navy Board, 2 November 1786, ADM 106/243; Navy Board, Minute, 6 November 1786, ADM 106/2622; Navy Board to Teer, 13 November 1787, ADM 106/2347, p. 233; Teer to Navy Board, 14 and 28 November 1787, ADM 106/243.

11. Sydney to Treasury, 21/18 August 1786, T 1/639, no. 2176; Steele to Navy Board, 26 August 1786, ADM OT.

12. Rose to Nepean, 24 October 1786, HO 35/7, to Navy Board, 24 October 1786, ADM A/2816; Navy Board, Minute, 25 October 1786, ADM 106/2622.

13. Adair and White, List, [c. 14 November], and Nepean to Steele, 14 November 1786, T 1/639, no. 2643.

14. Steele to Navy Board, 20 November 1786, ADM OT; Navy Board to Steele, 21 November 1786, T 1/639, no. 2683.
15. Navy Board, Minute, 15 January 1787, ADM 106/2623.
16. See Lloyd and Coulter, pp. 92–3.
17. Nepean to Steele, 14 November 1786, T 1/639, no. 2643; Steele to Nepean, 18 December 1786, HO 35/7; Nepean to Phillip, 21 December 1786, HO 43/2, pp. 186–7.
18. See *St James's Chronicle*, 16 January 1787 and *London Chronicle*, 16–18 January 1787; *Smyth (1)*, p. 389.
19. Steele to Nepean, 31 August 1786, HO 35/7.
20. Banks, Instructions, [c. 1 March 1787], NHM, DTC vol. 5, p. 213; and see *Smyth (2)*, p. 16.
21. Phillip, Memorandum, [c. 1 October 1786], CO 201/2, fos 92–3, and to Nepean, [30 October 1786], HO 42/10, fo. 301.
22. Banks, 'Scheme of plants for Botany Bay', and List, [c. 28 November 1786], Sutro, Banks SS 1/48, 49.
23. Tony Courtis, Letter, 29 January 1987.
24. *Péron*, p. 273.
25. *Péron*, pp. 37, 271–6, 273–85, 293–5; and see Fletcher, p. 229.
26. For an extended discussion of this progress, see Frost (1994 (2)).
27. Nepean to Middleton, [c. 7 December 1786], ADM 106/243.
28. Steele to Navy Board, 26 August 1786, ADM OT; Navy Board, Minutes, 11 and 26 September 1786, ADM 106/2622.
29. Phillip to Nepean, [30 October 1786], HO 42/10, fo. 302; Nepean to Middleton, [c. 7 December 1786], ADM 106/243; Rose to Navy Board, 16 December 1786, ADM OT; Navy Board, Minute, 19 December 1786, ADM 106/2622, and to Rose, 19 December 1786, T 1/639, no. 2957; Ross, Memorandum, and to Phillip, 22 December 1786, CO 201/2, fos 71–3.
30. Stephens to Ross, 29 December 1786, ADM 2/1178, p. 78; Middleton to Nepean, 4 January 1787, CO 201/2, fo. 193; Navy Board, Minute, 4 January 1787, ADM 106/2623, and Thomas to Trotter, 4 January 1787, USNA, Record group 45/446; Navy Board, Minute, 25 January 1787, ADM 106/2623, and to Teer, 25 January 1787, ADM 106/2347, p. 189.
31. Navy Board, Minute, 8 November 1786, ADM 106/2622; Teer to Navy Board, 26 October 1786, ADM 106/243; Phillip to Sydney, 15 May 1788, CO 201/3, fo. 24.
32. 'Estimate of clothing to serve a male convict for one year', T 1/639, no. 2176.
33. Ibid.
34. Navy Board, Minute, 7 September 1786, *HRNSW*, vol. 2, pp. 367–8, and Minute, 26 December 1786, ADM 106/2622, and Thomas to Wadham, *et al.*, 26 December 1786, USNA, Record group 45/446.
35. This item is not included in the original list – or at least, in the transcription of it published in *HRNSW*. Later lists of women's clothing indicate that it should have been.
36. I.e., common/coarse shirts, trousers, frocks.
37. Navy Board to Darby, 2 November 1786, ADM 106/2347, fo. 82; Thomas to Stiles, 21 November 1786, USNA, Record group 45/446.
38. Nepean to Middleton, 21 December 1787, NMM, MID 1/131; Navy Board, Minute, 26 December 1786, ADM 106/2622, and Thomas to the various contractors, 26 December 1786, USNA, Record group 45/446.

39. Steele to Navy Board, 26 August 1786, ADM OT.
40. Thomas to Harrison, Gordon and Stanley, 13 September 1786, USNA, Record group 45/446; Middleton to Nepean, [c. 18 October 1786], CO 201/2, fo. 99.
41. Navy Board, Minute, 18 October 1786, ADM 106/2622, and Thomas to Harrison, Gordon and Stanley, 18 and 19 October 1786, USNA, Record group 45/446; Teer to Navy Board, 26 October 1786, ADM 106/243; Phillip to Nepean, [30 October 1786], HO 42/10, fos 301–2; Thomas to Harrison, Gordon and Stanley, 31 October 1786, USNA, Record group 45/446; Harrison, Gordon and Stanley to Navy Board, [c. 13 November 1786], CO 201/2, fo. 19; Navy Board, Minute, 13 November 1786, ADM 106/2622, and to Rose, 13 November 1786, T 1/639, no. 2624.
42. Thomas to Harrison, Gordon and Stanley, 29 December 1786 and 24 January 1787, USNA, Record group 45/446; Phillip to Nepean, 4 January 1787, CO 201/2, fo. 103.
43. See Frost (1987), pp. 55, 99; Phillip, Memorandum, [c. 1 October 1786], CO 201/2, fo. 90; Francis Wheatley, Captain Arthur Phillip, 1786 (SLNSW, Mitchell Library).
44. Phillip to Nepean, [30 October 1786], HO 42/10, fo. 301; Nepean to Sydney, 9 November 1786, SLNSW, Mitchell MS An 53/1; Richmond to Pitt, 3 December 1786, PRO 30/8/171, fo. 97; Rogers, 'Proportion of Ordnance, Ammunition and Stores demanded for the Equipment for Botany Bay', 21 December 1786, CO 201/2, fos 66–8.
45. Steele to Ordnance Board, 7 November 1786, T 27/38, p. 391; Stephens to Smith and Collins, 23 November 1786, ADM 2/1178, pp. 6–7.
46. Teer to Navy Board, 26 October 1786, ADM 106/243; Navy Board, Minute, 26 October 1786, ADM 106/2622; 'Articles sent by [the] First Fleet to Botany Bay', *HRNSW*, vol. 2, p. 388.
47. After agitation by domestic wool and silk manufacturers, parliament banned the printing of calicoes in England, but continued to permit that of fustians with a warp of linen and a weft of cotton. Hence 'fustian' came to comprehend cloth that would earlier have been classified as calico.
48. Nepean to Sackville Hamilton, 24 October 1786 (draft), HO 100/18, fo. 372; Privy Council, Instructions to Phillip, 25 April 1787, CO 201/1, fo. 35.
49. Account of proceedings, 6 February 1783, *JHC*, vol. 39 (1782–4), pp. 157–8. (I am grateful to Ken Cozens for this information.)
50. Nepean to Sharrow, 27 October 1786, HO 43/2, p. 175; Sharrow to Nepean, 30 October 1786, HO 42/9, fo. 92, and [c. 5 November 1786], HO 42/8, fo. 12.
51. Phillip to Nepean, [30 October 1786], HO 42/10, fo. 301; Singleton to Nepean, 5 November 1786, HO 42/10, fo. 383.
52. Phillip to Banks, 2 September 1787, SLNSW, Mitchell MS C 213, p. 5; *King*, pp. 56, 106; Phillip to Nepean, 17 November 1788, CO 201/3, fo. 166.
53. 'Articles sent by [the] First Fleet to Botany Bay', *HRNSW*, vol. 2, p. 388; *Lady Penrhyn* Log, 25 March 1788, ADM 51/4376, fo. 38.
54. Steele to Navy Board, 27 January 1787, ADM A/2817.
55. Navy Board, Minute, 4 December 1786, ADM 106/2622, and Thomas to Harrison, Gordon and Stanley, 4 December 1786, USNA, Record group 45/446.
56. Phillip to Nepean, [30 October 1786], HO 42/10, fos 301–2; Nepean, 'Articles to be provided for the purchase of stock etc. for the intended settlement at Botany Bay', [c. 31 October 1786], CO 201/1, fo. 48, and to Rose, 31 October 1786, T 1/639, no. 2553; Steele to Rashleigh, 8 November 1786, T 27/38, p. 395; Rashleigh to Steele, 13 November 1786, T 1/639, no. 2621; Navy Board, Minute, 8 December 1786,

ADM 106/2622, and Teer to Thomas, 8 December 1786, ADM 106/243; Navy Board to Teer, 8 December 1786, ADM 106/2347, p. 169; *London Chronicle*, 23–25 November 1786.

57. Stephens to Greenway, 20 November 1786, ADM 2/1177, p. 556, and to Prater, 5 and 22 December 1786 and 5 January 1787, ADM 2/1178, pp. 30, 62, 85.

58. Navy Board to Steele, 1 November 1786, T 1/639, no. 2558; Steele to Navy Board, 2 November 1786, ADM OT.

59. Steele to Navy Board, 8 November 1786, ADM OT; Cologan, Pollard and Cooper to Treasury, 17 October 1786, T 1/639, no. 2498; Navy Board to Steele, 13 November 1786, T 1/639, no. 2618.

60. Navy Board, Minute, 30 November 1786, ADM 106/2622; Phillip to Nepean, 2 December 1786, CO 201/2, fo. 45.

61. Dawes, 'List of Instruments proper for making astronomical Observations at Botany Bay', [c. 1 November 1786], RS, Misc. MS vol. 7, no. 56A; Board of Longitude, Minutes, 14 November 1786, CUL, RGO series 14, vol. 6, pp. 100–4.

62. Ibid.; and Parker to Phillip, 21 November 1786, CUL, RGO series 14, vol. 9, fo. 33.

63. Dawes, Receipt, 8 March 1800, CUL, RGO series 14, vol. 14, fo. 204.

64. Society for the Propagation of the Gospel, Minutes, 14, 21 and 28 November 1786, SLNSW, Bonwick box 47, pp. 28–32.

65. [Banks and Dickson], '*Sirius* seeds continued', [c. 28 December 1786], T 1/639, fo. 253.

66. 'Proportion of each specie of Provisions', ADM 30/44; and Rodger, pp. 83, 90.

67. *Colnett*, p. 73; Yarwood, p. 176.

7. Loading the Ships and Embarking the People

1. Admiralty, Minute, 25 October 1785, ADM 3/102, and to Navy Board, 25 October 1786, ADM 2/262, fos 485–6.

2. Deptford Officers to Navy Board, 25 October 1786, ADM 106/3321, fo. 95; Phillip to Admiralty, 11 November 1786, ADM 1/2308; Deptford Officers to Navy Board, 22 November 1786, ADM 106/3321, fo. 103; Navy Board to Stephens, 25 October 1786, ADM 106/2213, fo. 241; *Bradley*, p. 2.

3. Admiralty, Minute, 27 October 1786, ADM 3/102, and to Navy Board, 27 October 1786, ADM A/2816.

4. Deptford Officers to Navy Board, 1 and 6 November 1786, ADM 106/3321, fos 97, 98.

5. Navy Board, Minute, 31 October 1786, ADM 106/2622.

6. *Lady Penrhyn* Log, ADM 51/4376, fo. 2.

7. Navy Board to Treasury, 20 November 1786, T 1/639, no. 2702; *Alexander* Log, ADM 51/4375, fo. 4.

8. Phillip to Nepean, 4 January 1787, CO 201/2, fo. 103.

9. Teer to Navy Board, 4 December 1786, ADM 106/243, and Navy Board to Teer, 4 December 1786, ADM 106/2347, p. 166.

10. Teer to Navy Board, 7 December 1786 (two letters), ADM 106/243.

11. The first sign of this decision is in a memorandum written by Nepean for Middleton about 7 December 1786, ADM 106/243.

12. Treasury, Minute, 18 August 1786, T 29/58, p. 23.

13. Nepean to Middleton, 9 December 1786, CO 201/2, fos 49–50; Middleton to Nepean, 11 December 1786, CO 201/2, fos 51–2.

14. Navy Board, Minute, 6 December 1786, ADM 106/2622; Rose to Nepean, 7 December 1786, HO 35/7.

15. Teer to Navy Board, 13 and 15 December 1786, ADM 106/243; Navy Board, Minute, 14 December 1786, ADM 106/2622; Stephens to Smith, 18 January 1787, ADM 2/1178, p. 107.

16. Navy Board, Minutes, 8 and 18 January 1787, ADM 106/2623, and to Richards, 8 January 1787, ADM 106/2347, p. 178.

17. Tench to Ross, 14 January 1787, ADM A/2816; Ross to Stephens, 17 January 1787, Stephens to Navy Board, 17 January 1787, ADM A/2817; Navy Board, Minute, 18 January 1787, ADM 106/2623, and to Richards, 18 January 1787, ADM 106/2347, p. 183.

18. Stephens to Collins, 2 January, to Greenway and Pownoll, 13 January, to Lewis, 18 January, to Mackenzie, 20 January, to Prater, 26 January and to Smith, 27 January 1787, ADM 2/1178, pp. 82, 98–100, 107, 112, 117, 120.

19. Navy Board, Minute, 22 January 1787, ADM 106/2623, and to Shortland and Richards, 22 January 1787, ADM 106/2347, pp. 185, 187.

20. Phillip to Nepean, 12 December, Nepean to Rose, 13 December 1786, T 1/639, nos 2892 a and b; Rose to Navy Board, 19 December 1786, ADM OT; Navy Board, Minute, 27 December 1786, ADM 106/2622; Deptford Officers to Navy Board, 29 December 1786, ADM 106/3407, p. 34.

21. Ross to Phillip, 22 December 1786, CO 201/2, fos 71–3, and to Stephens, 11 January 1787, ADM 108/1D, fo. 192; Nepean to Rose, 17 January 1787, HO 36/5, pp. 235–6; Navy Board, Minutes, 17 January and 14 February 1787, ADM 106/2623.

22. Harrison, Gordon and Stanley to Navy Board, 6 November, and Navy Board to Treasury, 6 November 1786, T 1/639, no. 2575; Rose to Navy Board, 7 November 1786, T 27/38, p. 392; Navy Board, Minute, 29 November 1786, ADM 106/2622, and Thomas to Stiles, 29 November 1786, USNA, Record group 45/446. A 'cocket' was a certificate stating that goods had been entered in the Customs register, and the requisite duties paid upon them.

23. Navy Board, Minute, 28 November 1786, ADM 106/2622, and Thomas to Fisher, 28 November 1786, USNA, Record group 45/446; Navy Board to Treasury, 30 November 1786, T 1/639, no. 2791; Steele to Excise Board, 30 November 1786, T 27/38, p. 408; Jackson to Steele, 2 December 1786, T 1/639, no. 2702; Rose to Navy Board, 7 December 1786, ADM OT; Steele to Customs Board, 2 February 1787, T 11/34.

24. Phillip to Nepean, [c. 30 October 1786], HO 42/10, fo. 302; to Nepean, 15 November 1786, and Nepean to Steele, 15 November 1786, T 1/639, no. 2649; Rose to Customs Board, 22 November 1786, T 11/34; Stiles to Rose, 23 November 1786, T 1/639, no. 2746.

25. Sydney to Lord President, 1 December 1786, HO 43/2, pp. 180–1; Privy Council, Draft Order, [6 December 1786], HO 42/10, fos 296–9.

26. Privy Council, Orders-in-Council, 6 and 22 December 1786, PC 2/131, pp. 492–505, 505–19, 544–7, 540–3; 12 February and 20 April 1787, PC 2/132, pp. 36–9, 39–41, 158–60, 160–3.

27. See, e.g., Orders-in-Council, 12 and 14 March, HO 13/5, pp. 85–6, 86–7, 98.

28. Privy Council, Warrants, 3 and 20 January, 24 February, 5 and 10 March and 4 April 1787, HO 13/5, pp. 1–6, 31–2, 65–8, 74–5, 77, 129.

29. Nepean to Middleton, 9 December 1786, CO 201/2, fo. 50; Middleton to Nepean, 11 December 1786, CO 201/2, fos 51–2.
30. Nepean to Clerks, 13 December 1786, HO 13/4, p. 355; Sydney to Law Officers, 16 December 1786, HO 49/1, pp. 274–5; Law Officers to Sydney, 19 December 1786, HO 48/1A, p. 858.
31. Contract, 27 January 1787, Kingston, KE 2/4/6. (I am indebted to Gary Sturgess for this reference.)
32. Stephens to Johnston, 8 December 1786, ADM 2/1178, p. 35, and to Navy Board, 8 December 1786, ADM A/2816; Johnson to Stephens, 18 December 1786, ADM OT.
33. Campbell, Returns of convicts on the hulks, 13 January 1787, T 1/641; *Alexander* Log, ADM 51/4375, fos 5–6.
34. *Lady Penrhyn* Log, ADM 51/4376, fos 5–6, 8; *Smyth (2)*, p. 15.
35. Admiralty to Hood, Smith, Phillip and Ball, 11 January 1787, ADM 2/1178, pp. 93–5; *Bradley*, p. 9.
36. Smith to Stephens, 27 February 1787, ADM 1/3290; Marshall to Stephens, 27 February 1787, ADM 1/989; *Prince of Wales* Log, 7 March 1787, ADM 51/4376, fo. 8; *Lady Penrhyn* Log, 17 and 20 March 1787, ADM 51/4376, fo. 8.
37. Nepean to Campbell, 20 February 1787, HO 13/5, p. 58; Campbell to Erskine, [c. 20 February 1787], SLNSW, Mitchell MS ZA 3229, pp. 270–1; Privy Council, Warrant, 24 February 1787, HO 13/5, pp. 65–8.
38. Nepean to Thomas, 21 February 1787, [privately owned]; to Stephens, 23 February 1787, ADM 1/4152, no. 49; to Lewis, 25 February 1787, WO 1/685, pp. 85–6; Stephens to Martin, 26 February 1787, ADM 2/587, pp. 395–6; Marshall to Stephens, 4 March 1787, ADM 1/989.
39. Quoted in Thomas, p. 22.
40. Nepean to Stephens, 3 March 1787, ADM 1/4152, no. 52; Marshall to Stephens, 4 March 1787, ADM 1/987.
41. *Scarborough* Log, ADM 51/4376, fo. 9, which states that 185 convicts were embarked.
42. Sydney to Bradley, 5 March 1787, HO 13/5, pp. 74–5; *Friendship* Log, ADM 51/4376, fos 8–9; *Charlotte* Log, ADM 51/4375, fo. 9.
43. Privy Council, Warrant, 27 April 1787, HO 13/5, p. 172; John Townsend and William Badger, Accounts, 1 May, Sydney to Treasury, 14 May 1787, T 1/646, no. 1235; *Prince of Wales* Log, ADM 51/4376, fos 9, 10, 11; Richards to Nepean, 8 May 1787, CO 201/2, fo. 334.
44. Stephens to Long and Furzer, 21 February 1787, ADM 2/1178, pp. 145–6; Admiralty, Minute, 2 March 1787, ADM 3/102, and Minute, 30 April 1787, ADM 3/103; *Bradley*, p. 11.
45. Ross to Nepean, 18 April 1787, CO 201/2, fos 305–7; Richards to Nepean, 26 April 1787, CO 201/2, fos 315–6.
46. Richards to Nepean, 26 April 1787, CO 201/2, fos 315–6; Ross, Return, 6 May 1787, CO 201/2, fo. 333; and see O'Brien (1950), pp. 279–84.
47. This was John Irwin, who was acting as surgeon on the ship.
48. Phillip, 'State of the Garrison and Convicts that are on board the Transports, June 10th 1787', CO 201/2, fo. 172. (The slight variations in the numbers are due to the lack of precise details for those put on board in the week before the ships sailed, and to deaths and births between the beginning of May and arrival at Tenerife – for a detailed discussion, see O'Brien (1950)).

8. At Portsmouth

1. Navy Board to Treasury Secretaries, 5 September 1786, T 1/639, no. 2267; e.g., Sydney to Colqhitt, and to the mayor of Chester, 11 October 1786, HO 13/4, pp. 236–7.
2. Nepean, Memorandum, [c. 1 January 1787], SLNSW, Dixson MS Q 522. [The *Hampshire Chronicle*'s description of the route on 15 January 1787 was clearly based on this memorandum.]
3. *General Evening Post*, 27 February 1787; Collins, Entry, 7 March 1787, Orderly Book, RMM, Archive 11/51/5.
4. Fowell to John Fowell, 17 April 1787, *Fowell*, p. 36; Nepean to Middleton, 18 April 1787, CO 201/2, fo. 302.
5. Clark, p. 77; Shaw (1966), p. 54; Hughes, p. 70; Thomas, p. 14.
6. Rose to Nepean, 7 December 1786, HO 35/7; Nepean to Rose, 7 December 1786, T 1/639, no. 2850; Navy Board to Rose, 11 December 1786, T 1/639, no. 2876; Teer to Middleton, 15 December 1786, ADM 106/243.
7. The dates of the ships' departures and arrivals are mostly taken from their logs, ADM 51/4375–6, from reports to the Navy Board, and from the First Fleet journals. There are sometimes variations between one source and another; and whether the log or journal was kept according to land time or sea time can also give rise to differences.
8. Nepean to Rose, 8 January 1787, HO 36/5, pp. 229–30; Steele to Stephens, and to Navy Board, 10 January 1787, T 27/38, p. 458; Admiralty, Minutes, 16 January 1787, ADM 3/102, and to Phillip and Hunter, 16 January 1787, ADM 2/117, p. 280; Admiralty to Phillip, 2 March 1787, ADM 2/117, pp. 314–5, and to Navy Board, 2 March 1787, ADM 108/1D, fo. 203.
9. Phillip to Navy Board, 15 February 1787, ADM 106/1291; Navy Board, Minute, 15 February 1787, ADM 106/2623; Hunter to Marshall, 21 February 1787, ADM 1/989; Admiralty, Minute, 23 February 1787, ADM 3/102, and Stephens to Navy Board, 23 February 1787, ADM 2/587, p. 389; Phillip to Stephens, 24 February 1787, ADM 1/2308; Navy Board, Minute, 24 February 1787, ADM 106/2623; Hunter to Marshall, 24 February 1787, ADM 1/989; Phillip to Stephens, 30 March 1787, ADM 1/2308; Admiralty to Navy Board, 31 March 1787, ADM 2/263, p. 148.
10. Admiralty, Minute, 6 January 1787, ADM 3/102, and Stephens to Navy Board, 6 January 1787, ADM 2/587, pp. 284–5; Navy Board, Minute, 6 January 1787, ADM 106/2623, and to Ball, 6 January 1787, ADM 106/2347, p. 177; Thomas to Deptford Officers, 6 January 1787, USNA, Record group 45/446; Deptford Officers to Navy Board, 11 January 1787, ADM 106/3364, fo. 89; Admiralty, Minute, 24 February 1787, ADM 3/102, and Stephens to Marshall, 24 February 1787, ADM 2/587, p. 392; and Marshall to Stephens, 25 February 1787, ADM 1/989.
11. Admiralty, Minute, 26 February 1787, ADM 3/102, and Stephens to Marshall, 26 February 1787, ADM 2/587, pp. 397–8.
12. Navy Board, Minutes, 23 February and 5 March 1787, ADM 106/2623.
13. Phillip to Stephens, 22 March 1787, ADM 1/2308; Admiralty, Minute, 22 March 1787, ADM 3/102.
14. Navy Board, Minutes, 5, 19 and 22 March 1787, ADM 106/2623, and to Shortland, 5, 19 and 22 March, and to Martin, 28 March 1787, ADM 106/2347, pp. 187, 211, 214, 217, 219.

15. Thomas to Shortland, 2 January 1787, USNA, Record group 45/446; Phillip to Nepean, 4 January 1787, CO 201/2, fo. 103; Stephens to Navy Board, 25 January 1787, ADM 2/1178, p. 116; Navy Board to Laforey, 26 January and 3 February 1787, ADM 106/2347, pp. 189, 192; Meredith and Walton to Stephens, 21 February 1787, ADM 108/1D, fo. 200; Navy Board, Minute, 26 February 1787, ADM 106/2623, and to Laforey, 26 February 1787, ADM 106/2347, p. 206.

16. Navy Board, Minutes, 8 and 31 January 1787, ADM 106/2623, and to Teer, 31 January 1783, ADM 106/2347, p. 192.

17. Ross to Stephens, 13 April 1787, CO 201/2, fo. 298; Stephens to Navy Board, 16 April 1787, ADM 108/1D, fo. 212; Navy Board, Minutes, 16 and 19 April 1787, ADM 106/2623, and to Martin, 16 and 19 April 1787, ADM 106/2347, pp. 233–4; Hunter to Phillip, 18 April 1787, [privately owned].

18. Navy Board, Minute, 28 March 1787, ADM 106/2623, and to Martin, 28 March 1787, ADM 106/2347, p. 219; Navy Board, Minutes, 9 March and 5 April 1787, ADM 106/2623, and 2 May 1787, ADM 106/2624, and to Shortland, 2 May 1787, ADM 106/2347, p. 228.

19. Admiralty, Minute, 26 February 1787, ADM 3/102, and Stephens to Marshall, 26 February 1787, ADM 2/587, pp. 397–8; Navy Board, Minute, 27 February 1787, ADM 106/2623; Marshall to Stephens, 28 February 1787, ADM 1/989; Navy Board, Minutes, 28 February, 2 and 5 March 1787, ADM 106/2623; Navy Board to Phillip, 2 March 1787, ADM 106/2347, pp. 209–10; Phillip to Stephens, 20 and 22 March 1787, ADM 1/2308; Navy Board, Minute, 16 March 1787, ADM 106/2623, and to Shortland, 22 March 1787, ADM 106/2347, p. 217; e.g., Navy Board to Shortland and Richards, 13 March 1787, ADM 106/2347, p. 213.

20. Stephens to Greenway, 28 February and 10 March, to Collins, 13 March, to Ross, 16 March 1787, ADM 2/1178, pp. 158, 183, 191, 195; Stephens to Smith, 13 March, and to Pownoll, 16 March 1787, ADM 2/1178, pp. 190, 196–7; Navy Board, Minutes, 20 March and 20 April 1787, ADM 106/2623.

21. Ross to Stephens, 13 April 1787, CO 201/2, fo. 299; Nepean to Stephens, 18 April 1787, ADM 1/4152, no. 63; Navy Board, Minute, 20 April 1787, ADM 106/2623; Richards to Nepean, 5 April 1787, CO 201/2, fo. 294.

22. Phillip to Nepean, 11 April 1787, CO 201/2, fo. 126.

23. Phillip to Nepean, 18 March 1787, CO 201/2, fo. 123; Middleton to Nepean, 20 March 1787, CO 201/2, fo. 243; Navy Board, Minute, 27 March 1787, ADM 106/2623.

24. *Clark*, pp. 247, 249.

25. Navy Board, Minute, 16 March 1787, ADM 106/2623; Stephens to Navy Board, 20 March 1787, ADM A/2817; Hunter to Stephens, 28 March 1787, ADM A/2818; Admiralty, Minute, 31 March 1787, ADM 3/102; Stephens to Navy Board, 2 April 1787, ADM A/2818.

26. Ball to Marshall, 27 March 1787, ADM 1/989; Admiralty, Minute, 29 March 1787, ADM 3/102, and Stephens to Marshall, 29 March 1787, ADM 2/587, p. 498; Marshall to Stephens, 2 April 1787, ADM A/2818; Admiralty, Minute, 3 April 1787, ADM 3/103, and Stephens to Marshall and Navy Board, 3 April 1787, ADM 2/587, pp. 519, 521–2.

27. White to Nepean, 27 February 1787, CO 201/2, fo. 220.

28. Fowell to John Fowell, 17 April 1787, *Fowell*, p. 36.

29. Stephens to Smith, 6 and 26 March, to Morrison, 14 March 1787, ADM 2/1178, pp. 76, 194, 202–3.

30. Clark to Phillip, 3 and 16 April 1787, Phillip to Clark, 10, 13 and 17 April, Howe to Clark, 16 April 1787, *Clark*, pp. 241–5.

31. *Clark*, pp. 19, 65, 94, 97.

32. Hunter to Phillip, 18 April 1787, [privately owned]; Navy Board, Minute, 19 April 1787, ADM 106/2623.

33. Sydney to Admiralty, 31 August 1786, ADM 1/4152, no. 25; Stephens to Tupper and Hughes, 8 October 1786, ADM 1/1177, p. 492; Ross to Stephens, 8 May 1787, CO 201/2, fo. 338.

34. *Alexander* marines, Petition, 7 April, *Prince of Wales* marines, Petition, 4 May, *Charlotte* marines, Petition, 7 May, *Scarborough* marines, Petition, 7 May 1787, CO 201/2, fos 327, 340, 342, 344; Phillip to Nepean, 8 May, Ross to Stephens, 8 May, Stephens to Nepean, 9 May 1787, CO 201/2, fos 150, 336, 338.

35. Sydney to Middleton, Middleton to Thomas, Thomas to Middleton, 23 April 1787, NLA, MS 1399; Sydney to Phillip, 5 May, Phillip to Nepean, 11 May 1787, CO 201/2, fos 146, 154–5.

36. *Tench*, pp. 11–12.

9. *Preparing Bodies for the Voyage*

1. Clark, p. 77; Shaw (1966), pp. 53–4; Mackay, pp. 69–70; Hughes, pp. 70–1; Hill, p. 45.

2. Phillip to Nepean, 18 March 1788, CO 201/2, fos 122–3.

3. Navy Board to Rose, 11 December 1786, T 1/639, no. 2876; Sydney to Treasury, 22 December 1786, T 1/639, no. 2984; Navy Board, Minute, 26 December 1786, ADM 106/2622, and Thomas to Wadham, *et al.*, 26 December 1786, USNA, Record group 45/446.

4. Navy Board, Minutes, 20 and 22 January 1787, ADM 106/2623; Teer to Navy Board, 22 January 1787, ADM 106/243.

5. Navy Board, Minute, 16 March 1787, ADM 106/2623, and to Shortland, 16 March 1787, ADM 106/2347, p. 214; Phillip to Nepean, 18 March 1787, CO 201/2, fos 122–3; Nepean to Middleton, 18 April 1787, NMM, MID 1/131.

6. Navy Board, Minutes, 9, 19 and 20 April 1787, ADM 106/2623, and to Shortland, 9 and 20 April, and to Martin, 19 April 1787, ADM 106/2347, pp. 223–5.

7. Treasury to Navy Board, 10 May 1787, ADM/OT; Navy Board, Minutes, 7, 9, and 14 May 1787, ADM 106/2624, and to Shortland, 7 May, and to Martin, 11 May 1787, ADM 106/2347, p. 229; Steele to Navy Board, 10 May 1787, ADM OT; Thomas to Yerbury, *et al.*, 11 and 16 May 1787, USNA, Record group 45/446.

8. *Howard*, pp. 236–7, 266, 272, 275, 276, 290, 341.

9. Navy Board, Minute, 8 February 1787, ADM 106/2623; Sydney to Admiralty, 19 March 1787, ADM 1/4152, no. 56; Admiralty to Navy Board, 20 March 1787, ADM 108/1D, fo. 208; Navy Board, Minute, 20 March 1787, ADM 106/2623; *Alexander* Log, ADM 51/4375, fos 8–10; and see Watt (1989), p. 140.

10. *Nagle*, p. 106.

11. Watt (1981), p. 12; Gordon, pp. 155–66.

12. C. R. Markham, ed., *The Hawkins' Voyages* (Burt Franklin, New York, 1970), p. 163.

13. *Banks*, vol. 1, pp. 243–4, 251, vol. 2, pp. 74, 301.

14. Phillip, Memorandum, [c. 1 October 1786], and to Sydney, 12 March 1787, CO 201/2, fos 88, 121.

15. *Collins*, p. 1.

16. Balmain to Shortland, Shortland to Navy Board, 17 February 1787, T 1/643, no. 409; Navy Board, Minutes, 19 and 22 February 1787, ADM 106/2623, and to Treasury Secretaries, 19 February 1787, T 1/643, no. 409; Admiralty, Minute, 21 February 1787, ADM 3/102, and Stephens to Navy Board, 21 February 1787, ADM 2/587, p. 379; Steele to Navy Board, 21 February 1787, ADM OT; Navy Board, Minute, 22 February, ADM 106/2623, and to Shortland and Richards, 22 February 1787, ADM 106/2347, pp. 203–4.

17. Phillip to Sydney, Nepean to Middleton, and Middleton to Nepean, 28 February 1787, CO 201/2, fos 96–7, 112, and [privately owned].

18. Navy Board, Minute, 6 March 1787, ADM 106/2623, and to Shortland, 6 March 1787, ADM 106/2347, p. 211.

19. Phillip to Nepean, 18 March 1787, CO 201/2, fo. 122; Navy Board, Minutes, 19 and 21 March 1787, ADM 106/2623, and to Shortland and Richards, 21 March 1787, ADM 106/2347, pp. 216–17; *Tench*, p. 12.

20. Middleton to Nepean, 28 February 1787, CO 201/2, fo. 96. For the date of the contract, see Navy Board, Minute, 27 November 1786, ADM 106/2622.

21. Phillip to Sydney, 12 March 1787, CO 201/2, fos 120–1.

22. Phillip to Admiralty, 27 December 1786, ADM 1/2308; Admiralty to Phillip, 23 February 1787, CO 201/2, fos 118–9; Navy Board, Minutes, 28 February and 2 March 1787, ADM 106/2623; Middleton to Nepean, 28 February 1787, CO 201/2, fo. 96.

23. Phillip to Sydney, Nepean to Middleton and Middleton to Nepean, 28 February 1787, CO 201/2, fos 96–7, 112, and [privately owned]; Navy Board, Minute, 28 February 1787, ADM 106/2623, and to Phillip and Richards, 28 February 1787, ADM 106/2347, p. 208; Phillip to Nepean, 1 March 1787, CO 201/2, fos 114–5.

24. Phillip to Sydney, 12 March 1787, CO 201/2, fo. 120; Navy Board, Minute, 25 April 1787, ADM 106/2623, and to Phillip, 25 April 1787, ADM 106/2347, pp. 227–8.

25. Privy Council, Instructions to Phillip, 25 April 1787, CO 201/2, fos 30–1; Nepean to Richards, 25 April 1787, HO 13/5, pp. 165–6; Phillip to Nepean, 11 May 1787, CO 201/2, fo. 154.

26. Lloyd and Coulter, p. 92.

27. White to Phillip, and Phillip to Stephens, 7 February 1787, ADM 1/2308; Phillip to Nepean, 7 February 1787, CO 201/2, fo. 108; Stephens to Navy Board, 10 February 1787, ADM A/2187; Navy Board, Minute, 12 February 1787, ADM 106/2623, and to Phillip, Martin and Laforey, 12 February 1787, ADM 106/2347, pp. 196–7; Nepean to Middleton, 13 February 1787, [privately owned]; Middleton to Nepean, 13 February 1787, CO 201/2, fo. 214; Navy Board, Minute, 28 February 1787, ADM 106/2623, and to Cawthorne, 28 February 1787, ADM 106/2347, p. 207; Navy Board, Minute, 12 March 1787, ADM 106/2623, and to White, Shortland and Cawthorne, 12 March 1787, ADM 106/2347, pp. 212–3.

28. Phillip to Nepean, 18 March 1787, CO 201/2, fos 122–4; Navy Board, Minutes, 19 and 21 March 1787, ADM 106/2623, and to Shortland and Richards, 21 March 1787, ADM 106/2347, pp. 216–7; Middleton to Nepean, 20 March 1787, CO 201/2, fo. 243.

29. Navy Board, Minute, 4 April 1787, ADM 106/2623, and to Cawthorne and Martin, 4 April 1787, ADM 106/2347, p. 222; Phillip to Nepean, 11 April 1787, CO 201/2, fo. 126; Nepean to Middleton, 18 April 1787, NMM MID 1/131; Navy Board, Minutes, 20 and 23 April 1787, ADM 106/2623, and to Shortland and Richards, 20 and 23 April 1787, ADM 106/2347, pp. 225–6; Phillip to Nepean, 11 May 1787, CO 201/2, fo. 154.

30. *Smyth (2)*, p. 47.
31. *Collins*, p. 1.
32. Navy Board, Minute, 28 February 1787, ADM 106/2623; Phillip to Nepean, 18 March 1787, CO 201/2, fo. 124.
33. *Bath Chronicle*, 5 April 1787.
34. White, Return, 15 November 1788, CO 201/3, fo. 160; *Collins*, p. 1.
35. Pemberton to Dundas, [September 1785], BL, OIOC G 9/1, pp. 18–25; Grimes to Grimes, 21 October 1792, *HRNSW*, vol. 1, part 2, p. 672; Wordsworth, p. 154.
36. Phillip to Sydney, 2 September 1787, CO 201/2, fo. 176; Collins to his father, 6 November 1787, SLNSW, Mitchell MS 700.
37. Watt (1989), p. 144; Phillip to Sydney, 2 September 1787, CO 201/2, fo. 176.
38. Knight, p. 131.

10. *Leaving the World*

1. See *Botany Bay: The Real Story*, pp. 117–8.
2. For details, see Frost (1987).
3. Phillip, Memorandum, [c. 1 October 1786], CO 201/2, fos 88–93; and other documents cited following.
4. Nepean, Memorandum, [c. 1 January 1787], SLNSW, Dixson Add. MS Q 522.
5. *Worgan*, p. 12.
6. Privy Council, Instructions to Phillip, 25 April 1787, CO 201/1, fos 30–2.
7. Nepean to Middleton, 4 May 1787, NMM MID 1/131; Middleton to Nepean, 4 May 1787, CO 201/2, fo. 329.
8. Sydney to Admiralty, 5 May 1787, CO 201/2, fo. 331; Admiralty, Minute, 7 May 1787, ADM 3/103, and to Phillip, 7 May 1787, ADM 2/117, p. 397.
9. *Smyth (2)*, pp. 44–5.
10. For more on the development of the chronometer, see Sobel.
11. Phillip to Sydney, 5 June, and to Nepean, 2 September 1787 CO 201/2, fos 162, 182.
12. *Bradley*, p. 12.
13. *Smyth (2)*, p. 16.
14. *Collins*, p. lvii; Phillip to Sydney, 5 June and 6 August 1787, CO 201/2, fos 162, 174.
15. Phillip to Nepean, 5 June 1787, CO 201/2, fo. 169.
16. Phillip to Sydney, 5 June, and to Nepean, 5 and 10 June 1787, CO 201/2, fos 162, 168, 170.
17. *Collins*, p. lxiii; *Tench*, p. 17; *White*, p. 54.
18. Phillip to Nepean, 2 September 1787, CO 201/2, fos 182–4; *Bradley*, p. 38.
19. *Smyth (2)*, pp. 29, 34; *Clark*, p. 36.
20. *Smyth (2)*, p. 29.
21. Phillip to Nepean, 2 September 1787, CO 201/2, fos 182–4; *Easty*, p. 30; *White*, p. 73; Phillip to Sydney, 2 September 1787, CO 201/2, fo. 176.
22. Phillip to Nepean, 2 September 1787, CO 201/2, fos 182–4.
23. Phillip to Banks, 31 August 1787, Sutro, Banks EN 1/29, and 2 September 1787, SLNSW, Mitchell MS C 213, pp. 3–5; *Collins*, p. lxxx.
24. Phillip to Stephens, 10 November 1787, ADM 1/2308; *King*, p. 21; *Collins*, p. lxxix; *White*, p. 90.
25. *White*, p. 90.
26. Southwell to Butler, 11 November 1787, BL, Add. MS 16381, fo. 25.

27. *Tench*, p. 26; *White*, p. 81 (of Rio de Janeiro).
28. Phillip to Nepean, 28 October 1786, HO 42/9, fo. 83; *Worgan*, p. 1; *Hunter*, p. 21; *Tench*, p. 28.
29. *Worgan*, p. 1; *Collins*, p. lxxx.
30. Southwell to his mother, 11 November 1787, BL, Add. MS 16381, fo. 23.
31. Cook to Walker, 20 November 1772, NLNZ Turnbull, MS Papers 0230–30; *Collins*, p. lxxxvi.
32. *White*, p. 101; *Tench*, p. 28.
33. *Worgan*, p. 1; Masson to Banks, 13 November 1787, Sutro, Banks EN 1/36.
34. *Tench*, p. 66.
35. *King*, pp. 24–31; Phillip to Middleton, 6 July 1788 [privately owned].
36. *Smyth (2)*, pp. 50–4.
37. *Tench*, p. 31.
38. Blackburn to his sister, 5 June 1787, AJCP, Reel M 970.
39. *Collins*, p. 1.
40. This summary is based on the journals of the First Fleet officers.

11. *No Cheaper Mode?*

1. Hancock, p. 11; Mackay, p. 51; Shaw (1984), p. 90, and cf. Shaw (1955), p. 43. Pitt's speech of 9 February 1791 is reported in *PH*, vol. 28 (1789–91), cols 1223–5.
2. Campbell was contracted to accommodate 250 convicts on the Justitia for £1818 per quarter, and 240 on the Censor for £1625 – i.e., 490 for a total of £13,772 per annum, or £28 per person. In practice, the actual cost might vary a little, according to whether the hulks were over or under complement, and to what was paid surgeons and clergymen. Reflecting what I take to be information from the Home Office, the Daily Universal Register announced on 23 November 1786 that 'The expense of keeping the convicts on board the hulks, amounted communibas annis, to about £28 each man per annum. The transporting of them to Botany Bay will cost the public, it is computed, £32 each nearly.' It seems best to settle on £28 as the base figure.
3. Moloney, p. 22.
4. Coggan and Campbell, Testimony, 12 May 1785, HO 7/1.
5. Nepean's queries, and Campbell's replies [before 22 January 1786], HO 42/10, fos 426–7; Campbell's detailed accounts of the cost of the ship, and his lists of the food and tools that would be needed, are in HO 42/8, no. 9 and HO 42/10, fo. 427; and his letter to Nepean, 22 January 1786, HO 42/8, no. 8.
6. [   ], Estimate, [undated, but August 1786], HO 42/10, fo. 425. (In some of these lists, the figures for £s only are given. Generally I have followed this practice. I have also supplied totals when these are not in the originals.)
7. [Nepean], Estimate, [undated, but August 1786], HO 42/7, fo. 23. There are some discrepancies between the figures in this list and those in the next.
8. [Nepean], 'Staff Establishment for the Settlement at New South Wales', [undated, but August 1786], HO 35/1.
9. [Nepean], Estimate, [undated, but August 1786], HO 42/7, fo. 24.
10. Nepean to Middleton, 12 December 1786, CO 201/2, fo. 53; Middleton to Pitt, 13 December 1786, [privately owned]. (In this list and those following, I have not adjusted the figure to the nearest pound. Rather, I have simply left off all shillings and pence.)

11. I have derived these figures from:
    Ships and marines: Stephens to Nepean, 28 December 1786, CO 201/2, fo. 43.
    Civil establishment: Nepean, 'An Account of Expenses Incurred in Transporting
    and Maintaining the Convicts Sent to New South Wales', February 1790,
    CO 201/4, fo. 189, where he gives the annual cost as £2877.10.0.
    Ordnance: Rogers, 'Estimate of the Expense of Ordnance …', [c. 21 December
    1786], CO 201/2, fo. 69.
12. [Middleton], 'An Account of the Expenses incurred and that will probably attend
    the Botany Bay establishment', 18 April 1787, [privately owned].
13. This is a composite list, compiled from: Middleton, 'Calculations given to
    Mr. Nepean Feby 1790 concerning convicts and Botany Bay', [privately owned];
    Nepean, Lists, [undated], CO 201/4, ff. 182–90, 191–9; and Navy Board, 'An Account
    of the Total Expense incurred in our department for the settlements in New South
    Wales …', 5 June 1793, HRNSW, vol. 2, pp. 38–9. I have also re-arranged the
    sequence of Middleton's items somewhat, so as to make the phases clearer.
14. This was the number of women first intended to be sent. In the event, 192 women
    convicts and marines' wives sailed, so that the cost in the clause is significantly
    understated.
15. This item does not appear in Middleton's list. However, it is included in the yet
    fuller one dated 5 June 1793 – see *HRNSW*, vol. 2, p. 38.
16. Middleton gave the figures for the nine transports and store ships separately.
17. Middleton calculated this expense variously at £31,663 (December 1786), £34,375
    (April 1787) and £39,209 (April 1787). I have therefore used the last figure.
18. From List, 5 June 1793, *HRNSW*, vol. 2, p. 39.
19. List, CO 201/4, fo. 195.
20. Ross to Nepean, 10 July 1788, *HRNSW*, vol. 1, part 2, p. 176; Blainey (1966), p. 17.
21. *PH*, vol. 28 (1789–91), cols 1221–5.
22. *Botany Bay: The Real Story*, pp. 152–4.
23. Memorandum, 14 February 1791, Court of Directors, Proposed terms, [c. 17 March
    1790]; and 'Observations on the Paper returned from the Court of Directors',
    BT 6/227; 'Heads of the proposed New Bill', 28 March 1791, BL, Add. MS 38350,
    pp. 284–7.
24. Dundas to Phillip, 10 January 1792, *HRNSW*, vol. 1, part 2, p. 585.

Conclusion

1. Mackay, p. 57.
2. Atkinson, pp. 59–61; Christopher, p. 335.
3. Phillip, Memorandum, [c. 1 October 1786], CO 201/2, fo. 92.
4. Camden to Sydney, 11 January 1787, Clements, Sydney vol. 14.
5. Roberts to Ross, [c. January 1785], HO 42/5, fo. 466; Barnes and others,
    Memorandum, [4 February 1785], HO 35/1.
6. Nepean to Steele, 10 June 1786, T 1/632, no. 1407.
7. See *Botany Bay: The Real Story*, pp. 146–7.
8. Pitt to Rolle, 6 May 1786, PRO 30/8/195, fo. 31.
9. Richards to Pitt, 28 September 1786, PRO 30/8/171, fo. 17.
10. Phillip, Memorandum, [c. 1 October 1786], CO 201/2, fo. 92.
11. Phillip to Nepean, 28 October 1786, HO 42/9, fo. 84; to Sydney, 1 November 1786,
    SLNSW, Dixson MS Q 162, pp. 1–2; to Clark, 13 April 1787, *Clark*, p. 243.

12. Phillip to Lansdowne, 3 July 1788, SLNSW, Mitchell MS 7241; to Sydney, 6 July 1788, SLNSW, Dixson MS Q 162, pp. 9–10; to Middleton, 6 July 1788, [privately owned].
13. Sydney to Admiralty, 31 August 1786, ADM 1/4152, no. 25.
14. Phillip, Memorandum, [c. 1 October 1786], fos 90, 92.
15. Phillip to Nepean, 1 March 1787, CO 201/2, fo. 115; Privy Council, Instructions to Phillip, 25 April 1787, fos 38–9.
16. Privy Council, Draft Additional Instructions to Phillip, 23 June 1789, HO 31/1, which were approved by the Privy Council on 8 August 1789, PC 2/134, pp. 188–92; Attorney-General, 'Draft of a Warrant for a Commission authorizing the Governor of New South Wales to remit Sentences', 8 November 1790, HO 48/1B, pp. 345–50; 30 Geo. III, c. 47, *Statutes at Large*, vol. 16 (London, 1784), p. 57.
17. Phillip to Sydney, 5 June, and to Nepean, 6 June and 2 September 1787, CO 201/2, fos 162, 168–9, 182.
18. Phillip to Nepean, 11 April 1787, CO 201/2, fo. 128.
19. *Fowell*, p. 57.
20. Sydney to Treasury, 31 October 1788, HO 35/9.
21. *Reading Mercury and Oxford Gazette*, 6 November 1786; *Hampshire Chronicle*, 2 April 1787; and cf. *Bath Chronicle*, 5 April 1787.
22. See Frost (1994), pp. 144–58.
23. Blainey (1966), p. 17.
24. Phillip to Nepean, 18 March 1787, CO 201/2, fo. 123.
25. Miles to the African Committee, 1 February 1783, T 70/33, pp. 53–4.
26. John Barnes and others, Memorandum, [4 February 1785], HO 35/1.
27. Reece, pp. 155–65.
28. Ibid., pp. 166–90.
29. Teer to Navy Board, 7 December 1786, ADM 106/243.
30. *Smyth (2)*, p. 47; *Collins*, p. 2.
31. See Frost (1995), p. 84.
32. Elizabeth Magra, Memorial, 31 March 1780, AO 13/56; Commissioners, Decision, 20 May 1783, AO 12/99.
33. Danforth, Memorial, 8 September 1783, quoted in Norton, p. [vii].
34. Phillip to Grenville, 20 June 1790, *HRNSW*, vol. 1, part 2, p. 351.
35. Knight, p. 136.

Select Bibliography

R.G. Albion, *Forests and Sea Power: The Timber Problem of the Royal Navy, 1652–1862* (Harvard University Press, Cambridge, Mass., 1926).

Alan Atkinson, *The Europeans in Australia, 1: The Beginnings* (Oxford University Press, Melbourne, 1997).

Bernard Bailyn, *Atlantic History: Concept and Contours* (Harvard University Press, Cambridge, Mass., 2005).

George Barrington, *The History of New South Wales* (London, 1802).

G.B. Barton, *History of New South Wales from the Records*, 2 vols (Charles Potter, Government Printer, Sydney, 1889–94).

Charles Bateson, *The Convict Ships, 1787–1868*, 2nd ed. (A.H. and A.W. Reed, Sydney, 1974 [1969]).

Daniel Baugh, *British Naval Administration in the Age of Walpole* (Princeton University Press, Princeton, NJ, 1965).

J.M. Beattie, *Crime and the Courts in England, 1660–1800* (Princeton University Press, Princeton, NJ, 1986).

Geoffrey Blainey, *The Tyranny of Distance: How Distance Shaped Australia's History* (Sun Books, Melbourne, 1966).

Geoffrey Blainey, 'A Reply: I came, I Shaw …', *Historical Studies*, vol. 13 (1968), pp. 204–6.

Geoffrey Blainey, 'Botany Bay or Gotham City?', *Australian Economic History Review*, vol. 8 (1968), pp. 154–63.

David Blair, *The History of Australasia* (McCreedy, Thompson and Niven, Glasgow, Melbourne and Dunedin, 1878).

G.C. Bolton, 'The Hollow Conqueror: Flax and the Foundation of Australia', *Australian Economic History Review*, vol. 8 (1968), pp. 3–16.

G.C. Bolton, 'Broken Reeds and Smoking Flax', *Australian Economic History Review*, vol. 9 (1969), pp. 64–70.

John Brewer, *The Sinews of Power: War, Money and the English State, 1688–1783* (Unwin Hyman, London, 1989).

Asa Briggs, *The Making of Modern England, 1783–1867: The Age of Improvement* (Harper and Row, New York, 1965 [1959]).

W.S. Campbell, 'Arthur Phillip', *JRAHS*, vol. 21 (1935), pp. 264–6.

A.K. Cavanagh, 'The Return of the First Fleet Ships', *The Great Circle*, vol. 11, no. 2 (1989), pp. 1–16.

J.D. Chambers and G.E. Mingay, *The Agricultural Revolution, 1750–1880* (Batsford, London, 1966).

Emma Christopher, *A Merciless Place: The Lost Story of Britain's Convict Disaster in Africa and How it Led to the Settlement of Australia* (Allen & Unwin, Sydney, 2010).

C.M.H. Clark, *A History of Australia, vol. 1: From the Earliest Times to the Age of Macquarie* (Melbourne University Press, Melbourne, 1962).

Stephen Conway, 'The Recruitment of Criminals into the British Army, 1775–81', *Bulletin of the Institute of Historical Research*, vol. 58 (1985).

R.M. Crawford, *Australia* (Hutchinson, London, 1952).

Victor Crittenden, *A Bibliography of the First Fleet* (Australian National University Press, Canberra, 1981).

Victor Crittenden, *The Voyage of the First Fleet, 1787–1788: Taken from Contemporary Accounts* (Mulini Press, Canberra, c. 1981).

F.K. Crowley, 'The Foundation Years, 1788–1821', in *Australia: A Social and Political History*, ed. Gordon Greenwood (Angus and Robertson, Sydney, 1955).

K.M. Dallas, 'The First Settlement in Australia, considered in relation to sea-power in world politics', *Tasmanian Historical Research Association: Papers and Proceedings*, no. 3 (1952).

John Ehrman, *The Younger Pitt: The Years of Acclaim* (Constable, London, 1969).

A. Roger Ekirch, 'Bound for America: A Profile of British Convicts Transported to the Colonies, 1718–1775', *William and Mary Quarterly*, 3rd series, vol. 42 (1985).

A. Roger Ekirch, *Bound for America: The Transportation of British Convicts to the Colonies, 1718–1775* (Clarendon Press, Oxford, 1987).

M. Barnard Eldershaw, *Phillip of Australia: An Account of the Settlement of Sydney Cove, 1788–92* (Harrup, London, 1938).

Toyin Falola and Kevin D. Roberts, eds, *The Atlantic World, 1450–2000* (Indiana University Press, Bloomington, 2008).

Roderick Flanagan, *The History of New South Wales*, 2 vols (London, 1862).

B.H. Fletcher, *Landed Enterprise and Penal Society* (Sydney University Press, Sydney, 1976).

Alan Frost, *Convicts and Empire: A Naval Question, 1776–1811* (Oxford University Press, Melbourne, 1980).

Alan Frost, 'Botany Bay: An imperial venture of the 1780s', *English Historical Review*, vol. 100 (1985).

Alan Frost, *Arthur Phillip, 1738–1814: His Voyaging* (Oxford University Press, Melbourne, 1987).

Alan Frost, *Sir Joseph Banks and the Transfer of Plants to and from the South Pacific, 1786–1798* (The Colony Press, Melbourne, 1993).

Alan Frost, *Botany Bay Mirages* (Melbourne University Press, Melbourne, 1994).

Alan Frost, 'The Planting of New South Wales: Sir Joseph Banks and the creation of an Antipodean Europe', in *Sir Joseph Banks: A Global Perspective*, eds R.E.R. Banks, et al. (Royal Botanic Gardens, Kew, London, 1994), pp. 133–47.

Alan Frost, *The Precarious Life of James Mario Matra: Voyager with Cook; American Loyalist; Servant of Empire* (The Miegunyah Press, Melbourne, 1995).

Alan Frost, *The Global Reach of Empire* (Melbourne University Publishing, Melbourne, 2003).

Mollie Gillen, 'The Botany Bay Decision, 1786: convicts, not empire', *English Historical Review*, vol. 97 (1982).

Mollie Gillen, *The Founders of Australia: A Biographical Dictionary of the First Fleet* (Library of Australian History, Sydney, 1989).

Mollie Gillen, 'His Majesty's Mercy: The circumstances of the First Fleet', *The Push*, no. 29 (1991), pp. 47–109.

E.C.K. Gonner, 'The Settlement of Australia', *English Historical Review*, vol. 23 (1888).

E.C. Gordon, 'Scurvy and Anson's Voyage Round the World, 1740–1744: An analysis of the Royal Navy's worst outbreak', *American Neptune*, vol. 44 (1984), pp. 155–66.

Sir W.K. Hancock, *Australia* (Ernest Benn, London, 1930).

Graeme Henderson and Myra Stanbury, *The* Sirius: *Past and Present* (Collins Australia, Sydney, 1988).

David Hill, *1788: The Brutal Truth of the First Fleet* (Heinemann, Sydney, 2008).

Edward Hughes, *Studies in Administration and Finance, 1558–1825* (Porcupine Press, Philadelphia, 1980 [1934]).

Robert Hughes, *The Fatal Shore: A History of the Transportation of Convicts to Australia, 1787–1868* (Harvill Collins, London, 1987).

W. Branch Johnson, *The English Prison Hulks*, 2nd ed. (Phillimore, London, 1970).

Thomas Keneally, *Australians, vol. 1: Origins to Eureka* (Allen and Unwin, Sydney, 2009).

Jonathan King, *The First Fleet: The Convict Voyage that Founded Australia, 1787–88* (Macmillan, Melbourne, 1982).

Robert J. King, 'George Vancouver and the contemplated settlement at Nootka Sound', *The Great Circle*, vol. 32, no. 1 (2010), pp. 6–34.

Roger Knight, 'The First Fleet: Its state and preparation, 1786–1787', in *Studies from Terra Australis to Australia*, eds John Hardy and Alan Frost (Australian Academy of the Humanities, Canberra, 1989), pp. 121–36, 256–62.

J.D. Lang, *An Historical and Statistical Account of New South Wales*, 2 vols (Cochrane and M'Crone, London, 1834).

John H. Langbein, '*Albion*'s Fatal Flaws', *Past and Present*, no. 98 (1983).

Philip Lawson, 'The Missing Link: The Imperial Dimension in Understanding Hanoverian Britain', *The Historical Journal*, vol. 29 (1986).

C. Lloyd and J.L.S. Coulter, *Medicine and the Navy, 1200–1900, vol. 3: 1714–1815* (Edinburgh, Livingstone, 1961).

Neil K. Macintosh, *Richard Johnson: Chaplain to the Colony of New South Wales* (Library of Australian History, Sydney, 1978).

David Mackay, *A Place of Exile: The European Settlement of New South Wales* (Oxford University Press, Melbourne, 1985).

R.W. Malcolmson, '"A set of ungovernable people": The Kingswood colliers in the eighteenth century', in *An Ungovernable People: The English and Their Law in the Seventeenth and Eighteenth Centuries*, ed. John Brewer and John Styles (Rutgers University Press, New Brunswick, NJ, 1980).

Ged Martin, ed., *The Founding of Australia: The Argument about Australia's Origins* (Hale and Iremonger, Sydney, 1978).

John Molony, *The Penguin Bicentennial History of Australia: The Story of 200 Years* (Viking, Melbourne, 1987).

John Moore, *The First Fleet Marines, 1786–1792* (University of Queensland Press, St Lucia, 1987).

Kenneth Morgan, 'The Organization of the Convict Trade to Maryland: Stevenson, Randolph and Cheston, 1768–1775', *William and Mary Quarterly*, 3rd series, vol. 42 (1985).

Mary Beth Norton, *The British-Americans: The Loyalist Exiles in England, 1774–1789* (Little, Brown and Company, Boston, 1972).

Eris O'Brien, *The Foundation of Australia (1786–1800): A Study of English Criminal*

Practice and Penal Colonization in the Eighteenth Century (Sheed & Ward, London, 1937).

Eris O'Brien, *The Foundation of Australia (1786–1800): A Study in English Criminal Practice and Penal Colonisation in the Eighteenth Century* (Sheed and Ward, London, 1937; 2nd ed., Angus and Robertson, Sydney, 1950).

Wilfrid Oldham, *Britain's Convicts to the Colonies* (Library of Australian History, Sydney, 1990).

Bob Reece, *The Origins of Irish Convict Transportation to New South Wales* (Palgrave, Basingstoke, 2001).

David Richardson, 'Cultures of Exchange: Atlantic Africa in the Era of the Slave Trade', in *Transactions of the Royal Historical Society*, 6th series, vol. 19 (Cambridge University Press, Cambridge, 2009).

Sir Herbert Richmond, *The Navy in India, 1763–1783* (Ernest Benn, London, 1931).

N.A.M. Rodger, *The Wooden World: An Anatomy of the Georgian Navy* (Naval Institute Press, Annapolis, 1986).

Michael Roe, 'Motives for Australian Settlement: A document', *Tasmanian Historical Research Association: Papers and Proceedings*, no. 4 (1952).

Michael Roe, 'Australia's Place in the "Swing to the East", 1788–1810', *Historical Studies*, vol. 8 (1958).

G.W. Rusden, *History of Australia*, 3 vols (Chapman and Hall, London, 1883).

Owen Rutter, ed., *The First Fleet* (Golden Cockerel Press, [n.p.], 1937).

Ernest Scott, *A Short History of Australia* (Oxford University Press, London, 1916).

H.M. Scott, 'The Importance of Bourbon Naval Reconstruction to the Strategy of Choiseul after the Seven Years' War', *Imperial History Review*, vol. 1 (1979).

J.R. Seeley, *The Expansion of England* (Macmillan, London, 1883).

A.G.L. Shaw, *The Story of Australia* (Faber & Faber, London, 1955).

A.G.L. Shaw, *Convicts and the Colonies: A Study of Penal Transportation from Great Britain and Ireland to Australia and Other Parts of the British Empire* (Faber and Faber, London, 1966).

A.G.L. Shaw, 'The Hollow Conqueror and the Tyranny of Distance', *Historical Studies*, vol. 13 (1968).

A.G.L. Shaw, 'The Reasons for the Foundation of a British Settlement at Botany Bay in 1788', *ARTS*, vol. 12 (1984).

Babette Smith, *Australia's Birthstain* (Allen and Unwin, Sydney, 2008).

Dava Sobel, *Longitude: The True Story of a Lone Genius Who Solved the Greatest Scientific Problem of His Time* (Fourth Estate, London, 1996).

Alexander and George Sutherland, *The History of Australia from 1606 to 1876* (George Robinson, Melbourne, 1877).

J.H. Thomas, *Portsmouth and the First Fleet, 1786–1787* (Portsmouth City Council, Portsmouth, 1987).

E.P. Thompson, 'The moral economy of the English crowd in the eighteenth century', *Past and Present*, no. 50 (1971).

E.P. Thompson, *Whigs and Hunters: The Origin of the Black Act* (A. Lane, London, 1975).

Sir James Watt *et al.*, eds, *Starving Sailors* (National Maritime Museum, London, 1981)

Sir James Watt, 'The Colony's Health', in *Studies from Terra Australis to Australia*, eds John Hardy and Alan Frost (Australian Academy of the Humanities, Canberra, 1989), pp. 137–51, 262–6.

P.L.C. Webb, 'The Rebuilding and Repair of the Fleet, 1783–1793', *Bulletin of the Institute of Historical Research*, vol. 50 (1977), pp. 194–209.
Charles Wilson, *Australia, 1788–1988: The Creation of a Nation* (Weidenfeld & Nicolson, London, 1987).
A.T. Yarwood, *Samuel Marsden: The Great Survivor* (Melbourne University Press, Melbourne, 1977).

Index

ALAN FROST is emeritus professor of history at La Trobe University in Melbourne. His previous books include *The Voyage of the Endeavour, Arthur Phillip, 1738–1814: His Voyaging, Botany Bay Mirages* and *The Global Reach of Empire*.